1968

SOCRATES

SOCRATES

AND

THE SOCRATIC SCHOOLS

NEWLY TRANSLATED

FROM THE THIRD GERMAN EDITION OF

D[R] E. ZELLER

BY

OSWALD J. REICHEL, B.C.L. & M.A.

VICAR OF SPARSHOLT, BERKS

THIRD CAREFULLY REVISED EDITION

NEW YORK

RUSSELL & RUSSELL · INC

FIRST PUBLISHED IN 1885
REISSUED, 1962, BY RUSSELL & RUSSELL, INC.
L. C. CATALOG CARD NO: 62-10700
PRINTED IN THE UNITED STATES OF AMERICA

PREFACE.

In offering to the English reader a new edition of that part of Dr Zeller's *Philosophie der Griechen* which treats of Socrates and the imperfect Socratic Schools, the translator is not unaware of the difficulties of the task which he has undertaken. For if, on the one hand, such a translation be too literal, the reader may find it more difficult to understand than the original, and expend labour in disentangling the thread of a sentence which were better spent in grasping its meaning. If, on the other hand, too much freedom be allowed, the charge may be justly preferred, that the rendering does not faithfully represent the original. The present translator has endeavoured to steer a middle course between these two extremes, aiming at reproducing the meaning of Dr Zeller's work, whilst reducing the sentences, and where it seemed necessary, by breaking them up. In order to avoid inaccuracies, he has once more carefully gone over the whole, and hopes that such slight changes as may have been made in this the third edition will be found to be in the way of amendment.

The writer is well aware how imperfectly he has been able to realise his own standard of excellence; but believing that there is a large class of students who find it a work of toil to read Dr ZELLER'S work in the original, he submits this attempt to meet their wants, soliciting for it a gentle criticism.

SPARSHOLT VICARAGE, BERKS:
March, 1885.

CONTENTS.

PART I.

THE GENERAL STATE OF CULTURE IN GREECE.

CHAPTER I.

THE INTELLECTUAL DEVELOPMENT OF GREECE IN THE FIFTH CENTURY B.C.

CHAPTER II.

CHARACTER AND PROGRESS OF GREEK PHILOSOPHY IN THE FIFTH CENTURY B.C.

PART II.

SOCRATES.

CHAPTER III.

THE LIFE OF SOCRATES.

CHAPTER IV.

THE CHARACTER OF SOCRATES.

CHAPTER V.

SOURCES AND CHARACTERISTICS OF THE PHILOSOPHY OF SOCRATES.

CHAPTER VI.

THE PHILOSOPHICAL METHOD OF SOCRATES.

CHAPTER VII.

SUBSTANCE OF THE TEACHING OF SOCRATES—ETHICS.

CHAPTER VIII.

SUBSTANCE OF THE TEACHING OF SOCRATES, CONTINUED. NATURE—GOD—MAN.

CHAPTER IX.

XENOPHON AND PLATO. SOCRATES AND THE SOPHISTS.

CHAPTER X.

THE TRAGIC END OF SOCRATES.

PART III.

THE IMPERFECT FOLLOWERS OF SOCRATES.

CHAPTER XI.

THE SCHOOL OF SOCRATES—POPULAR PHILOSOPHY. XENOPHON—ÆSCHINES.

CHAPTER XII.

THE MEGARIAN AND THE ELEAN-ERETRIAN SCHOOLS.

CHAPTER XIII.

THE CYNICS.

CHAPTER XIV.

THE CYRENAICS.

CHAPTER XV.

RETROSPECT.

PART I.

THE GENERAL STATE OF CULTURE IN GREECE.

CHAPTER I.

THE INTELLECTUAL DEVELOPMENT OF GREECE IN THE FIFTH CENTURY.

THE intellectual life of Greece had reached a point towards the close of the fifth century before Christ at which the choice between two alternatives lay before it, either giving up philosophy altogether, or attempting a fresh treatment upon entirely new lines. The older schools were not indeed for the most part extinct; but dependence in their systems had been shaken; a general disposition to doubt had set in. From the Sophists men had learnt to call everything in question—to attack or defend with equal readiness every opinion. Belief in the truth of human ideas, or in the validity of moral laws, had been lost. Not only inquiries respecting nature, which had engaged the attention of thinkers for upwards of a century and a half, had become distasteful, but even philosophy itself had given place to a mere superficial glibness of thought and expression and

CHAP. I.

Problem proposed to philosophy in the fifth century.

the acquisition of attainments useful only for the purposes of social life. Yet this state of things naturally suggested the need of a new method, which would avoid the defects and onesidedness of previous systems by a more cautious treatment of scientific questions. The way thereto had not only been prepared indirectly by the clearing away of previous speculation, but the very instrument of research had been sharpened by the quibbles and subtleties of sophistry; ample material, too, for the erection of a new structure lay to hand in the labours of preceding philosophers. Moreover, by the practical turn taken by Sophistic enquiries a new field of research had been opened up, the more careful cultivation of which gave promise of a rich harvest for speculative philosophy. Would a creative genius be forthcoming, able to make use of these materials, and to direct thought into a new channel? Before this question Greek philosophy stood at the time when Socrates appeared.

A. *The answer determined by political events.*

(1) *Political unsettledness.*

The answer was determined in great part by the course which political circumstances, moral life, and general culture had taken. Between these and philosophy the connection is at all times close; yet lately, in the case of the Sophistic teaching, it had become more than ever apparent. The most sweeping changes had taken place in the fifth century in Greece. Never has a nation had a more rapid or more brilliant career of military glory in union with high culture than had the Greeks. Yet never has that career been sooner over. First came the great deeds of the Persian war, then the rich bloom of art of the age of Pericles; following immediately an internal conflict which wasted the strength and prosperity of the free states of Greece in unhallowed domestic strife, which sacrificed anew the independence so hardly won from the foreigner, for ever undermined freedom, confused all moral notions, and irretrievably ruined the character of the people. A progress which elsewhere required centuries was here compressed within a few generations. When the pulse of national life beats so fast, the public character must undergo a quick and perceptible change; and when so much that is great happens in so short a time, an abundance of ideas is sure to crop up, awaiting only a regulating hand to range themselves into scientific systems.

(2) *Athens a centre of union.*

Of greatest importance for the future of philosophy was the position won by Athens since the close of the Persian war. In that great conflict the consciousness of a common brotherhood had dawned upon the Hellenes with a force unknown before. All that fancy had painted in the legend of the Trojan war seemed to be there in actual history: Hellas standing as a united nation opposed to the East. The headship of this many-membered body had fallen in the main to Athens, and accordingly that city had become the centre of every intellectual movement, 'the Prytaneum of the wisdom of Greece.'[1] This circumstance had a most beneficial effect on the further development of philosophy.

[1] So called by Hippias in *Plato*, Prot. 337, D.

CHAP. I.

No doubt a tendency may have been already noticed on the part of the several schools to come forth from their isolation; in the natural philosophers of the fifth century it may be seen that an active interchange of thought was being carried on between the East and the West of Greece; and now that the Sophists had begun to travel from one end to the other of the Hellenic world, carrying to Thessaly the eloquence of Sicily, to Sicily the doctrines of Heraclitus, these various sources of culture could not fail gradually to flow together into one mighty stream. Still it was of great importance that a firm bed should be hollowed out for this stream and its course directed towards a fixed end. This result was brought about by the rise of the Attic philosophy. No sooner had the various lines of pre-Socratic inquiry met and crossed in Athens, as the common centre of the Grecian world, than it became possible for Socrates to found a more comprehensive philosophy; and to Athens ever afterwards Greek philosophy clung so firmly, that down to the time of the New Academy that city was the birthplace of all schools historically important, as it was their last place of refuge, too, before the final extinction of ancient philosophy.

B. *The answer determined by literature.*

(1) *The tragedians.*

To make clear, from the literary remains we possess, the change which took place in Greek ideas during the fifth century, and to estimate the worth and extent of the contributions rendered to philosophy by the general culture of the time, the great Athenian tragedians may be first appealed to. For tragedy is better suited than any other kind of poetry to arouse ethical reflection, to pourtray the moral feelings of a people, and to express the highest sentiments of which an age, or at least individual prominent spirits in an age, are capable. Every deeper tragic plot rests on the conflicting calls of duty and interest. To make clear the origin of such a plot, to unfold the position psychologically, to produce the general impression intended, the poet must keep these two points of view before us, allowing each to advocate its cause in lively speech and counter-speech: he must go into the analysis of moral consciousness, weigh what is right and what is faulty in human action, and expose it to view. As a poet he will do so, always having regard to the particular case before him. Yet this he cannot do without comparing one case with another, without going back to general experience, to the generally received notions respecting right and wrong—in short, to general moral conceptions. Hence tragic poetry must always give a lasting impetus to scientific speculation on moral conduct and its laws; and at the same time afford itself for such speculation material both ample and to a certain extent already prepared, and only requiring use, or correction.[1] Moreover, moral convictions being originally bound up with religious convictions in the case of the Greeks as in the case of other nations, and this connection particularly affecting tragedy owing to

[1] On this point compare the excellent remarks of *Grote*, Hist. of Greece, P. II. c. 67, vol. viii. 137, ed. 1870; vol. vii. 7, ed. 1872.

CHAP. I.

the legendary subjects with which it deals, it follows that all that has been said respecting the connection between tragedy and principles of morality, applies also to the connection between tragedy and principles of theology: nay more, in exactly the same way tragedy must busy itself with the nature and state of men whose deeds and fate it depicts. In all these respects a most decided and thorough change in Greek thought may be observed in the three generations, whose character finds such fitting expression in the three successive tragedians, Æschylus, Sophocles, and Euripides. Without going so far as to attribute to the poets themselves every word which they put into the mouths of their heroes, still the general tone of their sentiments may be gathered partly from their general treatment of the materials, partly from their individual utterances, with no lack of certainty.

(a) *Æschylus.*

In Æschylus there is an earnestness of purpose, a depth of religious feeling, an overwhelming force and majesty, worthy of a man of ancient virtue, who had himself taken part in the great battles with the Persians. At the same time there is a something sullen and despotic about him, which a time of heroic deeds and sacrifices, of mighty capabilities and inspiriting results, could neither soften down nor yet dispense with. The spirit of his tragedies is that of an untamed and boisterous mind seldom moved by softer feelings, but spell-bound by reverence for the Gods, by the recognition of an unbending moral order, by resignation to a destiny from which there is no escape. Never were the Titan-like insolence of unbridled force, the wild fury of passion and frenzy, the crushing might of fate, the dread of divine vengeance, more thrillingly painted than by Æschylus. At the bottom of all his sentiments lies reverence for the divine powers; yet these are grouped almost monotheistically together, in his grand vision, as one almighty power. What Zeus says happens; his will always comes to pass, even though it escape the notice of men;[1] no mortal can do aught against him;[2] none can escape the decision of heaven, or rather of destiny,[3] over which Zeus himself is powerless.[4] In face of this divine power man feels himself weak and frail; his thoughts are fleeting as the shadow of smoke; his life is like a picture which a sponge washes out.[5] That man mistake not his position, that he learn not to overrate what is human,[6] that he chide not the gods when in affliction,[7] that his mind soar not too high, that the grain of guilt planted by pride ripens to a harvest of tears,[8]—such is the teaching which, with glowing words, flashes on us in every page of the poet.

Not even an Æschylus, however, was able to grasp these ideas in their purity, or to rise above the contradiction which runs not only through Greek tragedy, but through the whole of the Greek view of life. On the one hand, even he gives utterance

[1] Suppl. 598; Agamemnon, 1485.

[2] Prometh. 550.

[3] Pers. 93; Fragm. 299 Dindorf (352 Nauck).

[4] Prometh. 511.

[5] Fragm. 295 (390); Agam. 1327.

[6] Niobe, Fr. 155 (154).

[7] Fragm. ·369 Dindorf. *Stobæus*, Serm. 108, 43, attributes the words to Euripides.

[8] Pers. 820.

CHAP. I.

to the ancient belief in the envy of heaven, which is so closely connected with the peculiarity of natural religion; sickness lurks under the rudest health; the wave of fortune, when it bears man highest on its crest, breaks on a hidden reef; would the man on whom fortune smiles escape ruin, he must voluntarily throw away part of what he has;[1] even the deity itself ordains guilt, when bent on utterly destroying a family.[2] On the other hand, Æschylus never tires of insisting on the connection between guilt and punishment. Not only in the old stories of Niobe and Ixion, of the house of Laius and of that of Atreus, does he paint with telling touches the pitilessness of divine vengeance, the mischief which follows in the wake of pride, the never-dying curse of crime; but also in the unexpected result of the Persian expedition he sees a higher hand, visiting with punishment the self-exaltation of the great king, and the insults offered to the gods of Greece. Man must suffer[3] according to his deeds; God blesses him who lives in piety with out guile and pride, but the transgressor of right, vengeance[4] though it tarry at first suddenly overtakes; some Diké strikes down with a sudden blow,[5] others she slowly crushes; from generation to generation the curse of crime gathers strength, so likewise virtue and happiness[6] descend to children and

[1] Agam. 1001; compare the story of Polycrates in Herodotus, iii. 40.
[2] Niobe, Fr. 160; blamed by *Plato*, Rep. 380, A.
[3] Agam. 1563; Choeph. 309; Fr. 282.
[4] Eumen. 530; Fr. 283.
[5] Choeph. 61.
[6] Agam. 750.

children's children; the Furies rule over the destiny of men, avenging the father's sins on the sons,[1] sucking the criminal's life-blood, stealthily clinging to his feet, throwing round him the snares of madness, pursuing him with punishment down to the shades.[2] So hard and pronounced is the thought of divine justice and of implacable destiny running through all these mighty poems.

All the more remarkable on that account is the vigour with which the poet breaks through the fetters which this view of the world imposes. In the Eumenides, these moral conflicts, the play of which Æschylus can so well pourtray,[3] are brought to a satisfactory issue, the bright Olympic Goddess appeasing the dark spirits of vengeance, and the severity of the ancient bloodthirsty Justice yielding to mercy. In the Prometheus, natural religion as a whole celebrates its moral transfiguration; the jealousy of the Gods towards mortals is seen to melt into graciousness; Zeus himself requires the aid of the Wise One, who, for his kindness to men, has had to feel the whole weight of his wrath; yet, on the other hand, the unbending mind of the Titan must be softened, and Zeus' rule of might be changed by willing submission into a moral rule. What the poet places in the legendary past is in reality the history of his own time and of his own mind. Æschylus stands on the boundary line between two periods of culture, and the story he tells

[1] Eum. 830.
[2] Eum. 264, 312.
[3] Choeph. 896; Eum. 198, 566.

CHAP. I.

of the mitigation of ancient justice, and of the new rule of the Gods, was repeated in another way, when the sternness of the generation of Marathon gave place to the bright sunshine of the age of Pericles.

(b) Sophocles.

To the spirit of this new age Sophocles has given the most fitting expression. Albeit his principles agree with those of his predecessor, his poems, nevertheless, convey a very different impression. The keynote of the poetry of Sophocles is likewise reverence for the Gods, whose hand and laws encompass human life. From them come all things, even misfortune;[1] their never-decaying power no mortal can withstand; nothing can escape its destiny;[2] from their eyes no deed and no thought can be hid;[3] their eternal laws,[4] the offspring of no mere human power, none dare transgress. Men, however, are weak and frail, mere shadows of a dream, a very nothing, capable only of a passing semblance of happiness.[5] No mortal's life is free from misfortune,[6] and even the happiest man cannot be called happy before his death;[7] nay, taking all things into account, which the changing day brings with it, the number of woes, the rarity of good fortune, the end to which all must come, it were well to repeat the old saying, 'Not to have been born is the best lot, and the next best is to die as soon as may be.'[8] The highest wisdom in life is,

[1] Ajax, 1036; Trach. 1278.
[2] Antig. 604, 951; Fr. 615.
[3] Electra, 657.
[4] Œd. T. 864; Ant. 450.
[5] Ajax, 125; Œd. T. 1186; Fr. 12, 616, 860.
[6] Ant. 611; Fr. 530.
[7] Œd. T. Trach. 1, 943; Fr. 532, 583.
[8] Œd. Col. 1215.

therefore, to control desire, to keep the passions in check, to love justice, to fear God, to be resigned to fate. Man should not exalt himself above human measure; only the modest man is acceptable to the Gods;[1] it is absurd to seek a higher instead of being content with a moderate lot; arrogance hurries on to sudden destruction; Zeus hates the vaunts of a boastful tongue,[2]—all these teachings Sophocles illustrates by the example of men who have been hurled from the summit of fortune, or who have been ruined by intemperance and overbearing. He, too, is full of the thought of the worth of virtue and of divine retribution. He knows that uprightness is better than riches, that loss is better than unjust gain, that heavy guilt entails heavy punishment, but that piety and virtue are worth more than all things else, and deserving a reward not only in this world, but also in the next;[3] he even declares that it is more important to please those in another world than those in this.[4] He is moreover convinced that all wisdom comes from the Gods, and that they always bring men to what is right,[5] albeit men must never cease from studying and pursuing it themselves.[6] He bids them to commit their griefs to Zeus, who from heaven above looks down and orders all things, and to bear what the Gods send with resignation,[7] and in this belief is

[1] Ajax, 127, 758; Œd. Col. 1211; Fr. 320, 528.

[2] Œd. T. 873; Ant. 127.

[3] Fr. 18, 210, 196; Philoc. 1440.

[4] Ant. 71.

[5] Fr. 834, 227, 809, 865; in the unintelligible θείᾳ ἡμέρᾳ probably there is a θεία μοῖρα.

[6] Fr. 731, 736.

[7] Elec. 174; Fr. 523, 862.

CHAP. I.

neither shaken by the good fortune of many bad men, nor yet by the misfortunes of many good ones.[1]

The same thoughts had inspired the poetry of Æschylus, and yet the spirit of the drama of Sophocles is a very different one from his. Sophocles has a higher artistic execution to show, a fuller dramatic handling, a more delicate delineation of the inner life, a more careful unravelling of action from characters and of characters by means of actions, more beauty of proportion, language clearer and more pleasing; whereas for stormy force, for wild grandeur, for majestic view of history, Æschylus stands unrivalled. Nor yet is the moral platform of the two tragedians quite the same. Both are penetrated with reverence for the divine powers; but in Æschylus this reverence is combined with dread which has first to be got over, and with antagonism which has to be overcome before the trustful resignation and the blissful peace of the piety of Sophocles can be attained. The power of fate seems with Æschylus much harsher, because less called for by the character of those whom it reaches; the reign of Zeus is a reign of terror, mitigated only by degrees, and man must perish if the Deity enter into too close relations with him.[2] Both poets celebrate the victory of moral order in the world over human self-will; but in Æschylus the victory is preceded by severer and more dreadful struggles. Moral

[1] Fr. 104.

[2] Compare the character of Io in the Prometheus, especially v. 887, &c.

order works, with him, as a stern and relentless power, crushing the refractory; whereas, with Sophocles, it completes its work with the quiet certainty of a law of nature, awakening rather pity for human weakness than terror. That conflict of the older bloodthirsty justice with the milder justice of modern times, round which the Eumenides of Æschylus play, Sophocles has left behind; with him justice is, from the very beginning, harmoniously united with mercy, and the most accursed of all mortals finds in the 'Œdipus Coloneus' reconciliation at last. His heroes, too, are of a different order from those of his predecessor. In Æschylus moral contrasts are so sharp, that human representatives of them do not suffice; hence he brings the Gods themselves into the battle-field, Zeus and the Titans, the daughters of Night and the denizens of Olympus; whereas the tragedy of Sophocles moves entirely in the world of men. Æschylus deals by preference with headstrong natures and passions uncontrolled; the strong point of Sophocles is to depict what is noble, self-contained, tender; strength is by him generally coupled with dignity, pain with resignation. Hence his female characters are so specially successful. Æschylus paints in a Clytæmnestra, the demoniacal side of woman's nature in all its repulsiveness; Sophocles in an Antigone pourtrays pure womanliness, knowing 'how to love, but not to hate,'[1] and putting even hatred to shame by the heroism of her love. In short, the poetry of Sopho-

[1] Ant. 523.

CHAP. I.

cles sets before us the sentiments of an epoch and a people which having, by most successful efforts, risen to a happy use of its powers, and so to fame and position, enjoys existence, and which has learned to look on human nature and all that belongs to it in a cheerful spirit, to prize its greatness, to mitigate its sufferings by wise resignation, to bear its weaknesses, to control its excesses by custom and law. From him, as from no other poet, the idea is borne to us of a beautiful natural agreement between duty and inclination, between freedom and order, which constitutes the moral ideal of the Greek world.

(*c*) *Euripides.*

Only some four Olympiads later comes Euripides. Yet what a remarkable change in ethical tone and view of life is apparent in his writings! As an artist, Euripides is far too fond of substituting calculation in place of the spontaneous outcome of the poet's mind and discriminating criticism in place of admiring contemplation. By scenes of an exciting and terrifying character, by chorus-songs often loosely connected with the action of the play, by rhetorical declamation and moralising he seeks to produce an effect which might be gained better and more legitimately from the unison of the whole. That harmony between the moral and the religious life which commended itself so agreeably to us in Sophocles, may be seen in a state of dissolution in the plays of the younger poet. Not that he is lacking in moral maxims and religious reflections. He knows full well that piety and the virtue of temperance are the best things for man; that he who is mortal must not be proud of advantages nor despair in misfortune; that he can do nothing without the Gods; that in the long run the good man fares well and the bad fares ill; that a modest lot is preferable to fitful greatness;[1] that the poor man's fear of God is worth more than the ostentatious sacrifices of many a rich man; that virtue and intelligence are better than wealth and noble birth.[2] He discourses at length of the benefits conferred by the Gods on men;[3] he speaks right well of their righteous and almighty rule,[4] and he even traces back human guilt to their will.[5]

However numerous such expressions may be in his writings, still they do not contain the whole of his view of the world, neither is the ethical peculiarity of his poetry to be found in them. Euripides has sufficient appreciation of what is great and morally beautiful, to be able to paint it, when it comes before him, in a true and telling manner. For all that, as a pupil of philosophers,[6] as a kindred

[1] Bacch. 1139. Io Schl. Hippolyt. 1100. Kirchh. Fr. 77, 80, 257, 305, 355, 395, 507, 576, 621, 942, 1014, 1016, 1027, Nauck.

[2] Fr. 329, 53, 254, 345, 514, 940.

[3] Suppl. 197.

[4] Troad. 880; Hel. 1442. Compare the concluding verses of this piece, which also occur at the end of the Andromache and Bacchæ. Fr. 797, 832, 875, 969.

[5] Hippol. 1427.

[6] The testimony of the ancients respecting the connection between Euripides and Anaxagoras has been quoted in *Zeller's* Philosophie der Griechen, vol. i. 790, 3. For the traces thereof, which are principally found in some of the fragments, compare *Hartung's* Euripides Restitut. 109, 118, 139. Anaxagoras, however, does not, like Euripides, make Earth and Ether, but Air and Ether come first after the original mixing of all things. The well-known and beautiful passage (Fragment 902) com-

CHAP. I.

spirit to the better Sophists, he is too far removed from the older lines of thought to be able to give himself freely and with full conviction to the traditional faith and morality. His sober understanding feels the improbability and unseemliness of many legends, and the artistic spirit has not such an exclusive hold on him that he can overlook this feature for the sake of the ideas that they embody, or for their poetic worth. The fortunes of men do not seem to him to be directly the revelation of a higher power, but rather to be proximately the result of natural causes, of calculation, of caprice, and of accident. Even moral principles appear wavering. If, on the whole, their authority is admitted, still the poet cannot conceal from himself that even an immoral course of conduct has much to say in its defence. The grand poetic way of contemplating the world, the moral and religious way of looking at human life, has given place to a sceptical tone, to a disintegrating criticism, to an appeal to plain facts as they are. Æschylus brought the Eumenides, all in the uncouth guise of antiquity, yet with most fearful effect, on to the stage; whereas the Electra of Euripides says to her brother, or rather the poet himself says, that they are mere fancies of his imagination.[1] Whilst Iphigeneia is preparing to sacrifice the captives, she reflects that the goddess

mending the investigator, who contemplates with innocence the eternal order of immortal nature, is referred to Anaxagoras. Compare also Fr. 7. Younger men, like Prodicus and Socrates, Euripides may have known, but cannot have been their pupil.

[1] Orest. 248, 387.

herself cannot possibly require this sacrifice, and that the story of the feast of Tantalus is a fable.[1] Likewise in the Electra[2] doubts are thrown by the tragic chorus on the miracle of the change in the course of the sun. In the Troades,[3] Hecuba questions the tale of the judgment of Paris, and explains the assistance of Aphrodite in carrying off Helen as meaning the attractive beauty of Paris. In the Bacchæ,[4] Teiresias gives a stupid half-natural explanation of the birth of Bacchus.[5] The Gods, says Euripides,[6] have no needs, and therefore the stories which impute to them human passions cannot possibly be true. Even the general notions of divine justice give him offence. This he will not regard as a punishment for particular acts, but rather as a universal law.[7] In other instances, the actions and commands of the Gods are held up to blame—blame, too, for the most part, not called for by the character of the acting persons, and going unpunished in the sequel, so that it necessarily appears as the poet's own conviction;[8] whence he concludes at one time that man need not disturb himself because of his faults, since the Gods commit the same; at another time, that the stories about the Gods cannot be true.[9] The prophetic art is

[1] Iphig. Taur. 372.
[2] 734.
[3] 963.
[4] 265.
[5] Frag. 209.
[6] Herc. Fur. 1328.
[7] Fr. 508, with which the saying (Fr. 964) is connected, that God cares only for great events, leaving unimportant things to chance.
[8] Io 448, 1315; Elect. 1298; Orest. 277, 409; Herc. Fur. 339, 654.
[9] Herc. Fur. 1301.

CHAP. I.

held in equally low estimation, and the opportunity is seized in the Helen,[1] to prove, on highly rationalistic grounds, that it is all a lie and deceit.[2]

With these legends and rites, however, belief in the Gods is most thoroughly interwoven. No wonder, therefore, that the poet often puts into the mouths of his heroes statements respecting the existence of the Gods, which would sound more natural coming from Protagoras than from men and women of the legendary past. Talthybius raises the question whether there be Gods, or whether Chance guides all things;[3] another doubts their existence,[4] because of the unjust distribution of good and bad fortune; Hecuba in her prayer wonders what the deity really is, whether Zeus, or natural necessity, or the spirit of mortal beings;[5] Hercules and Clytæmnestra leave it open whether there be Gods, and who Zeus is;[6] even the Ether is explained to be Zeus.[7] One thing at least these utterances prove, that Euripides had wandered far away from the ancient faith in the Gods. Allowing that he is sincere when he says that only a fool can deny the deity and give credence to the deceitful assertions of philosophy respecting what is hidden,[8] still his attitude appears to have been preponderatingly sceptical and critical

[1] 743.

[2] *Sophocles*, Antig. 1033, makes Cleon attack the prophet, but his accusations are refuted by the sequel. Not so with Euripides.

[3] Hel. 484.

[4] Fr. 288; compare Fr. 892.

[5] Troad. 877.

[6] Herc. Fur. 1250; Iph. Aul. 1034; Orestes, 410, and the fragment of Melanippe Fr. 483.

[7] Fr. 935, 869.

[8] Fr. 905, 981.

towards the popular faith. Probably he allowed that there was a God; certainly he attached no value to the legendary notions respecting the Gods; holding that the essence of God could not be known, and assuming the oneness of the divine nature either by glossing over or by plainly denying the ruling Pantheism.[1]

Nor did the popular ideas respecting the state after death fare better at his hands. Naturally enough, he makes use of them when a poet can use them, but then it is also said, that we know not how it is with another life, we only follow an unfounded opinion. In several places Euripides expresses the view,[2] derived partly from Orphic-Pythagorean traditions, and partly from the teaching of Anaxagoras and Archilaus,[3] that the spirit returns at death to the ether whence it came;[4] leaving it apparently an open question, whether at all, or to what extent, consciousness belongs to the soul when united with the ether.[5] That the sphere of morals did not

[1] Fr. 904 says the ruler of all things is now called Zeus, now Hades, which would point to the opinion that the popular Gods are only different names for the one God. Helios and Apollo are identified (Fr. 781, 11) according to the tradition of Orpheus.

[2] Hippolyt. 192.

[3] Compare *Zeller's* Philosophie der Griechen, Part I. pp. 388, 430, 822, 846.

[4] Suppl. 532, the genuineness of which Kirchhoff wrongly suspects; Hel. 1012; Fr. 836.

[5] He says in the Helen: The soul of the dead no longer lives, but yet it has an eternal consciousness (γνώμη ἀθάνατος) after it has united with the immortal Ether. From this he deduces the belief in retribution after death, and he asks (Fr. 639, compare Fr. 452, 830), whether on the whole life is not a death and death a life. On the other hand, in the Troades, 638, it is stated that the dead man is feelingless, like an unborn child; in Fr. 536, that he is a nothing, earth

remain unaffected by these doubts may be gathered from the general character of his tragedies more definitely than from those particular utterances which in some measure sufficed to give offence even to his cotemporaries.[1] The tragic movement in Euripides, lies less in a conflict of moral forces such as Æschylus and Sophocles knew how to depict so expressively, but depends rather on personal passions, arrangements, and experiences. His heroes have not that ideal character which makes them types of a whole class. Hence, in most cases, that higher necessity, which called forth admiration in the case of Æschylus and Sophocles, is not active in the development of the Euripidean drama, but the final result is brought about by some external means, either by divine interposition or by some human trick. Thus, rich as he may be in poetic beauties, successful in painting individual characters, experienced in knowledge of human life and human weaknesses, thrilling in many of the speeches and scenes in his tragedies; yet most undeniably he has come down from the moral and artistic height of his two great predecessors, by introducing into tragedy

and a shade; Fr. 734 appears only to recognise the immortality of fame: and in the Heraclid. 591, he leaves it an open question whether the dead have feelings or not.

[1] As, for instance: ἡ γλῶσσ' ὀμώμοκε, &c. Hippol. 607, or the language of Eteocles in Phœn. 504, 525, that men will do anything for power, and even commit crimes for a throne; or that of the old man in Io 1051, that it befits the fortunate man to shun wrong, but that all means of vengeance are lawful in case of injury. It is true Euripides does not give these as his own sentiments. Yet even his cotemporaries noticed their resemblance to the moral teaching of the Sophists.

habits of inward reflection, of studied effect, and of artificial language, which Agatho with mincing elegance, and Critias with sophistic moralising, were not slow to follow.[1]

(2) *The Didactic Poets.*

Cotemporary with Æschylus, or even a little before him, the poets Epicharmus, Simonides, and Pindar flourished: soon after him Bacchylides. The first of these, Epicharmus, it has been shown in an earlier work,[2] takes a rational view of the world, and entertains clear notions on morals, and theology, thanks to his knowledge of philosophy. Simonides,[3] so far as his views can be gathered from scattered fragments, appears mainly to insist on that moderation and self-restraint which result from consideration for human weakness and frailty. Our life is full of toils[4] and cares; its fortune is uncertain; swiftly it hurries away; even prudence[5] is too easily lost by men; their hardly-won virtue is imperfect and unstable; it changes with circumstances; the best man is he on whom the Gods bestow prosperity. A faultless man must not be looked for; enough to find one moderately righteous.[6] The same vein of feeling is found in Bacchylides, on whom descended the mantle of Simonides. He knows that no one is altogether happy, that few are spared some heavy changes of fortune, and bursts, yet not alone, into

(a) *Simonides.*

(b) *Bacchylides.*

[1] *Zeller's* Geschichte der Philosophie, Part I. p. 925, and Nauck. Trag. Frag. 599.

[2] *Zeller's* Philosophie der Griechen, Part I. p. 427 (German).

[3] Called by later writers, as well as by Æschylus, a poet of the good old time. *Aristoph.* Clouds, 1352.

[4] Fr. 32, 36, 38, 39, 85.

[5] Fr. 42.

[6] Fr. 5.

CHAP. I.

the complaint: 'Not to have been born were the happiest lot.'[1] Hence the highest practical wisdom consists, in his view, in equanimity, in contentment with the present, in absence of care for the future.[2] At the same time he shares the conviction that man can discover what is right, and that Zeus, the all-seeing ruler of the world, is not to blame for the misfortunes of mortals.[3] These are the very sentiments of the older moral poets, without any noticeable change in the moral platform.[4]

(c) Pindar.

A spirit far more peculiar and more powerful, and more nearly akin to Æschylus, finds utterance in the poems of Pindar. At the bottom of Pindar's, as of Æschylus', view of the world, lies a most exalted notion of the deity. 'God is the all;'[5] nothing for Him is impossible; Zeus governs all things according to his will; He bestows success or failure;[6] law, which governs mortals and immortals, accomplishes its purposes with mighty hand.[7] Nor are the deeds of men hid from the all-seeing eyes of God.[8] Only beautiful and noble traits can be attributed to the deity; he who accuses it of human vices cannot escape punishment.[9] Such being the

[1] Fr. 1, 2, 3, 21.

[2] Fr. 19.

[3] Fr. 29.

[4] *Zeller*, Part I. p. 90.

[5] *Clemens*, Stromat. v. 610: Πίνδαρος . . . ἀντικρὺς εἰπών, τί θεός; ὅτι τὸ πᾶν. Although Clement appears to give the words beginning τί as a quotation, it seems hardly likely that they can have stood in Pindar. Perhaps Pindar used the words θεός τό πᾶν in the same sense that Sophocles said (Trach. 1278) οὐδὲν τούτων ὅ τι μὴ Ζεύς, to express, All depends upon God.

[6] Fr. 119; Pyth. ii. 49, 88; Nem. x. 29.

[7] Fr. 146.

[8] Ol. i. 64; Pyth. iii. 28; ix. 42.

[9] Ol. i. 28, where, with a curious combination of credu-

exalted position of the deity, man occupies thereto a two-fold attitude. On the one hand he has a nature related to that of the Gods; one is the race of men,[1] the race of Gods is another, yet both descend from the same mother; hence in nature and spirit mortals are not altogether unlike immortals. On the other hand, looking at their power, there is an infinite difference,[2] for changeful is our lot, and joy and sorrow lie for us ever near together.[3] True wisdom, therefore, consists in not transgressing the bounds of what is human, in looking to the Gods for all that is good, in taking with contentment what they bestow. 'Seek not to be a God,' exclaims the poet: mortality becomes mortals; he who soars to heaven will, like Bellerophon, have a precipitate fall.[4] Only where God leads is blessing and success;[5] in His hand rests the issue of our labour, according as it is determined by destiny.[6] From the deity comes all virtue and knowledge;[7] and doubtless for this very reason, as being a gift of God, natural talent is placed by Pindar far above all

lity and rationalism, the story of the feast of the Gods in the house of Tantalus is declared to be a fable, the occasion for which was supplied by the carrying off of Pelops by Poseidon.

[1] This, rather than the identity of both races, must be the meaning of the words ἓν ἀνδρῶν ἓν θεῶν γένος: men form a race by themselves; the Gods form another different therefrom.

[2] Nem. vi. 1. According to Frag. 108, the soul, the εἴδωλον αἰῶνος, comes from God alone, and proves its higher nature during the sleep of the body in prophetic dreams.

[3] Ol. ii. 30; Fr. 210.

[4] Ol. v. 24; Isthm. v. 14; vii. 42.

[5] Fr. 85, where probably ἐν stands for ἐς.

[6] Pyth. xii. 28.

[7] Ol. ix. 28, 103: Pyth. i. 41; Fr. 118.

CHAP. I.

acquirements, and the creative spirits on whom it has been bestowed, above all other spirits, as the eagle of Zeus is above the croaking ravens.[1] We must resign ourselves to what God disposes, content ourselves with our lot, whatever it be. Strive not against God; bear His yoke without kicking against the pricks; adapt yourself to circumstances; seek not what is impossible; in all things observe moderation; beware of envy, which deals the strongest blow to those most highly placed;—these are the counsels of the poet.[2] Nay more, to give greater weight to his moral counsels, he not unfrequently appeals to a future retribution of the wicked as well as of the good, sometimes following herein the received notions respecting Tartarus, Elysium, and the islands[3] of the blessed, at other times connecting therewith a belief in the migration of souls.[4] In the main, Pindar's platform, both religious and moral, is not different from that of Æschylus, albeit the thought of divine veageance does not stand out with him in such tragic force.

(3) *Historians.*

Would we study this view of life going over to a later form, no better example can be selected than

[1] Ol. ii. 86; ix. 100; Nem. i. 25; iii. 40.

[2] Pyth. ii. 34, 88; iii. 21, 59, 103; xi. 50; Fr. 201.

[3] Ol. ii. 56; Fr. 106, 120. Fr. 108 seems only to presuppose the current notions, with this difference, that a more intense life is attributed to souls in Hades than was the view of Homer and the mass of the people. Fr. 109 is probably interpolated by some Alexandrian Jew.

[4] Fr. 110, Ol. ii. 68. According to the latter passage, in which Pindar is most explicit, reward or punishment follows in Hades. Some few distinguished men are allowed to return to life, and may, by a threefold life of innocence, enjoy the higher bliss on the islands of the blessed.

CHAP. I.

(a) Herodotus.

Herodotus. This friend of Sophocles, in writing history, often allows himself to be guided by the notions of olden times. He admits the rule of divine providence in the order of nature,[1] and equally clearly in the fortunes of men, and especially in punishment, which overtakes the guilty, even though he have acted in the excess of an excusable passion.[2] Popular forms of worship he honours,[3] knowing that every nation likes its own rites best; only a madman, he says, can treat these with disdain.[4] Credulous, too, he is, so far as to relate, in all good faith, divers wonders and prophecies,[5] among them some of the most extraordinary kind. Even his piety is of an antique type, affected with that fear of the divine powers which is so peculiarly suited to natural religion, where the exaltation of Gods above men is not conceived of as an essential difference, but is more physical than moral. Man is not destined to enjoy perfect good fortune; his life is exposed to changes innumerable; before death no one may be called happy; nay it is even a general matter for doubt whether death is not better for a man than life.[6] He who in prosperity or imagination soars above the lot of men, is invariably struck by the envy of the deity, which, jealous of

[1] *Her.* iii. 108.

[2] ii. 120; iv. 205; vi. 84; viii. 129; vii. 133.

[3] For this reason he hesitates to utter the names of Egyptian Gods in a context which might desecrate them, ii. 86, or to speak of Egyptian mysteries.

[4] iii. 38.

[5] vii. 12, 57; viii. 37, 65; ix. 100. Here belong the prophecies of Bakis and Musæus, viii. 77; ix. 43, respecting the genuineness of which he entertains no doubt.

[6] ii. 31.

CHAP. I.

its privileges, will not brook a mortal rival.[1] All this is quite in agreement with the spirit which breathes through the older poetry of Greece.

For all that, Herodotus neither can nor will conceal the fact that he is the child of an epoch, in which thought has already begun to shake the foundations of simple faith. Notwithstanding the simplicity with which he tells many a wonder,[2] there are times when he cannot resist the impulse to explain away the marvels of legend, either referring them to natural causes in the rationalising spirit of the Sophists, or at least mentioning with approval such explanations given by others. Thus the wanderings of Io and the rape of Europa are explained at the very beginning of his work to mean the carrying off by pirates of these two royal maidens. In the story of Gyges the wonderful power of the ring is referred to a very common trick.[3] The prophetic doves of Dodona turn into Egyptian priestesses.[4] The Egyptian stories respecting Paris and Helena are preferred to those of Homer and the general tradition of the Greeks,[5] on grounds far removed from ancient poetry. Where the Thessalian legend makes Poseidon interpose, he sees the working of an earthquake,[6] and remarks, not without irony, that those who believe Poseidon produces earthquakes, may believe he interposed in this case also. Add to this that he occasionally

[1] On the θεῖον φθονερόν, conf. i. 32, 34; iii. 40; vii. 10, 5, 46.

[2] i. 60.

[3] i. 8.

[4] ii. 56.

[5] ii. 120.

[6] vii. 129.

expresses the opinion that all men know equally little about the Gods,[1] and it will be patent, how much doubt had already taken the place of the ancient faith.

(b) *Thucydides.*

In Thucydides, the next great historian, doubt has gone over into the matter of fact treatment of history. The high moral tone of his style no one will deny. Even in its unfinished form his history of the Peloponnesian war has all the effect of an impressive tragedy. This effect, however, is secured by a simple setting forth of historical facts, without introducing the interposition of the Gods to explain events. Thucydides knows how indispensable religion is for the public good. He shows, by his very description, how deeply he deplores the decay, not only of morals but also of religion in his country.[2] Yet the rule of the deity and of moral order in the world he only allows to be seen in the progress of events. Convinced that human nature is always the same, he exhibits moral laws by showing how in any particular case before him ruin naturally resulted from the weakness and the passions of men, which he knows so well and can judge so impartially.[3] Nowhere is a belief betrayed in those extraordinary occurrences, in which the hand of God manifests itself in Herodotus. Where his cotemporaries see the fulfilment of a prophecy, he contents himself with sober criticism.[4] To depend on oracles instead

[1] ii. 3 (Schl.).

[2] See the well-known passages ii. 53; iii. 82.

[3] iii. 82, 84; and in the description of the Sicilian expedition, its motives and results, vi. 15, 24, 30; vii. 75, 87.

[4] For instance, ii. 17, 54.

of using remedies, he calls the folly of the masses;[1] he openly expresses disapproval of the disastrous superstition of Nicias.[2] In the panegyric of the dead,[3] which is quite as much a memorial of his own views as of those of Pericles, there is not a word on the legendary history of Athens, that hackneyed theme of earlier panegyrists; but instead thereof, there is a statesmanlike tone in the way in which he clings to facts and practical problems. His history is a brilliant evidence of a mature judgment, of high intellectual culture, of a varied experience of life, of a calm, unimpassioned, penetrating, and sober view of the world. It is a work which kindles the highest respect not only for the writer, but for the whole period, which could rear up such a genius.

Not that this work conceals the darker sides of that period. Read but the descriptions it gives[4] of the confusion of all moral notions in the factious struggles of the Peloponnesian war, of the desolation of Athens by the plague, of the decline of piety and self-sacrifice, of the wild riot of all the selfish passions, to be satisfied of the decay of moral excellence, even in that period of might and culture. Beyond all question, along with this outward change of conduct, general convictions were shaken also. To place this fact beyond doubt, Thucydides puts in the mouth of several of his speakers, and particularly

[1] v. 103, where the Athenian is, without doubt, expressing the writer's opinion.

[2] vii. 50.

[3] ii. 35.

[4] ii. 53; iii. 82.

of those coming from Athens, naked avowals of the most selfish principles, such as could only come from the lips of some one of the younger Sophists. All who have the power seek to rule; no one is restrained by considerations of right from pursuing his advantage by hook or by crook; the rule of the stronger is the universal law of nature; at bottom every one determines what is right and honourable by his own interests and enjoyments; even the best regulated states act on this idea, at least in their foreign relations. These and such like utterances are put into the mouths of Athenian popular men and ambassadors on every opportunity.[1] Even those who suffer from Athenian selfishness are in the end hardly able to blame it.[2] Have we not here moral and political conditions the exact counterpart of the sophistic type of philosophy?

(4) The Comedians.

Nor were other prudent men blind to the dangers which this progress of events involved, little though they were able to stem it, or to run counter to the spirit of their times. Among such was Aristophanes. This poet is an enthusiastic admirer of the good old time as he paints it with its steady morality, its strict education, its military prowess, its orderly and prudent administration.[3] He warms to his subject whenever he speaks of the days of Marathon.[4] With ruthless satire, now in the form of bantering jest, now in that of bitter earnestness, he lashes the

Aristophanes.

[1] i. 76; iii. 40; v. 89, 105, 111; vi. 85.

[2] iv. 61.

[3] Clouds, 882; Knights, 1316.

[4] Wasps, 1071; the Acharnians, 676.

CHAP. I.

innovations which have supplanted time-honoured institutions—democracy running riot with demagogues and sycophants;[1] poetry, empty, effeminate, free-thinking, faithless to its moral purpose, degraded from its artistic height;[2] sophistic culture with its fruitless speculations, dangerous alike to faith and morals, the producer of shameless quibblers, atheistic rationalisers,[3] or conscienceless perverters of justice, instead of steady citizens and sober-minded men. Love for what is ancient is with him undeniably an affair of personal conviction. Of this his zeal is proof, the warmth and classic beauty of those passages which tell the praise of the olden time and its ways. Stronger proof still lies in the general tone of his comedies. Proud, and not without reason, of the courage with which he discharged his citizen's duty against Cleon,[4] he forces even the reader of to-day to acknowledge that he was an honourable man fighting for a principle.

Whilst hotly taking the field against the spirit of innovation, he at the same time not only presupposes this spirit in his audience, but actually represents and promotes it himself. Demagogues and sycophants he lashes; yet in lashing them tells us that every place is full of them; that democracy has a hundred heads, ever full of vitality; that the Athenian people, like a childish old man, are ever the victim of the most impudent of their flatterers; that

[1] Wasps; Clouds, 568. The Sycophants are taken to task on every opportunity.

[2] Frogs; Achar. 393.

[3] Clouds; Birds, 1282, 1553; Frogs, 1491.

[4] Wasps, 1029, 1284; Peace, 951; Achar. 959; Clouds, 542.

the true-hearted men of the older generation are quite as intent on their judicial dues as the whole worshipful body of citizens are on their lawsuits; that the young champions of Spartan severity are as debauched as the demagogues;[1] that the sovereign people, since the re-establishment of Solon's constitution, has gone on as capriciously as before, only wanting female government to complete the folly.[2] Even in his plays he himself indulges in the arts of the demagogue and the sycophant; Socrates he slanders, and many another as heartily as any rhetorician could do; and to outbid those who squandered the public property in order to bribe the people, he tells the citizens of Athens that if things were fairly done,[3] they ought to receive far more than they did. For a reform in religion and morals, the prospects with him are bad. He praises the moral training of the ancients, but observes with a smile that morality is little at home amongst his hearers,[4] and finds the vices from which his people suffered at bottom very natural.[5] Women he brings on the stage to lash their licentiousness; but that licentiousness he represents as so deep and so general, that there can hardly be hope of improvement. He makes an onslaught on the philosophers who deny the Gods, but in one of his first comedies he gives us to understand, that belief in his time rested on tottering feet.[6]

[1] Wasps; Birds, 38.
[2] Eccles. v. 456; conf. *Plato,* Rep. viii. 563, B.
[3] Wasps, 655.
[4] Clouds, 1055.
[5] Compare Birds, 137; Frogs, 148; Knights, 1384.
[6] Knights, 32.

CHAP. I.

Not only here and there,[1] but in whole acts and plays,[2] he exposes the Gods, together with their priests, with audacious recklessness, bringing them down with rough wit to a human level and indeed to what is low and common ; laying bare the moral weaknesses in which they resemble men nakedly and minutely ; making the world of Gods, like that of men, turn in such a wild whirl, that neither the spectator who takes delight in this perverted world, nor yet the poet, can have any real respect for beings who are so readily and recklessly at the service of his imagination. Much of this may be attributed to the license of comedy ; [3] yet more than enough remains to show that the poet himself, as well as his audience, had strayed far from the ancient morality which he so regretfully wishes to recall ; that his enthusiasm for it, like Rousseau's wild dream of returning to a state of nature, is only the outcome of discontent with the present, only the expression of a romantic idea, not a sentiment penetrating everyday life, and ruling every thought and feeling. Thus, take them where you will, the age and the surroundings from which Attic philosophy came forth appear penetrated by a spirit of innovation, rendering it impossible for the most decided lovers of antiquity to adhere to the life and beliefs of their ancestors.

Amongst other signs of this change, one pheno-

[1] Clouds, 369, 396, 900, 1075 ; Birds, 554, 1608 ; Eccles. 778 ; Plut. 123, 697.

[2] In the Frogs, Peace, and the Birds.

[3] *Plut.* 665.

C. The problem solved by the new forms of religious worship.

menon deserves to be noticed, which appeared about the time of the Peloponnesian war—the increasing spread of mystery worship; and of soothsaying in connection therewith. Hitherto in extraordinary cases the alleged predictions of the older prophets had been looked up,[1] as is the wont of men; now the mischief and abuse carried on therewith reached an incredible pitch.[2] To judge by the numerous allusions in the writers of this and the following generation, the Orphic and Corybantic mysteries probably gained at this time both in ground and supporters.[3] In itself this was a noticeable innovation in more than one respect. Viewed as a matter of

[1] *Herod.* viii. 7; ix. 437, mentions prophecies of Bakis and Musæus respecting the Persian war.

[2] This is particularly evident in Aristophanes, who loses no opportunity of lashing the prophets. Not to mention cursory attacks, as in Clouds, 330; Birds, 521; Knights, 109, 818, 960, 967 (comp. Lysist. 767), he shows what liberal use Cleon and other demagogues made of superstition to flatter the self-love of the people, and to direct its will by the so-called prophecies of Bakis. In Peace, 1047, he introduces a prophet Hierocles, who, from interested motives, opposes the conclusion of peace, and is evidently meant for a real person; in the Birds, 959, a prophet, who intrudes himself at the founding of a city, to pick up a trifle. Such like phenomena may have given occasion to the polemic of Euripides.

[3] Amongst others, Philolaus (*Zeller*, Part I. 388) and Plato (Phædo, 69, C.; Rep. ii. 363, C.; 364, B.; Laws, vi. 782, C.), and more particularly Euripides and Aristophanes. The former (Hippol. 949) describes Hippolytus as a pupil of Orpheus, and (Fr. 475) introduces a mystic, who, initiated into the orgies of Idæan Zeus of Zagreus, and the Curetes, devotes himself to an Orphic life. The latter not only depicts (in the Frogs, 145, 312) the life of the initiated and uninitiated in Hades as rudely and vividly as the consecrated priests do in Plato, but also (in Peace, 374) hints at the opinion that man cannot die quietly without receiving initiation before death, and (in Wasps, 119) alludes to the custom of initiating the sick for the purpose of healing them

CHAP. I.

form it was one thing to seek counsel from public oracles making use of ancient rites naturalised from time immemorial in fixed spots; a very different thing to fall back on the alleged answers of individual prophets and private forms of worship without fixed locality, propagated by vagrant priests, practised in self-constituted confraternities, and claiming to elevate all who took part in them as the special elect above the mass of mankind, both in this world and in the next. What was this increasing fondness for private forms of worship and irregular prophecy but a proof that the public religion was not altogether satisfactory, whilst at the same time it contributed to intensify the evil? Viewed as to its real nature, this mystical piety has departed from the received form of faith and life. In it, the notions of the Gods begin to lose their distinctness by fusion;[1] perhaps even to it the tendency to pantheism may be referred, which has been already noticed in individuals in the fifth century.[2] The conception of human life and of human

[1] This is more immediately true in the case of Dionysus. In mystic theology this God, as the representative of the changing life of nature, dying in winter, reviving in spring, was honoured under the name of Dionysus Zagreus, and treated as one of the Gods of the nether world. On this account the Dionysus-mysteries are so important for the future life. To the initiated in them (*Plato*, Phædo, 69, C.; comp. *Aristoph.* Frogs) may be promised life in Hades with the Gods, among whom must surely be found the God in whose service they were enlisted. At a later time, following Heraclitus' example, Dionysus was identified with Plato. See *Zeller's* Gesch. d. Phil. vol. i. 51, 3; 592, 5.

[2] Besides the extracts from Euripides already quoted, p. 19, 1, compare the fragment in *Clemens*, Stromat. v. 603, D, which *Nauck*. Fragm. Trag. 588, attributes in all proba-

nature has changed owing to a clearer belief in immortality, introduced by the dogmas of the migration of souls and of future retribution ;[1] and of this change traces may be seen even in the poetry of the time of Euripides.[2] Lastly, in connection herewith an ascetic code of morals[3] has come into vogue, enjoining abstinence from animal food,[4] celibacy,[5] the avoidance of certain defilements,[6] and the wearing of white clothing. Philosophy, it is true, could only appropriate in an intellectual form the general idea of this asceticism, the renunciation of what belongs to the senses. Not till a later time did it embrace it as a whole with all its external belongings,

bility to Æschylus' son Euphorion: Ζεύς ἐστιν αἰθὴρ, Ζεὺς δὲ γῆ, Ζεύς τ' οὐρανὸς, Ζεύς τοι τὰ πάντα χὤτι τῶνδ' ὑπέρτερον.

[1] Comp. *Zeller*, vol. i. 54, 388, 581, 654.

[2] Besides Euripides (p. 19, 1), Melanippides (Fr. 6 in *Bergk*, Lyr. Gr. p. 982) appears to have regarded the soul as immortal. Io, too (Fr. 4 in *Bergk*, p. 464), appropriates the Pythagorean belief in immortality. A resolution of souls into ether may also be implied in the popular belief mentioned by Aristophanes (Peace, 832), that the dead become stars.

[3] See *Euripid.* Hippol. 949 ; Fr. 475 ; *Plato*, Laws, vi. 782, C.; comparing therewith the principles of Empedocles and Pythagoras.

[4] Probably *Eurip.* Fr. 884, refers to this.

[5] That this was a part of Orphic perfection may be gathered from Euripides, who holds up Hippolytus as a type of an Orphic, probably only because this despiser of Aphrodite (Hippol. 10, 101), by his typical chastity, reminds of Orphic virginity. A vow of chastity also occurs in Electra, v. 254, and it is well known that marriage was forbidden to many priestesses, though more rarely to priests.

[6] Φεύγω γένεσίν τε βροτῶν καὶ νεκροθήκης οὐ χριμπτόμενος (*Eurip.* Fr. 475, 16), consequently the same καθαρεύειν ἀπὸ κήδους καὶ λεχοῦς (touching a corpse or woman who has been confined), which the Pythagorean of Alexander Polyhister in *Diog.* viii. 33 requires. Birth and death, for reasons closely allied, are regarded as polluting. Compare *Eurip.* Iphig. Taur. 372 ; *Thuc.* iii. 104.

CHAP. I.

in the system of the Neopythagoreans. Such, however, was the state of intellectual life and mental development in Greece that, before that time came, it had entered itself on another and a more brilliant career.

CHAPTER II.

CHARACTER AND PROGRESS OF GREEK PHILOSOPHY IN THE FIFTH CENTURY.

THE age of Socrates inherited from earlier days a rich store of religious ideas, of moral principles, and scientific conceptions; at the same time it had fallen away at every point from the earlier tone of thought and custom. Traditional lines seemed now to be all too narrow; new paths were looked for; new problems pressed for solution. The legendary ideas respecting the Gods and the state after death, had lost all meaning for the great majority of the educated;[1] the very existence of the Gods had been denied by many; ancient customs had fallen into disuse; the orderliness of civil life, the simplicity and purity of domestic life, had given place to a wanton dissoluteness of conduct, and an unscrupulous pursuit of pleasure and profit. Principles subversive of all law and of all right were being unblushingly advocated with the ready approval of the younger generation. The severity and grandeur of the earlier art, the lucid beauty, the classic grace, the self-contained dignity of the later art, began to resolve themselves into the study of mere effect;

[1] Conf. *Plato*, Rep. i. 330, D.

CHAP. II.

and under the influence of sophistry, philosophy had come to disbelieve, not only in individual systems, but also in the whole course of previous inquiry, and even in the possibility of knowledge at all.

Far, however, from being exhausted, the mental vigour of Greece was only fully emancipated by the throes and struggles of the fifth century. Its horizon was extended; its energy was stimulated; its views and conceptions enriched. Its whole consciousness had gained a new field since its success in deeds of renown and distinguished exploits. If the meridian of classic art and of free political life was past towards the close of this period, still the newly awakened culture of the understanding was full of intellectual promise for the future; for sophistry had been destructive, not constructive, only suggesting, not bringing to maturity. Some new and thorough change was called for to satisfy not only practical but also intellectual requirements. Ancient propriety of conduct, and the received philosophic teaching having been once ousted by the altered spirit of the times, simple return thereto became impossible. But to despair on this account of all knowledge, and of all principles of morality, was most precipitate. Allowing even that the received view of both was inadequate, it by no means followed, that all science and all morality was impossible. On the contrary, the more the pernicious consequences of such a view were exposed, the more urgent became the duty of avoiding them by a thorough transformation of the whole tone of feeling and thought, without, however, attempting the impossible task of simply restoring the past.

A. Distinction of Socratic from pre-Socratic philosophy.

(1) The pre-Socratic traditional; the Socratic resting on knowledge.

For this purpose some new path must be struck out; and what that path should be, a far-sighted eye could discern with sufficient clearness by the aid of past experience. Traditional propriety of conduct had given way before the spirit of innovation, because it rested upon instinct and custom, and not on any clear recognition of necessity. To undertake a permanent restoration of moral life, it must be founded upon knowledge. Earlier philosophy had been unable to satisfy the needs of the times, because it had been directed exclusively to a study of nature; because to the mass of men it did not give sufficient preparation for the work of life, nor to the thinking spirit any clue to the problem of its being and destiny. New philosophy must meet this want, must direct its attention to the sphere of mind and morals, and work into shape the ample store of ethical ideas underlying religion, poetry, and received custom. Earlier systems had succumbed before the doubts of sophistry, because their method was too partial, too little depending on definite conceptions respecting the nature and problem of knowledge to be able to withstand a searching criticism which destroyed their several platforms by means of each other, and argued from the change and uncertainty of the phenomena of the senses that knowledge must be impossible. No building that would last could be erected except by laying the foundations deeper, except by finding

CHAP. II.

some means of supplementing these several points of view by each other, of harmonising them when contradictory in some higher bond of union,[1] and of grasping the unchangeable essence of things amid changing appearances. The means wanted were supplied by Dialectic, the art of forming conceptions, and the result was philosophical Idealism. Thus the knowledge of the faults and deficiencies in existing conditions led naturally to the turn taken by philosophy after the time of Socrates. Scientific ethics became necessary because of the giving way of moral convictions; a wider inquiry, because of the narrowness of the philosophy of nature; a critical method, because of the contradiction of dogmatic systems; a philosophy of conceptions, because of the uncertainty of the observations of the senses; Idealism, because of the unsatisfactory nature of a materialistic view of the world.

(2) *The pre-Socratic philosophy a study of nature; the Socratic of conceptions.*

Precisely these features distinguish the Socratic philosophy from that which went before it. The pre-Socratic philosophy was simply and solely a philosophy of nature;[2] the transitional philosophy of the Sophists was the first to leave nature for ethical and dialectical questions. After Socrates the dialectical tendency is supreme. His own attention was exclusively occupied with determining conceptions and inquiries respecting virtue. With rare exceptions the imperfect Socratic schools confined themselves to the same field. Plato, founding

[1] Comp. *Zeller's* Phil. der Griechen, Part I. pp. 854, 860.

[2] In the sense given, *ibid.* I 155.

his system in conceptions, completing it in morals, forms a marked contrast to the natural philosophers who went before him. Even in Aristotle, who treats of physics in detail and with an evident preference for the subject, they are only a single branch of a system, and in point of value subordinate to metaphysics.

Such an extension of ground showed that the whole platform of philosophy had changed. Why else should the mind have embraced other and more comprehensive materials, had it not changed in itself and therefore become discontented with what had been? For the same reason the philosophic method was now a different one. In previous times the mind had dealt directly with its object as such. In the Socratic and post-Socratic systems it deals primarily with conceptions, and only with objects indirectly, through the medium of conceptions. The older systems asked, without further preliminary, what predicates belonged to things; for instance, Whether what is real admits of motion or not?—How and out of what the world is made? The Socratic philosophy ever asks, in the first place, what things are in themselves according to their conception, thinking not otherwise to obtain information respecting their properties and conditions than by the help of the conception of things thoroughly mastered.[1] No conception of a thing can, however,

B. *Characteristic of this period is its doctrine of conceptions.*

[1] Compare, not to mention other passages, the clear statement in the Phædo, 99 D: After having vainly busied himself with the inquiries of the natural philosophers, he

CHAP. II.

be obtained, except by grouping together the various aspects and qualities of that thing, by smoothing down apparent contradictions, by separating what is permanent from what is changing; in a word, by that critical method, which Socrates introduced, and which Plato and Aristotle elaborated and developed.

(1) *Definition of a conception.*

Former philosophers having gone forth from particular prominent features to arrive at the essence of things, and having failed because of their one-sidedness, it was now required that all the properties of an object should be taken into account and weighed from every side, before a judgment could be formed thereupon. Thus the philosophy of conceptions steps into the place of dogmatism. In this way criticism, which by means of sophistry had destroyed the older philosophy, was taken into the service of the new philosophy; the various aspects under which things may be regarded were brought together and referred to each other; but not content with the negative conclusion that our notions cannot be true because they contain opposite determinations, the new philosophy aimed at uniting these opposites in one, and showing that true science is not affected by contradiction, inasmuch as it only refers to that which unites opposites in itself, to the exclusion of contradiction. This pursuit of knowledge through

declares himself convinced, that he has only got into deeper darkness by directing his inquiries into things in themselves. (τὰ ὄντα σκοπῶν . . . βλέπων πρὸς τὰ πράγματα τοῖς ὄμμασι καὶ ἑκάστῃ τῶν αἰσθήσεων ἐπιχειρῶν ἅπτεσθαι αὐτῶν.) ἔδοξε δή μοι χρῆναι εἰς τοὺς λόγους καταφυγόντα ἐν ἐκείνοις σκοπεῖν τῶν ὄντων τὴν ἀλήθειαν (the true essence of things), i.e. instead of πράγματα, λόγοι, instead of ὄντα, ἀλήθεια τῶν ὄντων.

conceptions is the common peculiarity of the Socratic, the Platonic, and the Aristotelian philosophy. That the lesser Socratic schools follow the same bent will be seen hereafter.

If only conceptions can give true knowledge, it follows that true being can only belong to that which is known by means of conceptions, that is, to the essence of things as it presents itself in thought. This essential being cannot, however, be looked for in matter. Anaxagoras had early realised that matter could only become a world by means of spirit; since then the old materialistic physics had been discredited by sophistry; nothing remained but to regard the form and purpose of things, the immaterial part in them as the essential part for determining the conception; nay, even to assign to it a true reality underlying the appearance. In this way the Socratic philosophy led logically to Idealism.

(2) *Theory of conceptions expanded by Socrates, Plato, and Aristotle.*

The beginnings of this Idealism are unmistakable even in Socrates. His indifference to physical inquiries and his preference for ethical ones prove conclusively that he attributed to the inner world a much higher value than to the outer would. Resolve his theory of final causes in nature into the metaphysical elements out of which it is composed; the conclusion is inevitable that not the material of which a thing is made, but the conception which gives it shape, makes a thing what it is, and that this accordingly represents its true nature. This Idealism is more pronounced in the school of Megara;

CHAP. II.

and in Plato it runs through all parts of his philosophy side by side with a current of pre-Socratic doctrines. Even Aristotle is not faithless to this view. Whilst denying the independent existence of the Platonic ideas, he nevertheless asserts that reality consists not in matter but in form, and that the highest reality belongs to mind free from matter. On this ground he maintains, quite in harmony with his predecessors, that even in natural science final causes are higher than material causes. Compared therefore with the natural philosophers of the pre-Socratic period, even Aristotle may fairly be called an Idealist.

Starting from a consideration of nature, the pre-Socratic philosophy made it its chief endeavour to inquire into the essence and causes of external things, for this purpose going back to their material properties. An entirely different character is displayed in the philosophy founded by Socrates. This begins with the study of self rather than the study of nature—with ethics rather than physics. It aims at explaining phenomena, first of all by means of conceptions, and only in the second place naturally. It substitutes an attitude of inquiry for dogmatic statement, idealism in the place of materialism. Mind is now regarded as the higher element compared with matter. The philosophy of nature has developed into a philosophy of conceptions.

As yet the claim was not advanced that the human mind is the measure of truth and the end of science. Far from reaching the subjective idealism

C. *Distinction of Socratic from post-Aristotelian philosophy.*

of Fichte—an idealism in fact only possible in modern times—the philosophy of this period is not nearly so subjective as in the post-Aristotelian schools.[1] In them the interests of speculation are subordinated to those of morals; knowledge is regarded only as a means to virtue and happiness; whereas the independent value of knowledge is fully admitted by the great philosophers of the present period. To them knowledge is an end in itself; speculation is the highest and noblest thing; action is made to depend upon knowledge, not knowledge to depend upon the aims of active life. Only a few one-sided followers of Socrates, who, however, prove nothing as to the general tendency, are an exception to this rule.

(1) *It still believes the attainment of knowledge to be possible.*

A simple belief in the possibility of knowledge is here displayed which was wanting in the post-Aristotelian philosophy. The doubts of the Sophists are refuted, but there is no need of overcoming doubt in the thinker's mind. The questions asked are, How can true knowledge be obtained? In what kind of mental representation must it be sought? How must the conception of it be determined? No doubt is felt as to the possibility of knowledge. The search for a test—the fundamental question of the later schools—is altogether unknown[2] to the

[1] Take for instance the Theætetus; the question raised there as to the conception of knowledge (ἐπιστήμη ὅ τί ποτε τυγάχνει ὄν; Theætet. 145, E.), is quite different from the doubt as to the possibility of knowledge involved in the inquiry for a standard.

[2] Compare *Zeller*, l. c.; Introduction to Part III. and I. 137.

CHAP. II.

thinkers of this time. Equally unknown to them are the answers to that problem. They did not, as did the Epicureans and Stoics, cut short the question by practically begging it. They did not, as did the Sceptics, despair of knowledge. They did not, as did the Neoplatonists, resort to higher revelations. They were content to look to precision of thought for the source of truth. Even that branch of science, the independent pursuit of which was so much neglected by later thinkers—physics—was studied in this epoch with success. Socrates and the majority of his pupils may have neglected it, but not so Plato; and Aristotle carried it to a point final in the main for nearly two thousand years. When the post-Aristotelian Ethics had finally broken away from the principles of the old Greek morality, owing partly to their world-wide comprehensiveness, partly to their rupture with politics, to the withdrawal of the moral consciousness from the outer world, to silent resignation and morose asceticism; a moment's recollection of the many-sided sympathies of Socrates, with his cheerful enjoyment of life, and his devoted attachment to his country, or of Plato's teaching concerning the state, or of Aristotle's concerning virtue and society, or of the relation between the Cyrenaic and the Epicurean doctrine of happiness,[1] brings home at once the difference of epochs.

(2) Morality not pursued independently.

It is true that the philosophy of this second period attempts to get beyond the received bounds in ethics. It supplements the propriety of custom

[1] Comp. *Zeller*, l. c. i. 139.

by a theory of morals and conscious action. It distinguishes more definitely than the current view between the outward deed and the intention. It requires a rising above the life of the senses to what is ideal. Light is thrown on the meaning and motives of moral consciousness. A universal philanthropy is taught, which is not lost in local patriotism; and accordingly the state is only regarded as an institution for the attainment of virtue and happiness, and not as the final moral cause. For all that this period is far removed from the apathy of either Stoic or Epicurean, from the imperturbability of the Sceptic, from the asceticism of the Neoplatonist. It seeks not to sever man in his moral activity from nature; with Aristotle it regards virtue as the perfection of a natural gift; with Plato it advances from the love of what is sensibly beautiful, to the love of what is morally beautiful. It requires the philosopher to work for his fellow men. The world-citizenship of a later time is absent; absent too is its nationality and political life. Even in this respect, it holds the classic mean between a slavish surrender to the outer world, and a narrow withdrawal therefrom.

Compared with the pre-Socratic era, the age of Socrates is characterised by the diversion of philosophy from external nature to thought or to ideas. Compared with the following age, it is marked by the objective character of its thought, that is, by the fact that the thinker is not concerned with himself and the certainty of his own knowing, but with

CHAP. II.

attaining to the knowledge of what is in itself real and true. In short its theory of a knowledge of conceptions determines its scientific platform. From this theory follows its breadth of view, reaching alike beyond the physical one-sidedness of the pre-Socratic, and the moral one-sidedness of the post-Aristotelian schools, its critical method in opposition to the earlier and later dogmatism, and its idealism, transfiguring the whole aspect of the outer world, without, however, entailing any withdrawal therefrom.

D. *Development of the Socratic philosophy.*

The development of this theory was carried out in a simple and natural order by three philosophic schools, the founders of which belong to three successive generations, and are personally connected as teachers and pupils.[1] First comes Socrates asserting that the standard of human thought and action lies in a knowledge of conceptions, and teaching his followers to acquire this knowledge by analysing notions critically. Hence Plato concluded that objective conceptions are in the true sense the only real things, a derivative reality belonging to all other things—a view which he upheld by a more critical analysis, and developed to a system. Lastly, Aristotle argued that in a thing the conception itself constitutes its real essence and makes it what it is. By an exhaustive analysis of the scientific method, he showed how conceptions were to be formed and applied to particulars, and by a most comprehensive inquiry into the several parts of the universe, he

[1] Comp. *Zeller*, I. 9, 136, 142.

examined the laws and connection of conceptions, and the thoughts which determine all that really is. Socrates had as yet no system. He had not even any material groundwork. Convinced that only in acquiring conceptions is true knowledge to be found, that true virtue consists in acting according to conceptions, that even the world has been ordered in accordance with definite conceptions, and therefore shows design, in any given case he tries by a critical testing of prevailing notions to gain a conception of the object with which he has to deal, and to this he devotes all his powers, to the exclusion of every other interest. But he never went beyond this formal treatment. His teaching was confined to these general postulates and assumptions. His importance lies not in a new view of things, but in a new conception of knowledge, and in the way he forms this conception, in his apprehension of the problem and method of science, in the strength of his philosophical bent, and in the simplicity of his philosophical life.

(1) *Socrates.*

The Socratic search for conceptions has grown in Plato to a discovery of them, to a certainty of possessing them, and gazing upon them. With him objective thoughts or ideas are the only real things. Mere idealess existence or matter as such is simply non-existent; all things else are made up partly of what is and partly of what is not; they therefore are only real in proportion to the part they have in the idea. Granting that this is in advance of the Socratic view, it is no less certain that it follows

(2) *Plato.*

CHAP. II.

logically from that view. The Platonic ideas, as Aristotle rightly understood them,[1] are the general conceptions, which Socrates had arrived at, separated from the world of appearance. They are also the central point of the speculations of Aristotle. With him the conception or the form constitutes the essence, the reality, and is as it were the soul of things; only form without matter, pure self-contemplating mind is absolutely real; only thought is to man the most intense reality, and therefore also the most intense pleasure in life. Yet there is this difference between Aristotle and Plato, that whereas Plato separates the conception from the appearance, regarding it as independent—as an ἰδέα, Aristotle places it *in* things themselves, without, however, implying that form stands in need of matter to become actual, since it is in itself actual. Aristotle will not remove the idea out of the phenomenal world because in a state of separation it cannot serve as a connecting link between individual things, nor yet be the cause and substance of things. Thus the theory is seen to be one and the same which Socrates, Plato, and Aristotle represent at different stages of growth. In Socrates it is undeveloped, but full of vitality, pushing itself forward through the husk of earlier philosophy; in Plato it has grown to a free and independent existence; and in Aristotle it has overspread the whole world of being and consciousness, exhausting itself in the effort, and moving towards a perfect transformation in

(3) *Aristotle.*

[1] Met. i. 6, 987, B. 1.

later systems. Socrates, so to speak, is the pregnant germ, Plato the rich bloom, Aristotle the ripe fruit of Greek philosophy at the perfection of its historical growth.

(4) *Difficulty caused by Socratic Schools.*

One phenomenon only will not fall into this historical chain, but threatens to break the continuity of Greek thought, viz. the imperfect attempts to expand the Socratic principle which are seen in the Megarian, the Cynic, and the Cyrenaic schools. In these schools no real and essential progress of the philosophic consciousness was to be found, philosophy being by them restricted to subjective training of thought and character, although in principle at any rate it had in the time of Socrates arrived at objective knowledge, such as could only be found in a system. Nor yet can they be said to be wholly unimportant. For not only were they, at a later period, starting points for Stoicism, Epicureanism, and Scepticism, but they also promoted independently thereof many scientific inquiries, by means of which they exercised an undeniable influence on Plato and Aristotle. Elsewhere, and even in this epoch, the same case occurs in the older Academy, and in the Peripatetic schools, both of which had no independent influence on the growth of philosophy, but yet cannot be overlooked in its history. Of all these phenomena one and the same thing must be said. Their chief importance lies not in their having theoretically expanded a principle, but in their having been practically helpful in advancing it, by preserving the older forms of culture for cotempor-

CHAP. II.

aries to see, here and there improving and widening them, and by thus keeping the philosopher's mind in sight of a many-sidedness, without which later systems would never have included the products of the earlier ones.

This permanence of philosophic schools is not therefore met with until philosophy had attained a certain general extension, in Greece not until the time of Socrates and Plato. Whereas Plato, by summing up all the pre-Socratic schools, put an end to their existence; after his time no theory was put forward which did not perpetuate itself in a school until the time that Neoplatonism put the coping-stone on Greek philosophy, in and with which all previous systems were extinguished. In later times, however many intellectual varieties rise up side by side, only a few of them possess a distinct life of their own. The rest are a traditional survival of previous views, and cannot, in considering the peculiar philosophical character of an age, be taken further into account. They need only be mentioned in a passing way. This statement applies to the imperfect followers of Socrates. Their doctrines are not an advancement in principle, but only incomplete reproductions of Socratic views, connected with Socrates in the same way that the elder Academy is with Plato, or the Peripatetic school with Aristotle.

PART II.

SOCRATES.

CHAPTER III.

THE LIFE OF SOCRATES.

CHAP. III.

THERE is no instance on record of a philosopher whose importance as a thinker is so closely bound up with his personal character as a man as it was in the case of Socrates. Every system, it is true, as being the work of a definite person, may best be studied in the light of the peculiarities, culture, misfortunes and circumstances of its author; yet in the case of others it is easier to separate the fruits of their intellectual life from the stock on which they grew; doctrines can generally be received and handed down quite unchanged by men of very different characters. In the case of Socrates this is not nearly so easy. His teaching aimed far less at definite doctrines, which can be equally well embraced by different men, than at a special tone of life and thought, at a philosophic character and an art of intellectual inquiry, in short, at a something not to be directly imparted and handed down unaltered,

CHAP. III.

but to be propagated freely, others being stirred up to an analogous development of their peculiarities. Hence the increased anxiety for accurate information as to the training of a character which has had so powerful an influence on history. Here a very common difficulty arises. What Socrates was, and how he acted in his riper years, is well known; but only the roughest outline is preserved of the circumstances of his life. Over the earlier part of it thick darkness rests. For the history of his intellectual and moral training, if we except a few scanty and for the most part untrustworthy statements of earlier writers, we are left entirely to conjecture.

A. *Early life of Socrates.*

The youth and early manhood of Socrates fall in the most brilliant period of Grecian history. Born during the last years of the Persian war,[1] he was

[1] The best ascertained date in the life of Socrates is the date of his death. According to *Demetrius Phalerius* and *Apollodorus* (in *Diog.* ii. 44), he died in Olympiad 95, 1 (*Diod.* xiv. 37), probably in the second half of the month Thargelion. For in this year must be placed the return of the Delian θεωρὶς, which (according to *Plato*, Phædo, 59, D.), arrived the day before the execution of Socrates. Comp. K. F. *Hermann*, De theoria Deliaca, Ind. Schol. Götting. 1846. About a month earlier (*Xenophon*, Mem. iv. 8, 2, says definitely thirty days), i.e. in the month Munychion, the judicial inquiry took place. Socrates must accordingly have been condemned in April or May 399 B.C., and have suffered death in May or June the same year. Since at the time of his death he had passed his seventieth year (*Plato*, Apol. 17, D.), but not long (Crito, 52, E., calls him in round numbers seventy), his birth cannot have fallen later than Ol. 77, 3, or 469 B.C. If his birthday is rightly fixed on the 6th Thargelion (Apoll. in *Diog.* ii. 44; *Plut.* Qu. Conv. viii. 1, 1; *Ælian*, V. H. ii. 25), and was not past at the time of the judicial inquiry, we should have to go back for it to 470 or even 471 B.C. (Comp. *Böckh.* Corp. Inscript. ii. 321; *Hermann*, l. c. 7).

The question then arises whether these statements respecting the date of his birth are nearly cotemporary with all those great men who adorned the age of Pericles. As a citizen of Athens he participated in all those elements of culture, which congregated in that great metropolis, thanks to its unrivalled fertility of thought. If poverty and low birth somewhat impeded his using them,[1] still

facts or a mere fiction; and whether the birthday of Socrates, the μαιευτικὸς, was not placed on the 6th of Thargelion to make it agree with that of Artemis, just as Plato's was made to agree with Apollo's. If so, he may have been born in 469 B.C. (Olymp. 77, 3). Anyhow, *Apollodorus* is wrong, placing it in 468 B.C. (Ol. 77, 4), (*Diog.* l. c.). Nor can the statement noticed by Diogenes that he was only sixty years of age outweigh the clear language of Plato; it probably rests upon a transcriber's mistake. Hermann's remark (Plat. Phil. 666, De Philos. Jon. ætat. ii. A., 39) that Socrates could not have been born in the third or fourth year of an Olympiad, since he was twenty-five (*Synes.* Calv. Enc. c. 17) at the time of his interview with Protagoras, which interview happened (*Plato*, Parm.) at the time of the Panathenæa, and consequently in the third year of an Olympiad, will not hold water. Supposing the interview to be even a fact, which is very doubtful, the remark of Synesius (Calv. Enc. c. 17) respecting the age of Socrates is a pure guess, and altogether refuted by the language of the Theætet. 183, F, and the Parmen. 127, C., πάνυ νέος, σφόδρα νέος.

[1] That his father Sophroniscus (*Xen.* Hellen. i. 7, 15; *Plato*, Lach. 180, D.; how Epiphanius, Exp. Fid. 1087, A., comes to call him Elbaglus, is difficult to say) was a sculptor, may be gathered from *Diog.* ii. 18. The services of his mother Phænarete as a midwife are known from Plato's Theætetus, 149, A. As regards circumstances, it is stated by Demetrius Phaler, in *Plutarch's* Life of Aristides, c. 1, that he not only possessed land, but had seventy minæ—a considerable sum—at interest; but this statement is at variance with the testimony of the best witnesses. The reasons for it are without doubt quite as weak as those for a similar statement respecting Aristides, and arose seemingly from some Peripatetic's wish to find authorities for his view of the worth of riches. Plato (Apol. 23, B., 38, A.; Rep. i. 337, D.) and Xenophon (Œc. ii. 2; xi. 3; Mem. i. 2, 1) represent him not only as very poor, πάνυ μικρὰ κεκτημένος and ἐν πενίᾳ μυρίᾳ, but they also give reasons for thinking so. Plato makes him say, perhaps he could pay a fine of a mina, and Xenophon depicts him as

in the Athens of Pericles, not even the lowest on the city roll was debarred from enjoying the rich profusion of art, which for the most part was devoted to the purposes of the state, nor yet from associating with men in the highest ranks of life. This free personal intercourse did far more to advance intellectual culture at that time than teaching in schools; Socrates had reached manhood before the Sophists introduced a formal system of instruction. Intelligible as it thus becomes, that an energetic man in the position of Socrates should have found many incitements to and means of culture, and even should have been carried away by the wonderful elevation of his native city, still nothing very accurate is known respecting the routes by which he advanced to his subsequent greatness.[1] We may suppose that he enjoyed the usual education in gymnastics and music,[2] although the stories which are told of his

estimating his whole property, inclusive of his cottage, at five minæ. The story of Libanius (Apol. Socr. t. iii. p. 7), according to which Socrates inherited eighty minæ from his father, and having lost them by lending, bore his loss with extreme composure, looks like a story intended to show the indifference of a philosopher to wealth. Had Plato and Xenophon known the story, we may be sure they would not have omitted to tell it.

[1] See the work of K. F. *Hermann*, De Socratis magistris et disciplina juvenili, Marb. 1837.

[2] Plato says so plainly in the Crito, 50, D. Even apart from this testimony there could be no doubt. Porphyry's statement (in *Theod.* Cur. Gr. Aff. i. 29, p. 8)—a statement undoubtedly derived from Aristoxenus—that Socrates was too uneducated to be able to read, need scarcely be refuted by authorities such as *Xen.* Mem. i. 6, 14; iv. 7, 3, 5. It is clearly an exaggeration of the well-known ἀπαιδευσία (*Plato*, Symp. 221, E., 199, A., Apol. 17, B.), which only belongs to the satirical outside of the philosopher, but was readily taken hold of and exaggerated by jealousy in later times.

teachers in music[1] deserve no credit. We hear further that he learnt enough of geometry to be able to grapple with difficult problems, and that he was not ignorant of astronomy;[2] but whether he acquired this knowledge in his youth, or only in later years, and who was his teacher, we cannot tell.[3] We see him, in mature years, in relations more or less close with a number of characters who must have exerted a most varied and stirring influence on his mind.[4] It

[1] According to *Max. Tyr.* xxxviii. 4, Connus was his teacher in music, and Euenus in poetry. Alexander (in *Diog.* ii. 19) calls him a pupil of Damon, whereas *Sextus* (Matth. vi. 13) makes Lampo his teacher. All these notices have undoubtedly come from passages in Plato which are irrelevant. Socrates calls Connus his teacher (Menex. 235, E., and Euthyd. 272, C.), but according to the latter passage he was a man at the time, so that he must have gone to Connus simply with a view to revive a skill long since acquired. It is more probable (however often such notices are given as historical, and with further details: *Cic.* ad Fam. ix. 22; *Quint.* i. 10; *Val. Max.* viii. 7; *Diog.* ii. 32; *Stob.* Flor. 29, 68) that the passages in Plato refer to the Connus of the comic poet Ameipsias, the origin of the whole fabrication. See *Hermann*, p. 24. Damon's name is mentioned in the Laches, 180, D., 197, D.; Rep. iii. 400, B., 424, C., in which passages, however, this musician appears as the friend rather than as the instructor of Socrates, and as an important political character, from his connection with Pericles. The Phædo, 60, C., and the Apology, 20, A., mention Euenus, yet not as a teacher, and hardly even as an acquaintance of Socrates. And lastly, Lampo mentioned by Sextus probably owes his existence to a mistake. Sextus may have written Damon instead of Connus (*Stobæus*, Flor. 29, 68, has Connus in the same connection)—or else Lamprus (a name which occurs in the Menexenus, though not as that of a teacher of Socrates), and transcribers made it Lampo. The celebrated prophet of this name cannot of course have been intended.

[2] *Xen.* Mem. iv. 7, 3, 5.

[3] *Maximus* l.c. says Theodore of Cyrene, but this is only an inference from Plato's Theætetus and not warranted by it.

[4] For instance, the Sophists, Protagoras, Gorgias, Polus, Hippias, Thrasymachus, but especially Prodicus. Cf. *Plato*, Prot., Gorg., Hip., Rep. i.; *Xen.* Mem. ii. 1, 21; iv. 4, 5, &c. Also Euripides, who was on

CHAP. III.

is beyond doubt that he owed much to such relations; but these friends cannot in strict accuracy be described as his teachers, although we may often find them so called;[1] neither is any light derived hence for the history of his early training. We further meet with expressions which show that he must have had a general acquaintance with the views of Parmenides and Heraclitus, of the Atomists, of Anaxagoras, and perhaps of Empedocles.[2] Whence he derived this knowledge, it is impossible to say. The stories that he received instruction in his younger years from Anaxagoras and Archelaus, can neither be supported by satisfactory evidence, nor are they probable in themselves.[3] Still more uncertain is his

such intimate terms with him that the comic poets charged him with borrowing his tragedies from Socrates. (Cf. *Diog.* ii. 18; *Ælian*, V. H. ii. 13.) Also Aspasia; cf. *Xen.* Œc. 3, 14; Mem. ii. 6, 36; *Æschines*, in *Cic.* de Invent. i. 31; in *Max. Tyr.* xxxviii. 4; conf. *Hermann* De Æsch. relig. 16; Hermesianax in *Athen.* xiii. 599. a; Diotima (*Plato*, Symp.). Respecting several of these we know not whether Plato was true to facts in bringing them into connection with Socrates.

[1] Socrates calls himself in Plato a pupil of Prodicus (*Zeller*, l. c. i. 873, D.), of Aspasia (Menex. 235, E.), and of Diotima (Symp. 201, D.), all of which statements have been repeated in past and present times. See *Hermann*, Soc. Mag. p. 11. We may suppose that the instruction given by the two ladies consisted in free personal intercourse, even allowing that Diotima is a real person, and the Menexenus a genuine dialogue; and the same remark applies equally to Prodicus. Maximus calls Ischomachus his teacher in agriculture, but he probably arrived at this conclusion by misunderstanding *Xen.* Œc. 6, 17. The story that he was a pupil of Diagoras of Melos (the Scholiast on *Aristoph.* Nubes, v. 828), is obviously false.

[2] *Xen.* Mem. i. 1, 14; iv. 7, 6.

[3] The authorities are: for Anaxagoras, *Aristid.* Or. xlv., p. 21, and the nameless authorities referred to by *Diog.* ii. 19 and 45, whom Suidas Σωκράτ. according to custom follows; for Archelaus, *Diog.* ii. 16, 19, 23, x. 12, and those mentioned by him, Io, Aristoxenus, and Diocles. Besides these Cicero,

supposed intercourse with Zeno and Parmenides. Even little is known of the philosophical writings

Sextus, Porphyry (in *Theod.* Cur. Gr. Aff. xii. 67, p. 175), Clement of Alexandria (Strom. i. 302, A.), Simplicius, Eusebius (Pr. Ev. x. 14, 13, xiv. 15, 11, xv. 61, 11), Hippolytus, the spurious Galen, and a few others; conf. *Krische*, Forsch. 210. The evidence in favour of Anaxagoras is very insufficient, and the language respecting him used by Socrates (*Plato*, Phædo, 97, B., and *Xenophon*, Mem. iv. 7, 6) makes it improbable that he knew him personally, or was acquainted with his views, except from books and hearsay, which of course does not exclude any casual or accidental meeting. The traditions respecting his relations to Archelaus are better authenticated; yet even here there is much that is suspicious. Of the two earliest authorities, Io and Aristoxenus, the former, who was an older cotemporary of Socrates, does not make Archelaus his instructor. All that is stated in *Diog.* ii. 23, on his authority, is that Socrates, when a young man, travelled with Archelaus to Samos. This assertion, however, flatly contradicts Plato (Crito, 52, B.), who says that Socrates never left Athens, except once to go to the Isthmian games or when on military duty. Müller, however, gets over the difficulty (Frag. Hist. Gr. ii. 49, N. 9) by supposing that Plato was only referring to Socrates when grown up.

It is just possible that Plato may not have known of a journey which Socrates took in his earlier years. That he should have knowingly omitted to mention it, as *Alberti*, Socr. 40, supposes, is hardly likely. It is also possible some mistake may have been made. Io may not have meant a journey to Samos, but his taking part in the expedition to Samos of 441 B.C., which, strange to say, is not mentioned in the Apology, 28, E. Or the error may lie with Diogenes, who applied to Socrates what Io had said of some one else. Or it may not be the Io of Chios, but some later individual who thus writes of Socrates. Certain it is, that Io's testimony does not prove Socrates to have been a pupil of Archelaus. Even if the relation were proved to have existed in Socrates' younger days, it would still be a question whether his philosophy was influenced thereby.

Aristoxenus goes further. According to his account in *Diog.* ii. 16, Socrates was the favourite of Archelaus, or, as Porphyry represents the matter, he became acquainted with Archelaus in his seventeenth year, lived with him many years, and was by him initiated into philosophy. We shall have occasion to notice hereafter how little dependence can be placed on the statements of Aristoxenus respecting Socrates. Were the other statement given on his authority which is to be found in Diogenes closely con-

CHAP. III.

with which he was acquainted.[1] A well-known passage in Plato's Phædo[2] describes him as advancing from the older natural science and the philosophy of Anaxagoras to his own peculiar views. But it is most improbable that this passage gives an historical account of his intellectual development, if for no other reason, at least for this one,[3] that the course of development there leads to the Platonic theory of conceptions; let alone the fact that it is by no means certain that Plato himself possessed any fuller information respecting the intellectual progress of his teacher.

No doubt he began life by learning his father's trade,[4] a trade which he probably never practised,

nected with this one, the statement that Socrates did not become a pupil of Archelaus till after the condemnation of Anaxagoras, his untrustworthiness would be at once exposed; for Socrates was seventeen when Anaxagoras left Athens, and had long passed his years of pupilage. The assertions of Aristoxenus, however, are in themselves improbable. For, supposing Socrates to have been on intimate terms with Archelaus, when young, twenty years before Anaxagoras was banished, how is it conceivable that he should not have known Anaxagoras?—and if he was instructed by him in philosophy, how is it that neither Xenophon nor Plato nor Aristotle ever mentions Archelaus? All the later authorities for the relation of the two philosophers appear to rest on Aristoxenus. As there is nothing in the teaching of Archelaus, with which the Socratic teaching can be connected, it seems probable that he had little to do with the philosophy of Socrates, even though Socrates may have known him and his teaching. Besides, Socrates (in Xen. Sym.) calls himself an αὐτουργὸς τῆς φιλοσοφίας, a self-taught philosopher.

[1] He seems to have known those of Anaxagoras. A supposed allusion to the writings of Heraclitus (in *Diog.* ii. 22) is uncertain, nor is it established that he ever studied the Pythagorean doctrines (*Plut.* Curios. 2).

[2] 96, A.

[3] As *Volquardsen* (Rhein. Mus. N. F. xix. 514; *Alberti*, Socr. 13; *Ueberweg*, Unters. d. Plat. Schr. 94; *Steinhart*, Plat. L., 297.

[4] Timon and Duris in *Diog.* ii. 19. Timæus, according to

and certainly soon gave up.[1] Considering it to be his special calling to labour for the moral and intellectual improvement of himself and others, this conviction forced itself so strongly upon him, as to appear to him in the light of a divine revelation.[2] He was, moreover, confirmed therein by a Delphic oracle, which, of course, must not be regarded as the cause of, but rather as an additional support to, his reforming zeal.[3] How and when this conviction first

Porphyry in *Cyril* c. Jul. 208, A. Plato (Rep. vi. 496, B.) seems to have had the case of Socrates in view.

[1] Porphyry leaves it open whether Socrates or his father practised sculpture; nor is anything proved by the story that the Graces on the Acropolis were his work (*Diog.* Paus. i. 22). No allusions are found in Aristophanes, Plato, or Xenophon to the sculptor's art. Hence we may conclude that if Socrates ever practised it, he gave it up long before the play of the Clouds was acted. Duris and Demetrius of Byzantium (in *Diog.* ii. 19), in stating that he was a slave, and that Crito took him from a workshop and brought him up, appear to confound him with Phædo.

[2] *Plato*, Apol. 33, C.: ἐμοὶ δὲ τοῦτο . . . . προστέτακται ὑπὸ τοῦ θεοῦ πράττειν καὶ ἐκ μαντείων καὶ ἐξ ἐνυπνίων καὶ παντὶ τρόπῳ, ᾧπερ τίς ποτε καὶ ἄλλη θεία μοῖρα ἀνθρώπῳ καὶ ὁτιοῦν προσέταξε ποιεῖν.

[3] According to the well-known story in the Apol. 20, E., which has been repeated countless times by succeeding writers, the matter stands thus: Chærephon had asked at Delphi if there was a wiser man than Socrates, and the priestess had answered in the negative. The Iambics which purport to contain the answer in *Diog.* ii. 37, and *Suid.* σοφός belong of course to a much later period. Whereupon, says Socrates, he had thought over the sense of the oracle, and, in the hope of finding it, he had conversed with all who made pretensions to knowledge. At last he has found that neither he himself nor any other man was wise, but that others believed themselves to be wise, whilst he was conscious of his want of wisdom. He considered himself therefore enlisted in the service of Apollo and pledged to a similar sifting of men, to save the honour of the oracle, since it had declared him, although one so wanting in wisdom, to be the wisest of men. Allowing that Socrates really said this—and there is no doubt that he said it in substance—it by no means follows that his philosophical activity dated from the time

CHAP. III.

dawned on him, cannot be determined. Most probably it grew gradually in proportion as he gained more knowledge of the moral and intellectual circumstances of his time, and soon after the beginning of the Peloponnesian war he had found in the main his philosophical centre of gravity.[1]

B. *Active life of Socrates.*

From that time forward he devoted himself to the mission he had assumed, regardless of everything else. His means of support were extremely scanty,[2] and his domestic life, in company with Xanthippe, was far from happy.[3] Yet neither her passionate

of the Pythian oracle. Else what should have led Chærephon to put the question, or the oracle to give the answer it did? So that if in the Apology he speaks as though the Delphic Oracle had first stirred him up to the sifting of men, that must be a figure of speech. Without going so far as Colotes (in *Plut* adv. Col. 17, 1), and *Athenæus* (v. 218) and many modern writers (*Brucker*, Hist. Phil. i. 534, *Van Dalen* and *Heumann*), and denying the historical character of the oracle altogether—and certainly the proofs are not very strict—we can at least attach no great importance to it. It may have been of service to Socrates just as his doctor's degree was to Luther, assuring him of his inward call, but it had just as little to do with making him a philosophical reformer as the doctor's degree had with making Luther a religious reformer. The story of the response given to his father when he was a boy (*Plut.* Gen. Socr. c. 20) is altogether a fiction.

[1] This is proved by the part which Aristophanes assigns to Socrates in the Clouds. If at that time, 424 B.C., he could be described as the chief of the new learning, he must have worked for years according to a definite method, and have gathered about him a circle of friends. In the Connus of Ameipsias, which seems to have been acted at the same time as the Clouds, he likewise appears as a well-known person, and Io in his travelling memorials had previously alluded to him. See p. 57, 1; 58, 3.

[2] See p. 55, 1.

[3] The name of Xanthippe is not only proverbial now. Later writers of antiquity (*Teles.* in *Stob.* Flor. 5, 64; *Seneca* De Const. 18, 5; Epist. 104, 177; *Porphyry* in *Theod.* Cur. Gr. Aff. xii. 65; *Diogenes* ii. 36); *Plutarch* Coh. Ira, 13, 461, who however tells the same of the wife of Pittacus, Tranq. An.

character was permitted to ruffle his philosophic

ii. 471; *Ælian*, V. H. xi. 12; *Athenæus*, v. 219; *Synesius*, &c.), relate of her so many little stories and disgraceful traits that one almost feels inclined to take up the cudgels in her behalf, as Heumann has actually done (Acta Phil. i. 103). What Xenophon (Mem. ii. 2; Sym. 2, 10) and Plato (Phædo, 60, A.) say, shows that she cannot have been altogether badly disposed. At least she was solicitous about her family, though at the same time she was extremely violent, overbearing, and intractable. It is remarkable that Aristophanes in the Clouds says nothing of the married life of Socrates, although this might have afforded him material for many a joke. Probably Socrates was not then married. His eldest son is called twenty-five years later (*Plato*, Apol. 34, D.; Phædo, 60, A.) μειράκιον ἤδη, and there were two young children. Besides Xanthippe, Socrates is said to have had another wife, Myrto, a daughter or grand-daughter of Aristides: *after* Xanthippe according to Aristotle (in *Diog*. ii. 26; conf. *Stob*. Floril. 86, 25, Posidon in Ps. *Plut*. De Nob. 18, 3; less accurate is Plutarch's Aristid. 27 which Athen. xiii. 555 follows); *before* her according to another view (also in Diog.); and at the same time with her according to Aristoxenus, Demetrius Phaler., Hieronymus Rhod., Satyrus, and Porphyry, in Cyril. c. Jul., vi. 186, D.; so that he had two wives at once. The mistake in the last view has been already exposed by Panætius (according to Plut.), and in modern times most thoroughly by Luzac (Lectiones Atticæ, Leyden, 1809). Not only is such a thing incompatible with the character of Socrates, but amongst his cotemporaries, foes and friends, Xenophon, Plato, Aristophanes, and other comic poets, including Timon, there is no allusion to a relation, which, had it existed, would most undoubtedly have caused a great sensation and have provoked attack and defence and derision in the highest degree. The laws of Athens never allowed bigamy, and the decree purporting to be in favour of it, by which Hieronymus attempts to give probability to his story (the same decree quoted by *Gell*. N. A. xv. 20, 6, in support of the alleged bigamy of Euripides), either never was passed or must bear a different meaning. The only question is, whether there can be any foundation for the story, and how its rise can be explained. Shall the Pseudo-Aristotle be believed, who says that Myrto was his second wife, and the two younger sons her children? But how can this be reconciled with the Phædo 60, A., leaving alone the fact that Myrto, as a daughter of Aristides, must have been older than Socrates (whose father in Laches, 180, D., is mentioned as a school companion of her brother), and far too old then to bear children? Or shall it, on the contrary, be conceded

CHAP. III.

composure,[1] nor could domestic cares hinder the

(with Luzac) that Myrto was Socrates' first wife, and that he married Xanthippe after her death? This, too, is highly improbable. For, in the first place, neither Xenophon nor Plato know anything about two wives of Socrates, although the Symposium would have invited some mention of them. In the second place, all the biographers (a few unknown ones in Diogenes excepted) and particularly the Pseudo-Aristotle, from whom all the rest appear to have taken the story, say that he married Myrto after Xanthippe, and that Sophroniscus and Menexenus were her children. Thirdly, Socrates cannot possibly have married the sister or the niece of Lysimachus, the son of Aristides, before the battle of Delium, since at the time of the battle (Lach. 180, D.) he did not know Lysimachus personally. Nor can his first marriage have been contracted after that date, since Xanthippe's eldest son was grown up at the time of her death. And lastly, in Plato's Theætet. 150, E., shortly before his death, Socrates mentions this Aristides, as one of those who had withdrawn from his intellectual influence without detriment to his relationship as a kinsman.

Thus the connection between Socrates and Myrto seems to belong altogether to the region of fable. The most probable account of the origin of the story is the following. We gather from the remains of the treatise περὶ εὐγενείας (*Stob.* Flor. 86, 24, 25; 88, 13), the genuineness of which was doubted by Plutarch, and certainly cannot be allowed, that this dialogue was concerned with the question, whether nobility belonged to those whose parents were virtuous. Now none were more celebrated for their spotless virtue and their voluntary poverty than Aristides and Socrates. Accordingly the writer brought the two into connection. Socrates was made to marry a daughter of Aristides, and since Xanthippe was known to be his wife, Myrto was made to be his second wife and the mother of his younger children. Others, however, remembered that Xanthippe survived her husband. They thought it unlikely that Socrates should be the son-in-law of a man dead before he was born, and they tried to surmount these difficulties in various ways. As regards the first difficulty, either it was maintained that Myrto was his second wife and that the younger children were hers, in which case it was necessary to place her side by side with Xanthippe, as Hieronymus actually did, inventing a popular decree to make it probable; or to avoid romance, this supposition had to be given up, and Myrto was said to be his first wife, who then can have borne him no children,

For note [1] see next page.

occupation which he recognised to be the business of his life. His own concerns were neglected lest he should omit anything in the service of God.[2] To be independent, he tried, like the Gods, to rise superior to wants;[3] and by an uncommon degree of self-denial and abstemiousness,[4] he so far succeeded that he could boast of living more pleasantly and more free from troubles than any one else.[5] It was thus possible for him to devote his whole powers to the service of others without asking or taking reward;[6]

since Lamprocles, his eldest son, according to Xenophon, was a child of Xanthippe. The second difficulty could be got over either by making Myrto a grand-daughter instead of a daughter of Aristides, or by making her father the grandson of Aristides the Just. *Plato*, Lach. 179, A.; Theæt., &c. The former was the usual way. The latter is the view of Athenæus.

[1] See *Xenophon* l. c., not to mention later anecdotes respecting this subject.

[2] *Plato*, Apol. 23, B.; 31, B.

[3] Conf. *Xen.* Mem. i. 6, 1–10, where he argues against Antiphon, that his is a thoroughly happy mode of life, ending with the celebrated words: τὸ μὲν μηδενὸς δέεσθαι θεῖον εἶναι, τὸ δὲ ὡς ἐλαχίστων ἐγγυτάτω τοῦ θείου.

[4] The contentment of Socrates, the simplicity of his life, his abstinence from sensual pleasures of every kind, his scanty clothing, his walking barefoot, his endurance of hunger and thirst, of heat and cold, of deprivations and hardships, are well known. Conf. *Xen.* Mem. i. 2, 1; 3, 5; *Plato*, Symp. 174, A., 219, B.; Phædrus, 229, A.; *Aristoph.* Clouds 103, 361, 409, 828, Birds 1282.

[5] *Xen.* Mem. i. 6, 4; iv. 8, 6.

[6] *Xen.* Mem. i. 2, 5; i. 5, 6; i. 6, 3; *Plato*, Apol. 19, D. 31, B.; 33, A.; Euthypro, 3, D.; Symp. 219, E. In the face of these distinct statements the story told by Aristoxenus (*Diog.* ii. 20) that from time to time he collected money from his pupils, can only be regarded as a slander. It is possible that he did not always refuse the presents of opulent friends—(*Diog.* ii. 74, 121, 34; *Sen.* de Benef. i. 8; vii. 24; *Quintil.* Inst. xii. 7, 9). Questionable anecdotes (*Diog.* ii. 24, 31, 65; *Stob.* Flor. 3, 61; 17, 17) do not disprove this, since no dependence can be placed on these authorities. He is said to have refused the splendid offers of the Macedonian Archelaus and the Thessalian Scopas (*Diog.* ii. 25; *Sen.* Benef. v. 6; *Arrian* or *Plut.* in *Stob.* Floril.

CHAP. III.

and this occupation so confined him to his native city that he rarely passed its boundaries or even its gates.[1]

To take part in state affairs,[2] he did not, however, feel to be his calling; not only believing it impossible to hold a statesman's position[3] in the Athens of his day without violating his principles, and disliking to truckle to the demands of a pampered mob;[4] but far more because he felt his own peculiar task to lie in a very different direction. Any one sharing his conviction that care for self-culture must precede care for the public weal, and that a thorough knowledge of self, together with a deep and many-sided experience, is a necessary qualification for public life,[5] must regard the educational treatment of individuals as a far more pressing business than the like treatment of the community, which without the other would be profitless;[6] considering it a better service to his country to educate able statesmen than actually to discharge a statesman's duties.[7] One so thoroughly fitted by nature,

97, 28; *Dio Chrys.* Or. xiii. 30), and this tale is confirmed as regards the first-named individual by Aristotle (Rhet. ii. 23), in a passage which Bayle (Dict. Archelaus Rem. D.) disputes without reason.

[1] In the Crito, 52, B.; 53, A., he says, that except on military duty he has only once left Athens, when he went as a deputy to the Isthmian games. From the Phædrus, 230, C., we gather that he rarely went outside the gates.

[2] *Plato*, Apol. 31, C.

[3] *Plato*, Apol. 31, D.; Rep. vi. 496, C.; Gorg. 521, C.

[4] *Plato*, Apol. 33, A., or, as the Gorgias 473, E., ironically expresses it: because he was too plain-spoken for a statesman. Conf. Gorg. 521, D.

[5] *Plato*, Apol. 36, Symp. 216, A.; *Xen.* Mem. iv. 2, 6; iii. 6.

[6] *Plato*, Apol. 29, C.; 30, D.; 33, C.; Gorg. 513, E.

[7] *Xen.* Mem. i. 6, 15.

taste, tone of thought and character, to elevate the moral tone and develop the mind of others by means of personal intercourse, could hardly feel at home in any other line of life.[1] Accordingly, Socrates never attempted to move from his position as a private citizen. By serving in several campaigns with the greatest bravery and endurance,[2] he discharged his

[1] Socrates asserts this explicitly in Plato. In Apol. 31, D., he remarks that his δαιμόνιον sent him back from a public life, and wisely too; for in a career spent in stemming the passionate impulses of the masses he would long since have been ruined. The δαιμόνιον which deters him is the sense of what is suited to his individuality. That this was a right kind of sense may be gathered from the consideration that a public career, in his case, would not only have been unsuccessful, but would also have been most injurious for himself; and Socrates usually estimates the moral value of conduct by success. If, as no doubt was the case, this consideration confirmed his dislike to a public career, still the primary cause of this dislike, the source of that insuperable feeling, which as a δαιμόνιον preceded every estimate of consequences, was without doubt something immediate. Had a public position suited his character as well as the life he chose, he would as little have been deterred by its dangers as he was by the dangers of that which he had adopted (Apol. 29, B.). He states, however, that his occupation afforded him great satisfaction with which he could not dispense, Apol. 38, A. ὅτι καὶ τυγχάνει μέγιστον ἀγαθὸν ὂν ἀνθρώπῳ τοῦτο, ἑκάστης ἡμέρας περὶ ἀρετῆς τοὺς λόγους ποιεῖσθαι καὶ τῶν ἄλλων, περὶ ὧν ὑμεῖς ἐμοῦ ἀκούετε διαλεγομένου καὶ ἐμαυτὸν καὶ ἄλλους ἐξετάζοντος, ὁ δὲ ἀνεξέταστος βίος οὐ βιωτὸς ἀνθρώπῳ.

[2] See the stories in *Plato*, Symp. 219, E.; Apol. 28, E.; Charm. i.; Lach. 181, A. Of the three expeditions mentioned in the Apology, that to Potidæa, 432 B.C., that to Delium, 424 B.C., and that to Amphipolis, 422 B.C., the two first are fully described. At Potidæa Socrates rescued Alcibiades, but renounced in his favour his claim to the prize for valour. His fearless retreat from the battle of Delium is mentioned with praise. Antisthenes (in Athen. v. 216, b) refers the prize affair to the time after the battle of Delium. Probably Plato is right, being generally well informed on such matters. The doubts which Athenæus raises respecting Plato's account are trivial. Of course other accounts derived from his account cannot be

CHAP. III.

duties to his country. As a citizen he met unrighteous demands alike of an infuriated populace or of tyrannical oligarchs, in every case of danger,[1] firmly and fearlessly; but in the conduct of affairs he preferred to take no part.

Neither would he come forward as a public teacher after the manner of the Sophists. Not only taking no pay, but giving no methodical course;[2] not professing to teach, but only to learn in common with his fellows; not forcing his convictions upon others, but simply examining theirs; not dealing out ready-made truth like coin fresh from the mint, but awakening a taste for truth or virtue and showing the way thereto; he sought to overthrow spurious, and to discover real knowledge.[3] Never weary of converse, he eagerly seized every opportunity for instructive and moral chit-chat. Day by day he was about in the market and public walks, in schools and workshops, ever ready to have a word with friend or stranger, with citizen or foreigner, but always prepared to give

quoted to support it. The story that Socrates rescued Xenophon at Delium (*Strabo*, ix. 2, 7; *Diog.*) seems to confound Xenophon with Alcibiades.

[1] *Xen.* Mem. i. 1, 18, and 2, 31; iv. 4, 2; Hellen. i. 7, 15; *Plato*, Apol. 32, A.; Gorg. 473, E.; epist. Plat. vii. 324, D.; see also *Luzac*, De Socrate cive, 92–123; *Grote's* Hist. of Greece, viii. 238–285.

[2] *Plato*, Apol. 33, A.: *ἐγὼ δὲ διδάσκαλος μὲν οὐδενὸς πώποτ' ἐγενόμην· εἰ δέ τίς μου λέγοντος καὶ τὰ ἐμαυτοῦ πράττοντος ἐπιθυμεῖ ἀκούειν . . . οὐδενὶ πώποτ' ἐφθόνησα*, *ibid.* 19, D. *Xen.* Mem. i. 2, 3 and 31. The assertion of the Epicurean Idomeneus, and of Favorinus in *Diog.* ii. 20, that he gave instruction in rhetoric, needs no further refutation.

[3] Proofs in all the dialogues. See particularly *Plato*, Apol. 21, B.; 23 B.; 29, D.; 30, E.; Rep. i. 336, B. The Socratic method will be discussed hereafter.

an intellectual or moral turn to the talk.[1] Whilst thus serving God in his higher calling, he was persuaded that he was also serving his country in a way that no one else could do.[2] For deeply as he deplored the decline of discipline and education in his native city,[3] he could place no reliance on the Sophists, the moral teachers of his time.[4] The attractiveness of his discourse gathered around him a circle of admirers, consisting for the most part of young men of family,[5] drawn to him by the most varied motives, standing to him in every kind of relation, and coming to him, some for a longer, others for a shorter time.[6] These friends he was anxious not only to educate, but to advise in everything pertaining to their good, even in worldly matters;[7] and out of this changing and, in great measure, loosely connected society, a nucleus was gradually formed of decided admirers,—a Socratic school, united, far less by a common set of doctrines, than by a common love for the person of its founder. With more

[1] *Xen.* Mem. i. 1, 10; iii. 10; *Plato*, Symp., Lysis., Charmides, Phædrus, Apol. 23, B.; 30, A. The *μαστροπεία* which Socrates boasts of, *Xen.* Symp. 3, 10; 4; 56, 8, 5, 42, is nothing else, this art consisting in making friends lovable, by virtue and prudence.

[2] *Plato*, Apol. 30, A.; Conf. 36, C.; 39, 3; 41, D.; Gorg. 521, D.

[3] *Xen.* Mem. iii. 5, 13.

[4] Mem. iv. 4, 5, which is not at variance with *Plato*, Apol. 19, D, nor yet with the passages quoted p. 69, 1.

[5] *Plato*, Apol. 23, C., *οἱ νέοι μοι ἐπακολουθοῦντες οἷς μάλιστα σχολή ἐστιν, οἱ τῶν πλουσιωτάτων.* Still we find among his ardent admirers, not only Antisthenes, but also Apollodorus and Aristodemus, who appear, according to *Plato*, Symp. 173, 8, to have been equally poor.

[6] Conf. *Xen.* Mem. i. 2, 14; iv. 2, 40; *Plato*, Theæt. 150, D.

[7] Conf. examples, Mem. ii. 3, 7, 8, 9; iii. 6, 7.

CHAP. III.

intimate friends he frequently had common meals,[1] which, however, can scarcely have been a fixed institution. Such as appeared to him to require other branches of instruction, or whom he believed unsuited for intercourse with himself, he urged to apply to other teachers, either in addition to or in place of himself.[2] This course of action he followed until his seventieth year with his powers of mind unimpaired.[3] The blow which then put an end to his life and his activity will be mentioned hereafter.

[1] *Xen.* Mem. iii. 14.

[2] *Plato*, Theætet. 151, B.; Xen. Mem. iii. 1; Symp. 4, 61.

[3] Xenophon and Plato mostly represent Socrates as an old man, as he was when they knew him, not showing any trace of weakness in his mental powers or in his activity up to the last moment. That this was a wrong view, Mem. iv. 8, 8, states distinctly.

CHAPTER IV.

THE CHARACTER OF SOCRATES.

CHAP. IV.

A. The greatness of the character of Socrates.

ANCIENT writers speak of the character of Socrates in terms of the greatest respect. There are, however, some exceptions, quite apart from the prejudice occasioned by his condemnation, which no doubt lingered some time after his death. Followers of Epicurus indulged their love of slander even at his expense,[1] and one voice from the Peripatetic School has scandalous stories to tell respecting his life: as a boy he was disobedient and refractory; as a youth, irregular in his habits; as a man, coarse, arrogant, passionate, and licentious.[2] The stories of this kind

[1] *Cicero* de N. D. i. 34, says that his teacher, the Epicurean Zeno, called him an Attic buffoon. Epicurus, however, according to *Diog.* x. 8, appears to have spared him, although he decried every other philosopher.

[2] The source from which these unfavourable reports, collected by *Luzac*, come, is Aristoxenus, Lect. Att. 246 (from whom we have already heard similar things, p. 59, note; 62, 3; 65, 6). From this writer comes the statement mentioned in *Porphyry*: ὡς φύσει γεγόνοι τραχὺς εἰς ὀργήν, καὶ ὁπότε κρατηθείη τῷ πάθει διὰ πάσης ἀσχημοσύνης ἐβάδιζεν—*Synesius* (Enc. Galv. 81 confines this to his younger years;—also the statement of *Cyril.* c. Jul. vi. 185, C.; *Theod.* Cur. Gr. Aff. xii. 63, p. 174: ὅτε δὲ φλεχθείη ὑπὸ τοῦ πάθους τούτου δεινὴν εἶναι τὴν ἀσχημοσύνην· οὐδενὸς γὰρ οὔτε ὀνόματος ἀποσχέσθαι οὔτε πράγματος; and another of Cyril. 186, C. *Theod.* l. c.) that Socrates was in other ways temperate, πρὸς δὲ τὴν τῶν ἀφροδισίων χρῆσιν σφοδρότερον μὲν εἶναι, ἀδικίαν δὲ μὴ προσεῖναι, ἢ γὰρ ταῖς γαμεταῖς ἢ ταῖς κοιναῖς χρῆσθαι μόναις, and then after the history of his bigamy he

CHAP. IV.

extant are so improbable, and the chief authority for them is so untrustworthy,[1] that we cannot even with certainty[2] infer that Socrates only became what he was after a severe struggle[3] with his natural dis-

concludes: εἶναι δέ φησιν αὐτὸν ἐν ταῖς ὁμιλίαις αἰνῶς τε φιλαπεχθήμονα καὶ λοίδορον καὶ ὑβριστικόν. From the same source, as witness *Plut.* Mal. Her. c. 9, p. 856, comes the charge which *Theod.* l. c. I. 29, p. 8 quotes from Porphyry, without naming Aristoxenus, εἶναι δὲ αὐτὸν πρὸς οὐδὲν μὲν ἀφυῆ, ἀπαίδευτον δὲ περὶ πάντα, so that he was hardly able to read, besides what follows (*ibid.* xii. 66, p. 174; conf. iv. 2, p. 56): ἐλέγετο δὲ περὶ αὐτοῦ ὡς ἄρα παῖς ὢν οὐκ εὖ βιώσειεν οὐδὲ εὐτάκτως· πρῶτον μὲν γάρ φασιν αὐτὸν τῷ πατρὶ διατελέσαι, ἀπειθοῦντα καὶ ὁπότε κελεύσειεν αὐτὸν λαβόντα τὰ ὄργανα τὰ περὶ τὴν τέχνην ἀπαντῶν ὁπουδήποτε ὀλιγωρήσαντα τοῦ προστάγματος περιτρέχειν αὐτὸν ὁπουδήποτε δόξειεν . . . ἦν δὲ καὶ τῶν ἐπιτιμωμένων καὶ τάδε Σωκράτει ὅτι εἰς τοὺς ὄχλους εἰσωθεῖτο καὶ τὰς διατριβὰς ἐποιεῖτο πρὸς ταῖς τραπέζαις καὶ πρὸς ταῖς Ἑρμαῖς. Herewith is connected the story of the physiognomist Zopyrus: (*Cic.* Tusc. vi. 37, 83; De Fat. iv. 10; *Alex. Aph.* De Fato, vi., *Pers.* Sat. IV. 24; conf. Max. Tyr. xxxi. 3), who declared Socrates to be stupid and profligate, and received from him the answer, that by nature he had been so, but had been changed by reason. This account can hardly be true. It looks as if it had been devised to illustrate the power of reason over a defective natural disposition, as illustrated in *Plato*, Symp. 215, 221, B. If the story was current in the time of Aristoxenus, he may have used it for his picture; but it is also possible that his description produced the story, which in this case would have an apologetic meaning. The name of Zopyrus would lead us to think of the Syrian magician, who, according to Aristotle in *Diog.* ii. 45, had foretold the violent death of Socrates.

[1] As may be already seen from the stories respecting the bigamy, the gross ignorance, the violent temper, and the sensual indulgences of Socrates.

[2] As *Hermann* does, De Socr. Mag. 30.

[3] Though this is in itself possible, we have no certain authority for such an assertion. The anecdote of Zopyrus is, as already remarked, very uncertain, and where is the warrant that Aristoxenus followed a really credible tradition? He refers, it is true, to his father Spintharus, an actual acquaintance of Socrates. But the question arises, whether this statement is more trustworthy than the rest. The chronology is against it, and still more so is the substance of what Spintharus says. It may also be asked whether Spintharus spoke the truth, when he professed to have witnessed outbursts of

position. Our best authorities only know him as the perfect man, to whom they look up with respect, and whom they regard as the exemplar of humanity and morality. 'No one,' says Xenophon, 'ever heard or saw anything wrong in Socrates; so pious was he that he never did anything without first consulting the Gods; so just that he never injured any one in the least: so master of himself that he never preferred pleasure to goodness; so sensible that he never erred in his choice between what was better and what was worse. In a word, he was of men the best and happiest.'[1]

He further represents Socrates as a pattern of hardiness, of self-denial, of self-mastery; as a man of piety and love for his country, of unbending fidelity to his convictions, as a sensible and trust-

anger in Socrates, who must then have been in the last years of his life. Certainly we have no more reason to believe him than his son. Lastly, Aristoxenus does not confine his remarks to the youth of Socrates, but they are of a most general character, or refer distinctly to his later years. *Luzac*, l. c. 261, would appear to have hit the truth when he makes Aristoxenus responsible for all these statements. For Aristoxenus appears not only to have carried his warfare with the Socratic Schools against the person of Socrates, but also to have indulged in the most capricious and unfounded misapprehensions and inferences. His overdrawn imagination makes Socrates as a boy dissatisfied with his father's business, and as a man pass his life in the streets. In the same way he finds that Socrates must have been a man without culture, because of expressions such as that in the Apology, 17, B., or that in the Symp. 221, E.; 199, A.; violent in temper, in support of which he refers to Symp. 214, D.; and dissolute because of his supposed bigamy, and the words in *Xen.* Mem. i. 3, 14; ii. 2, 4, and p. 51, 2.

[1] Mem. i. 1, 11; iv. 8, 11. R. *Lange's* objections to the genuineness of the concluding chapters of the Memorabilia (iv. 8) (De Xenoph. Apol., Berl. 1873) do not appear sufficiently strong to preclude their being cited as an authority.

CHAP. IV.

worthy adviser both for the bodies and souls of his friends, as an agreeable and affable companion, with a happy combination of cheerfulness and seriousness; above all, as an untiring educator of character, embracing every opportunity of bringing all with whom he came into contact to self-knowledge and virtue, and especially opposing the conceit and thoughtlessness of youth.

Plato says the same of him. He too calls his teacher the best, the most sensible, and the most just man of his age,[1] and never tires of praising his simplicity, his moderation, his control over the wants and desires of the senses; imbued with the deepest religious feelings in all his doings, devoting his whole life to the service of the Gods, and dying a martyr's death because of his obedience to the divine voice; and like Xenophon, he describes this service as the exercise of a universal moral influence on others, and particularly on youth. In his picture, too, the solemn side in the character of Socrates is lighted up by a real geniality of manner, an Attic polish, a cheery kindness and a pleasing humour. Of his social virtues and his political courage Plato speaks in the same terms as Xenophon, adding an admirable description of Socrates on military service.[2] Every trait he mentions gives a picture of moral greatness, as wonderful as it is original, with as little of pretence and imitation about it as there is of self-satisfaction and display.[3]

[1] See the end of the Phædo.

[2] See page 67, note 2.

[3] Most of the traits and anecdotes recorded by later

CHAP. IV.

B. *His character reflecting Greek peculiarities.*

Owing to its being a native growth, the Socratic type of virtue bears throughout the peculiar impress of the Greek mind. Socrates is not the lifeless ideal of virtue, to which a superficial rationalism would reduce him, but he is a thorough Greek and Athenian, taken as it were from the very core of his nation, possessed of flesh and blood, and not merely the universal moral type for all time. His much-lauded moderation is free from the ascetic element, which it always seems to suggest in modern times. Good company he enjoys, although he avoids noisy carousals;[1] if the pleasures of the senses are not to him an aim in life, no more does he avoid them, when they come in his way, nay, not even when in excess. The call for small cups in Xenophon's banquet is not made for fear of indulging too largely, but only that exhilaration may not be too rapid.[2] Plato describes him as boasting that he can equally

writers are in harmony with this view of Socrates. Some of them are certainly fictions. Others may be taken from writings of pupils of Socrates, which have been since lost, or from other trustworthy sources. They may be found in the following places:—*Cic.* Tusc. iii. 15, 31; Off. i. 26 and 90; *Seneca*, De Const. 18, 5; De Ira, i. 15, 3; iii. 11, 2; ii. 7, 1; Tranqu. An. 5, 2; 17, 4; Epist. 104, 27; *Plin.* H. Nat. vii. 18; *Plut.* Educ. Pu. 14, p. 10; De Adulat. 32, p. 70; Coh. Ira, 4, p. 455; Tranqu. An. 10, p. 471; Garrulit. 20; *Diog.* ii. 21, 24, 27, 30; vi. 8; *Gell.* N. A. ii. 1.; xix. 9, 9; *Val. Max.* viii. 8; *Ælian*, V. H. i. 16; ii. 11, 13, 36; iii. 28; ix. 7, 29; xii. 15; xiii. 27, 32; *Athen.* iv. 157 c.; *Stob.* Flor. 17, 17 and 22; *Basil.* De Leg. Græc. libr. Op. II. 179, a.; *Themist.* Orat. vii. 95, a.; *Simpl.* in Epict. Enchir. c., 20, p. 218. A few others have been or will be referred to.

[1] *Plato*, Symp. 220, A.; conf. 174, A.

[2] *Xen.* Mem. 2, 26: ἢν δὲ ἡμῖν οἱ παῖδες μικραῖς κύλιξι πυκνὰ ἐπιψεκάζωσιν, οὕτως οὐ βιαζόμενοι ὑπὸ τοῦ οἴνου μεθύειν, ἀλλ' ἀναπειθόμενοι πρὸς τὸ παιγνιωδέστερον ἀφιξόμεθα.

CHAP. IV.

well take much or little, that he can surpass all in drinking, without ever being intoxicated himself;[1] at the close of the banquet he represents him, after a night spent over the bowl, as pursuing his daily work, leaving all his companions under the table, as if nothing had happened. Moderation is here depicted not as consisting in total abstinence from pleasure, but in perfect mental freedom, neither requiring pleasure, nor being ever overtaken by its seductive influence. In other points also his abstemiousness is recorded with admiration.[2] That his morality was far below our strict standard of principles numerous passages in Xenophon's 'Memorabilia'[3] prove. His relations with youth bear the Greek peculiarity of affection for boys. However much his character is above all suspicion of actual vice,[4]—and he can even treat with irony a supposed love-affair of his own,[5]—

[1] Symp. 176, C.; 220, A.; 213, E.

[2] *Xen.* Mem. i. 2, 1; 3, 14. We have already seen that Aristoxenus and his followers cannot prove the contrary.

[3] i. 3, 14; ii. 1, 5; 2, 4; iii. 11; iv. 5, 9. Conf. Conv. iv. 38.

[4] The cotemporaries of Socrates seem to have found nothing to object to in Socratic affection. Not only is there no allusion to it in the judicial charge, but not even in Aristophanes, who would undoubtedly have magnified the smallest suspicion into the gravest charge. The other comic poets, according to *Athen.*, v. 219, knew nothing of it. Nor does Xenophon deem it necessary to refute this calumny, and therefore the well-known story of Plato's banquet has for its object far more the glorification than the justification of his teacher. On the other hand, the relation of Socrates to Alcibiades, in the verses purporting to be written by Aspasia, which *Athenæus* communicates on the authority of Herodicus, have a very suspicious look, and *Tertullian* Apol. c. 46 mistakenly applies the words διαφθείρειν τοὺς νέους to pæderastia. In *Juvenal* (Sat. ii. 10) *Socratici cinædi* refer to the manners of his own time.

[5] *Xen.* Mem. iv. 1, 2; Symp.

at the same time, there was a certain element of æsthetic pleasure about his relations with youthful beauty which at least was the ground and origin, even though an innocent one, of deeper affection.[1] The odious excrescences of Greek morality called forth his severest censure; yet at the same time, according to Xenophon,[2] and Æschines,[3] and Plato,[4] Socrates described his own relations to his younger friends by the name of Eros, or a passionate attachment grounded on æsthetic attractions. Similarly in his ethical or political views, Grecian peculiarities may be noticed, nor is his theology free from the trammels of popular faith. How deeply these lines had influenced his character may be gathered not only from his simple obedience[5] to the laws of his country throughout life, and his genuine respect for the state religion,[6] but far more also from the trials

4, 27; *Plato*, Symp. 213, C.; 216, D.; 222, B.; Charm. 155, D.

[1] *Xen.* Mem. i. 2, 29; 3, 8; Sym. 8, 19, 32, with which Plato agrees.

[2] Symp. 8, 2 and 24; Mem. iv. 1, 2.

[3] In his Alcibiades he speaks of the love of Socrates for Alcibiades. See *Aristid.* Or. xlv. περὶ ῥητορικῆς, p. 30, 34.

[4] Prot. beginning; Symp. 177, D.; 218, B.; 222, A.; not to mention other expressions for which Plato is answerable.

[5] *Plato*, Apol. 28, E.

[6] *Xenophon*, Mem. i. 1, 2, assures us not only that Socrates took part in the public sacrifices, but that he was frequently in the habit of sacrificing at home. In Plato he invokes Helios, Symp. 220, D.; and his last words, according to the Phædo, 118, A., were a solemn charge to *Crito* to offer a cock to Æsculapius. Often is belief in oracles mentioned, which he always conscientiously obeyed (Mem. i. 3, 4; *Plato*, Apol. 21, B.) and the use of which he recommended to his friends (*Xen.* Mem. ii. 6, 8; iv. 7, 10; Anabas. iii. 1, 5). He was himself fully persuaded that he possessed an oracle in the truest sense, in the inward voice of his δαιμόνιον, and he also believed in dreams and similar prognostications. (*Plato*, Crito, 44, A.; Phædo, 60, D.; Apol. 33, C.)

CHAP. IV.

of his last days, when for fear of violating the laws, he scorned the ordinary practices of defence, refusing after his condemnation to escape from prison.[1] The epitaph which Simonides inscribed on the tomb of Leonidas might well be inscribed on that of Socrates also: He died to obey his country.[2]

C. *Prominent traits in his character.*

Deeply as Socrates is rooted in the national character of Greece, there is about him something un-Greek, and almost modern in appearance. This foreign element it was which made him appear to his cotemporaries a strange person, altogether unlike anyone else. So new and unintelligible was this trait that it was described as his extreme singularity.[3] According to Plato's account,[4] it consisted in a want of agreement between the outward appearance and the inward and real nature, and so formed a marked contrast to the mutual interpenetration of both, which constitutes the usual classic ideal. On the one hand we see in Socrates indifference to the outer world, originally foreign to the habits of his countrymen; on the other hand, a meditativeness

[1] This motive is represented by *Xenophon* (Mem. iv. 4, 4) and *Plato* (Apol. 34, D.; Phædo, 98, C.) as the decisive one, although the Crito makes it appear that a flight from Athens would have done no good to himself, and much harm to his friends and dependants. The Apology speaks as though entreaties to the judges would have been unworthy of the speaker and his country.

[2] *Xenophon* says: *προείλετο μᾶλλον τοῖς νόμοις ἐμμένων ἀποθανεῖν ἢ παρανομῶν ζῆν.*

[3] *Plato*, Symp. 221, C.: Πολλὰ μὲν οὖν ἄν τις καὶ ἄλλα ἔχοι Σωκράτη ἐπαινέσαι καὶ θαυμάσια . . . . τὸ δὲ μηδενὶ ἀνθρώπων ὅμοιον εἶναι, μήτε τῶν παλαιῶν μήτε τῶν νῦν ὄντων, τοῦτο ἄξιον παντὸς θαύματος . . . . οἷος δὲ οὑτοσὶ γέγονε τὴν ἀτοπίαν ἄνθρωπος καὶ αὐτὸς οἱ λόγοι αὐτοῦ οὐδ' ἐγγὺς ἂν εὕροι τις ζητῶν, οὔτε τῶν νῦν οὔτε τῶν παλαιῶν.

[4] Symp. 215, A.; 221, E.

unknown before. Owing to this indifference there is about him a something prosaic and dry, and, if the expression may be allowed, philistine-like, sharply contrasting with the contained beauty and the artistic grace of life in Greece. Owing to his contemplative turn there is about him something akin to the revelation of a higher life, having its seat within, in the recesses of the soul, and not fully explained in its manifestations, and which even Socrates himself regarded as superhuman. In their account of these two peculiarities both Plato and Xenophon are agreed. Even from an outward point of view, the Silenus-like appearance of Socrates, which Plato's Alcibiades,[1] and Xenophon's Socrates himself [2] describe with so much humour, must rather have concealed than exposed the presence of genius to the eye of a Greek. But more than this, a certain amount of intellectual stiffness, and an un-Greek indifference to what is sensibly beautiful, may be noticed in his speech and behaviour. Take for instance the catechising process given in the 'Memorabilia,' [3] whereby a knowledge of his duties is brought home to a cavalry officer, or the formality with which things,[4] long familiar to his hearers, are proved, or the way in which the idea of the beautiful is resolved into that of the useful.[5] Or hear him, on grounds of expediency, advising conduct, which

[1] Symp. 215; conf. Theæt. 14, 3, E.

[2] Symp. 4, 19; 2, 19; *Epictetus* (Diss. iv. 11, 19) gives Socrates a pleasing appearance, but this is of course quite untenable.

[3] iii. 3.

[4] Symp. iii. 10, 9; iii. 11.

[5] iii. 8, 4.

CHAP. IV.

to us seems simply abominable;[1] in the Phædrus[2] refusing to walk out because he can learn nothing from trees and the country; in the Apology[3] taking exception to the works of poets and artists because they are the results of natural genius and inspiration, and not of reflection.[4] Or see him in Xenophon's Symposium,[5] despite the universal custom of the ancients,[6] dancing alone at home, in order to gain healthful exercise, and justifying his conduct by the strangest of reasons; unable even at table[7] to forget considerations of utility. Taking these and similar traits into account, there appears in him a certain want of imagination, a one-sided prominence of the critical and intellectual faculties, in short a prosiness which clashes with the poetry of Greek life, and the refined taste of an Athenian. Even Plato's Alcibiades[8] allows that at first sight the discourses of Socrates appear ridiculous and rude, treating as they invari-

[1] i. 3, 14.

[2] 230, D.

[3] This point will be subsequently discussed.

[4] 22, C.

[5] 2, 17.

[6] Compare Menexenus, 236, C.: *ἀλλὰ μέντοι σοί γε δεῖ χαρίζεσθαι, ὥστε κἂν ὀλίγου εἴ με κελεύοις ἀποδύντα ὀρχήσασθαι, χαρισαίμην ἄν*; and *Cicero* pro Mur. 6: Nemo fere saltat sobrius, nisi forte insanit. De Offic. iii. 19: Dares hanc vim M. Crasso, in foro, mihi crede, saltaret. *Plut*. De Vit. Jud. 16, 533; also the expressions in *Xenophon*: Ὀρχήσομαι νὴ Δία. Ἐνταῦθα δὴ ἐγέλασαν ἅπαντες. And when Charmides found Socrates dancing: *τὸ μέν γε πρῶτον ἐξεπλάγην καί ἔδεισα, μὴ μαίνοιο, κ. τ. λ.* Of the same character was his instruction in music under Connus, if the story were only true of his having received lessons with the schoolboys. *Plato*, Euthyd. 272, C.

[7] *Xen*. Symp. 3, 2.

[8] Symp. 221, E. Conf. Kallicles in Gorgias 490, C.: *περὶ σιτία λέγεις καὶ ποτὰ καὶ ἰατροὺς καὶ φλυαρίας . . . . ἀτεχνῶς γε ἀεὶ σκυτέας τε καὶ γναφέας καὶ μαγείρους λόγων καὶ ἰατροὺς οὐδὲν παύει, ὡς περὶ τούτων ἡμῖν ὄντα τὸν λόγον.*

ably do of beasts of burden, smiths, tailors, and tanners, and apparently saying the same thing in the same words. Was not this the very objection raised by Xenophon?[1] Very strange must that plain unadorned common sense have appeared to his cotemporaries which carefully avoided all choice figures, and only used the simplest and most common expressions.

This peculiarity was not, however, the result of any lack of taste, but of the profound originality of his ideas, for which customary figures were insufficient. Sometimes again the soul of the philosopher, diving into its own recesses, so far lost itself in this labour as to be insensible to external impressions, and at other times gave utterance to enigmas, which appeared strange to it in a wakeful state.[2] It not unfrequently happened that deep in contemplation he remained, for a longer or shorter time, lost to the outer world,[3] and standing like one of absent mind. According to Plato, he once remained in this state, standing on the same spot, from one day to the

[1] Mem. i. 2, 37: Ὁ δὲ Κριτίας· ἀλλὰ τῶν δέ τοι σε ἀπέχεσθαι, ἔφη, δεήσει, ὦ Σώκρατες, τῶν σκυτέων καὶ τῶν τεκτόνων καὶ τῶν χαλκέων, καὶ γὰρ οἶμαι αὐτοὺς ἤδη κατατετρῖφθαι διαθρυλουμένους ὑπὸ σοῦ. Again in iv. 4, 6: καὶ ὁ μὲν Ἱππίας· ἔτι γὰρ σύ, ἔφη, ὦ Σώκρατες, ἐκεῖνα τὰ αὐτὰ λέγεις ἃ ἐγὼ πάλαι ποτέ σου ἤκουσα. The like complaint and the like answer is met with in *Plato's* Gorgias, 490, E. Conf. 497, C.: σμικρὰ καὶ στενὰ ἐρωτήματα.

[2] Accordingly in the Aristotelian problems, xxx. 1, 953, a, 26, he is reckoned amongst the melancholy, which is not at variance with the gentle firmness (τὸ στάσιμον) which *Aristotle* (Rhet. ii. 15) assigns to him.

[3] *Plato*, Symp. 174, D. *Volquardsen*, D. Dæmon. d. Socr. 25, 63, and *Alberti*, Socr. 148 have entirely mistaken the meaning of the text in supposing that it attributes to Socrates any ecstatic states.

CHAP. IV.

D. *The δαιμόνιον of Socrates.*

next.[1] So energetically did he struggle with himself to attain an insight into his every motive. In doing this, he discovered a residuum of feelings and impulses, which he watched with conscientious attention without being able to explain them from what he knew of his own inner life. Hence arose his belief in those divine revelations, which he thought to enjoy. And not only was he generally convinced that he stood and acted in the service of God, but he also held that supernatural suggestions were communicated to him, not only through the medium of public oracles,[2] but also in dreams,[3] and more particularly by a peculiar kind of higher inspiration, which goes by the name of the Socratic δαιμόνιον.[4]

(*a*) *Incorrect views of the δαιμόνιον.*

Even among the ancients this inspiration was regarded by many as derived from intercourse with a special and personally-existing genius,[5] of which

[1] Symp. 220, C. The circumstances may be regarded as a fact; still we do not know from what source Plato derived his knowledge of it, nor whether the authority which he followed had not exaggerated the time of Socrates' standing. Favorinus in *Gell.* N. A. ii. 1, makes the one occasion into many, and says stare solitus, etc. *Philop.* De an. R. 12, places the occasion during the battle of Delium.

[2] Conf. p. 77, 6, and 90.

[3] Conf. p. 61, 2. In the passage here quoted Socrates refers to dreams in which the deity had commanded him to devote himself to his philosophical activity. In the Crito 44, A., a dream tells him that his death will follow on the third day.

[4] *Volquardsen,* Das Dæmonium d. Socr. und seine Interpreten. Kiel, 1862. *Ribbing,* Ueber Socrates' Daimonion (Socratische Studien II., Upsala Universitets Årskrift, 1870.

[5] The bill of accusation against Socrates seems to have understood the δαιμόνιον in this sense, since it charges him with introducing ἕτερα καινὰ δαιμόνια in the place of the Gods of the state; nor does

Socrates boasted; in modern times this view was for a long time the prevailing one.[1] Somewhat humiliating it no doubt was in the eyes of rationalising admirers, that a man otherwise so sensible as Socrates should have allowed himself to be ensnared by such a superstitious delusion. Hence attempts were not wanting to excuse him, either on the ground of the universal superstition of his age and

Ribbing's (Socrat. Stud. II. 1) remark militate against this, that Meletus (in *Plato*, Apol. 26, B.) thus explained his language: Socrates not only denies the Gods of Athens but all and every God; the heavenly beings, whose introduction he attributes to Socrates not being regarded as Gods, just as at a later time Christians were called ἄθεοι though worshipping God and Christ. Afterwards this view appears to have been dropped, thanks to the descriptions of Xenophon and Plato, and does not recur for some time, even in spurious works attributed to these writers. Even *Cicero*, Divin. i. 54, 122, does not translate δαιμόνιον by genius, but by 'divinum quoddam,' and doubtless Antipater, whose work he was quoting, took it in the same sense. But in Christian times the belief in a genius became universal, because it fell in with the current belief in dæmons. So, too, it is found in *Plut.* De Genio Socratis, c. 20; *Max. Tyr.* xiv. 3; *Apuleius*, De Deo Socratis, the Neoplatonists, and the Fathers, who, however, are not agreed whether his genius was a good one or a bad one. Plutarch, and after him Apuleius, mention the view that by the δαιμόνιον must be understood a power of vague apprehension, by means of which he could guess the future from prognostications or natural signs.

[1] Compare *Tiedemann*, Geist der spekulat. Philosophie, ii. 16; *Meiners*, Ueber den Genius des Sokr. (Verm. Schriften, iii. 1); Gesch. d. Wissensch. II. 399, 538; *Buhle*, Gesch. d. Phil. 371, 388; *Krug*, Gesch. d. alten Phil. p. 158. *Lasaulx* too (Socrates' Leben, 1858, p. 20) in his uncritical and unsatisfactory treatise respecting the δαιμόνιον, believes it to be a real revelation of the deity, or even a real genius, and even *Volquardsen* sums up as the result of his careful, and in many respects meritorious, disquisition, that a real divine voice warned Socrates. The older literature in *Olearius*, 148, 185, and *Brucker*, I. 543, including many supporters of the opinion that the genius of Socrates was only his own reason. Further particulars in *Krug*, l. c. and *Lélut*, Démon de Socrate, 163.

CHAP. IV.

nation, or else of his having a physical tendency to fanaticism.[1] Some even went so far as to assert that the so-called supernatural revelations were a shrewd invention,[2] or a product of his celebrated irony.[3] It is hard to reconcile such a view with the

[1] The first-named excuse is universal. Marsilius Ficinus (Theol. Platon. xiii. 2, p. 287) had assumed in Socrates, as well as in other philosophers, a peculiar bodily disposition for ecstasy, referring the susceptibility for supernatural revelations to the melancholy temperament. The personality of the dæmon is not however called into question by him or by his supporters (*Olearius*, 147). Modern writers took refuge in the same hypothesis in order to explain in Socrates the possibility of a superstitious belief in a δαιμόνιον. For instance, *Tiedemann*, 'The degree of exertion, which the analysis of abstract conception requires, has, in some bodies, the effect of mechanically predisposing to ecstasy and enthusiasm.' 'Socrates was so cultivated that deep thought produced in him a. dulness of sense, and came near to the sweet dreams of the ἐκστατικοί.' 'Those inclined to ecstasy mistake suddenly rising thoughts for inspirations.' 'The extraordinary condition of the brain during rapture affects the nerves of the abdomen and irritates them. To exercise the intellect immediately after a meal or to indulge in deep thought produces peculiar sensations in the hypochondriacal.' In the same strain is *Meiners*, Verm. Schr. iii. 48, Gesch. d. Wissensch. ii. 538. Conf. *Schwarze*, Historische Untersuchung: war Socrates ein Hypochondrist? quoted by *Krug*, Gesch. d. alten Phil. 2 A. p. 163.

[2] *Plessing*, Osiris and Socrates, 185, who supposes that Socrates had bribed the Delphic oracle in order to produce a political revolution, and vaunted his intercourse with a higher spirit. Chauvin in *Olearius*.

[3] *Fraguier*, Sur l'ironie de Socrate in the Mémoires de l'Académie des Inscriptions, iv. 368, expresses the view that Socrates understood by the δαιμόνιον his own natural intelligence and power of combination, which rendered it possible for him to make right guesses respecting the future; somewhat ironically he had represented this as a matter of pure instinct, of θεῖον or θεία μοῖρα, and employed for this purpose δαιμόνιον and similar expressions. He remarks, however, that Socrates had no thought of a genius familiaris, δαιμόνιον here being used as an adjective and not as a substantive. Similarly *Rollin* in his Histoire ancienne, ix. 4, 2; and *Barthélemy*, Voyage du jeune Anacharsis, treats the expressions used respecting the

tone in which, on the testimony of both Plato and Xenophon, Socrates speaks of the suggestions of the δαιμόνιον, or with the value which he attaches to these suggestions on the most important occasions.[1] To explain the phenomenon by the irritability of a sickly body falls not far short of deriving it from the fancy of a monomaniac, and reduces the great reformer of philosophy to the level of a madman.[2] All these explanations are now superfluous, Schleiermacher having shown,[3] with the universal approval of the most competent judges,[4] that by the δαιμόνιον in the sense of Socrates, no genius, no separate or distinct personality can be understood, but only vaguely some heavenly voice or divine revelation. No passage in Plato or Xenophon speaks

(b) Regarded by Socrates as an inward oracle.

δαιμόνιον in Plato's Apology as *plaisanterie*, and considers it an open question whether Socrates really believed in his genius. On others sharing the view, see *Lélut*, l. c. p. 163.

[1] *Xen.* Mem. iv. 8, 4. *Plato*, Apol. 31, C.; 40, A.; 41, D.

[2] Many have spoken of the superstition and fanaticism of Socrates in a more modest way, but comparatively recently *Lélut* (Du Démon de Socrate, 1836) has boldly asserted, 'que Socrate était un fou'—a category in which he places amongst others not only Cardan and Swedenborg, but Luther, Pascal, Rousseau and others. His chief argument is that Socrates not only believed in a real and personal genius, but in his hallucinations believed that he audibly heard its voice. Those who rightly understand Plato, and can distinguish what is genuine from what is false, will not need a refutation of these untruths.

[3] *Platon's* Werke, i. 2, 432.

[4] *Brandis*, Gesch. d. Gri. Rom. Phil. ii. a. 60. *Ritter*, Gesch. d. Phil. ii. 40. *Hermann*, Gesch. u. Syst. d. Plato i. 236. *Socher*, Über Platon's Schriften, p. 99. *Cousin* in the notes to his translation of Plato's Apology p. 335. *Krische*, Forschungen, 227. *Ribbing*, 16. Conf. *Hegel*, Gesch. d. Phil. ii. 77. *Ast* too (Platon's Leben und Schriften, p. 482), who takes δαιμόνιον for a substantive meaning the deity, does not see therein a genius, but only a θεῖον.

of Socrates holding intercourse with a genius.[1] We only hear of a divine or heavenly sign,[2] of a voice heard by Socrates,[3] of some supernatural guidance by which many warnings were vouchsafed to him.[4] All that these expressions imply is, that Socrates was conscious within of divine revelations, but of how produced and whence coming they say absolutely nothing,[5] nay their very indefiniteness proves plainly enough that neither Socrates nor his pupils had any very clear notion on the subject.[6] These revelations,

[1] The passage Mem. i. 4. 14; *ὅταν οἱ θεοὶ πέμπωσιν, ὥσπερ σοὶ φῂς πέμπειν αὐτοὺς συμβούλους*, proves nothing, as *συμβούλους* is used as a metonym for *συμβουλάς*. Plato's Alcibiades, do not go further; and the Theages. 128, D., with all its romance respecting the prophecies of the *δαιμόνιον*, expresses itself throughout indefinitely, nor need the *φωνὴ τοῦ δαιμονίου* p. 128, E. be taken for a person. The spuriousness of the Theages. notwithstanding Socher's defence needs no further exposure, especially after being exhaustively shown by *Hermann*, p. 427.

[2] *Plato*, Phædr. 242, B.: *τὸ δαιμόνιόν τε καὶ τὸ εἰωθὸς σημεῖόν μοι γίγνεσθαι ἐγένετο, καί τινα φωνὴν ἔδοξα αὐτόδε ἀκοῦσαι.* Rep. iv. 496, C.: *τὸ δαιμόνιον σημεῖον.* Euthy. 272, E.: *ἐγένετο τὸ εἰωθὸς σημεῖον, τὸ δαιμόνιον.* Apol. 50; *τὸ τοῦ θεοῦ σημεῖον — τὸ εἰωθὸς σημεῖον.* *Ibid.* 41, D. c. *τὸ σημεῖον.*

[3] *Plato*, Apol. 31, D.: *ἐμοὶ δὲ τοῦτ' ἐστὶν ἐκ παιδὸς ἀρξάμενον, φωνή τις γιγνομένη.* *Xen.* Apol. 12: *θεοῦ φωνή.*

[4] *Plato*, l. c.: *ὅτι μοι θεῖόν τι καὶ δαιμόνιον γίγνεται.* Also 40, A.: *ἡ εἰωθυῖά μοι μαντικὴ ἡ τοῦ δαιμονίου.* Theæt. 151, A.: *τὸ γιγνόμενόν μοι δαιμόνιον.*—Euthyphro 3, B.: *ὅτι δὴ σὺ τὸ δαιμόνιον φῂς σαυτῷ ἑκάστοτε γίγνεσθαι.*—*Xen.* Mem. i. 1, 4: *τὸ δαιμόνιον ἔφη σημαίνειν·* iv. 8, 5.: *ἠναντιώθη τὸ δαιμόνιον.* Symp. 8, 5. Even the spurious writings, Xenophon's Apology and

[5] Doubtless Socrates regarded God or the deity as its ultimate source. But he expresses no opinion as to whether it came herefrom directly or mediately.

[6] It is much the same thing whether *τὸ δαιμόνιον* be taken for a substantive or an adjective. The probable rights of the case are, as *Krische*, Forsch. 229 remarks, that Xenophon uses it as a substantive = *τὸ θεῖον* or *ὁ θεὸς*, whereas Plato uses it as an adjective, explaining it as *δαιμόνιον σημεῖον*, and says *δαιμόνιόν μοι γίγνεται.* The grammar will admit of either. Conf. *Arist.* Rhet. ii. 23,

moreover, always refer to particular actions,[1] and according to Plato assume the form of prohibitions.

1398 a, 15. When, therefore, *Ast* cites Xenophon against Plato's explanation of δαιμόνια as δαιμόνια πράγματα, he probably commits a μετάβασις εἰς ἄλλο γένος. The very difference between Xenophon and Plato proves how loosely Socrates spoke of the δαιμόνιον.

[1] This applies to all the instances of its intervention mentioned by Plato and Xenophon. They are the following: (1) In *Xen.* Mem. iv. 8, 5, Socrates, when urged to prepare a defence, replies: ἀλλὰ νὴ τὸν Δία, ἤδη μου ἐπιχειροῦντος, φροντίσαι τῆς πρὸς τοὺς δικαστὰς ἀπολογίας ἠναντιώθη τὸ δαιμόνιον. (2) In *Plato*, Apol. 31, D., asked why he did not busy himself with political matters, Socrates replies: The δαιμόνιον was the reason: τοῦτ' ἔστιν ὅ μοι ἐναντιοῦται τὰ πολιτικὰ πράττειν. (3) *Ibid.* (after his condemnation): a singular occurrence took place, ἡ γὰρ εἰωθυῖά μοι μαντικὴ ἡ τοῦ δαιμονίου ἐν μὲν τῷ πρόσθεν χρόνῳ παντὶ πάνυ πυκνὴ ἀεὶ ἦν καὶ πάνυ ἐπὶ σμικροῖς ἐναντιουμένη, εἴ τι μέλλοιμι μὴ ὀρθῶς πράξειν, νυνὶ δὲ . . . οὔτε ἐξιόντι ἕωθεν οἴκοθεν ἠναντιώθη τὸ τοῦ θεοῦ σημεῖον, οὔτε ἡνίκα ἀνέβαινον ἐνταυθοῖ ἐπὶ τὸ δικαστήριον, οὔτ' ἐν τῷ λόγῳ οὐδαμοῦ μέλλοντί τι ἐρεῖν· καίτοι ἐν ἄλλοις λόγοις πολλαχοῦ δή με ἐπέσχε λέγοντα μεταξύ. (4) In *Plato*, Theæt. 151, A. he says: if such as have withdrawn from my society again return, ἐνίοις μὲν τὸ γιγνόμενόν μοι δαιμόνιον ἀποκωλύει ξυνεῖναι, ἐνίοις δὲ ἐᾷ. Add to these cases a few others in which Socrates himself more or less jokes about the δαιμόνιον, and which deserve to be mentioned because it there appears in the same character as elsewhere. (5) *Xen.* Symp. 8, 5, where Antisthenes throws in Socrates' teeth: τοτὲ μὲν τὸ δαιμόνιον προφασιζόμενος οὐ διαλέγῃ μοι τοτὲ δ' ἄλλου του ἐφιέμενος. (6) *Plato*, Phædr. 242, B., when Socrates wished to depart: τὸ δαιμόνιόν τε καὶ εἰωθὸς σημεῖόν μοι γίγνεσθαι ἐγένετο ἀεὶ δέ με ἐπίσχει ὃ ἂν μέλλω πράττειν καί τινα φωνὴν ἔδοξα αὐτόθεν ἀκοῦσαι, ἥ με οὐκ ἐᾷ ἀπιέναι πρὶν ἂν ἀφοσιώσωμαι, ὥς τι ἡμαρτηκότα εἰς τὸ θεῖον. (7) *Ibid.* Euthyd. 272, E.; as Socrates was about to leave the Lyceum, ἐγένετο τὸ εἰωθὸς σημεῖον τὸ δαιμόνιον, he therefore sat down again, and soon after Euthydemus and Dionysodorus really came in. In all these cases the δαιμόνιον appears to have been an inward voice deterring the philosopher from a particular action. Even the more general statement that the δαιμόνιον always made its warnings heard whenever Socrates thought of a political career, falls in with this conception of it. In a similar sense the passage in the Republic vi. 496, D. should be understood, where Socrates remarks that most of those who had the capacity for philosophy were diverted therefrom by other interests, unless peculiar circumstances kept them, such as sickness, which was a hin-

CHAP. IV.

Sometimes the *δαιμόνιον* stops him from saying or doing something.[1] It only indirectly points out what should be done, by approving what it does not forbid. In a similar way it indirectly enables Socrates to advise his friends by not hindering him from approving their schemes, either by word or by silence.[2] The subjects respecting which the

drance to political life. τὸ δ' ἡμέτερον οὐκ ἄξιον λέγειν τὸ δαιμόνιον σημεῖον· ἢ γάρ πού τινι ἄλλῳ ἢ οὐδενὶ τῶν ἔμπροσθεν γέγονε. The heavenly sign keeps Socrates true to his philosophical calling, by opposing him whenever he thinks of following anything else, such as politics. Consequently, not even this passage obliges us to give another meaning to its utterances than they bear according to Plato's express words, which describe them as conveying a judgment respecting the admissibility of a definite action, either contemplated or commenced by Socrates. Even at the commencement of the spurious 'Alcibiades,' not more than this is said, and in the Theages. 128, D. the prophecies of the δαιμόνιον have reference only to particular future actions (not only of Socrates, but of others), from which it dissuades. These two latter authorities, are, however, of no value.

[1] Apol. 31, D.: ὅτι μοι θεῖόν τι καὶ δαιμόνιον γίγνεται . . . . ἐμοὶ δὲ τοῦτ' ἐστὶν ἐκ παιδὸς ἀρξάμενον φωνή τις γιγνομένη, ἣ ὅταν γένηται ἀεὶ ἀποτρέπει με τούτου ὃ ἂν μέλλω πράττειν, προτρέπει δὲ οὔποτε. Phædr. 242, C.

[2] From the Platonic statements respecting the δαιμόνιον which have just been given, Xenophon's statements differ, making it not only restraining but inciting, and not confined to the actions of Socrates only. Mem. i. 1, 4 (Apol. 12): τὸ γὰρ δαιμόνιον ἔφη σημαίνειν, καὶ πολλοῖς τῶν ξυνόντων προσηγόρευε τὰ μὲν ποιεῖν, τὰ δὲ μὴ ποιεῖν, ὡς τοῦ δαιμονίου προσημαίνοντος· καὶ τοῖς μὲν πειθομένοις αὐτῷ συνέφερε, τοῖς δὲ μὴ πειθομένοις μετέμελε. *Ibid.* iv. 3, 12: σοὶ δ' ἔφη (Euthydemus), ὦ Σώκρατες, ἐοίκασιν ἔτι φιλικώτερον ἢ τοὶς ἄλλοις χρῆσθαι (sc. οἱ θεοὶ) εἴγε μηδὲ ἐπερωτώμενοι ὑπό σου πρυσημαίνουσί σοι ἅ τε χρὴ ποιεῖν καὶ ἃ μή. Still both statements may be harmonised as in the text. Evidently Plato is more accurate. His language is far more definite than that of Xenophon, and is throughout consistent, witness the various cases mentioned in the previous note. Xenophon, as is his wont, confined himself to what caught the eye, to the fact that the δαιμόνιον enabled Socrates to judge of actions whose consequences were uncertain, all the more so because he aimed before all things at proving Socrates' divination to be the

heavenly voice makes itself heard are in point of value and character very different. Besides a matter of such deep personal interest to Socrates as his judicial condemnation, besides a question having such a far-reaching influence on his whole activity as that whether he should take part in public life or not, it expresses itself on occasions quite unimportant.[1] It is in fact a voice so familiar to Socrates and his friends,[2] that, whilst regarded as a something enigmatical, mysterious, and unknown before, affording, too, a special proof of divine providence, it can nevertheless be discussed without awe and mystery in easy and even in flippant language. The facts of the phenomenon resolve themselves into this, that not unfrequently Socrates was kept back from carrying out some thought or intention by a vague feeling for which he could not account, in which he discerned a heavenly sign and a divine hint. Were he asked why this sign had been vouchsafed to him, the reply would have been ready—to deter himself or others from that which would be harmful.[3] In order, therefore, to vindicate the claims of the *δαίμονιον*,

same as other forms of divination, and so defending his teacher from the charge of religious innovation. As to the special peculiarity of the Socratic δαιμόνιον and its inner processes, we can look to Plato for better information.

[1] πάνυ ἐπὶ σμικροῖς. See p. 87, 1.

[2] πάνυ πυκνή. *Ibid.*

[3] It will be subsequently shown that Socrates was on the one hand thoroughly convinced of the care of God for man down to the smallest matters, and on the other hand was accustomed to estimate the value of every action by its consequences. It followed herefrom that to his mind the only ground on which God could forbid an action was because of its ill-consequences.

CHAP. IV.

and to justify its *raison d'être*, he sought to show that the actions which it approved or occasioned were the most beneficial and advantageous.[1] The *δαίμονιον* appeared therefore to him as an internal revelation from above respecting the result of his actions—in a word, as an internal oracle. As such it is expressly included, both by Xenophon[2] and Plato,[3] under the general head of divination, and placed side by side with divination by sacrifice and the flight of birds. Of it is therefore true what Xenophon's Socrates remarks respecting all divination, that it may only be resorted to for things which man cannot discover himself by reasoning.[4]

[1] See *Xen.* Mem. iv. 8, 5, where Socrates observes that the δαιμόνιον forbad him to prepare a defence, and then proceeds to discuss the reasons why the deity found an innocent death better for him than a longer life. In *Plato*, Apol. 40, 3, he concludes, from the silence of the δαιμόνιον during his defence, that the condemnation to which it led would be for him a benefit.

[2] *Xen.* Mem. i. 1, 3 ; iv. 3, 12 ; i. 4, 14. Conf. Apol. 12.

[3] Apol. 40, A. ; Phæd. 242, C. ; Euthyphro, 3, B.

[4] *Xen.* Mem. i. 1, 6 : τὰ μὲν ἀναγκαῖα συνεβούλευε καὶ πράττειν ὡς ἐνόμιζεν ἄριστ' ἂν πραχθῆναι· περὶ δὲ τῶν ἀδήλων ὅπως ἂν ἀποβήσοιτο μαντευσομένους ἔπεμπεν εἰ ποιητέα. For this reason, therefore, divination was required: τεκτονικὸν μὲν γὰρ ἢ χαλκευτικὸν ἢ γεωργικὸν ἢ ἀνθρώπων ἀρχικὸν ἢ τῶν τοιούτων ἔργων ἐξεταστικὸν ἢ λογιστικὸν ἢ οἰκονομικὸν ἢ στρατηγικὸν γενέσθαι, πάντα τὰ τοιαῦτα μαθήματα καὶ ἀνθρώπου γνώμῃ αἱρετέα ἐνόμιζε εἶναι· τὰ δὲ μέγιστα τῶν ἐν τούτοις ἔφη τοὺς θεοὺς ἑαυτοῖς καταλείπεσθαι ὧν οὐδὲν δῆλον εἶναι τοῖς ἀνθρώποις. The greatest things, however, as he immediately explains, are the consequences of actions, the question whether they are useful or detrimental to the doer. Accordingly, Socrates observes that it is madness to think to be able to dispense with divination, and to do everything by means of one's own intelligence (and as he afterwards adds, ἀθέμιστα ποιεῖν): δαιμονᾶν δὲ τοὺς μαντευομένους, ἃ τοῖς ἀνθρώποις ἔδωκαν οἱ θεοὶ μαθοῦσι διακρίνειν, examples of which are then given. Conf. iv. 3, 12, where μαντική, and also the Socratic μαντική, is said to refer to consequences (τὰ συμ-

CHAP. IV.

(c) Limited in its application.

Herewith the whole field of philosophical inquiry is excluded from the province of the δαιμόνιον. This field Socrates, more than any one of his predecessors, claimed for intelligent knowledge and a thorough understanding. As a matter of fact, no instance occurs of a scientific principle or a general moral law being referred to the δαιμόνιον. Nor must the sage's conviction of his own higher mission be confounded with his belief in the heavenly sign, nor the deity by whom he considered himself commissioned to sift men be identified with the δαιμόνιον.[1] That Socrates thought to hear the heavenly voice from the time when he was a boy, ought to be sufficient warning against such an error;[2] for at that time he cannot possibly have had any thought of a philosophic calling. That voice, moreover, according to Plato, always deterring, never prompting,[3] cannot have been the source of the positive command of the deity to which Socrates referred his activity as a teacher.[4] Nor is it ever deduced therefrom, either by Xenophon or by Plato. Socrates indeed says that the deity had assigned to him the task of sifting men, that the deity had forced him to this line of life;[5] but he never says that he had received

φέροντα, τὰ ἀποβησόμενα), and the appropriate means (ᾗ ἂν ἄριστα γίγνοιντο).

[1] This was often done in former times; for instance by *Meiners*, Verm. Schrift. iii. 24, and still more so by *Lélut*, l. c. p. 113, who sees in the θεὸς from whom Socrates derived his vocation a proof of his belief in a genius. The same mistake is committed by *Volquardsen*, l. c. p. 9, 12, against whose view see *Alberti*, Socr. 56.

[2] ἐκ παιδὸς. See above p. 88, 1.

[3] See p. 88, 2.

[4] See p. 61, 2; 82, 5.

[5] *Plato*, Apol. 23, B.; 28, D. 33, C.; Theætet. 150, C.

CHAP. IV.

this commission from the δαιμόνιον.[1] To the δαιμόνιον he only owes a debt for help received in his philosophic calling, whereby he was dissuaded from proving faithless to his calling by meddling with politics.[2]

Lastly, the δαιμόνιον has been often regarded as the voice of conscience,[3] but this view is at once too wide and too narrow. Understanding by conscience the moral consciousness in general, and more particularly the moral sense as far as this finds expression in the moral estimate of our every action, its monitions are not confined to future things as are the monitions of the Socratic δαιμόνιον. Indeed, it more frequently makes itself felt in the first place by the approval or disapproval following upon actions. Again, conscience exclusively refers to the moral value or worthlessness of an action, whereas the heavenly sign in Socrates always bears reference to the consequences of actions. Therein Plato, no less than Xenophon, sees a peculiar kind

[1] It is not true, as *Volquardsen*, l. c. B., says, that in *Plato*, Apol. 31, D., Socrates mentions the δαιμόνιον as the first and exclusive αἴτιον of his mode of life. He there only attributes to the δαιμόνιον his abstinence from politics, not his attention to philosophy.

[2] See p. 81, 2.

[3] *Stapfer*, Biogr. Univers. T. xlii. Socrate, p. 531; *Brandis*, Gesch. d. Griech. Röm. Phil. ii. a, 60 (Gesch. d. Entwick. d. Griech. Phil. i. 243 is a modification of the above). *Breitenbach*, Zeitschrift für das Gymnasialwesen, 1863, p. 499; *Rötscher*, Arist. 256. *Ribbing*, too, l. c. 27, defends this view, observing, however, that the δαιμόνιον (1) only manifests itself as conscientia antecedens and concomitans, not as conscientia subsequens; and (2) that its meaning is not exhausted with the conception of conscience, but that it figures as 'practical moral tact in respect of personal relations and particular actions.'

of prophecy. Allowing that Socrates was occasionally mistaken as to the character of the feelings and impulses which appeared to him as revelations, that now and then he was of opinion that the deity had forbidden him something for the sake of its harmful consequences when the really forbidding power was his moral sense, yet the same cannot be said of all the utterances of the δαιμόνιον. In deterring him from taking up politics, no doubt the real restraint lay in the feeling that a political career was incompatible with his conviction of an important higher calling, to which he had devoted his life. It may, therefore, be said that in this case a scruple of conscience had assumed the form of a heavenly voice. But in forbidding him to prepare a speech for judicial defence, this explanation will no longer apply. Here the only explanation which can be given of the heavenly voice, is that such a taking in hand of his own personal interests did not commend itself to his own line of thought, and that it appeared unworthy of him to defend himself otherwise than by an unvarnished statement of the truth requiring no preparation.[1] All this, however, has little to do with

[1] *Volquardsen* l. c. confounds two things in explaining the prohibition to prepare a defence mentioned by *Xen.* Mem. iv. 8, 4, in the sense of *Plato*, Apol. 17, A., as meaning that it was not a question of a simple defence, but of a defence in the usual legal style with all the tricks and manœuvres of an orator. In Xenophon's account there is not a word of this Had this been his meaning, it must somehow have been indicated in the sequel; it would have been said that the δαιμόνιον kept him from defending himself, because a defence in keeping with his principles would have been useless; it is by no means a matter of course that he would not have been able to get up a speech very much worthy of himself.

CHAP. IV.

judgments respecting what is morally admissible or not, and has much to do with the questions as to what is suited or unsuited to the individual character of the philosopher. Still less can the decision respecting the readmission of seceded pupils [1] be referred to conscience. The question here really was as to the capacity of the respective persons to profit by his instructions. It involved, therefore, a criticism of character. The jokes, too, which Socrates and his friends permitted themselves as to the *δαιμόνιον* [2] would be wholly out of place, were the *δαιμόνιον* conscience. As far as they are authentic, they are evidence that the *δαιμόνιον* must be distinguished from moral sense or conscience; and it is quite in harmony herewith to hear Socrates say,[3] that the heavenly voice often made itself heard on occasions quite unimportant. Remembering further that Socrates more perhaps than anyone else was bent on referring actions to clear conceptions, excluding accordingly from the field of prophecy, and therefore from the field of the *δαιμόνιον*, everything capable of being known by personal inquiry,[4] we shall see how little reason there is for thinking the *δαιμόνιον* had principally or wholly to do with moral decision.

The heavenly voice appears rather to be the

But as *Cron* in Eos. i. 175 observes: what idea must we form to ourselves of Socrates, if he required the assistance of the *δαιμόνιον* to keep him back from that which he clearly saw to be incompatible with his principles?

[1] See above p. 86, No. 2 and 4

[2] *Ibid.* No. 5 and 7.

[3] *Ibid.* No. 3.

[4] See p. 90, 4.

CHAP. IV.

(d) Philosophical explanation of the δαιμόνιον.

general form, which a vivid, but unexplored sense of the propriety of a particular action assumed for the personal consciousness of Socrates.[1] The actions to which this sense referred could, as we have seen, be most varied in matter and importance. Quite as varied must the inward processes and motives have been out of which it grew. It might be some conscientious scruple overpowering the philosopher's feelings without his being fully conscious thereof. It might be some apprehension of the consequences of a step, such as sometimes instantaneously flashes on the experienced observer of men and of circumstances, before he can account to himself for the reasons of his misgiving. It might be that an action in itself neither immoral nor inappropriate, jarred on his feelings, as being out of harmony with his special mode of being and conduct. It might be that on unimportant occasions all those unaccountable influences and impulses came into play, which contribute all the more to our mental attitude and decision in proportion as the object itself affords less definite grounds for decision. In this respect the *δαιμόνιον* has been rightly called 'the inner voice of individual tact,'[2] understanding by tact a general sense of propriety in word and

[1] The last remark follows not only from what has been stated, p. 90, 4, but it is also inconceivable that Socrates could have referred to a higher inspiration impulses the sources of which he had discovered. Nor does it conflict herewith, that after the heavenly voice has made itself heard, he afterwards considers what can have led the Gods to thus reveal their will.

[2] *Hermann*, Platonismus i. 236: similarly *Krische*, Forschung. i. 231.

CHAP. IV.

action as exemplified in the most varied relations of life in small things as well as in great.[1] This sense Socrates early noticed in himself as unusually strong,[2] and subsequently by his peculiarly keen and unwearied observation of himself and other men he developed it to such a pitch of accuracy, that it was seldom or as he believed never at fault. Its psychological origin was, however, concealed from his own consciousness. It assumed for him from the beginning the appearance of a foreign influence, a higher revelation, an oracle.[3]

Herein is seen the strength of the hold which the beliefs of his countrymen had over Socrates;[4] herewith, too, are exposed to view the limits of his self-knowledge. Feelings whose origin he has not discovered are seen to exercise over him an irresistible power. On the other hand, the *δαιμόνιον*, when it does speak, takes the place of the usual signs and portents. Hegel[5] not without reason

[1] The objections hereto raised by *Volquardsen*, pp. 56, 63, and *Alberti*, Socr. 68, are partly answered by the argument which has preceded. Besides, they have more reference to words than to things. So far as this is the case, there is no use in disputing. By tact we understand not only social but moral tact, not only acquired but natural tact, and this word seems very appropriate to express the sense which Socrates described as the *δαιμόνιον*.

[2] See p. 89, 2.

[3] *Hegel*, Gesch. d. Phil. ii. 77: The genius of Socrates is not Socrates himself . . . but an oracle, which, however, is not external, but subjective, his oracle. It bore the form of knowledge, which was, however, connected with a certain unconsciousness.

[4] *Krische* l. c.: What is not in our power, what our nature cannot bear, and what is not naturally found in our impulses or our reflections, is involuntary, or, according to the notion of the ancients, heavenly: to this category belong enthusiasm and prophecy, the violent throb of desire, the mighty force of feelings.

[5] *Hegel* l. c. and Recht's Philosophie, § 279, p. 369.

sees herein a proof that the determining motives of action, which in the case of the Greek oracles were things purely external, have come to be sought in man himself. A high importance is here given to forebodings incapable of being resolved into clear conceptions; in them a very revelation of deity is seen. Have we not here a proof that the human mind, in a way hitherto foreign to Greeks, had come to occupy itself with itself, carefully observing what transpired within? The power which these feelings early exercised over Socrates, the devotion with which he even then listened for the inner voice, afford an insight into the depths of his emotional nature. In the boy we see the embryo of the man, for whom self-knowledge was the most pressing business of life, for whom untiring observation of the moral and mental conditions, analysis of notions and actions, reasoning as to their character and testing of their value, were primary necessities.[1]

The same tone of mind also shows itself in other peculiarities of Socrates, which to his cotemporaries appeared so strange. At times he was seen lost in thought, utterly unconscious of what was transpiring around him; at times going on his way regardless of the habits of his fellows; his whole appearance displaying a far-reaching indifference to externals, a one-sided preference of the useful to the beautiful. What do all these traits show if not the importance which he attached to the study of self, to the solitary work of thought, to a free determination of self

[1] Conf. *Plato*, Apol. 38, A. See above, p. 61, 3.

independent of foreign judgments? Remarkable as it may seem to find the stiffness of the man of brains and the enthusiasm of the man of feeling united in one and the same person, both features may be referred to a common source. What distinguishes Socrates in his general conduct from his fellow-citizens was this power of inward concentration. This struck his cotemporaries as being so strange, and thereby an irreparable breach was made in the artistic unity of Greek life.

What the general importance of this peculiarity may be, and what traces it has left in history, are other questions leading to an inquiry into the Socratic philosophy.

CHAPTER V.

THE SOURCES AND CHARACTERISTICS OF THE PHILOSOPHY OF SOCRATES.

CHAP. V.

A. *Xenophon and Plato as authorities.*

To give an accurate account of the philosophy of Socrates is a work of some difficulty, owing to the well-known divergence of the earliest accounts. Socrates committed nothing to writing himself;[1] of the works of his pupils, in which he is introduced as speaking, only those of Xenophon and Plato are preserved.[2] These are, however, so little alike, that we gather from the one quite a different view of the teaching of Socrates from what the other gives. Among early historians of philosophy it was the fashion to construct a picture of Socrates, without principles and criticism, indiscriminately from the writings of Xenophon and Plato, no less than from

[1] The unimportant poetical attempts of his last days (*Plato*, Phædo, 60, C.) can hardly be counted as writings, even if they were extant. They appear, however, to have been very soon lost. The Pæan at least, which *Themist.* (Or. ii. 27, c.) considers genuine, was rejected by the ancient critics, according to *Diog.* ii. 42. The spuriousness of the Socratic letters is beyond question, and that Socrates committed nothing to writing is clear from the silence of Xenophon, Plato, and all antiquity, not to mention the positive testimony of *Cic.* de Orat. iii. 16, 60; *Diog.* i. 16; *Plut.* De Alex. Virt. i. 4. A conclusive discussion on this point in refutation of the views of Leo Allatius is given by Olearius in *Stanl.* Hist. Phil. 198.

[2] For instance, those of Æschines, Antisthenes, Phædo.

CHAP. V.

later, and for the most part indifferent, authorities. Since the time of Brucker, however, Xenophon has come to be regarded as the only perfectly trustworthy authority for the philosophy of Socrates; to all others, Plato included, at most only a supplementary value is allowed. Quite recently, however, Schleiermacher has lodged a protest against this preference of Xenophon.[1] Xenophon, he argues, not being a philosopher himself, was scarcely capable of understanding a philosopher like Socrates. The object, moreover, of the Memorabilia was a limited one, to defend his teacher from definite charges. We are therefore justified in assuming *à priori* that there was more in Socrates than Xenophon describes. Indeed, there must have been more, or he could not have played the part he did in the history of philosophy, nor have exerted so marvellous an attractive power on the most intellectual and cultivated men of his time. The character, too, which Plato gives him would otherwise have too flatly contradicted the picture of him present to the mind of his reader. Besides, Xenophon's dialogues create the impression that philosophic matter has, with detriment to its meaning, been put into the unphilosophic language of every-day life; and that there are gaps left, to supply which we are obliged to go to Plato. Not that we can go so far as Meiners,[2] and say that only those parts of the

[1] On the philosophical merits of Socrates, *Schleiermacher*, Werke, iii. 2, 293, first printed in Abhandlungen der Berliner Academie, Philos. Kl. 1818, p. 50. Conf. Gesch. d. Phil. p. 81.

[2] Geschichte der Wissen-

dialogues of Plato can be considered historical, which are either to be found in Xenophon, or immediately follow from what Xenophon says, or which are opposed to Plato's own views. This hypothesis would only give us the Socrates of Xenophon slightly modified, whilst the deeper spring of Socratic thought would still be wanting. The only safe course to pursue is that adopted by Schleiermacher—to ask, What *may* Socrates have been, in addition to what Xenophon reports, without gainsaying the character and maxims which Xenophon distinctly assigns to him? and What *must* he have been to call for and to justify such a description as is given of him in the dialogues of Plato? Schleiermacher's estimate of Xenophon[1] has been since adopted by several other writers; and even before Schleiermacher, Dissen[2] had declared that he could only find in the pages of Xenophon a description of the outward appearance of Socrates. Schleiermacher's

schaften in Griechenland und Rom, ii. 420.

[1] *Brandis*, in Rhein. Mus. von *Niebuhr und Brandis*, i. b. 122. Conf. Gesch. d. Gr.-Röm. Philos. ii. a. 20; *Ritter*, Gesch. d. Phil. ii. 44; *Ribbing*, Ueber d. Verhältniss zwischen den Xenophont. und den Platon. Berichten über Socrates. Upsala Universitets Årskrift, 1870, specially p. 1, 125. *Alberti*, too (Socrates, 5), takes in the main the side of Schleiermacher, whilst allowing that Plato's account can only be used for history with extreme caution—a caution which he has himself failed to observe in using the Phædo (see above, p. 60). In respect of the personality of Socrates rather than his teaching, *Van Heusde* (Characterismi principum philosophorum veterum, p. 54) gives a preference to Plato's picture as being truer to life than Xenophon's Apology.

[2] De philosophia morali in Xenophontis de Socrate commentariis tradita, p. 28 (in *Dissen's* Kleineren Schriften, p. 87).

CHAP. V.

canon has been equally approved of for discovering the truly Socratic teaching, supplemented however by the further remark,[1] that Aristotle's statements supply a matter-of-fact verification for that teaching. On the other hand, Xenophon's historical accuracy has been stoutly maintained by several critics.[2]

In deciding between these two views, a difficulty presents itself. The accuracy of one or the other of our accounts can only be ascertained by a reference to the true historical picture of Socrates, and the true historical picture can only be known from these conflicting accounts. This difficulty would be insurmountable, if the two narratives had the same claim to be considered historical in points which they state varyingly. Aristotle's scanty notices respecting the Socratic philosophy would have been insufficient to settle the question, even assuming that he had other sources of information at command beside the writings of Xenophon and Plato—albeit there is not the least evidence for such an assumption. If one thing is clearer than another it is, however, this,—that Plato only claims to be true to facts in those points wherein he agrees with Xenophon, as, for instance, in the Apology and the Symposium. On others no one could well assert that he wished all

[1] By *Brandis*, l. c.

[2] *Hegel*. Gesch. d. Phil. ii. 69; *Rötscher*, Aristophanes und sein Zeitalter, p. 393; *Hermann*, Gesch. und Syst. des Platonismus, i. 249; *Labriola*, La dottrina di Socrate (Napoli, 1871), 22. Conf. *Fries*, Gesch. d. Phil. i. 259. For further literature on this point consult *Hurndall*, De philosophia morali Socratis (Heidelberg, 1853), p. 7, and *Ribbing*, l. c.

to be taken as literally true which he puts into the mouth of Socrates. As to Xenophon, it must be granted that, either from want of philosophic sense, or from his exclusively practical tastes, not unfrequently the scientific meaning and the inner connection of the principles of Socrates escape his notice. It should not be forgotten that the Memorabilia were primarily intended to be a defence of his teacher against the charges brought against him, charges which were the cause of his condemnation, and passed current years after his death. For this purpose a description was requisite, not so much of his philosophy as of his morals and religion, setting forth his piety, his integrity, his obedience to the laws, his services to his friends and fellow-citizens rather than his intellectual convictions; and Xenophon candidly confesses that this is the main object of his treatise.[1] Even the question whether, with the means at his command, a lifelike reproduction of the dialogues of Socrates can be expected from Xenophon, cannot be answered affirmatively without some limitation. His treatise was not written until six years after the death of Socrates, and we have not the least indication that it was based on notes made either by himself or others in the time immediately following the dialogues.[2] What was committed to writing years

[1] Mem. i. 1, 1 and 20; 2, 1; 3, 1; iv. 4, 25; 5, 1; 8, 11.

[2] It cannot be inferred from *Plato*, Symp. 172, C.; 173, B.; Theæt. 143, A., that Socrates' friends (as *Volquardsen*, Dæmon d. Sokr. 6, says) took down his discourses at home and filled up their sketches by further inquiries. Nay, the very dis-

afterwards from his own or his friends' memory has not the claim to accuracy of a verbal report, but rather owes to the writer its more definite form and setting. No doubt it was his intention to give a true account of Socrates and his teaching. He says that he writes from his own recollection. He expressly observes in a few cases that he was present during the conversation, and had heard similar things from others, mentioning his authority.[1] If, then, many a Socratic discourse is unknown to him or has escaped his memory, if one or other line of thought has not been thoroughly understood, or its philosophical importance misunderstood, it may nevertheless be assumed that Xenophon, as a pupil of Socrates, accustomed to mix with him for years, and able to communicate all that he actually communicates, neither repeats on the whole what is false, nor leaves any essential side of the Socratic teaching untouched. From Plato, so far as his description is historical or permits a reference to the Socrates of history, many a trait supplementary of Xenophon's narrative may be expected, and many an explanation of the real meaning of sayings, which his fellow-

courses which are vouched for by this supposed care, cannot possibly be historical. Such statements do not therefore mean more than similar ones in Parm. 126, B. Neither does Mem. i. 4, 1 refer to writings of pupils of Socrates, but to the views of opponents. Mem. iv. 3, 2 appears to refer not even to writings, but to oral communications.

[1] Mem. i. 3, 6: *ὡς δὲ δὴ καὶ ὠφελεῖν ἐδόκει μοι τοὺς ξυνόντας . . . . τούτων δὴ γράψω ὁπόσα ἂν διαμνημονεύσω.* iv. 3, 2; others have reported similar conversations respecting the Gods, at which they were present: *ἐγὼ δὲ ὅτε πρὸς Εὐθύδημον τοιάδε διελέγετο παρεγενόμην.* iv. 8, 4: *λέξω δὲ καὶ ἃ Ἑρμογένους τοῦ Ἱππονίκου ἤκουσα περὶ αὐτοῦ.*

pupil understood too literally only from the side of their practical utility. Hence objection can hardly be taken to the above-quoted canon of Schleiermacher.[1] Nevertheless, it is highly improbable that in essential points there should be an irreconcilable difference between Xenophon's description and that which we may take for historically established as Plato's.[2] The real state of the case can only be ascertained by examining the statements of various authorities in detail to test their worth and their agreement, and this inquiry naturally coincides with the exposition of the Socratic teaching from which it can only be distinguished in point of form. It will not be separated from it here. Socrates will be described from the three accounts of Xenophon, Plato, and Aristotle. If the attempt to form an harmonious picture from these sources succeeds, Xenophon will be vindicated. Should it not succeed, it will then be necessary to ask which of the traditional accounts is the true one.[3]

B. Philosophical platform.

To begin with the question as to the philosophical platform and fundamental principle of Socrates. Here the sketches of our main authorities seem to

[1] P. 101.

[2] As *Ribbing*, l. c. asserts. Hard is it to reconcile herewith that Ribbing declines to question 'the essentially historical accuracy' of Xenophon's description.

[3] The course here followed is also in the main that taken by *Strümpell*, Gesch. d. Prakt. Philos. d. Gr. i. 116. He considers it impossible to distinguish in point of speculation what belongs to Socrates and what belongs to Plato. As regards morals, he hopes to gain a true general view of Socrates by taking the maxims which are attributed to him by Xenophon, Plato, and Aristotle, unanimously following them out to their consequences, and testing the traditions by these.

give grounds for the most opposite views. According to Plato, Socrates appears as an expert thinker, at home in all branches of knowledge; whereas, in Xenophon he is represented far less as a philosopher than as an innocent and excellent man, full of piety and common sense. Hence Xenophon's account is specially appealed to in support of the view which regards Socrates as a popular moral man, holding aloof from all speculative questions, and in fact as far less of a philosopher than a teacher of morality and instructor of youth.[1] It certainly cannot be denied that Socrates *was* full of the most lively enthusiasm for morality, and made it the business of his life to exercise a moral influence upon others.[2] Had he only discharged this function after the unscientific manner of a popular teacher, by imparting and inculcating the received notions of duty and virtue, the influence which he exerted would be inexplicable, not only over weaklings and hairbrains, but over the most talented and cultivated of his cotemporaries. It would be a mystery what induced Plato to connect the deepest philosophical inquiries with his person, or what led all later philo-

[1] How common this view was in past times, needs not to be proved by authorities which abound from Cicero down to Wiggers and Reinhold. That it is not yet altogether exploded may be gathered not only from writers like *Van Heusde*, Characterismi, p. 53, but even *Marbach*, a disciple of the Hegelian philosophy, asserts in his Gesch. d. Philos. i. 174, 178, 181, that Socrates 'regarded the speculative philosophy which aimed at general knowledge as useless, vain, and foolish,' and that he 'took the field not only against the Sophists as pretenders to knowledge, but against all philosophy;' in short, that 'he was no philosopher.'

[2] Conf. Apol. 23, D.; 30, E.; 38, A.; and above, p. 50.

sophers, from Aristotle down to the Stoics and Neoplatonists, to regard him as the founder of a new epoch, and to trace their own peculiar systems to the movement set on foot by him.

Even about himself and his doings more than one feature is at variance with this view. It would follow therefrom that knowledge is only of value in as far as it is instrumental for action; but so far was Socrates from sharing this belief that he considered actions only then to have a value when they proceed from correct knowledge; referring moral action or virtue to knowledge, making its perfection depend on perfection of knowledge. According to the ordinary assumption, he would in his intercourse with others have been ultimately intent on moral training; yet so far was it otherwise that it appears from his own words that love of knowledge was the original motive for his activity.[1] Accordingly, we observe him in conversation pursuing inquiries, which not only have no moral purpose,[2] but which,

[1] *Plato*, Apol. 21, where Socrates deduces his whole activity from the fact that he pursued a real knowledge.

[2] Examples are to be found in the conversations (Mem. iii. 10), in which Socrates conducts the painter Parrhasius, the sculptor Clito, and Pistias, the forger of armour, to the conceptions of their respective arts. It is true Xenophon introduces these conversations with the remark that Socrates knew how to make himself useful to artisans. But the desire to make himself useful can only have been a very subordinate one; he was no doubt really actuated by the motive mentioned in the Apology, a praiseworthy curiosity to learn from intercourse with all classes whether they were clearly conscious of what their arts were for. Xenophon himself attests this, Mem. iv. 6, 1: σκοπῶν σὺν τοῖς συνοῦσι, τί ἕκαστον εἴη τῶν ὄντων οὐδεπώποτ' ἔληγεν. This pursuit of the conceptions of things, aiming not at the application of knowledge, but at knowledge itself, is quite enough to prove that

CHAP. V.

in their practical application, could only serve immoral purposes.[1] These traits are not met with exclusively in one or other of our authorities, but they are equally diffused through the accounts given by the three main sources. Socrates can therefore not have possibly been the unscientific moral teacher for which he was formerly taken. Knowledge must have had for him a very different value and importance from what it would have had on such a supposition. It may not even be said that the knowledge which he sought was ultimately only pursued for the sake of action, and only valued as a means to morality.[2] He who pursues knowledge in this sense, as a means to an end which lies beyond, and not from an independent impulse and love of knowing, will never study the problem and method of philosophic research so carefully and so independently as Socrates did; will never be a

Socrates was not only a preacher of virtue, but a philosopher. Even Xenophon found some difficulty in bringing it into harmony with his practical view of things, as his words show: from which it may be seen that Socrates made his friends more critical. But criticism is the organ of knowledge.

[1] Mem. iii. 11 contains a paragraph adapted more than any other to refute the idea that Socrates was only a popular teacher. Socrates hears one of his companions commending the beauty of Theodota, and at once goes with his company to see her. He finds her acting as a painter's model, and he thereupon enters into a conversation with her, in which he endeavours to lead her to a conception of her trade, and shows her how she will best be able to win lovers. Now, although such a step would not give that offence to a Greek which it would to us, still there is not the least trace of a moral purpose in his conduct. *Brandis'* (Gesch. d. Entw. i. 236) remarks are little to the point. A purely critical interest leads Socrates to refer to its general conception every action across which he comes, regardless of its moral value.

[2] *Ribbing*, Socrat. Stud. i. 46.

reformer of philosophy as he was. Nay, more, had he thus confined himself to practical interests, he would have been incapable of exerting the deep reforming influence over Ethics which according to the testimony of history he did exert. His importance for Ethics comes not so much from the fact that he insisted on a re-establishment of moral life—this Aristophanes and without doubt many others did,—but from his recognising that an intellectual basis for moral principles must be an indispensable condition for any real reform of morals. This presupposes that practical problems are settled and vindicated by knowledge; in other words, that knowledge not merely subserves action, but leads and governs it—a view never as yet held by any one who did not attribute to knowledge an independent value of its own. If, therefore, Socrates, as a matter of fact, confined himself on principle to inquiries having for man a practical value, it can only be inferred that he was not himself fully conscious of the range of his thought. In practice he went beyond these limits, treating ethical questions in such a manner as no one could do unless fired with an independent love of knowledge.

The area is thus determined within which the fundamental conception of the Socratic philosophy must be looked for. True knowledge is the treasure to discover which Socrates goes forth in the service of the Delphic God; to gain the knowledge of the essence of things, he, with his friends, unweariedly labours; to true knowledge he ultimately refers all

CHAP. V.

C. *Theory that knowledge consists in conceptions.*

moral demands. The force with which he asserted this demand constitutes him the creator in Greece of an independent system of morality. For him it is not enough that men should do what is right; they must also know why they do it. He demands that they should not follow a dark impulse, an undefined enthusiasm or the aptitude of habit, but should act from clear consciousness; and because of its deficiency in this characteristic, he refuses to allow true wisdom to the art of his time, however high it otherwise stood.[1] In a word, the idea of knowledge forms the central point of the Socratic philosophy.[2] Since, however, all philosophy aims at knowledge, to give precision it must be further added, that, whereas the pursuit of true knowledge

[1] In *Plato*, Apol. 22, B., Socrates observes: In his sifting of men he had turned to the poets, but had soon found that they were usually not able to account for their own works. Ἔγνων οὖν . . . . ὅτι οὐ σοφίᾳ ποιοῖεν ἃ ποιοῖεν, ἀλλὰ φύσει τινὶ καὶ ἐνθουσιάζοντες, ὥσπερ οἱ θεομάντεις καὶ χρησμῳδοί· καὶ γὰρ αὐτοὶ λέγουσι μὲν πολλὰ καὶ καλὰ, ἴσασι δὲ οὐδὲν ὧν λέγουσιν. Besides, no one knows the limits of his knowledge, but thinks to understand all things. He had also observed the same in the χειροτέχναι, the representatives of sculpture and art.

[2] *Schleiermacher*, Werke, iii. 2, 300: 'The awakening of the idea of knowledge, and its first utterances, must have been the substance of the philosophy of Socrates.' *Ritter* agrees with this, Gesch. d. Philosophie, ii. 50. Brandis only differs in unessential points, Rhein. Mus. von *Niebuhr und Brandis*, i. 6, 130; Gr.-Röm. Phil. ii. a, 33. To him the origin of the doctrine of Socrates appears to be a desire to vindicate against the Sophists the absolute worth of moral determinations; and then he adds: to secure this purpose the first aim of Socrates was to gain a deeper insight into his own consciousness, in order to be able to distinguish false and true knowledge with certainty. Similarly *Brandis*, Gesch. d. Phils. Kant. i. 155. The important feature in Socrates was this, that to him morality appeared to be a certain kind of knowledge, proceeding from the thought of the good inborn in the soul.

had been heretofore unconscious and instinctive, with Socrates it first became conscious and methodical. By him the idea of knowledge as knowledge was first brought out, and received precedence of every other idea.[1]

This statement, again, requires further explanation. If the love of knowledge was shared also by previous philosophers, why, it may be asked, did it not before develop into a conscious and critical pursuit? The reason which may be assigned is this: The knowledge which earlier philosophers pursued, was, in itself, different from the knowledge which Socrates required. They were not compelled by their idea of knowledge as Socrates was to direct their attention to the intellectual processes and conditions by which it was truly to be acquired. Such a necessity was, however, imposed on Socrates by the principle which the most trustworthy accounts unanimously report as the soul of all his teaching—the principle, viz. that all true knowledge must proceed from correct conceptions, and that nothing can be known unless it can be referred to its general conception, and judged thereby.[2] In this principle, simple as

[1] *Schleiermacher*, l. c. 299; *Brandis.*

[2] *Xenoph.* Mem. iv. 6, 1: Σωκράτης γὰρ τοὺς μὲν εἰδότας, τί ἕκαστον εἴη τῶν ὄντων, ἐνόμιζε καὶ τοῖς ἄλλοις ἂν ἐξηγεῖσθαι δύνασθαι· τοὺς δὲ μὴ εἰδότας οὐδὲν ἔφη θαυμαστὸν εἶναι αὐτούς τε σφάλλεσθαι καὶ ἄλλους σφάλλειν· ὧν ἕνεκα σκοπῶν σὺν τοῖς συνοῦσι τί ἕκαστον εἴη τῶν ὄντων, οὐδεπώποτ' ἔληγε . . . § 13: ἐπὶ τὴν ὑπόθεσιν ἐπάνηγε πάντα τὸν λόγον, *i.e.*, as is explained by the context, he referred all doubtful points to universal conceptions, in order to settle them by means of these; iv. 5, 12; ἔφη δὲ καὶ τὸ διαλέγεσθαι ὀνομασθῆναι ἐκ τοῦ συνιόντας κοινῇ βουλεύεσθαι, διαλέγοντας κατὰ γένη τὰ πράγματα. δεῖν οὖν πειρᾶσθαι ὅτι μάλιστα πρὸς τοῦτο ἑαυτὸν ἕτοιμον παρασκευάζειν.

it may appear, an entire change was demanded in the intellectual procedure.[1] The ordinary way is to take things as being what they appear to the senses to be; or if contradictory experiences forbid doing so, to cling to those appearances which make the strongest impression on the observer, declaring these to be the essence, and thence proceeding to further conclusions. Hitherto this was exactly what philosophers had done. Even those who attacked the senses as untrustworthy had invariably started from one-sided observations, without being conscious of the necessity

Comp. i. 1, 16, and the many instances in the Memorabilia. *Aristotle* (Met. xiii. 4, 1078, b, 17, 27): Σωκράτους δὲ περὶ τὰς ἠθικὰς ἀρετὰς πραγματευομένου καὶ περὶ τούτων ὁρίζεσθαι καθόλου ζητοῦντος πρώτου . . . . ἐκεῖνος εὐλόγως ἐζήτει τὸ τί ἐστιν . . . δύο γάρ ἐστιν ἅ τις ἂν ἀποδοίη Σωκράτει δικαίως, τούς τ' ἐπακτικοὺς λόγους καὶ τὸ ὁρίζεσθαι καθόλου. Both are, however, at bottom the same. The λόγοι ἐπακτικοὶ are only the means for finding universal conceptions, and therefore Aristotle elsewhere (Met. i. 6, 987, b, 1; xiii. 9, 1086, b, 3; De Part. Anim. i. 1, 642, a, 28) justly observes that the seeking for universal conceptions or for the essence of things is the real service rendered to philosophy by Socrates. Accordingly, in the dialogues which Xenophon has preserved, we always see him making straight for the general conception, the τί ἐστιν. Even in *Plato's* Apology, 22, B., he describes his sifting of men as διερωτᾷν τί λέγοιεν, that is to say he asks for the conception of the deeds of the practical man, or of the poetry of the poet. Conf. Meno, 70, A.: Phædr. 262, B.; 265, D. It can, however, hardly be proved from Plato that Socrates really distinguished ἐπιστήμη from δόξα, as Brandis (Gr.-Röm. Phil. ii. a, 36; Gesch. d. Entw. i. 235) would have it; for we cannot decide whether passages like Meno, 98, B. represent the view of Socrates or that of Plato. Antisthenes, too, who, according to *Diogenes*, vi. 17, wrote a treatise περὶ δόξης καὶ ἐπιστήμης, may owe this distinction to the Eleatics. It can hardly be found in *Xen.* Mem. iv. 2, 33. In point of substance, no doubt the distinction was implied in the whole conduct of Socrates, and in passages such as *Xen.* Mem. iv. 6, 1; *Plato*, Apol. 21, B.

[1] Conf. what has been said above, p. 39, and in Gesch. d. Phil. i. 860.

of grounding every conclusion on an exhaustive inquiry into its subject. By means of sophistry this dogmatism had been overthrown. It was felt that all impressions derived from the senses were relative and personal, that they do not represent things as they are, but as they appear; and that, consequently, whatever we may assert, the opposite may be asserted with equal justice. For, if for one person at this moment *this* is true, for another person at another moment *that* is true.

Similar sentiments are expressed by Socrates relative to the value of common opinions. He is aware that they cannot furnish us with knowledge, but only involve us in contradictions. But he does not hence draw the inference of the Sophists, that no knowledge is possible, but only that it is not possible in that way. The majority of mankind have no true knowledge, because they confine themselves to assumptions, the accuracy of which they have never examined; only taking into consideration one or another property of things, but not their essence. Amend this fault; consider every object in all its bearings, and endeavour from this many-sided observation to determine the true essence; you will then have conceptions instead of vague notions—a regular examination, instead of an unmethodical and unconscious procedure—a true instead of an imaginary knowledge. In thus requiring knowledge of conceptions, Socrates not only broke away from the current view, but, generally speaking, from all previous philosophy. A thorough observation from every side, a critical examination, a methodical inquiry conscious of its own basis, was demanded; all that had hitherto been regarded as knowledge was rejected because it fell short of these conditions; and at the same time the conviction was expressed that, by observing these conditions real knowledge could be secured.

D. Moral importance of this theory.

For Socrates this principle had not only an intellectual, but a more immediate moral value. It is in fact one of the most striking things about him that he is unable to distinguish between morality and knowledge, and can neither imagine knowledge without virtue, nor virtue without knowledge.[1] In this respect also he is the child of his age, his greatness consisting herein, that he gave effect with penetration and spirit to its requirements and its legitimate endeavours. Advancing civilisation having created a demand for a higher education amongst the Greeks, and the course of intellectual development having diverted attention from the study of nature and fixed it on that of mind, a closer connection became necessary between philosophy and conduct. Only in man could philosophy find its highest object; only in philosophy could the support be found which was needed for life. The Sophists had endeavoured to meet this want with great skill and vigour; hence their extraordinary success. Nevertheless, their moral philosophy was too deficient in tenable ground; by doubting it had loosened its intellectual roots only too effectually; hence it

[1] Particular proof of this will be given subsequently.

degenerated with terrific speed, entering the service of every wicked and selfish impulse. Instead of moral life being raised by the influence of philosophy, both conduct and philosophy had taken the same downward course.

This sad state of things Socrates thoroughly understood. Whilst his cotemporaries, either blind with admiration for the Sophistic teaching were insensible to its dangers, or else through dread of these, and with a singular indifference to the wants of the times and the march of history, denounced the innovators in the tone of Aristophanes, he with keener penetration could distinguish between what was right and what was wrong in the spirit of the age. The insufficiency of the older culture, the want of firm ground in ordinary virtue, the obscurity of the prevailing notions so full of contradictions, the necessity for intellectual education, all were felt and taught by him as much as by any one of the Sophists. But to this teaching he set other and higher ends, not seeking to destroy belief in truth, but rather to show how truth might be acquired by a new intellectual process. His aim was not to minister to the selfishness of the age, but to rescue the age from selfishness and sloth, by teaching it what was truly good and useful; not to undermine morality and piety, but to establish them on a new foundation of knowledge. Thus Socrates was at once a moral and an intellectual reformer. His one great thought was how to transform and restore moral conduct by means of knowledge; knowledge and

CHAP. V.

right conduct were so closely associated in his mind that he could find no other object for knowledge save human conduct, and no guarantee for conduct save in knowledge.[1] How great the services were which he rendered to both morality and science by this effort, how wholesome was the influence which he exercised on the intellectual condition of his people and of mankind generally, history attests. If in the sequel the difference between morality and intellect was recognised quite as fully as their unity, yet the tie by which he connected them has never been broken; and if in the last centuries of the old world philosophy took the place of the waning religion, giving a stay to morality, purifying and quickening

[1] To revert to the question mooted above, as to whether he primarily regarded knowledge as a means to moral action, or moral action as a result of knowledge, so much may be said, that his peculiarity consisted herein, that for him this dilemma did not exist, that for him knowledge as such was at once a moral need and a moral force, and that therefore virtue was neither a simple consequence of knowledge, nor an end to be attained by means of knowledge, but was directly and in itself knowledge. If, therefore, Labriola (Dottrina di Socrate, 40) describes the only inner motive of Socrates' action as 'the moral need of certainty, and the conviction that this is only attainable by a clear and indubitably certain knowledge,' his statement may be accepted as true. On the other hand, *Ribbing's* (Socrat. Studien, i. 46) view does not seem to carry conviction, that according to both Plato and Xenophon, Socrates took in the first place a practical view of life, and that 'the theory of knowledge was only developed by him for the sake of a practical purpose.' We have already seen that, according to Socrates, true knowledge coincides with right intention. But, for the reasons set forth on p. 106, we cannot allow that knowledge with him has no independent value, and is only pursued as a means to a practical purpose; which must be the view of Ribbing, in as far as he contradicts the one given above. Nor do the passages quoted by Ribbing (*Plato*, Apol. 22, D.; 28, D.; 29, E.; 31, A.; 38, A.) suggest this view.

the moral consciousness, this great and beneficial result, in as far as it can be assigned to any one individual, was due to the teaching of Socrates.

E. The subjective character of the theory of Socrates.

The interest of philosophy being thus turned away from the outer world and directed towards man and his moral nature, and man only regarding things as true and binding of the truth of which he has convinced himself by intellectual research, there appears necessarily in Socrates a deeper importance attached to the personality of the thinker. In this modern writers have thought to discern the peculiar character of his philosophy.[1] Very different, however, is the personal importance of the thinker with Socrates from the caprice of the Sophists, different too from the extreme individualism of the post-Aristotelian schools. Socrates was aware that each individual must seek the grounds of his own principles for himself, that truth is not something given from without, but must be found by the exercise of individual thought. He required all opinions to be examined anew, no matter how old or how common they were, proofs only and not authorities claiming belief. Still, he was far from making man, as Protagoras did, the measure of all things. He did not even, as did the Stoics and Epicureans, declare personal conviction and practical need to be the ultimate standard of truth, nor yet, as did the Sceptics, resolve all truth into probability; but to him knowledge was an end in itself; so too he was persuaded that true knowledge could be obtained

[1] *Hegel*, Gesch. d. Phil. ii. 40; *Rötscher*, Aristoph. pp. 245, 388.

CHAP. V

by a thoughtful consideration of things. Moreover, he saw in man the proper object of philosophy, but instead of making of personal caprice a law, as the Sophists did, he subordinated caprice to the general law residing in the nature of things and of moral relations.[1] Instead too of making, with later philosophers, the self-contentment of the wise man his highest end, he confined himself to the point of view of old Greek morality, which could not conceive of the individual apart from the community,[2] and which accordingly regarded activity for the state as the first duty of a citizen,[3] and the law of the state as the natural rule of conduct.[4] Hence the Stoic apathy and indifference to country were entirely alien from Socrates. If it can be truly said 'that in him commences an unbounded reference to the person, to the freedom of the inner life,'[5] it must also be added that this statement by no means exhausts the theory of Socrates. Thus the disputes as to whether the Socratic doctrine rests on a purely personal or a really independent basis[6] may be settled, by allowing that, compared with former systems, his teaching exhibits a deeper importance attaching to the perso-

[1] Proofs may be found *Xen.* Mem. ii. 2; ii. 6, 1–7; iii. 8, 1–3; iv. 4, 20.

[2] Compare the conversation with Aristippus, *Xen.* Mem. ii. 1, 13; and *Plato's* Crito, 53, A.

[3] It has been already seen that Socrates placed his own activity under this point of view. See pp. 66, 69; *Xen.* Mem. i. 6, 15; *Plato,* Apol. 30, A.

[4] Mem. iv. 4, 12, and 3, 15, with which the previous remarks respecting the peculiar conduct of the sage may be compared.

[5] *Hegel,* l. c.

[6] Compare the views of *Rötscher,* l. c., and *Brandis* for the opposite view. 'Ueber die vorgebliche Subjektivität der Sokrat. Lehre,' in Rhein. Mus. ii. 1, 85.

nality of the thinker, but yet by no means belongs to those which are purely relative. It aims at gaining a knowledge which shall do more than satisfy a personal want, and which shall be true and desirable for more than the thinker; but the ground on which it is sought is the personal thought [1] of the individual.

This theory is indeed not further worked out by Socrates. He has established the principle, that only the knowledge which has to do with conceptions is true knowledge. To the further inference that only the being of conceptions is true being,[2] and that therefore only conceptions are true, and to a systematic exposition of conceptions true in themselves, he never advanced. Knowledge is here something sought, a problem to be solved by the thinker; philosophy is philosophic impulse, and philosophic method, a seeking for truth, not yet a possessing it; and this deficiency lends countenance to the view that

[1] Hegel says nothing very different, when in distinguishing (Gesch. d. Phil. ii. 40, 166) Socrates from the Sophists he says: 'In Socrates the creation of thought is at once clad with an independent existence of its own,' and what is purely personal is 'externalised and made universal by him as the good.' Socrates is said to have substituted 'thinking man is the measure of all things' in place of the Sophistic doctrine 'man is the measure of all things.' In a word, his leading thought is not the individual as he knows himself experimentally, but the universal element which is found running through all individuals. With this view agree also *Rötscher*, l. c. p. 246, 392, and *Hermann*, Gesch. und Syst. des Plat. i. 239.

[2] The objections of *Alberti*, Sokr. 94, to the above vanish if the word 'only' is properly emphasised. He only asserts what is already well known, that Socrates did not develop his theory of conceptions to the theory of ideas, nor contrast the universal thought in the conception, as being the only thing truly real with individual things.

the platform of Socrates was that of a narrow reference to the person. Still it should never be forgotten that the aim of Socrates was always to discover and set forth that which is in itself true and good. Mankind is to be intellectually and morally educated, but the one and only means thereto is to attain a knowledge of truth.

The primary aim of Socrates being to train men to think, rather than to construct a system, the main point with him was a philosophic method to determine the way which would lead to truth. The substance of his teaching thus appears to have been partly confined to questions having an immediate bearing on human conduct; partly it does not go beyond the general and theoretical demand, that all action should be determined by a knowledge of conceptions. There is no systematic development of individual points of morality and no attempt to give a reason for them.

CHAPTER VI.

THE PHILOSOPHICAL METHOD OF SOCRATES.

THE peculiarity of the method pursued by Socrates consists, generally speaking, in deducing conceptions from the common opinions of men. With the formation of conceptions, and the intellectual exercise of individuals he was content; there is no systematic treatment of conceptions. The theory of a knowledge of conceptions appears here as a demand presupposing as existing the consciousness of its necessity, and seeking an insight into the essence of things. At the same time, the mind does not go beyond this seeking. It has not the power to develop a system of absolute knowledge, nor has it a method sufficiently matured to form a system. For the same reason, the process of induction is not reduced within clearly defined rules. All that Socrates has clearly expressed is the general postulate, that every thing must be reduced to its conception. Further details as to the mode and manner of this reduction and its strict logical forms, were not yet worked out by him into a science, but were applied practically by dint of individual skill. The only thing about him at all resembling a logical rule, the maxim that the process of critical inquiry must

CHAP. VI.

always confine itself to what is universally admitted,[1] sounds far too indefinite to invalidate our assertion.

A. The Socratic knowledge of self, resulting in a knowledge of not knowing.

This process involves three particular steps. The first is the Socratic knowledge of self. Holding as he did that only the knowledge of conceptions constitutes true knowledge, Socrates was fain to look at all supposed knowledge, asking whether it agreed with his idea of knowledge, or not. Nothing appeared to him more perverse, nothing more obstructive to true knowledge from the very outset, than the belief that you know what you do not know.[2] Nothing is so necessary as self-examination to show what we really know and what we only think we know.[3] Nothing, too, is more indispensable for practical relations than to become acquainted

[1] Mem. iv. 6, 15: *ὁπότε δὲ αὐτός τι τῷ λόγῳ διεξίοι, διὰ τῶν μάλιστα ὁμολογουμένων ἐπορεύετο, νομίζων ταύτην τὴν ἀσφάλειαν εἶναι λόγου.*

[2] *Xen.* Mem. iii. 9, 6: *μανίαν γε μὴν ἐναντίον μὲν ἔφη εἶναι σοφίᾳ, οὐ μέντοι γε τὴν ἀνεπιστημοσύνην μανίαν ἐνόμιζεν. τὸ δὲ ἀγνοεῖν ἑαυτὸν καὶ ἃ μὴ οἶδε δοξάζειν τε καὶ οἴεσθαι γιγνώσκειν, ἐγγυτάτω μανίας ἐλογίζετο εἶναι.* Generally speaking, those are called mad who are mistaken about what is commonly known, not those who are mistaken about things of which most men are ignorant. Also *Plato*, Apol. 29, B.: *καὶ τοῦτο πῶς οὐκ ἀμαθία ἐστὶν αὕτη ἡ ἐπονείδιστος, ἡ τοῦ οἴεσθαι εἰδέναι ἃ οὐκ οἶδεν;*

[3] In this sense Socrates, speaking in *Plato*, Apol. 21, B., says that according to the oracle he had interrogated all with whom he was brought into contact to discover whether they had any kind of knowledge; and that in all cases he had found along with some kind of knowledge an ignorance, which he would not take in exchange for any kind of knowledge—an opinion that they knew what they did not know. On the other hand, he considered it to be his vocation, *φιλοσοφοῦντα ζῆν καὶ ἐξετάζοντα ἐμαυτὸν καὶ τοὺς ἄλλους* (28, E.); and he says elsewhere (38, A.) that there could be no higher good than to converse every day as he did: *ὁ δὲ ἀνεξέταστος βίος οὐ βιωτὸς ἀνθρώπῳ.*

with the state of our inner self, with the extent of our knowledge and capacities, with our defects and requirements.[1] One result of this self-examination being the discovery that the actual knowledge of the philosopher does not correspond with his idea of knowledge, there follows further that consciousness of knowing nothing, which Socrates declared to be his only knowledge. Any other knowledge he denied possessing,[2] and therefore refused to be the teacher of his friends,[3] only wishing, in common with them,

[1] *Xenophon*, Mem. iv. 2, 24, inquiring into the Delphic γνῶθι σεαυτόν, says that self-knowledge is attended with the greatest advantages, want of it with the greatest disadvantages: οἱ μὲν γὰρ εἰδότες ἑαυτοὺς τά τε ἐπιτήδεια ἑαυτοῖς ἴσασι καὶ διαγιγνώσκουσιν ἅ τε δύνανται καὶ ἃ μή· καὶ ἃ μὲν ἐπίστανται πράττοντες (self-examination always refers in the first place to knowledge, because with knowledge right action is given) πορίζονταί τε ὧν δέονται καὶ εὖ πράττουσιν. See also *Plato*, Phædrus, 229, E.; he had not time to give to the explanation of myths of which others were so fond, not being even able to know himself according to the Delphic oracle; Symp. 216, A.; when Alcibiades complains: ἀναγκάζει γάρ με ὁμολογεῖν, ὅτι πολλοῦ ἐνδεὴς ὢν αὐτὸς ἔτι ἐμαυτοῦ μὲν ἀμελῶ, τὰ δ' Ἀθηναίων πράττω.

[2] *Plato*, Apol. 21, B.: ἐγὼ γὰρ δὴ οὔτε μέγα οὔτε σμικρὸν σύνοιδα ἐμαυτῷ σοφὸς ὤν.—21, D.: τούτου μὲν τοῦ ἀνθρώπου ἐγὼ σοφώτερός εἰμι· κινδυνεύει μὲν γὰρ ἡμῶν οὐδέτερος οὐδὲν καλὸν κἀγαθὸν εἰδέναι, ἀλλ' οὗτος μὲν οἴεταί τι εἰδέναι οὐκ εἰδώς, ἐγὼ δὲ ὥσπερ οὖν οὐκ οἶδα, οὐδὲ οἴομαι.—23, B.: οὗτος ὑμῶν, ὦ ἄνθρωποι, σοφώτατός ἐστιν, ὅστις, ὥσπερ Σωκράτης, ἔγνωκεν, ὅτι οὐδενὸς ἄξιός ἐστι τῇ ἀληθείᾳ πρὸς σοφίαν. And a little before: τὸ δὲ κινδυνεύει, ὦ ἄνδρες Ἀθηναῖοι, τῷ ὄντι ὁ θεὸς σοφὸς εἶναι, καὶ ἐν τῷ χρησμῷ τούτῳ τοῦτο λέγειν, ὅτι ἡ ἀνθρωπίνη σοφία ὀλίγου τινὸς ἀξία ἐστὶ καὶ οὐδενός.—Symp. 216, D.: ἀγνοεῖ πάντα καὶ οὐδὲν οἶδεν, ὡς τὸ σχῆμα αὐτοῦ.—Theætet. 150, C.: ἄγονός εἰμι σοφίας, καὶ ὅπερ ἤδη πολλοί μοι ὠνείδισαν, ὡς τοὺς μὲν ἄλλους ἐρωτῶ, αὐτὸς δὲ οὐδὲν ἀποκρίνομαι περὶ οὐδενὸς διὰ τὸ μηδὲν ἔχειν σοφόν, ἀληθὲς ὀνειδίζουσι· τὸ δὲ αἴτιον τούτου τόδε· μαιεύεσθαί με ὁ θεὸς ἀναγκάζει, γεννᾷν δὲ ἀπεκώλυσεν. Comp. Rep. i. 337, E.; Men. 98, B. That this trait in Plato has been taken from the Socrates of history, may be gathered from the Platonic dialogues, in which his teacher is by no means represented as so ignorant.

[3] See above, p. 68.

CHAP. VI.

to learn and inquire.[1] This confession of ignorance was far from being a sceptical denial of knowledge,[2] with which the whole philosophic career of Socrates would be irreconcilable. On the contrary, it contains a simple avowal as to his own personal state, and collaterally as to the state of those whose knowledge he had had the opportunity of testing.[3] Nor again must it be regarded as mere irony or exaggerated modesty.[4] Socrates really knew nothing, or, to express it otherwise, he had no developed theory, and no positive dogmatic principles. The demand for a knowledge of conceptions having once dawned upon him in all its fulness, he missed the marks of true knowledge in all that hitherto passed for wisdom and knowledge. Being, however, also the first to make this demand, he had as yet attained no definite subject-matter for knowledge. The idea of knowledge was to him an unfathomable problem, in the face of which he could not but be conscious of his ignorance.[5] And thus a certain affinity between his view and the sophistic scepticism may

[1] *κοινῇ βουλεύεσθαι, κοινῇ σκέπτεσθαι, κοινῇ ζητεῖν, συζητεῖν,* &c. *Xen.* Mem. iv. 5, 12; 6, 1; *Plato*, Theæt. 151, E.; Prot. 330, B.; Gorg. 505, E.; Crat. 384, B.; Meno, 89 E.

[2] As the new Academicians would have it, *Cic.* Acad. i. 12, 44; ii. 23, 74.

[3] The already quoted language of the Apology, 23, A., does not contradict this; for the *possibility* of knowledge is not there denied; only the *limited character* of human knowledge is asserted in comparison with the divine.

[4] As *Grote* remarks (Plato, i. 270, 323), referring to *Arist.* Soph. El. 34, 183, b, 7: ἐπεὶ καὶ διὰ τοῦτο Σωκράτης ἠρώτα, ἀλλ' οὐκ ἀπεκρίνετο· ὡμολόγει γὰρ οὐκ εἰδέναι. Conf. *Plato*, Rep. 337.

[5] Compare *Hegel*, Gesch. d. Phil. ii. 54; *Hermann*, Plato, 326.

be observed. This scepticism, in as far as it denied the possibility of all knowledge, Socrates opposed, whilst agreeing with it in as far as it referred to previous philosophy. Natural philosophers, he believed, transcended in their speculation the limits of human knowledge, in proof of which he appealed to the fact of their being at variance with one another respecting the most important questions. Some hold being to be one, others make of it a boundless variety; some teach that everything, others that nothing, is subject to motion; some that all things, others that nothing, comes into being or perishes.[1] Just as the Sophists destroyed the conflicting statements of the natural philosophers by means of each other, so Socrates infers from the contest of systems, that no one of them is in possession of the truth. Their great difference consists herein, the Sophists making Not-knowing into a principle, and considering the highest wisdom to consist in doubting everything; Socrates adhering to his demand for knowledge, clinging to the belief in its possibility, consequently regarding ignorance as the greatest evil.

B. The search for knowledge. Sifting of his fellow-men. Eros and Irony.

Such being the importance of the Socratic Not-knowing, it involves in itself a demand for enlightenment; the knowledge of ignorance leads to a search

[1] *Xen.* Mem. i. 1, 13, says that Socrates did not busy himself with questions of natural science, but on the contrary he held those who did so to be foolish; ἐθαύμαζε δ' εἰ μὴ φανερὸν αὐτοῖς ἐστιν, ὅτι ταῦτα οὐ δυνατόν ἐστιν ἀνθρώποις εὑρεῖν· ἐπεὶ καὶ τοὺς μέγιστον φρονοῦντας ἐπὶ τῷ περὶ τούτων λέγειν οὐ ταὐτὰ δοξάζειν ἀλλήλοις, ἀλλὰ τοῖς μαινομένοις ὁμοίως διακεῖσθαι πρὸς ἀλλήλους· then follows what is quoted in the text.

CHAP. VI.

for true knowledge. The consciousness of Not-knowing continuing, and the philosopher having an idea of knowledge without finding it present in himself, the search for knowledge naturally assumes the form of an application to others, with a view of ascertaining whether the knowledge wanting at home is to be found with them.[1] Hence the necessity of inquiry in common by means of the dialogue.[2] For Socrates, this mode of intercourse has not merely an educational value, gaining easier access and a more fruitful effect for his ideas, but it is to his mind an indispensable condition of the development of thought, and one from which the Socrates of history never departs.[3] Speaking more accurately, its nature consists in a sifting of men such as is described in the Apology,[4] or in a bringing to the birth, as it is called in the Theætetus;[5] in other words, the philosopher by his questions obliges others to unfold their inner self before him:[6] he asks after their real opinions, after the reasons of their beliefs and actions,

[1] The connection is very apparent in the Apol. 21, B., if only the inner thought of the philosophy of Socrates is put in the place of the oracular response.

[2] Compare p. 124, 2.

[3] Compare besides the Memorabilia, *Plato*, Apol. 24, C.; Protag. 335, B., 336, B. Theæt. l. c.

[4] Similarly *Xen*. Mem. iv. 7, 1: *πάντων μὲν γὰρ ὧν ἐγὼ οἶδα μάλιστα ἔμελεν αὐτῷ εἰδέναι, ὅτου τις ἐπιστήμων εἴη τῶν συνόντων αὐτῷ*. Xenophon only took it to prove *ὅτι αὐτάρκεις ἐν ταῖς προσηκούσαις πράξεσιν αὐτοὺς εἶναι ἐπεμελεῖτο*: and the inquiry into human nature has this meaning in Mem. iii. 6; iv. 2; but clearly this is not its original object.

[5] See p. 150; 123, 2.

[6] *Plato*, Lach. 187, E.; he who enters into conversation with Socrates *μὴ παύεσθαι ὑπὸ τούτου περιαγόμενον τῷ λόγῳ, πρὶν ἂν ἐμπέσῃ εἰς τὸ διδόναι περὶ αὑτοῦ λόγον, ὅντινα τρόπον νῦν τε ζῇ*, nor is there any escape from the most thorough *βασανίζεσθαι*.

and in this way attempts by an interrogatory analysis of their notions to bring out the thought latent therein, of which they are themselves unconscious.[1] In as far as this process presupposes that the knowledge which the questioner lacks may be found in others, it resembles an impulse to supplement one's own defects by their help. This intercourse with others is, for a philosopher with whom knowing coincides with purposing, not only an intellectual but also a moral and personal need. To inquire in common is at once to live in common. Love of knowledge is at once impulse to friendship, and in the blending together of these two sides consists the peculiarity of the Socratic Eros.[2]

In as far as others do not possess the knowledge sought for, and the questions of Socrates only serve to expose their ignorance, the process bears also the character of irony. Irony, however, must not be understood to be merely a conversational trick;[3] still less is it that derisive condescension or affected sim-

[1] It is assumed, as a matter of course, that every one can give an account of what he knows and is, *Plato*, l. c. 190, C.; Charm. 158, E.

[2] See above, p. 76. Besides Brandis ii. a, 64, reminds us with justice that treatises on ἔρως are mentioned not only by Plato and Xenophon, but also by Euclid, Crito, Simmias, and Antisthenes, which shows the importance of it for the Socratic schools. The chief passage is in Xenophon, Symp. c. 8, where the advantages of a spiritual and the disadvantages of a sensual love are unfolded, apparently (as a careful survey of the Platonic Symposium will show) by Xenophon, speaking for himself, but undoubtedly following in the train of Socrates. Even Æschines and Cebes had treated of ἔρως in the Socratic sense. See *Plut.* Puer. Ed. c. 15, p. 11, and the fragment of Æschines in *Aristid.* Or. xlv. p. 34.

[3] *Hegel*, Gesch. d. Phil. ii. 53, 57; Conf. *Arist.* Eth. iv. 13; 1127, b, 22.

CHAP. VI.

plicity, which as it were lures others on to the ice in order to laugh at their falls; or that absolute reference to the person and destruction of all general truth, which for a time bore this name in the romantic school. Its proper nature consists rather herein, that without any positive knowledge, and prompted only by a desire for knowledge, Socrates applies to others in the hope of learning from them what they know, but that in the attempt to discover it, upon a critical analysis of their notions, even [1]

[1] Plato at least gives this deeper meaning to the irony of Socrates. See Rep. i. 337, A.: αὕτη ἐκείνη ἡ εἰωθυῖα εἰρωνεία Σωκράτους, καὶ ταῦτ' ἐγὼ ἤδη τε καὶ τούτοις προὔλεγον, ὅτι σὺ ἀποκρίνασθαι μὲν οὐκ ἐθελήσοις, εἰρωνεύσοιο δὲ καὶ πάντα μᾶλλον ποιήσοις ἢ ἀποκρίνοιο εἴ τίς τί σε ἐρωτᾷ. And again, 337, E.: ἵνα Σωκράτης τὸ εἰωθὸς διαπράξηται, αὐτὸς μὲν μὴ ἀποκρίνηται, ἄλλον δὲ ἀποκρινομένου λαμβάνῃ λόγον καὶ ἐλέγχῃ· to which Socrates replies: πῶς γὰρ ἂν . . . τις ἀποκρίναιτο πρῶτον μὲν μὴ εἰδὼς μηδὲ φάσκων εἰδέναι, &c. Symp. 216, E.: εἰρωνευόμενος δὲ καὶ παίζων πάντα τὸν βίον πρὸς τούς ἀνθρώπους διατελεῖ, which, as the context shows, refers partly to the fact that Socrates pretended to be in love, without being so in the Greek sense of the term, and partly to the words ἀγνοεῖ πάντα καὶ οὐδὲν οἶδεν. The same, omitting the word εἰρωνεία, is said in the passage of the Theætetus already mentioned, and in the Meno, 80, A.: οὐδὲν ἄλλο ἢ αὐτός τε ἀπορεῖς καὶ τοὺς ἄλλους ποιεῖς ἀπορεῖν, and also in the Apol. 23, E., in which, after the Socratic sifting of others has been described, it goes on to say: ἐκ ταυτησὶ δὴ τῆς ἐξετάσεως πολλοὶ μὲν ἀπέχθειαί μοι γεγόνασι . . . ὄνομα δὲ τοῦτο . . . σοφὸς εἶνα. οἴονται γάρ με ἑκάστοτε οἱ παρόντες ταῦτα αὐτὸν εἶναι σοφὸν ἃ ἂν ἄλλον ἐξελέγξω. Likewise *Xenophon*, Mem. iv. 4, 10: ὅτι τῶν ἄλλων καταγελᾷς, ἐρωτῶν μὲν καὶ ἐλέγχων πάντας, αὐτὸς δὲ οὐδενὶ θέλων ὑπέχειν λόγον οὐδὲ γνώμην ἀποφαίνεσθαι περὶ οὐδενός. *Ibid.* 11. Conf. i. 2, 36: ἀλλά τοι σύ γε, ὦ Σώκρατες, εἴωθας εἰδὼς πῶς ἔχει τὰ πλεῖστα ἐρωτᾶν. Hence *Quintilian*, ix. 2, 46, observes that the whole life of Socrates seemed an irony, because he always played the part of an admirer of the wisdom of others. Connected with this is the use which Socrates made of irony as a figure of speech. Conf. *Plat.* Gorg. 489, E.; Symp. 218, D.: *Xen.* Mem. iv. 2. Only its meaning must not be limited to this. Compare also *Hermann*, Plat. 242, 326, and par-

their supposed knowledge vanishes. This irony is, therefore, speaking generally, the dialectical or the critical factor in the Socratic method, assuming the peculiar form it here does owing to the presupposed ignorance of him who uses it for his instrument.

C. *The formation of conceptions and the method of proof by conceptions.*

Conscious as Socrates might be of possessing no real knowledge, he must at least have believed that he possessed the notion and the method of true knowledge. Without this conviction he would neither have been able to confess his own ignorance, nor to expose that of others, both being only rendered possible by comparing the knowledge he found with the idea of knowledge residing within himself. The fact that this idea was nowhere to be found present was in itself a challenge to him to set about realising it; hence resulted as the third point in his philosophic course the attempt to create real knowledge. For real knowledge he could only allow that to pass which emanated from the conception of a thing; hence the first step here is the formation of conceptions or induction.[1] For even if Socrates does not always make for formal definitions, he at least always seeks some universal quality applicable to the conception and to the essence of the thing, in order to settle the point in hand by referring the particular case to this universal quality.[2] The class-quality is therefore to him of the greatest importance.

ticularly *Schleiermacher*, Gesch. d. Phil. 83, and for the use of the word also *Leop. Schmidt*, in Ind. Lection, Marburg, 1873.

[1] Compare the remarks of *Aristotle* already mentioned, p. 111, 2.

[2] ἐπὶ τὴν ὑπόθεσιν ἐπανῆγε πάντα τὸν λόγον. See p. 111, 2.

CHAP. VI.

The starting point for this induction is supplied by the commonest notions. He begins with examples taken from daily life, with well-known and generally admitted truths. On every disputed point he goes back to such instances, and hopes in this way to attain a universal agreement.[1] All previous science being doubtful, nothing remains but to begin anew with the simplest experiences. On the other hand, induction has not as yet advanced so far as to understand how to derive conceptions from an exhaustive and critically tested series of observations. This is a later requirement due partly to Aristotle, partly to more modern philosophy. The wider basis of a comprehensive knowledge of facts was as yet wanting, nay, was even despised; Socrates was in the habit of developing his thoughts in personal conversation with distinct reference to the case before him and to the capacity and needs of his fellow-speakers; hence he was confined to the assumptions which the circumstances and his own limited experience supplied; he was fain to take isolated notions and admissions as his point of departure, and could only go as far as others could follow. Hence in most cases he relies more on particular instances than on an exhaustive analysis of experience.[2] This chance-

[1] Compare what has been quoted, pp. 81, 2; 122, 1, and the whole of the Memorabilia. Plato, too, gives instances of this procedure. See *Xen.* Œc. 19, 15: ἡ ἐρώτησις διδασκαλία ἐστὶν . . . ἄγων γάρ με δι' ὧν ἐγὼ ἐπίσταμαι, ὅμοια τούτοις ἐπιδεικνὺς ἃ οὐκ ἐνόμιζον ἐπίστασθαι, ἀναπείθεις, οἶμαι ὡς καὶ ταῦτα ἐπίσταμαι. As to the principle that from the less you proceed to an understanding of the more important, see *Plato*, Gorg. 947, C.

[2] As for example in the comparison of the politician with the physician, pilot, &c.

element in his principles he, however, endeavours to eliminate by collecting opposite instances, so as to correct and supplement varying experiences by one another. The question, for instance, before him being the conception of injustice: He is unjust, says Euthydemus, who lies, deceives, robs, and such like. Yet, rejoins Socrates, it is right to lie, to deceive, and to rob an enemy. Accordingly the conception must be more accurately defined thus: He is unjust who does such things to his friends. Even such action is, however, permitted under circumstances. A general is not unjust when he encourages his army by a lie, nor a father who gives his son medicine by deception, nor a friend who robs his friend of the weapon with which he would have committed suicide. We must, therefore, introduce a further limitation. Unjust is he who deceives or robs his friends in order to do them harm.[1] Or the conception of a ruler has to be discovered. General opinion regards a ruler as one who has the power to give orders. But this power, Socrates shows, is conceded only to the steersman on board ship, only to the physician in case of sickness, and in every other case only to those conversant with the special subject. He, therefore, only is a ruler who possesses the knowledge necessary for ruling.[2] Or it must be determined what belongs to a good suit of armour. The smith says, it must be of a proper size. But suppose the man intending to wear it is deformed. Why then, the answer is, it it must be of the proper size for his deformity. It

[1] Mem. iv. 2, 11. [2] *Ibid.* iii. 9, 10.

CHAP. VI.

therefore has the proper size when it fits. But now, supposing a man wishes to move, must the armour fit exactly? Not so, or he would be hampered in his movements. We must, therefore, understand by fitting what is comfortable for use.[1] In a similar way we see Socrates analysing the common notions of his friends. He reminds them of the various sides to every question; he brings out the opposition which every notion contains either within itself or in relation to some other; and he aims at correcting, by additional observations, assumptions resting on a one-sided experience, at completing them, and giving to them a more careful definition. By this process he arrives at what belongs to the essence of every object, and what does not; thus conceptions are formed from notions.

For the purpose of proof, too, the class-qualities of conceptions are also the most important things. In order to investigate the correctness of a quality or the necessity of a course of action, Socrates falls back on the conception of the thing to which it refers;[2] and therefrom deduces what applies to the given case.[3] As in seeking conceptions he always

[1] Mem. iii. 10, 9.

[2] l.c. iv. 6, B.

[3] For instance, in order to reprove Lamprocles for his conduct to Xanthippe, he first (Mem. ii. 1) lets him give a definition of ingratitude, and then shows that his conduct falls under this conception; in order to put his duties before a cavalry officer, he begins (Mem. iii. 3, 2) by stating what is his employment, and enumerating its different parts; in order to prove the being of the Gods, he begins with the general principle that all that serves an end must have an intelligent cause (Mem. i. 4, 4); in order to determine which of two is the better citizen, he first inquires into the peculiar features of a good citizen (iv. 6, 14).

progresses from what is known and universally admitted,[1] so, too, he does here. Hence his method of proof takes the most varied turns,[2] according as it starts from one or another point of departure. He allows a general principle to be taken for granted, and includes under it the particular case;[3] he refutes foreign assertions by bringing home to them contradictions with themselves or with other undoubted assumptions or facts;[4] he builds up the premisses from which he deduces his conclusions by means of induction, or concludes straight off by an apparent analogy.[5] A theory of this method of proof he has not given, nor distinguished the various kinds of proof. The essential point about it is only this, that everything is measured and decided by conceptions. To find the turns by which this end is reached is a matter of personal critical dexterity. Aristotle, therefore, in making the chief merit of Socrates in this respect consist in the formation of conceptions and in induction,[6] must on the whole be allowed to be right.

Asking further as to the objects on which Socrates practised his method, we encounter in the Memorabilia of Xenophon a motley array of materials—investigations into the essence of virtue, the duties of man, the existence of Gods, disputes with Sophists, advice of the most varied kind given to friends and

[1] See above, pp. 132; 122, 1.

[2] Conf. *Schwegler*, Gesch. d. Griech. Phil. 2 Aufl. p. 121.

[3] As in the cases quoted on p. 132, 3.

[4] For instance, Mem. i. 2, 34 and 36; iv. 2, 31; 4, 7.

[5] Mem. iv. 2, 22; iv. 4, 14; i. 2, 32.

[6] See p. 111, 2.

acquaintances, conversations with generals as to the responsibilities of their office, with artificers and tradesmen as to their arts, even with loose women as to their mode of life. Nothing is too small to arouse the curiosity of the philosopher and to call for a thorough and methodical examination. As Plato at a later time found in all things without exception essential conceptions, so, too, Socrates, purely in the interest of knowledge, even where no educational or other good was apparent, referred everything to its conception.[1] He looked upon the life and pursuits of man as the real object of his inquiries, and other things only in as far as they affected the conditions and problems of human life. Hence his philosophy, which in point of scientific form was a criticism of what *is* (διαλεκτική), became in its actual application a science of human actions (ἠθική).

[1] See p. 110.

CHAPTER VII.

THE SUBSTANCE OF THE TEACHING OF SOCRATES: ETHICS.

CHAP. VII.

A. *Fundamental restriction of the subject-matter to Ethics.*

SOCRATES, says Xenophon,[1] did not discourse concerning the nature of the All, like most other philosophers before him; he did not inquire into the essence of the world and the laws of natural phenomena; he declared it folly to search into such subjects; for it is unreasonable to quiz things divine before fully understanding things human; besides, the conflicting opinions of natural philosophers prove that the object of their research transcends the capacity of human knowledge. After all, these inquiries are of no practical use. Quite in keeping with this view, the Socrates of Xenophon tests even geometry and astronomy[2] by the standard of immediate utility, as being the knowledge respectively requisite for surveying and navigation. To carry these sciences farther than this he considers to be a useless waste of time, or even impious; for man can never come upon the track of the mighty works of the Gods, nor do the Gods desire that he should attempt such knowledge. Hence in all such

[1] Mem. i. 1, 11. Conf. p. 125, 1.

[2] *Ibid.* iv. 7.

CHAP. VII.

attempts, extravagances such as those of Anaxagoras are sure to come to view.[1]

The accuracy of this description of Socrates has, however, not passed unchallenged by modern writers.[2] Granting, it is said, that Socrates really expressed these and similar sentiments, can they be rightfully so understood as though he would altogether deprecate speculative inquiry into nature? Would not such an assertion too manifestly contradict his own fundamental view, the idea of the oneness of all knowledge? Would it not lead, if propounded as Xenophon has done, to consequences manifestly unreasonable? Even Plato[3] bears testimony to the fact that Socrates did not attack natural science in itself, but only the ordinary treatment of it; nor can Xenophon himself deny that he did devote his attention to nature,[4] hoping by con-

[1] Mem. iv. 7, 6: ὅλως δὲ τῶν οὐρανίων, ᾗ ἕκαστα ὁ θεὸς μηχανᾶται, φροντιστὴν γίγνεσθαι ἀπέτρεπεν· οὔτε γὰρ εὑρετὰ ἀνθρώποις αὐτὰ ἐνόμιζεν εἶναι, οὔτε χαρίζεσθαι θεοῖς ἂν ἡγεῖτο τὸν ζητοῦντα ἃ ἐκεῖνοι σαφηνίσαι οὐκ ἐβουλήθησαν. Such subtleties only lead to absurdities, οὐδὲν ἧττον ἢ Ἀναξαγόρας παρεφρόνησεν ὁ μέγιστον φρονήσας ἐπὶ τῷ τὰς τῶν θεῶν μηχανὰς ἐξηγεῖσθαι—which is then supported by various remarks, proving the extravagance of the notion that the sun is a fiery stone.

[2] *Schleiermacher*, Werke, iii. 2, 305–307; Gesch. d. Phil. p. 83; *Brandis*, Rhein. Mus. i. 2, 130; Gr.-Röm. Phil. ii. a, 34; *Ritter*, Gesch. d. Phil. ii. 48, 64; *Süvern*, Ueber die Wolken des Aristophanes, p. 11; *Krische*, Forsch. 105; *Alberti*, Sokr. 93, 98, likewise gives a partial adherence to this view: it might have been expected to go further after what has been said, p. 50, 2.

[3] Phædo, 96, A.; 97, B.; Rep. vii. 529, A.; Phileb. 28, D.; Leg. xii. 966, E.

[4] Mem. i. 4; iv. 3. No argument can be drawn from Mem. i. 6, 14: τοὺς θησαυροὺς τῶν πάλαι σοφῶν ἀνδρῶν, οὓς ἐκεῖνοι κατέλιπον ἐν βιβλίοις γράψαντες, ἀνελίττων κόινῇ σὺν τοῖς φίλοις διέρχομαι, for these σοφοὶ need not necessarily be the earlier natural philosophers. Σοφοὶ is also used of poets, chroniclers,

sidering the relations of means to ends in nature to gain an insight into its reasonable arrangement. Allowing, therefore, that Socrates, as was the fact, had no special talent for natural science, and hence did not study it to any great extent, at least the germ of a new form of this science may be discovered in him. In his notion of the relation of means to ends in nature must have lain 'the thought of a universal diffusion of intelligence throughout the whole of nature,' 'the theory of an absolute harmony of man and nature, and of man's occupying such a position in nature as to be a microcosm of the world.' [1] If he stopped at the germ, confining his study of nature to mere practical requirements, this must have been, according to his own opinion, only as a preliminary step. He must have only intended that man ought not to reach forth into the distance until a critical foundation has been securely laid at home in the depths of his own inner life; or else he must have referred to popular and not to philosophical study.[2]

Unfortunately this view of modern writers rests on assumptions which have no foundation. In the first place, not only Xenophon, but Aristotle also,[3]

&c., and it is expressly stated that Socrates perused their works in order to find in them what was morally useful for himself and his friends.

[1] *Schleiermacher* and *Ritter*.

[2] *Krische*, 208, as though Socrates made any distinction between training for a philosopher and training for a good man.

[3] Met. i. 6 (987, b, 1): Σωκράτους δὲ περὶ μὲν τὰ ἠθικὰ πραγματευομένου, περὶ δὲ τῆς ὅλης φύσεως οὐθέν, xiii. 4; De Part. Anim. i. 1 (642, a, 28): ἐπὶ Σωκράτους δὲ τοῦτο μὲν [τὸ ὁρίσασθαι τὴν οὐσίαν] ηὐξήθη, τὸ δὲ ζητεῖν τὰ περὶ φύσεως ἔληξε. Conf. Eth. Eud. i. 5; 1216, b,

CHAP. VII.

not to mention later writers,[1] assert that Socrates never pursued the study of nature. Aristotle is, however, the very authority called in to arbitrate when Xenophon and Plato differ. What right have we, then, to stand aghast at his testimony as soon as he declares against Plato? Yet even Plato indirectly admits in the Timæus that natural science was foreign to Socrates. If he elsewhere puts in his mouth sayings referring to nature, there is still no evidence that these utterances are historically true. Not even in the passage in the Phædo can such evidence be found, unless what follows—that Socrates had fallen back on the theory of Ideas—can be taken for history.[2] In one respect Xenophon fully agrees with Plato, in saying that Socrates demanded a consideration of the relation of means to ends in nature. If it be said that the relation of means to ends should not be understood in the lower sense of a later age, as it was indeed understood by Xenophon, but that higher speculative ideas should be sought therein, where, we ask, is the historical justification of this view? Lastly, if an appeal is made to the logical consequences of the Socratic theory, do they not prove that Socrates must have been quite in earnest in disparaging a speculative study of nature, and in his popular notion of the relation of means to ends? Had he indeed placed at the head of his system, in this

[1] *Cic.* Tusc. v. 4, 10; Acad. i. 4, 15; iv. 29, 123; De Fin. v. 29, 87; Rep. i. 10; *Senec.* Ep. 71, 7; *Sext.* Math. vii. 8; *Gell.* N. A. xiv. 6, 5; and, according to Demetrius of Byzantium, *Diog.* ii. 21.

[2] Phædo, 100, B.

CHAP. VII.

explicit form, the idea of the mutual dependence of all knowledge, it would be impossible to account for his low estimate of physics. If, on the contrary, he was concerned, not about knowledge in general, but about the education and training of men by means of knowledge, is it not most natural that his inquiries should be exclusively directed to the conditions and activities of man,[1] nature being only taken into account in as far as it was useful to man? Doubtless this view of the relation of means to ends was, for natural and scientific inquiries, like a seed sown broadcast, which sprang up and bore fruit in the systems of Plato and Aristotle; but to Socrates himself this new department of natural

[1] In this respect Socrates is like Kant, and Kant's position in history not unlike his. As Kant, after destroying the older Metaphysics, only retained Ethics, so Socrates, after setting aside natural science, turned his attention exclusively to morals. In the one case, as in the other, the one-sidedness with which the founder begins has been supplemented by the disciples, and the treatment at first adopted for Ethics has been extended to the whole of philosophy. Just as it may be said of Socrates, that, despite his so definitely attested declining of all cosmical and theological speculation on principle, he nevertheless, whilst actually refraining from such inquiries, could not conceal from himself that they were involved, as a necessary consequence, in his intellectual principles; with the same justice may it be said of Kant, that, notwithstanding his Critic of Pure Reason, he must, whilst disputing the Metaphysics of Wolff, have necessarily seen that his principles would lead him consistently to the Idealism of Fichte and the natural philosophy of Schelling; both of whom, and the first-named even against Kant's own protests, appealed to these consequences. For all that, it is a dangerous business, from a consideration of logical consequences and the historical results of a principle, to correct the clearest statements as to the doctrine of its originator, the question really being whether and to what extent the founder realised these consequences.

CHAP. VII.

science presented itself only as a subsidiary branch of ethical inquiry, without his being conscious of its range. His conscious interest applies only to Ethics. The study of the relation of means to ends in nature was, according to his view, subservient to a moral purpose—that of urging his friends to piety.[1] It cannot be altogether neglected in considering his teaching; neither can it be allowed, in the sense in which it was used by Socrates, an independent value, nor for this reason preferred to Ethics.

The same remark applies to theology, which here stills coincides with natural science. The motives which deterred him from the one must have deterred him from the other also.[2] If, notwithstanding, he expressed definite views as to the Gods and the worship of the Gods, these views were the outcome of a practical love of piety. Theology was only treated by him as an appendix to Ethics.

Comparatively very few definite opinions in theology can be brought home to Socrates with certainty. Indeed, how could it be otherwise, considering that a systematic treatment of Ethics is impossible without some foundation either in meta-

[1] *Xen.* Mem. i. 4, 1 and 18; iv. 3, 2 and 17.

[2] *Xen.* Mem. i. 1, 11; nothing impious was ever heard from Socrates; *οὐδὲ γὰρ περὶ τῆς τῶν πάντων φύσεως . . . διελέγετο . . . ἀλλὰ καὶ τοὺς φροντίζοντας τὰ τοιαῦτα* [or, as it is said, § 15: *οἱ τὰ θεῖα ζητοῦντες*] *μωραίνοντας ἀπεδείκνυε.* He asked whether they had fully mastered human things, as having advanced to such inquiries, *ἢ τὰ μὲν ἀνθρωπινὰ παρέντες τὰ δαιμόνια δὲ σκοποῦντες ἡγοῦνται τὰ προσήκοντα πράττειν·* and 16: *αὐτὸς δὲ περὶ τῶν ἀνθρωπείων ἀεὶ διελέγετο, σκοπῶν τί εὐσεβὲς τί ἀσεβές,* &c.

CHAP. VII.

physics or psychology for it to rest upon? The chief service which Socrates here rendered was a formal one—that of referring moral action in general to knowledge: no sooner, however, does it become a question of deducing particular moral acts and relations from knowledge, than he contents himself with falling back upon prevailing custom, or else there crops up a reference to purposes, the shortcomings of which were, it may be admitted, partially corrected in the sequel.

B. The leading thought of Ethics: All virtue is knowledge.

The leading thought of the ethics of Socrates may be expressed in the sentence—All virtue is knowledge.[1] This assertion is most closely connected with his whole view of things. His efforts aim from the first at re-establishing morality and rooting it more deeply by means of knowledge. The experiences of his time have convinced him that the conventional probity of moral conduct, resting as it does on custom and authority, cannot hold its own. His sifting of men discovered, even

[1] *Arist.* Eth. N. vi. 13; 1144, b, 17, 28: Σωκράτης . . . φρονήσεις ᾤετο εἶναι πάσας τὰς ἀρετάς . . . Σωκράτης μὲν οὖν λόγους τὰς ἀρετὰς ᾤετο εἶναι, ἐπιστήμας γὰρ εἶναι πάσας, *Ibid.* iii. 11; 1116, b, 4; Eth. Eud. i. 5; 1216, b, 6: ἐπιστήμας ᾤετ' εἶναι πάσας τὰς ἀρετάς, ὥσθ' ἅμα συμβαίνειν εἰδέναι τε τὴν δικαιοσύνην καὶ εἶναι δίκαιον. Conf. *Ibid.* iii. 1; 1229, a, 14; vii. 13; M. Mor. i. 1; 1182, a, 15; i. 35; 1198, a, 10; *Xen.* Mem. iii. 9, 5, ἔφη δὲ καὶ τὴν δικαιοσύνην καὶ τὴν ἄλλην πᾶσαν ἀρετὴν σοφίαν εἶναι· τά τε γὰρ δίκαια καὶ πάντα ὅσα ἀρετῇ πράττεται καλά τε καὶ ἀγαθὰ εἶναι· καὶ οὔτ' ἂν τοὺς ταῦτα εἰδότας ἄλλο ἀντὶ τούτων οὐδὲν προελέσθαι, οὔτε τοὺς μὴ ἐπισταμένους δύνασθαι πράττειν, ἀλλὰ καὶ ἐὰν ἐγχειρῶσιν ἁμαρτάνειν. i. 1, 16: he always conversed of justice, piety, καὶ περὶ τῶν ἄλλων, ἃ τοὺς μὲν εἰδότας ἡγεῖτο καλοὺς καὶ ἀγαθοὺς εἶναι, τοὺς δὲ ἀγνοοῦντας ἀνδραποδώδεις ἂν δικαίως κεκλῆσθαι. The latter iv. 2, 22. *Plato*, Lach. 194, D.: πολλάκις ἀκήκοά σου λέγοντος ὅτι ταῦτα ἀγαθὸς ἕκαστος ἡμῶν ἅπερ σοφός, ἃ δὲ ἀμαθὴς ταῦτα δὲ κακός. Euthyd. 278, E.

CHAP. VII.

in the most celebrated of his contemporaries,[1] a spurious in place of a genuine virtue. To attain true morality man must seek the standard of action in clear and certain knowledge.[2] The principle which has thus dawned upon him is, however, only understood in a narrow and exclusive spirit. Knowledge is for him not only an indispensable condition and a means to true morality, but it is the whole of morality. Where knowledge is wanting, there not only is virtue imperfect, but there is absolutely no virtue at all. Plato was the first, and after him more completely Aristotle, to improve upon the Socratic doctrine of virtue.

In support of his position, Socrates maintained that without right knowledge right action is impossible, and conversely, that where knowledge exists, right action follows as a matter of course; the former because no action or possession is of any use, unless it be directed by intelligence to a proper object;[3] the

[1] *Plato*, Apol. 21, C.; 29, E.

[2] See p. 114.

[3] It is only in Plato (Euth. 280, B.; Meno, 87, C.) that Socrates expressly takes this ground. Hence the Moralia Magna (i. 35; 1198, a, 10) appear to have derived the corresponding view; but it not only sounds very like Socrates, but it is also implied in Xenophon; Socrates there (Mem. iv. 2, 26) explaining more immediately in connection with self-knowledge that it alone can tell us what we need and what we can do, placing us so in a position to judge others correctly, and qualifying us for expedient and successful action. Nor is this contradicted by what follows, when it is refused that wisdom is an ἀναμφισβητήτως ἀγαθόν, many a one, like Dædalus and Palamædes, having been ruined for the sake of wisdom. For this is clearly said by way of argument, and σοφία is taken in its ordinary acceptation, including every art and every kind of knowledge. Of knowledge, in his own sense of the term, Socrates would certainly never have said that it was not good because it brought men some-

latter, because everyone only does what he believes he must do, what is of use to himself:[1] no one intentionally does wrong; for this would be the same thing as making oneself intentionally unhappy:[2] knowledge is, therefore, always the strongest power in man, and cannot be overcome by passion.[3]

times into peril, as the virtue, identical therewith, also does. What is said, iii. 9, 14, respecting εὐπραξία in contrast to εὐτυχία, that it is κράτιστον ἐπιτήδευμα, also refers to knowledge. For εὐπραξία consists in μαθόντα τι καὶ μελετήσαντα εὖ ποιεῖν, or as Plato's Euthydemus 281, A., explains it: ἐπιστήμη teaches to make a right use of all goods, and as κατορθοῦσα τὴν πρᾶξιν it produces εὐπραγία and εὐτυχία. *Xenophon*, i. 1, 7; 6, 4, expresses this view more definitely. Æschines, too, in *Demetrius* de Elocu. 297, Rhet. Gr. ix. 122, puts the question into the mouth of Socrates when speaking of the rich inheritance of Alcibiades: Did he inherit the knowledge how to use it?

[1] *Xen.* Mem. iii. 9, 4; see above, p. 141, 1; iv. 6, 6; εἰδότας δὲ ἃ δεῖ ποιεῖν οἴει τινὰς οἴεσθαι δεῖν μὴ ποιεῖν ταῦτα; Οὐκ οἴομαι, ἔφη. Οἶδας δέ τινας ἄλλα ποιοῦντας ἢ ἃ οἴονται δεῖν; Οὐκ ἔγωγ', ἔφη. Ibid. 3, 11; *Plato*, Prot. 358, C.

[2] *Arist.* M. Mor. i. 9: Σωκράτης ἔφη οὐκ ἐφ' ἡμῖν γενέσθαι τὸ σπουδαίους εἶναι ἢ φαύλους· εἰ γάρ τις, φησίν, ἐρωτήσειεν ὁντιναοῦν, πότερον ἂν βούλοιτο δίκαιος εἶναι ἢ ἄδικος, οὐθεὶς ἂν ἕλοιτο τὴν ἀδικίαν. More indefinite are the remarks in Eth. Nic. iii. 7; 1113, b, 14; conf. Eth. Eud. ii. 7; 1223, b, 3, on the statement ὡς οὐδεὶς ἑκὼν πονηρὸς οὐδ' ἄκων μάκαρ. *Brandis* remarks with justice (Gr.-Röm. Phil. ii. a, 39) that this refers in the first place to the arguments of the Platonic Socrates (see Meno, 77, B.; Prot. 345, D.; 353, C.), but that the same is asserted by *Xenophon*, Mem. iii. 9, 4; iv. 6, 6 and 11; and by *Plato*, Apol. 25, E.: ἐγὼ δὲ . . . τοῦτο τὸ τοσοῦτον κακὸν ἑκὼν ποιῶ, ὡς φῂς σύ; ταῦτα ἐγώ σοι οὐ πείθομαι, ὦ Μέλητε . . . εἰ δὲ ἄκων διαφθείρω . . . δῆλον ὅτι ἐὰν μάθω παύσομαι ὅ γε ἄκων ποιῶ. Conf. Dial. de justo, Schl. *Diog. Laert.* ii. 31.

[3] *Plato*, Prot. 352, C.: ἆρ' οὖν καὶ σοὶ τοιοῦτόν τι περὶ αὐτῆς [τῆς ἐπιστήμης] δοκεῖ, ἢ καλόν τε εἶναι ἡ ἐπιστήμη, καὶ οἷον ἄρχειν τοῦ ἀνθρώπου καὶ ἐάνπερ γιγνώσκῃ τις τἀγαθὰ καὶ τὰ κακὰ μὴ ἂν κρατηθῆναι ὑπὸ μηδενός ὥστε ἄλλ' ἄττα πράττειν; ἢ ἃ ἂν ἡ ἐπιστήμη κελεύῃ, ἀλλ' ἱκανὴν εἶναι τὴν φρόνησιν βοηθεῖν τῷ ἀνθρώπῳ; The latter is then affirmed with the consent of Socrates. (The further reasoning is probably only Platonic.) *Arist.* Eth. Nic. vii. 3: ἐπιστάμενον μὲν οὖν οὔ φασί τινες οἷόν τε εἶναι [ἀκρατεύεσθαι]. δεινὸν γάρ, ἐπιστήμης ἐνούσης, ὡς ᾤετο

CHAP. VII.

As regards that virtue which appears to be furthest removed from knowledge, the virtue of bravery, he more especially insisted that, in all cases, he who knows the true nature of an apparent danger and the means of avoiding it is braver than he who has not such knowledge.[1] Hence he concludes that virtue is entirely dependent upon knowledge; and accordingly he defines all the particular virtues in such a way as to make them consist in knowledge of some kind, the difference between them being determined by the difference of their objects. He is pious who knows what is right towards God; he is just who knows what is right towards men.[2] He is brave who knows how

Σωκράτης, ἄλλο τι κρατεῖν. Eth. Eud. vii. 13: ὀρθῶς τὸ Σωκρατικόν. ὅτι οὐδὲν ἰσχυρότερον φρονήσεως. ἀλλ' ὅτι ἐπιστήμην ἔφη, οὐκ ὀρθόν, ἀρετὴ γάρ ἐστι καὶ οὐκ ἐπιστήμη. If, therefore, anyone seems to act contrary to his better judgment, Socrates does not allow that is really the case. He rather infers the contrary. His conduct being opposed to right reason, he concludes that he is wanting in this quality; Mem. iii. 9, 4: προσερωτώμενος δέ, εἰ τοὺς ἐπισταμένους μὲν ἃ δεῖ πράττειν, ποιοῦντας δὲ τἀναντία, σοφούς τε καὶ ἐγκρατεῖς εἶναι νομίζοι· οὐδέν γε μᾶλλον, ἔφη, ἢ ἀσόφους τε καὶ ἀκρατεῖς. In Xenophon, this is so put, as if Socrates had admitted the possibility of a case of knowing right and doing wrong. The real meaning of the answer, however, can only be the one given above.

[1] *Xen.* Mem. iii. 9, 2; Symp. 2, 12: Socrates remarks, in reference to a dancing girl who is deliberating about sword points: οὔτοι τούς γε θεωμένους τάδε ἀντιλέξειν ἔτι οἴομαι, ὡς οὐχὶ καὶ ἡ ἀνδρεία διδακτόν. *Plato*, Prot. 349, E., where it is proved by various examples—divers, knights, peltastæ—that οἱ ἐπιστήμονες τῶν μὴ ἐπισταμένων θαῤῥαλεώτεροί εἰσιν. *Arist.* Eth. Nic. iii. 11; 1116, b, 3: δοκεῖ δὲ καὶ ἡ ἐμπειρία ἡ περὶ ἕκαστα ἀνδρεία τις εἶναι· ὅθεν καὶ ὁ Σωκράτης ᾠήθη ἐπιστήμην εἶναι τὴν ἀνδρείαν. Conf. Eth. Eud. iii. 1; 1229, a, 14.

[2] εὐσεβὴς = ὁ τὰ περὶ τοὺς θεοὺς νόμιμα εἰδώς· δίκαιος = ὁ εἰδὼς τὰ περὶ τοὺς ἀνθρώπους νόμιμα. Mem. iv. 6, 4 and 6. The εὐσέβεια, the definition of which is here given, is the same as the ὁσιότης, the conception of which is sought in Plato's Euthyphro.

to treat dangers properly;[1] he is prudent and wise who knows how to use what is good and noble, and how to avoid what is evil.[2] In a word, all virtues are referred to wisdom or knowledge, which are one and the same.[3] The ordinary notion that there are many kinds of virtue is incorrect. Virtue is in truth but one.[4] Nor does the difference between one

If, therefore, *Grote*, Plato, i. 328, remarks *à propos* of the latter, that Xenophon's Socrates was neither asking after the general conception of the holy, nor indeed could presuppose it, his observation is contradicted by appearances. It does not, however, follow herefrom that Socrates wished the Gods to be honoured νόμῳ πόλεως. Why could he not have said, piety or holiness consists in the knowledge of that which is right towards the Gods, and to this belongs, in respect of the honouring of the Gods, that each one pray to them after the custom of his country? A pious mind is not the same thing as worship. The piety may be the same when the forms of worship are different.

[1] *Xen.* Mem. iv. 6, 11: οἱ μὲν ἄρα ἐπιστάμενοι τοῖς δεινοῖς τε καὶ ἐπικινδύνοις καλῶς χρῆσθαι ἀνδρεῖοί εἰσιν, οἱ δὲ διαμαρτάνοντες τούτου δειλοί. *Plato*, Prot. 360, D.: ἡ σοφία ἄρα τῶν δεινῶν καὶ μὴ δεινῶν ἀνδρεία ἐστίν. The same thing is conveyed by the definition in Laches, 194, E. (which is not much imperilled by the objections raised thereto from a Socratic point of view). Courage is ἡ τῶν δεινῶν καὶ θαῤῥαλέων ἐπιστήμη; only θαῤῥαλέος must not be rendered 'bold' (as *Schaarschmidt*, Samml. d. plat. Schr. 409, does). It means rather, according to 198, B., as it so often does, ἃ μὴ δέος παρέχει. Conf. *Bonitz*, Plat. Stud. iii. 441.

[2] Mem. iii. 9, 4: σοφίαν δὲ καὶ σωφροσύνην οὐ διώριζεν, ἀλλὰ τὸν τὰ μὲν καλά τε καὶ ἀγαθὰ γιγνώσκοντα χρῆσθαι αὐτοῖς καὶ τὸν τὰ αἰσχρὰ εἰδότα εὐλαβεῖσθαι σοφόν τε καὶ σώφρονα ἔκρινε.

[3] Mem. iv. 6, 7: ἐπιστήμη ἄρα σοφία ἐστίν; Ἔμοιγε δοκεῖ. No man can know everything; ὃ ἄρα ἐπίσταται ἕκαστος τοῦτο καὶ σοφός ἐστιν.

[4] Plato develops this thought in his earlier writings, Prot. 329, B.; 349, B.; 360, E.; which, however, kept much more closely to the platform of Socrates; it is also evidently contained in Xenophon. His meaning, as may be gathered from Mem. iii. 9, 4, is certainly not: some one may possess the knowledge in which one virtue consists, whilst lacking the knowledge in which another consists; but he assumes, just as Plato's Socrates does in the Protagoras, that where one virtue is, all must be there, all depending on the knowledge of the good. From this doctrine

CHAP. VII.

person and another, one time of life and another, one sex and another, affect the question. For in all cases it is one and the same thing, which makes the conduct virtuous,[1] and in all persons the same natural capacity for virtue must be assumed to exist.[2] The main point then invariably is to cultivate this disposition by education. Some may bring with them more, others fewer gifts for any particular activity; yet all alike require exercise and training; the most talented require it most, would they not be lost in ruinous errors.[3] There being no greater obstacle to true knowledge than imaginary knowledge, nothing can in a moral point of view be more urgently necessary than self-knowledge, to dispel the unfounded semblance of knowledge and to bring home to man his wants and needs. Right action according to Socratic principles invariably

of Socrates the Cynic and Megarian notions of the oneness of virtue arose.

[1] *Plato*, Meno, 71, D., and *Aristotle*, Pol. i. 13, probably following the passage in Plato, 1216, a, 20, which he must in some way have harmonised with the Socratic teaching: ὥστε φανερόν, ὅτι ἐστὶν ἠθικὴ ἀρετὴ τῶν εἰρημένων πάντων, καὶ οὐχ ἡ αὐτὴ σωφροσύνη γυναικὸς καὶ ἀνδρός, οὐδ' ἀνδρία καὶ δικαιοσύνη, καθάπερ ᾤετο Σωκράτης . . . πολὺ γὰρ ἄμεινον λέγουσιν οἱ ἐξαριθμοῦντες τὰς ἀρετάς.

[2] *Xen.* Sym. 2, 9: καὶ ὁ Σωκράτης εἶπεν· ἐν πολλοῖς μὲν, ὦ ἄνδρες, καὶ ἄλλοις δῆλον, καὶ ἐν οἷς δ' ἡ παῖς ποιεῖ, ὅτι ἡ γυναικεία φύσις οὐδὲν χείρων τῆς τοῦ ἀνδρὸς οὖσα τυγχάνει, ῥώμης δὲ καὶ ἰσχύος δεῖται. Conf. *Plato*, Rep. v. 452, E.

[3] Mem. iii. 9, 1; iv. 1, 3; iv. 2, 2. The question whether virtue is a natural gift or a result of instruction—the identical question to which Plato devoted a thorough discussion in the Meno and Protagoras—appears to have become a favourite topic of discussion, thanks to the appearance of the Sophistic teachers of virtue. Such at least it seems in *Xenophon*, iii. 9, 1, and in the Meno. Pindar had previously drawn the contrast between natural and acquired gift. See above, p. 23.

follows upon knowledge just as wrong action follows from absence of knowledge; he who knows himself will, without fail, do what is healthful, just as he who is ignorant of himself will, without fail, do what is harmful.[1] Only the man of knowledge can do anything worth doing; he alone is useful and esteemed.[2] In short, knowledge is the root of all moral action; want of knowledge is the cause of every vice; were it possible wittingly to do wrong, that were better than doing wrong unwittingly; for in the latter case the first condition of right action, the moral sentiment, is wanting, whilst in the former case it would be there, the doer being only for the moment faithless to it.[3] What, however, the

[1] Mem. iv. 2, 24. For examples of conversations, in which Socrates endeavoured to bring his friends to a knowledge of themselves, see Mem. iii. 6; iv. 2.

[2] Mem. i. 2, 52: the accuser charged Socrates with inducing his followers to despise their friends and relations; for he had declared, those only deserve to be honoured who can make themselves useful by means of knowledge. Xenophon allows that he showed how little useless and ignorant people were esteemed by their own friends and relatives; but he says that Socrates did not thereby intend to teach them to despise dependants, but only to show that understanding must be aimed at, ὅτι τὸ ἄφρον ἄτιμόν ἐστι.

[3] Mem. iv. 2, 19: τῶν δὲ δὴ τοὺς φίλους ἐξαπατώντων ἐπὶ βλάβῃ πότερος ἀδικώτερός ἐστιν, ὁ ἑκών, ἢ ὁ ἄκων; The question is afterwards thus settled: τὰ δίκαια πότερον ὁ ἑκὼν ψευδόμενος καὶ ἐξαπατῶν οἶδεν, ἢ ὁ ἄκων; Δῆλον ὅτι ὁ ἑκών. Δικαιότερον δὲ [φῂς εἶναι] τον ἐπιστάμενον τὰ δίκαια τοῦ μὴ ἐπισταμένου; Φαίνομαι. Conf. *Plato*, Rep. ii. 382; iii. 389, B.; iv. 459, C.; vii. 535, E.; Hipp. Min. 371, E. It is only an imaginary case to suppose that anyone can knowingly and intentionally do what is wrong; for according to the principles of Socrates, it is impossible to conceive that the man who possesses knowledge as such should, by virtue of his knowledge, do anything but what is right, or that anyone should spontaneously choose what is wrong. If, therefore, an untruth is told knowingly and intentionally, it can only be an apparent

CHAP. VII.

knowledge is in which virtue consists, whether experimental or speculative, purely theoretical or practical—is a question upon which Socrates has not touched. In Xenophon he most ingenuously places learning and skill together,[1] although Plato had distinguished them,[2] and to prove that virtue consists in knowledge, that it requires knowledge, and can be acquired by instruction, he chooses by preference, even in the pages of Plato, examples of practical acquirements and of mechanical dexterity.[3]

C. *The Good and Eudæmonism.*

(1) *Virtue determined theoretically.*

All that has so far been laid down is in the nature of formal definition: all virtue is knowledge; but of what is it the knowledge? To this Socrates gives the general answer, knowledge of the good. He is virtuous, just, brave, and so forth, who knows what is good and right.[4] Even this addition is as

and seeming untruth, which Plato allows as a means to higher ends (Rep. ii. 382; iii. 389, B.; iv. 459, C.), whereas want of knowledge is the only proper lie, a proper lie being always unintentional, Rep. ii. 382; v. 535, E. See *Zeller's* Phil. Stud. p. 152.

[1] At the beginning of the Meno.

[2] Mem. iii. 9, 1, Socrates answers the question whether bravery is a διδακτὸν or φυσικόν: the disposition thereto is quite as various as is bodily power. νομίζω μέντοι πᾶσαν φύσιν μαθήσει καὶ μελέτῃ πρὸς ἀνδρίαν αὔξεσθαι, in proof of which it may be noted that no nation with weapons to which it is unaccustomed ventures to encounter those who are familiar with them. So, too, in everything else, it is the ἐπιμέλεια, the μανθάνειν καὶ μελετᾶν, whereby natural gifts are really developed to mastery. In Mem. iv. 1, 3, μάθησις and παίδεια are generally required, but even here no difference is made between theoretical and practical knowledge.

[3] So Protag. 349, E.; Mem. iii. 9, 1 and 11: ἄρχοντες are those ἐπιστάμενοι ἄρχειν, the steersman in a ship, in agriculture, sickness, and athletics, those who have made it their profession, women in spinning. The question here raised is discussed at length by *Strümpell*, Gesch. d. Prakt. Phil. d. Gr. vor Arist. 146.

[4] See p. 114.

wide and indefinite as what went before. Knowledge which makes virtue, is knowledge of the good; but what is the good? The good is the conception of a thing viewed as an end. Doing what is good, is acting up to the conception of the corresponding action, in short, knowledge in its practical application. The essence of moral action is therefore not explained by the general definition, that it is a knowledge of the good, the right, and so forth. Beyond this general definition, however, Socrates did not advance in his philosophy. Just as his speculative philosophy stopped short with the general postulate that knowledge belongs to conceptions only, so his practical philosophy stopped short with the indefinite requirement of conduct conformable to conceptions. From such a theory it is impossible to deduce a definite rule of moral action. To obtain such a rule no other alternative remains but either to adopt the necessary principles from the prevailing morality without further investigation; or, in as far as principles according to the knowledge-theory must be made good before the tribunal of thought, to refer to experience and the well-known consequences of actions.

(2) Practically the Good is determined either by custom or utility.

As a matter of fact, both courses were followed by Socrates. On the one hand, he explained the conception of the right by that of the lawful.[1] The

[1] Mem. iv. 6, 6: Δίκαια δὲ οἶσθα, ἔφη, ὁποῖα καλεῖται;—Ἃ οἱ νόμοι κελεύουσιν, ἔφη.—Οἱ ἄρα ποιοῦντες ἃ οἱ νόμοι κελεύουσι δίκαιά τε ποιοῦσι καὶ ἃ δεῖ; Πῶς γὰρ οὔ; In Mem. iv. 4, 12, Socrates says: φημὶ γὰρ ἐγὼ τὸ νόμιμον δίκαιον εἶναι, and when Hippias asks to be told what is meant by νόμιμον; νόμους δὲ

CHAP. VII.

best service of God, he says, is that which agrees with custom;[1] and he will not withdraw himself even from an unjust sentence, lest he should violate the laws.[2] On the other hand, as a necessary consequence of this view of things, he could not be content with existing moral sanctions, but was fain to seek an intellectual support for morality. This support he could only find by considering consequences; in doing which he frequently proceeds most superficially, arriving at ethical principles by a line of argument which differs in results rather than in principles from the moral philosophy of the Sophists.[3] When asked whether there could be a good, which is not good for a definite purpose, he distinctly stated that he neither knew, nor desired to know of such a one:[4] everything is good and

πόλεως, ἔφη, γιγνώσκεις;—Οὐκοῦν, ἔφη [Socrates]. *νόμιμος μὲν ἂν εἴη ὁ κατὰ ταῦτα* [*ἃ οἱ πολῖται ἐγράψαντο*] *πολιτευόμενος, ἄνομος δὲ ὁ ταῦτα παραβαίνων; Πὰν μὲν οὖν, ἔφη.—Οὐκοῦν καὶ δίκαια μὲν ἂν πράττοι ὁ τούτοις πειθόμενος, ἄδικα δ' ὁ τούτοις ἀπειθῶν;—Πάνυ μὲν οὖν.*

[1] Mem. iv. 3, 16: Euthydemus doubts whether anyone can worthily honour the Gods. Socrates tries to convince him. *ὁρᾷς γὰρ, ὅτι ὁ ἐν Δελφοῖς θεὸς ὅταν τις αὐτὸν ἐπερωτᾷ πῶς ἂν τοῖς θεοῖς χαρίζοιτο ἀποκρίνεται νόμῳ πόλεως.* The same principle is attributed to Socrates, i. 3, 1.

[2] See p. 78, 1.

[3] As Dissen has already shown, in the treatise referred to, p. 101, 2. Compare *Wiggers*, Socrates, p. 187; *Hurndall*, De Philosophia Mor. Socr. *Grote* (Hist. of Greece, viii. 605) agrees with this statement, only refusing to allow us to speak of Sophistic morals as if they were uniform.

[4] Mem. iii. 8, 1–7, where it is said, amongst other things. *εἴ γ' ἐρωτᾷς με, εἴ τι ἀγαθὸν οἶδα, ὃ μηδενὸς ἀγαθόν ἐστιν, οὔτ' οἶδα, ἔφη, οὔτε δέομαι . . . Λέγεις σὺ, ἔφη* [*'Αρίστιππος*] *καλά τε καὶ αἰσχρὰ τὰ αὐτὰ εἶναι; καὶ νὴ Δί' ἔγωγ', ἔφη* [*Σωκράτης*] *ἀγαθά τε καὶ κακά . . ,* meaning, as the sequel shows (not as *Ribbing*, l. c. p. 105, translates it: good and evil are the same), but the same thing is good and evil, in as far as for one pur-

beautiful in relation to the special needs which it subserves, and therefore one and the same thing may be good for one and bad for another. He declared in a manner most pronounced, that the good is identical with the profitable, the beautiful with the useful; everything therefore is good and beautiful in relation to the objects for which it is profitable and useful;[1] confirming his doctrine of the involuntary nature of evil—one of the leading principles of his ethics—by the remark that everyone does that which he thinks advantageous for himself.[2]

There is, therefore, according to his view, no absolute, but only a relative good; advantage and disadvantage are the measures of good and evil.[3] Hence in the dialogues of Xenophon he almost always bases his moral precepts on the motive of utility. We should aim at abstinence, because the abstinent man has a more pleasant life than the incontinent:[4] we should inure ourselves to hardships, because the hardy man is more healthy, and because he can more

pose it is useful, that is good, and for another harmful; πάντα γὰρ ἀγαθὰ μὲν καὶ καλά ἐστι, πρὸς ἃ ἂν εὖ ἔχῃ, κακὰ δὲ καὶ αἰσχρὰ, πρὸς ἃ ἂν κακῶς.

[1] *Xen.* Mem. iv. 6, 8, concluding: τὸ ἄρα ὠφέλιμον ἀγαθόν ἐστιν ὅτῳ ἂν ὠφέλιμον ᾖ . . . τὸ χρήσιμον ἄρα καλόν ἐστι πρὸς ὃ ἂν ᾖ χρήσιμον; conf. iv. 1, 5; 5, 6; Symp. 5, 3; *Plato*, Prot. 333, D.; 353, C., where Socrates meets Protagoras with the statement: ταῦτ' ἐστὶν ἀγαθὰ ἅ ἐστιν ὠφέλιμα τοῖς ἀνθρώποις, and afterwards explains good to be that which affords pleasure or averts pain.

[2] *Xen.* Mem. iii. 9, 4: something similar is found in Plato's Protagoras, 358, B.

[3] On the other hand, little importance can be attached to the treatment of happiness as the highest end of life in Mem. iii. 2, 4. All Greek philosophers do the same, including Plato, Aristotle, and even the Stoics.

[4] Mem. i. 5, 6; ii. 1, 1; conf. iv. 5, 9.

CHAP. VII.

easily avoid dangers, and gain honour and glory:[1] we should be modest, because boasting does harm and brings disgrace.[2] We should be on good terms with our relatives, because it is absurd to turn to harm what has been given us for good;[3] we should try to secure good friends, since a good friend is the most useful possession:[4] we should not withdraw from public affairs, since the well-being of the community is the well-being of the individual:[5] we should obey the laws, since obedience is productive of the greatest good to ourselves and to the State; and we should abstain from wrong, since wrong is always punished in the end.[6] We should live virtuously, because virtue carries off the greatest rewards both from God and man.[7] To argue that such-like expressions do not represent the personal convictions of the philosopher, but are intended to bring others to virtue by meeting them on their own ground, who could not be moved by higher motives, is evidently an untenable argument, considering the definiteness with which Socrates expresses himself.[8] Unless, therefore, Xenophon is misleading on essential points, we must allow that Socrates was in earnest in explaining the good as the useful, and

[1] Mem. iii. 12; ii. 1, 18; conf. i. 6.

[2] Mem. i. 7.

[3] Ibid. ii. 3, 19.

[4] Ibid. ii. 4, 5; ii. 6, 4 and 10.

[5] Ibid. iii. 7, 9; ii. 1, 14.

[6] Ibid. iv. 4, 16 and 20; iii. 9, 12.

[7] Mem. ii. 1, 27, gives an extract from a writing of Prodicus, the substance of which Socrates appropriates. Conf. i. 4, 18; iv. 3, 17.

[8] This point will be subsequently discussed.

consequently in the corresponding derivation of moral duties.

(3) *Inconsistency of Socratic Morality.*

True it is that in the mouth of Socrates other statements are met with, going beyond this superficial ground of moral duties, placing the essential advantage of virtue, the purpose which it serves and because of which it is good and beautiful in its influence on the intellectual life of man.[1] This would clearly and undoubtedly be the view of Socrates could we attribute to him the maxim so familiar to the Socrates of Plato,[2] that righteousness is health, unrighteousness disease of the soul, and consequently that all wrong-doing invariably injures him who does it, whereas the right is necessarily and always useful. Language of this kind occurring in the Republic and Gorgias does not justify our doing so. In these dialogues much is put into the mouth of Socrates which he never said and never can have said. Nor can the plea be admitted that Plato would never have held such exalted moral conceptions, unless his teacher before him had held them. Otherwise the theory of ideas and much besides which is found in Plato would have to be attributed to Socrates. We cannot even vouch for it that all the details contained in the Crito come from Socrates, its author not having been present at the conversation therein described. Apparently

[1] On what follows compare *Ribbing*, pp. 83, 91, 105, whose researches are here thankfully acknowledged, whilst all his conclusions are not accepted.

[2] See *Zeller's* Phil. d. Griech p. 561 of second edition.

CHAP. VII.

committed to writing no long time after the death of Socrates, and not going beyond his point of view, this dialogue is remarkable for containing the very same principles:[1] a circumstance which at least shows that they have a foundation in the teaching of Socrates. To the same effect the Apology expresses itself, Socrates there summing up the purpose of his life as being to convince his fellow-citizens that the education of the soul is more important than money or property, honour or glory;[2] declaring at the same time in plainest terms, that whether death is an ill or not he knows not, but that injustice is, he knows well.[3]

Similar language is found in Xenophon. In his pages too Socrates declares the soul to be the most valuable thing in man, the divine part of his being, because it is the seat of reason and only the Reasonable is of value.[4] He requires, therefore, that the

[1] Crito, 47, D.: as in the treatment of the body, the physician's advice must be followed, so in questions of right and wrong the advice of him ᾧ εἰ μὴ ἀκολουθήσομεν, διαφθεροῦμεν ἐκεῖνο καὶ λωβησόμεθα, ὃ τῷ μὲν δικαίῳ βέλτιον ἐγίγνετο τῷ δὲ ἀδίκῳ ἀπώλλυτο. If, moreover, life in a diseased body has no value: μετ' ἐκείνου ἄρα βιωτὸν ἡμῖν διεφθαρμένου, ᾧ τὸ ἄδικον λωβᾶται τὸ δὲ δίκαιον ὀνίνησιν, provided this is not a φαυλότερον but a πολὺ τιμιώτερον than that; 49, A.: wrongdoing always injures and disgraces him who commits it.

[2] Apol. 29, D.: as long as he lived, he would not cease φιλοσοφῶν καὶ ὑμῖν παρακελευόμενος . . . λέγων οἷάπερ εἴωθα, ὅτι, ὦ ἄριστε ἀνδρῶν, . . . χρημάτων μὲν οὐκ αἰσχύνει ἐπιμελούμενος, . . . καὶ δόξης καὶ τιμῆς, φρονήσεως δὲ καὶ ἀληθείας καὶ τῆς ψυχῆς, ὅπως ὡς βελτίστη ἔσται, οὐκ ἐπιμελεῖ οὐδὲ φροντίζεις· he would rather blame a man in every case where it was necessary ὅτι τὰ πλείστου ἄξια περὶ ἐλαχίστου ποιεῖται, τὰ δὲ φαυλότερα περὶ πλείονος.

[3] Ibid. 29, B.

[4] Mem. i. 4, 13: God has not only taken care of the human body, ἀλλ' ὅπερ μέγιστόν ἐστι καὶ τὴν ψυχὴν κρατίστην τῷ ἀνθρώπῳ ἐνέφυσε· i. 2, 53 and 55, where the statement ὅτι τὸ

first care should be for the soul.[1] He is convinced that conduct is better, the more you aim at the education of the soul, and more enjoyable, the more you are conscious thereof.[2] The intellectual perfection of man depends in the first place on knowledge, wisdom is the highest good, without compare more valuable than aught besides.[3] Learning is recommended not only on account of its utility, but far more because of the enjoyment which it directly confers.[4] These expressions fully agree with what has been quoted from Plato; they also appear quite consistent in a philosopher who bases the whole of moral conduct so decidedly upon knowledge, and so expressly leads man to self-knowledge and to self-control.[5]

What then must be made of accounts in which Socrates recommends moral duties entirely on grounds

ἄφρον ἄτιμόν ἐστι is proved by the fact that you bury the body as soon as the soul ἐν ῃ μόνῃ γίνεται φρόνησις has left it; iv. 3, 14: ἀνθρώπου γε ψυχή, εἴπερ τι καὶ ἄλλο τῶν ἀνθρωπίνων τοῦ θείου μετέχει.

[1] Mem. i. 2, 4: Socrates recommends bodily exercise within certain limits: ταύτην γὰρ τὴν ἕξιν ὑγιεινήν τε ἱκανῶς εἶναι καὶ τὴν τῆς ψυχῆς ἐπιμέλειαν (which accordingly regulates the care of the body) οὐκ ἐμποδίζειν ἔφη.

[2] Mem. iv. 8, 6: ἄριστα μὲν γὰρ οἶμαι ζῆν τοὺς ἄριστα ἐπιμελουμένους τοῦ ὡς βελτίστους γίγνεσθαι, ἥδιστα δὲ τοὺς μάλιστα αἰσθανομένους, ὅτι βελτίους γίγνονται. i. 6, 9: οἴει οὖν ἀπὸ πάντων τούτων τοσαύτην ἡδονὴν εἶναι, ὅσην ἀπὸ τοῦ ἑαυτόν τε ἡγεῖσθαι βελτίω γίγνεσθαι καὶ φίλους ἀμείνους κτᾶσθαι;

[3] Mem. iv. 5, 6; σοφίαν δὲ τὸ μέγιστον ἀγαθὸν κ. τ. λ.; iv. 2, 9, where Euthydemus is commended by Socrates for preferring treasures of wisdom to treasures of gold and silver; for the latter do not make men better, τὰς δὲ τῶν σοφῶν ἀνδρῶν γνώμας ἀρετῇ πλουτίζειν τοὺς κεκτημένους.

[4] Mem. iv. 5, 10: ἀλλὰ μὴν ἀπὸ τοῦ μαθεῖν τι καλὸν καὶ ἀγαθόν . . . οὐ μόνον ὠφέλειαι ἀλλὰ καὶ ἡδοναὶ μέγισται γίγνονται. Conf. ii. 1, 19.

[5] Conf. pp. 66; 122; 141.

CHAP. VII.

of outward adaptation to a purpose, such as we frequently find in Xenophon? Are we to assume that all such explanations are only intended for those who were too unripe to understand the philosopher's real meaning, to show that even on the hypothesis of the ordinary unsatisfactory definition of purpose, virtuous conduct is the best? that Xenophon mistook these preliminary and introductory discussions for the whole of the Socratic philosophy of life, and hence drew a picture of that philosophy representing his own but not the platform of the real Socrates? [1] This view has no doubt its truth, but it is hardly the whole truth. It is easy to believe that Xenophon found the tangible testing of moral precepts by their consequences both clearer and more intelligible than to try them by their working on the inner condition of man. It is, therefore, natural to expect his description to give the preference to the more intelligible explanation even at the cost of the other; throwing the other more into the background than the actual state of the case warrants. Double value must therefore be allowed to such Socratic utterances as he reports pointing to a deeper moral life. Still he cannot be considered so bad a guide as to report utterances which Socrates never expressed, nor can a meaning be put on these utterances which shall

[1] This is, in the main, the view of Brandis, Rhein. Mus. v. *Niebuhr u. Brandis*, i. b, 138; Gr.-Röm. Phil. ii. a, 40; Gesch. d. Entwickl. i. 238; *Ribbing*, Sokrat. Stud. i. 115; *Volquardsen*, Dæmon d. Sokr. 4, who reproduces Xenophon's sayings as incorrectly as he does Zeller's.

bring them into full accord with Plato's description of the Socratic ethics.

Take for instance the dialogues with Aristippus,[1] where Socrates is asked to point out a thing good, and afterwards a thing beautiful, and both times answers that goodness and beauty consist in nothing save a subserviency to certain purposes.[2] What inducement had Socrates here to withhold his own opinion? Was Aristippus one of the unripe unphilosophic heads, not in a condition to understand his views? Was he not, next to Plato and Euclid, one of the most independent and intellectually educated thinkers in the Socratic circle? Why should Socrates say to him: everything is good and beautiful for that to which it bears a good relation, and hence the same thing may in relation to one be a good, to another an evil? Why does he not add: one thing there is which is always and unconditionally good, that which improves the soul? Or did he add it, and Xenophon omit it, although the main point?[3] and was this so in other cases?[4] We could only be justified in so saying, were it shown that Socrates could not possibly have spoken as Xenophon makes him speak, or that his utterances cannot possibly have had the meaning which they have according to Xenophon's account.[5] To show this it is not sufficient to appeal to the contradiction with which

[1] Mem. iii. 8.
[2] See p. 150, 4.
[3] As Mem. iv. 6, 8.
[4] *Brandis*, l. c.
[5] As *Brandis*, l. c. asserts. Conf. *Dissen*, l. c. 88; *Ritter*, Gesch. d. Phil. ii. 70.

CHAP. VII.

Socrates is otherwise charged. It is no doubt a contradiction to call virtue the highest end of life, and at the same to recommend it because of the advantages it brings:[1] and Plato recognising this contradiction has avoided it.[2] Still the question really is, whether and to what extent Socrates has avoided it;

[1] What Brandis has elsewhere asserted appears to be less open to objection, viz. that Socrates distinguishes mere good fortune from really faring well, and that he only allows happiness in its ordinary sense a place among things relatively good. The former statement is in Mem. iii. 9, 14; but this distinction even by a decided advocate of Eudæmonism, such as Aristippus, could be admitted, if we assume that true and lasting happiness is to be attained not by the uncertain favour of chance, but by our own activity and understanding, and that man must not make himself dependent on extreme circumstances, but ensure a lasting enjoyment of life by rising superior to himself and his surroundings. If Brandis (Entw. i. 237) declares this impossible, he need simply be referred to the fact that in the Cyrenaic and Epicurean schools such views are actually met with. See below, ch. xiv. B. 5, and *Zeller's* Stoics, Epicureans, &c., p. 44. For the latter statement Brandis appeals to Mem. iv. 2, 34. Here Euthydemus has to be convinced of his ignorance in respect of good and evil. After it has been proved that all things considered by Euthydemus to be goods, wisdom included, may, under certain circumstances, be disadvantageous, Euthydemus continues: κινδυνεύει—ἀναμφιλογώτατον ἀγαθόν εἶναι τὸ εὐδαιμονεῖν, to which Socrates replies: εἴ γε μή τις αὐτὸ ἐξ ἀμφιλόγων ἀγαθῶν συντιθείη, or as it is immediately explained, εἴ γε μὴ προσθήσομεν αὐτῷ κάλλος ἢ ἰσχὺν ἢ πλοῦτον ἢ δόξαν ἢ καί τι ἄλλο τῶν τοιούτων, since among all these things there is none which is not the source of much evil. Far from denying, this proceeds on the distinct understanding that happiness is the highest good—which Greek ethics invariably presuppose; neither is it called simply an ἀμφίλογον ἀγαθόν, except in the case that it is compounded of ἀμφίλογα ἀγαθά, *i.e.* of such things as under certain circumstances lead to evil, and are not simply ἀγαθά, but sometimes κακά. This statement is not at variance with passages which estimate the value of every thing and of every action by its consequences, a standard being the very thing which Socrates is here laying down.

[2] As Plato has already remarked, Rep ii. 362, E.; Phædo, 68 D.

we have no reason for assuming that he cannot possibly have been involved in a contradiction. For have we not a case in point in Kant's rejecting most decidedly every experimental standard for testing the moral value of an action and then calling in experience to decide what maxims lend themselves to the principle of universal legislation, by appealing to the consequences which would follow were they universally adopted? Is there not a contradiction in the same writer, at one time waging war *à outrance* against Eudæmonism, at another founding the belief in the existence of God on the demand for a bliss corresponding to merit? Is not the critic of pure reason, in asserting the independent existence of a thing and at the same time unconditionally denying that it can be known, entangled in so flat a contradiction that Fichte was of the opinion that if the independent existence of a thing were really assumed, he would rather regard it as the work of a strange coincidence than of human brains? Can the historian therefore make the philosopher of Königsberg say what he did not say? Can he violently set aside these contradictions instead of explaining them? And would it be so inconceivable that the same thing should occur about the Socratic doctrine? The philosopher wishes to found moral conduct upon knowledge. In point of form his conception of knowledge is so indefinite that it includes, besides philosophical convictions, every kind of skill derived from experience.[1] In point of matter it

[1] See p. 148.

CHAP. VII.

suffers from a similar indefiniteness. The subject matter of practical knowledge is the good, and the good is the useful, or, what is the same thing, the expedient.[1] But in what this consists, Socrates, according to all accounts, has not expressed with sufficient precision to avoid all ambiguity in his Ethics. In passages of Plato from which the views of the Socrates of history can be gathered with some certainty, he does not go beyond saying that intellectual culture, care for the soul, must be the most important end for man. Still to refer all human actions to this end ultimately and finally is impossible for his unsystematic moral reasoning depending on proverbs and unsupported by any comprehensive psychological research. Thus the highest moral end comes to have associated with it apparently spontaneously other ends having to do with man's well-being in the most varied ways, and moral activity itself appears as a means towards attaining these ends.[2] If therefore Xenophon reports a number of Socratic dialogues in which the case is thus represented, we may still maintain that the Socratic basis of ethics is not herewith exhausted; but we have no right to question the accuracy of his description, supported as it

[1] Conf. p. 120, 4; 1 and 2. The identity of the good and the useful is also presupposed in the passages quoted from Plato on p. 154, although the conception of the useful is somewhat extended there.

[2] Compare the sound remarks of *Strümpell*, Gesch. d. Prakt. Phil. d. Gr. 138, resulting in this: Socrates made no such distinction in kind in the conception of the ἀγαθόν, as to regard the ἀγαθὸν belonging to virtues as moral good, all other good as good for the understanding only, and consequently as only useful and expedient.

is by many traces in Plato, nor yet to twist it into its opposite by assuming that we have here only the beginnings of dialogues the real object of which must be a very different one. Rather is the accuracy of that description vouched for by the circumstance,[1] that among the Socratic Schools side by side with the morals of the Cynics and the criticism of the Megarians, a place was found too for the Cyrenaic doctrine of pleasure; and that the founders of these schools to all appearances were firmly persuaded that they reproduced the true spirit of the Socratic teaching. Had that teaching afforded them no foothold, this phenomenon would be hard to understand. In its essence the Socratic morality is anything but selfish. That fact does not, however, prevent its assuming the form of Eudæmonism in its theoretical

[1] To which *Hermann*, Plat. i. 257, rightly draws attention. When, however, this writer finds in the principle of utility (ibid. p. 254 Ges. Abh. 232), or as he prefers to call it in the predominance of relative value, not merely a weak point in the philosophy of Socrates, but at the same time an instance of Socratic modesty, one feels inclined to ask, wherein does this modesty consist? And when he connects herewith the more general doctrine, constituting in his view the main difference between the Socratic dialectic and the Sophistic, and also the foundation of the Socratic teaching on the truth of universal conceptions, he appears to advocate a doctrine neither to be found in the Memorabilia (iii. 8, 4–7; 10, 12; iv. 6, 9; 2, 13), nor in the Hippias Major of Plato (p. 288)—the latter by the way a very doubtful authority. It is indeed stated in these passages, that the good and the beautiful are only good and beautiful for certain purposes by virtue of their use, but not that every application of these attributes to a subject has only a relative validity. Under no circumstances would the passage authorise a distinction between the Socratic and the Sophistic philosophy; one of the characteristics of the Sophists consisting in their allowing only a relative value to all scientific and moral principles.

CHAP. VII.

explanation. We do not complain of it as wanting in moral content, but as wanting in philosophic precision.

D. Particular moral relations.

To give a systematic account of moral actions was not a part of the intention of Socrates. His views were from time to time expanded as occasion required. Chance has, to a certain extent, decided which of his dialogues should come down to us. Still it may be assumed that Socrates kept those objects more especially in view, to which he is constantly reverting by preference according to Xenophon. Here, in addition to the general demand for moral knowledge, and for knowledge of self, three points are particularly prominent—1. The independence of the individual as secured by the control of his wants and desires; 2. The nobler side of social life, as seen in friendship; 3. The furtherance of the public weal by a regulated commonwealth. To these may be added the question, 4. Whether, and In how far, Socrates exceeded the range of the ordinary morality of the Greeks by requiring love for enemies?

(1) *Individual independence.*

Not only was Socrates himself a model of self-denial and abstemiousness, but he endeavoured to foster the same virtues in his friends. What other subject was more often the topic of conversation than abstemiousness in the dialogues of Xenophon?[1] And did not Socrates distinctly call moderation the corner-stone of all virtue?[2] On this point the

[1] See the authorities p. 151, 4; 152, 1.

[2] Mem. i. 5, 4: ἆρά γε οὐ χρὴ πάντα ἄνδρα, ἡγησάμενον τὴν ἐγκράτειαν ἀρετῆς εἶναι κρηπῖδα, ταύτην πρώτην ἐν τῇ ψυχῇ κατασκευάσασθαι; This does not contradict the assertion that all

ground he occupied was nearly the same as that which afterwards became so important for the schools of the Cynics and Stoics; man can only become master of himself by being independent of wants, and by the exercise of his powers; while depending on the conditions and pleasures of the body, he resembles a slave.[1] A philosopher who considers knowledge to be the highest good, will naturally insist upon the mind's devoting itself, uninterrupted by the desires and appetites of the senses,[2] to the pursuit of truth in preference to every other thing; and the less value he attaches to external things as such, and the more exclusively he conceives happiness to be bound up with the intellectual condition of man,[3] the more will he feel the call to carry these principles into practice, by really making himself independent of the external world. Other motives, however, which served as a standard for moralists of a later epoch, were unknown to Socrates. He was not an ascetic in relation to the pleasures of the

virtue consists in knowledge. If Socrates had at all reflected, he would have explained moderation as a kind of knowledge. The above quoted passage might then be taken to mean, that the conviction of the worthlessness of sensual enjoyments must precede every other moral knowledge.

[1] *Xen.* Mem. i. 5, 3; i. 6, 5; ii. 1, 11; i. 2, 29; iii. 13, 3; and, in particular, iv. 5, 2; Symp. 8, 23.

[2] This connection appears clearly Mem. iv. 5, 6. When Socrates had shown that want of moderation makes man a slave, whilst moderation makes him free, he continues: *σοφίαν δὲ τὸ μέγιστον ἀγαθὸν οὐ δοκεῖ σοι ἀπείργουσα τῶν ἀνθρώπων ἡ ἀκρασία εἰς τοὐναντίον αὐτοὺς ἐμβάλλειν;* for how can any one recognise and choose what is good and useful, if he is ruled by the desire of what is pleasant?

[3] See pp. 142, 3; 152.

CHAP. VII.

senses, and displayed less strictness than might have been anticipated, neither shrinking from enjoyment nor yet feeling it needful. To continue master of himself in the midst of enjoyment, by the lucid clearness of his thought—that was the aim which his moderation proposed to itself.[1]

Strongest appears this feature of the Socratic abstinence in the language used in reference to sensual impulses. However exemplary his own conduct in this respect may have been, yet, in theory, he does not object to the gratification of these impulses out of wedlock, only requiring that it be not carried so far as to exceed the requirements of the body, nor prove a hindrance to higher ends.[2] The leading thought of his moral teaching is not so much strict purity as freedom of mind.

(2) *Friendship.*

This in itself purely negative condition of morality receives a positive supplement when the individual places himself in connection with others. The simplest form of this connection is friendship. Socrates, as we have already remarked, can only defend this relation on the ground of its advantages; yet there can be no mistaking the fact that it had a

[1] See p. 75.

[2] Mem. i. 3, 14: *οὕτω δὴ καὶ ἀφροδισιάζειν τοὺς μὴ ἀσφαλῶς ἔχοντας πρὸς ἀφροδίσια ᾤετο χρῆναι πρὸς τοιαῦτα, οἷα μὴ πάνυ μὲν δεομένου τοῦ σώματος οὐκ ἂν προσδέξαιτο ἡ ψυχὴ, δεομένου δὲ οὐκ ἂν πράγματα παρέχοι.* The last remark applies partly to the prejudicial workings of passion, which make a slave of man, and deter him from what is good, and partly to the harm they do to property, honour, and personal security. Socrates considers it ridiculous to incur danger and trouble for the sake of an enjoyment, which could be procured in a much simpler manner from any common girl. Mem. ii. 1, 5; 2, 4. The use which the Cynics made of these principles will be seen hereafter.

deeper meaning, both for himself and for his philosophy. For this, if for no other reason, it was eagerly pursued, and discussed in all the Socratic schools. When knowledge and morality so fully coincide as they do from Socrates' point of view, an intellectual association of individuals is inconceivable without a more extended community of life. These personal relations become, too, more necessary in proportion as the thinker fails to be satisfied with his own thinking, and feels a need for investigation in common with others and for mutual interchange of ideas. Just as in the case of the Pythagorean league, from a common pursuit of morality and religion, a lively feeling of clanship, a fondness for friendship and brotherhood was developed; as in other cases, too, like causes produced like results; so, in the Socratic school, the blending of moral and intellectual interests was the ground of a more intimate connection of pupil and teacher, and pupils amongst themselves, than could have resulted from an association of a purely intellectual character. The question can hardly be asked, which came first with him, which afterwards; whether friendship-needs made the philosophy of Socrates take the form of continuous dialogue, or the need of common inquiry drew him towards all who felt the same want. It is his peculiarity—and this it is which makes him the philosophic lover drawn by Plato—that he could neither in research dispense with association with others, nor in friendly intercourse dispense with research.

Accordingly, careful discussions of his are pre-

CHAP. VII.

served as to the value and nature of friendship.[1] In these he always comes back to the point, that true friendship can only exist amongst virtuous men, being for them altogether natural and necessary; true friends, he says, will do everything for one another. Virtue and active benevolence[2] are the only means for securing friends. From this platform the prevailing custom is then criticised. Socrates not only allows friendship to assume the Greek form of affection for boys and men, but he adopts that form of it himself, hardly out of mere deference to others.[3] In applying, however, his own moral principles to this relation, he opposes the prevailing errors, and demands a reformation, to transform the sensual conception of Eros into the moral conception of Friendship.[4] True love, he declares, can only then be said to exist when the good of the loved object is sought disinterestedly; not when, with reckless selfishness, aims are pursued and means employed by which both persons become contemptible to one another. Only by unselfish love can fidelity and constancy be secured. To plead that the one by complaisance buys the kind assistance of the other towards his perfection is wholly a mistaken view; for immorality and im-

[1] Mem. ii. 4–6.

[2] Similar explanations are worked into the Platonic Lysis, but probably in too free a manner for us to be able to gain from them any information respecting Socrates.

[3] *Xen.* Symp. 8, 12, the leading thought of which at least is Socratic. Mem. i. 2, 29; 3, 8; ii. 6, 31.

[4] Symp. 8, 27: *οὐ γὰρ οἷόν τε πονηρὰ αὐτὸν ποιοῦντα ἀγαθὸν τὸν σύνοντα ἀποδεῖξαι, οὐδέ γε ἀναισχυντίαν καὶ ἀκρασίαν παρεχόμενον ἐγκρατῆ καὶ αἰδούμενον τὸν ἐρώμενον ποιῆσαι.*

CHAP. VII.

(3) *Civil Life and the State.*

modesty can never be means to moral ends.[1] It seems that with these principles Socrates was enunciating to his cotemporaries a new truth, or at least recalling to their memories one long since forgotten.[2] In his low estimate of marriage he agreed with his fellow-countrymen. This was no doubt partly the cause of the Greek affection for boys; partly, too, it was a result fostered thereby.[3] Whilst assuming in women a moral disposition similar to that of men,[4] whilst even maintaining with intellectual women an instructive interchange of opinions, he still speaks of married life in terms more in keeping with the husband of Xanthippe, than with the friend of Aspasia. He allows that a clever woman is as useful for the household as a man, and he reproaches men for not caring about the education of their wives,[5] but he considers the procreation of children the end of marriage,[6] and his own conduct shows little love for domestic life.[7] His social and his personal instincts are satisfied by friendly intercourse with men; in their society he sees a means of fulfilling his peculiar mission as an educator of mankind; apart herefrom, with the

[1] See p. 76.

[2] Conf. *Plato*, Symp. 178, C.; 180, C.; 217, E.

[3] Conf. *Plato*, Symp. 192, A.

[4] See p. 146, 2.

[5] *Xen.* Œc. 3, 10; but the question may be raised, in how far the substance of these remarks applies to Socrates himself. Symp. 2, 9.

[6] Mem. ii. 2, 4.

[7] If in addition to the trait described by *Plato*, Phædo, 60, A., the character of Xanthippe (which has no pretensions to great tenderness) be considered, the joking character of the conversation in *Xen.* Symp. 2, 10, being thrown into the scale against the passages in *Plato*, Apol. 34, D., the balance of probability is, that Socrates lived almost entirely in public, and almost never at home.

CHAP. VII.

peculiarity of a Greek, he considers the state, and not the family, to be the chief object of moral action.

Of the importance of the state, and the obligations towards the same, a very high notion indeed is entertained by Socrates: he who would live amongst men, he says, must live in a state, be it as a ruler or as ruled.[1] He requires, therefore, the most unconditional obedience to the laws, to such an extent that the conception of justice is reduced to that of obedience to law,[2] but he desires every competent man to take part in the administration of the state, the well-being of all individuals depending on the well-being of the community.[3] These principles were really carried into practice by him throughout life. With devoted self-sacrifice his duties as a citizen were fulfilled, even death being endured in order that he might not violate the laws.[4] His philosophic labours were regarded as the fulfilment of a duty to the state;[5] and in Xenophon's Memorabilia we see him using every opportunity of enlisting the able into the service of the state, of deterring the incompetent, of awakening officials to a sense of their duties, and of giving them help in the administration of their offices.[6] The political character of these efforts he describes most tellingly, by including[7] all virtues under the conception of the ruling art.[8]

[1] Mem. ii. 1, 12.

[2] See p. 119, 1.

[3] Mem. iii. 7, 9.

[4] See p. 77.

[5] See pp. 66, 7; 69, 2.

[6] Mem. iii. 2–7.

[7] βασιλικὴ τέχνη in Mem. ii. 1, 17; iv. 2, 11. *Plato*, Euthyd. 291, B., πολιτικὴ stands for βασιλική.

[8] Accordingly the story told by *Cicero*, Tusc. v. 37, 108, and

Whilst thus doing homage to the old Greek view of the state, he in other respects departs from it widely. If knowledge is the condition of all true virtue, it is also the condition of all political virtue; the more so as the conception of political virtue is the higher of the two. Hence everyone who aspires to the position of a statesman is required to prepare himself for this calling [1] by a thorough self-sifting and a course of intellectual labour; and, conversely, Socrates only recognises capacity or right to political position where this condition is fulfilled. Neither the possession of power, nor the good fortune of acquiring it by lot or popular election, but knowledge only, makes the ruler.[2] As

Plut. de Exil. c. 5, p. 600, *Epict.* Diss. i. 9, 1 (conf. Muson. in *Stob.* Floril. 40, 9), that in answer to the question, to what country he belonged, he replied that he was a citizen of the world, cannot command credit, and the question itself sounds strange as addressed to Socrates in Athens. In *Plato's* Crito and Apol. 37, C., he uses language very different from the later cosmopolitan philosophers. Probably one of these attributed to him the above story.

[1] Mem. iii. 6, particularly towards the end; iv. 2, 6; *Plato*, Symp. 216, A. See p. 56, 6.

[2] Mem. iii. 9, 10: βασιλεῖς δὲ καὶ ἄρχοντας οὐ τοὺς τὰ σκῆπτρα ἔχοντας ἔφη εἶναι, οὐδὲ τοὺς ὑπὸ τῶν τυχόντων αἱρεθέντας, οὐδὲ τοὺς κλήρῳ λαχόντας, οὐδὲ τοὺς βιασαμένους, οὐδὲ τοὺς ἐξαπατήσαντας, ἀλλὰ τοὺς ἐπισταμένους ἄρχειν: in all other cases obedience is given to men of professional knowledge;—which is then illustrated by the example of physicians, pilots, and others. Similarly in Mem. iii. 5, 21; iv. 2, 2; iii. 1, 4; ibid. 4, 6: λέγω ἔγωγε, ὡς ὅτου ἄν τις προστατεύῃ ἐὰν γιγνώσκῃ τε ὧν δεῖ καὶ ταῦτα πορίζεσθαι δύνηται, ἀγαθὸς ἂν εἴη προστάτης. Similar views are advocated by Plato with the same illustrations, Polit. 297, D., and they appear to have been generally held in the school of Socrates. Accordingly the accuser *Xen.* Mem. i. 2, 9, charges Socrates with having contributed to bring existing institutions into contempt: λέγων ὡς μωρῶν εἰς τοὺς μὲν τῆς πόλεως ἄρχοντας ἀπὸ κυάμου καθίστασθαι, κυβερνήτῃ δὲ μηδένα θέλειν κεχρῆσθαι κυαμευτῷ μηδὲ

CHAP. VII.

regards the rule of the majority, his judgment is, that it is impossible for a statesman desirous for right and justice to hold his own against it; hence, where it prevails, what else can an upright man do but withdraw into private life?

A political principle was here advocated, which brought Socrates not only into collision with the Athenian democracy, but with the whole political administration of Greece. In place of the equality of all, or the preference accorded to birth and wealth, he demanded an aristocracy of intelligence; in place of citizen-rulers, a race of intellectually educated officials; in place of a government of tribes and people, a government by professional adepts, which Plato, consistently developing the principles of Socrates, attempted to realise in his philosophic community.[1] Socrates is here observed following in the track which the Sophists first struck out; for they were the first to offer and to declare intellectual training necessary as a preparation for a statesman's career. Still what he aimed at was substantially very different from what they aimed at. For him the aim of politics was not the power of the individual, but the well-being of the community; the object of training was not to acquire personal dexterity, but to attain truth; the means of culture was not the art of persuasion, but the science of what is. Socrates aimed at a knowledge by means

τέκτονι μηδ' αὐλητῇ μηδ' ἐπ' ἄλλα τοιαῦτα, and Xenophon does not deny the accuracy of this statement, but only attempts to prove the harmlessness of such principles.

[1] *Plato*, Apol. 31, E.; conf. Rep. vi. 496, C.

of which the state might be reformed, the Sophists at one by means of which it might be governed.

The aristocratic tone of this view of the state appears to be contradicted by the ease with which Socrates rose above the social prejudices of his nation, meeting the prevailing contempt for trade by the maxim that no useful employment, be it what it may, is a thing to be ashamed of, but only idleness and inactivity. Still both come from a common source. For just as Socrates will have the position of the individual in the state settled according to his works, so he will have every action appreciated which leads to a good result.[1] Here, as elsewhere, the conception of good is his highest standard.

(4) Love for enemies.

One consequence of the political character of Greek morality was that the virtuous man's duty was customarily summed up as doing good to friends and harm to foes. This very definition is put into the mouth of Socrates [2] by Xenophon, who likewise considers it natural to feel pain at the success of enemies.[3] On the other hand, in one of the earliest and most historical of Plato's dialogues,[4] Socrates

[1] Mem. i. 2, 56. In keeping with this he urges a friend (ii. 7) to employ the maids of his house in wool-work, and another (ii. 8) to seek for occupation as a steward, refuting in both cases the objection, that such an occupation was unbecoming for free men. Xenophon held a different view (see Œc. 4, 2, and 6, 5), and it is well known that Plato did also. Socrates speaks as the son of a poor labourer, Xenophon and Plato as men of rank and property.

[2] Mem. ii. 6, 35: *καὶ ὅτι ἔγνωκας ἀνδρὸς ἀρετὴν εἶναι νικᾶν τοὺς μὲν φίλους εὖ ποιοῦντα τοὺς δὲ ἐχθροὺς κακῶς.*

[3] Mem. iii. 9, 8: *φθόνον δὲ σκοπῶν ὅ,τι εἴη, λύπην μέν τινα, ἐξεύρισκεν αὐτὸν ὄντα, οὔτε μέντοι τὴν ἐπὶ φίλων ἀτυχίαις οὔτε τὴν ἐπ' ἐχθρῶν εὐτυχίαις γιγνομένην.*

[4] Crito, 49, A. Also Rep. i. 334, B.

CHAP. VII.

declares it to be wrong to injure another: injury is the same thing as wrong-doing, and wrong-doing may never be permitted, not even towards one who has been guilty of wrong-doing. It is hard to reconcile accounts so divergent;[1] for taking it for granted that the Socrates of Xenophon is only speaking from a popular point of view, it would still appear that Xenophon cannot have been conversant with explanations such as Plato gives. No doubt Plato's account even in the Crito cannot be regarded as strictly conformable to truth; yet it may well be questioned whether such a flagrant deviation from his master's teaching[2] as this can be set down against him. That it is just possible cannot be denied; we must therefore rest content with uncertainty as to what were the real views of Socrates on this subject.[3]

[1] The remark of Meiners (Gesch. der Wissenschaft. ii. 456) is a pure guess that Socrates considered it allowable to do harm (bodily) to enemies, but not to injure them in respect of their true well-being; for Xenophon expressly allows κακῶς ποιεῖν while Plato as expressly forbids it.

[2] See p. 154.

[3] Still less have we any right to assert—as *Hildebrand* appears inclined to do (Xenophont. et Arist. de Œconomia publica Doctrina, part i. Marb. 1845)—that Socrates was in principle opposed to slavery. If he held many things, which Greek prejudices considered servile, not to be unworthy of a free man, it by no means follows that he disapproved of slavery. The view that slavery is contrary to nature (mentioned by *Aristotle*, Polit. i. 3) is not attributed to Socrates as its author. Had he been the author this would undoubtedly have been stated. The whole context is not in keeping with Socrates, to whom the distinction between φύσει and νόμῳ is foreign. We ought rather to think of the Cynics.

CHAPTER VIII.

CONTINUATION. ON NATURE. GOD AND MAN.

CHAP. VIII.

A. Subordination of means to ends in nature.

INQUIRIES into nature, we have seen, did not form part of the scheme of Socrates. Yet the line of his speculations led him to a peculiar view of nature and its design. One who so thoughtfully considered the problem of human life from all sides could not leave unnoticed its countless relations to the outer world; and judging them by the standard which was for him the highest—the standard of utility for man—could not but come to the conclusion that the whole arrangement of nature was subservient to the well-being of the human race—in short that it was adapted to a purpose and good.[1] To his mind, all that is good and expedient appears of necessity to be the work of reason; for just as man cannot do what is useful without intelligence, no more can what is useful exist without intelligence.[2] His view

[1] For Socrates, as has been already shown, understands by the good what is useful for man.

[2] See Mem. i. 4, 2, in which the argument from analogy is most clearly brought out. Socrates is desirous of convincing a friend of the existence of the Gods, and hence proposes the question: Whether more intelligence is not required to produce living beings than to produce paintings like those of Polycletus and Zeuxis? Aristodemus will only allow this conditionally, and in one special case, εἴπερ γε μὴ τύχῃ τινὶ ἀλλ

of nature was essentially that of a system of means working for ends, not with profound research exploring the real bearings of the several departments, and the innate purpose of the existence and growth of every natural being, but referring all things experimentally to the well-being of man as their highest end, and explaining their subservience to this purpose in an equally matter of fact way as due to an arrangement of reason which, like an artificer, has accidentally assigned to them their own purposes. As in the Socratic ethics, the wisdom regulating human actions becomes a superficial reasoning as to the use of particular acts, so, too, Socrates can only conceive of the wisdom which formed the world in a manner equally superficial. He shows [1] what care has been taken to provide for man, in that he has light, water, fire, and air, in that not only the sun shines by day, but also the moon and the stars by night; in that the heavenly bodies serve for divisions of seasons, that the earth brings forth food and other necessaries, and that the change of seasons prevents excessive heat or cold. He reminds of the advantages derived from cattle, from oxen, from pigs, horses, and other animals. To prove the wisdom of the Craftsman

ὑπὸ γνώμης ταῦτα γεγένηται· but he is immediately met by Socrates with the question: τῶν δὲ ἀτεκμάρτως ἐχόντων ὅτου ἕνεκά ἐστι καὶ τῶν φανερῶς ἐπ' ὠφελείᾳ ὄντων πότερα τύχης, καὶ πότερα γνώμης ἔργα κρίνεις; Πρέπει μὲν, he is obliged to confess, τὰ ἐπ' ὠφελείᾳ γινόμενα γνώμης εἶναι ἔργα. Compare also *Plato*, Phædo, 29, A., although, according to what has been said, p. 60, this passage is not strictly historical, and *Arist.* M. Mor. i. 1; 1183, b, 9.

[1] Mem. i. 4; iv. 3.

who made man,[1] he refers to the organism of the human body, to the structure of the organs of sense, to the erect posture of man, to the priceless dexterity of his hands. He sees a proof of a divine Providence in the natural impulse for propagation and self-preservation, in the love for children, in the fear of death. He never wearies of exalting the intellectual advantages of man, his ingenuity, his memory, his intelligence, his language, his religious disposition. He considers it incredible that a belief in God and in Providence should be naturally inborn in all men, and have maintained itself from time immemorial, clinging not to individuals only in the ripest years of their age, but to whole nations and communities, unless it were true. He appeals also to special revelations vouchsafed to men for their good, either by prophecy or portent. Unscientific, doubtless, these arguments may appear, still they became in the sequel of importance for philosophy.

As Socrates by his moral inquiries, notwithstanding all their faults, is the founder of a scientific doctrine of morals, so by his theory of the relation of means to ends, notwithstanding its popular character, he is the founder of that ideal view of nature which henceforth pervades the natural philosophy of the Greeks, and which with all its abuses has proved itself so valuable for the actual study of nature. Not aware himself that he was engaged on

[1] In Mem. i. 4, 12, a remark is found indicative of the popular character of these general considerations: *τὸ δὲ καὶ τὰς τῶν ἀφροδισίων ἡδονὰς τοῖς μὲν ἄλλοις ζῴοις δοῦναι περιγράψαντας τοῦ ἔτους χρόνον, ἡμῖν δὲ συνεχῶς μέχρι γήρως ταῦτα παρέχειν.*

CHAP. VIII.

natural science, he only studied the relation of means to ends in the world in the moral interest of piety. From what has been before said it follows that his view of nature was closely connected with the theory of the knowledge of conceptions, even its defects being due to the universal imperfection of his intellectual method.

B. *God and the worship of God.*

(1) *Popular use of the term Gods.*

Asking further what idea we should form to ourselves of creative reason, we are met by the reply that Socrates mostly speaks of Gods in a popular way, as many,[1] no doubt thinking in the first place of the Gods of the popular faith.[2] Out of this multiplicity the idea of the oneness of God,[3] an idea not unknown to the Greek religion, rises with him into prominence, as is not infrequently met with at that time.[4] In one passage he draws a curious distinction between the creator and ruler of the universe and the rest of the Gods.[5] Have we not here a union of polytheism and monotheism, which his mythology so readily suggested to a Greek re-

[1] Mem. i. 1, 19; 3, 3; 4, 11; iv. 3, 3.

[2] Mem. iv. 3, 16.

[3] Compare *Zeller's* Introduction to his Philos. d. Griechen, p. 3.

[4] Mem. i. 4, 5, 7, 17: ὁ ἐξ ἀρχῆς ποιῶν ἀνθρώπους—σοφοῦ τινος δημιούργου καὶ φιλοζώου—τὸν τοῦ θεοῦ ὀφθαλμὸν, τὴν τοῦ θεοῦ φρόνησιν.

[5] Mem. iv. 3, 13. The Gods are invisible; οἵ τε γὰρ ἄλλοι ἡμῖν τὰ ἀγαθὰ διδόντες οὐδὲν τούτων εἰς τοὐμφανὲς ἰόντες διδόασιν, καὶ ὁ τὸν ὅλον κόσμον συντάττων τε καὶ συνέχων, ἐν ᾧ πάντα καλὰ καὶ ἀγαθά ἐστι, καὶ ἀεὶ μὲν χρωμένοις ἀτριβῆ τε καὶ ὑγιᾶ καὶ ἀγήρατον παρέχων, θᾶττον δὲ νοήματος ἀναμαρτήτως ὑπηρετοῦντα, οὗτος τὰ μέγιστα μὲν πράττων ὁρᾶται, τάδε δὲ οἰκονομῶν ἀόρατος ἡμῖν ἐστιν. *Krische's* argument (Forsch. 220) to prove that this language is spurious, although on his own showing it was known to Phædrus, Cicero, and the writer of the treatise on the world, appears inconclusive.

ducing the many Gods to the position of instruments of the One Supreme God? CHAP. VIII.

(2) *God conceived as the Reason of the world.*

In as far as the reasonable arrangement of the world led Socrates to the notion of One Supreme Being, the idea which he formed to himself of this Being (herein resembling Heraclitus and Anaxagoras) was as the reason of the world, holding the same relation to the world that the soul does to the body.[1] Herewith are connected his lofty and precise ideas of God as a being invisible, all-wise, all-powerful, present everywhere. As the soul, without being seen, produces visible effects in the body, so does God in the world. As the soul exercises undisputed sway over the small portion of the world which belongs to it as an individual body, so God exercises dominion over the whole world. As the soul is present in all parts of its body, so God is present throughout the Universe. And if the soul, notwithstanding the limitations by which it is hemmed in, can perceive what is distant, and imagine things of the most varied kind, surely the knowledge and care of God must be able to embrace all and more.[2]

[1] Mem. i. 4, 8.: *σὺ δὲ σαυτὸν φρόνιμόν τι δοκεῖς ἔχειν, ἄλλοθι δὲ οὐδαμοῦ οὐδὲν οἴει φρόνιμον εἶναι . . . καὶ τάδε τὰ ὑπερμεγέθη καὶ πλῆθος ἄπειρα* (the elements, or generally, the parts of the world) *δι' ἀφροσύνην τινὰ οὕτως οἴει εὐτάκτως ἔχειν;* 17: *κατάμαθε ὅτι καὶ ὁ σὸς νοῦς ἐνὼν τὸ σὸν σῶμα ὅπως βούλεται μεταχειρίζεται· οἴεσθαι οὖν χρὴ καὶ τὴν ἐν τῷ παντὶ φρόνησιν τὰ πάντα ὅπως ἂν αὐτῇ ἡδὺ ᾖ, οὕτω τίθεσθαι· καὶ μὴ τὸ σὸν μὲν ὄμμα δύνασθαι ἐπὶ πολλὰ στάδια ἐξικνεῖσθαι, τὸν δὲ τοῦ θεοῦ ὀφθαλμὸν ἀδύνατον εἶναι ἅμα πάντα ὁρᾶν· μηδὲ, τὴν σὴν μὲν ψυχὴν καὶ περὶ τῶν ἐνθάδε καὶ περὶ τῶν ἐν Αἰγύπτῳ καὶ Σικελίᾳ δύνασθαι φροντίζειν, τὴν δὲ τοῦ θεοῦ φρόνησιν μὴ ἱκανὴν εἶναι ἅμα πάντων ἐπιμελεῖσθαι.*

[2] Compare the words in Mem. i. 4, 18: If you apply to the Gods for prophecy, *γνώσῃ τὸ θεῖον ὅτι τοσοῦτον καὶ τοιοῦτόν*

CHAP. VIII.

Had not a belief in the providential care of God been already[1] taken for granted, in the argument for His existence from the relation of means to ends? Was not the best explanation of this care to be found in the analogous care which the human soul has for the body? A special proof of this providence Socrates thought to discern in oracles:[2] by them the most important things, which could not otherwise be known, are revealed to man. It must be equally foolish to despise oracles, or to consult them in cases capable of being solved by our own reasoning.[3] Hence followed, as a matter of course, the worship of God, prayer, sacrifices and obedience.[4]

(3) *The worship of God.*

As to the form and manner of worship, Socrates, as we already know,[5] wished every one to follow the customs of his people. True, he propounds higher maxims corresponding with his own idea of God. He would not have men pray for special, least of all for external benefits, but only ask for what is good: for who but God knows what is advantageous for man, or knows it so well? With regard to sacrifices, he declared that the greatness of the sacrifice is unimportant compared with the spirit of the sacrificer, and that the more pious the man, the more

ἐστιν, ὥσθ' ἅμα πάντα ὁρᾶν καὶ πάντα ἀκούειν καὶ πανταχοῦ παρεῖναι, καὶ ἅμα πάντων ἐπιμελεῖσθαι· and the words, Ibid. iv. 3, 12: *ὅτι δέ γε ἀληθῆ λέγω . . . γνώσῃ, ἂν μὴ ἀναμένῃς, ἕως ἂν τὰς μορφὰς τῶν θεῶν ἴδῃς·* also i. 1, 19.

[1] Mem. iv. 3; i. 4, 6, and 11.

[2] Ibid. iv. 3, 12, and 16; i. 4, 14.

[3] Ibid. i. 1, 6. Conf. p. 78, 3; 66, 5.

[4] Compare Mem. iv. 3, 14; ii. 2, 14.

[5] See p. 150, 1; 77, 7.

acceptable will the offering be, so that it correspond with his means.[1] Abstaining on principle from theological speculations,[2] and not seeking to explore the nature of God, but to lead his fellow men to piety, he never felt the need of combining the various elements of his religious belief into one comprehensive conception, or of forming a perfectly consistent picture, and so avoiding the contradictions which that belief may easily be shown to contain.[3]

C. Dignity of man. His immortality.

A certain divine element Socrates, like others before him, thought to discern within the soul of man.[4] Perhaps with this thought is connected his belief in immediate revelations of God to the human soul, such as he imagined were vouchsafed to himself. It must have been a welcome theory to a philosopher giving strict heed to the moral and spiritual nature of man; but it does not appear that Socrates ever brought forward any argument to support it, neither do we find in him strict proof for the immortality of the soul, although he was inclined to this belief partly from his high opinion of the dignity of man, partly, too, on grounds of expe-

[1] Mem. i. 3, 2; iv. 3, 17.

[2] See p. 140, 2.

[3] We have no reason for supposing with *Dénis* (Histoire des Théories et des Idées morales dans l'Antiquité, Paris et Strasb. 1856, i. 79), that Socrates, like Antisthenes, spared polytheism from regard to the needs of the masses, whilst believing in only one God. To argue so would be to belie not only the definite and repeated assertions of Xenophon, but also Socrates' unflinching love of truth.

[4] Mem. iv. 3, 14: ἀλλὰ μὴν καὶ ἀνθρώπου γε ψυχὴ, εἴπερ τι καὶ ἄλλο τῶν ἀνθρωπίνων, τοῦ θείου μετέχει.

CHAP. VIII.

diency.[1] In Plato's Apology,[2] at a moment when the suppression of his beliefs can least be supposed, he expressed himself on this question with much doubt and caution.[3] Herewith agrees so well the language used by the dying Cyrus in Xenophon,[4] that we may safely assume that Socrates considered the soul's existence after death to be indeed probable, without, however,[5] pretending to any certain knowledge on the point. It was accepted by him as an article of faith, the intellectual grounds for which belonged to those problems which surpass man's capacities.[6]

[1] Compare *Hermann* in Marburger Lectionskatalog, 1835–6, Plat. 684.

[2] 40, C.; after his condemnation.

[3] Death is either an external sleep, or a transition to a new life, but in neither case is it an evil.

[4] Cyrop. viii. 7, 10. Several reasons are first given in favour of immortality; they need a great deal of confirmation to be anything like rigid proofs. (Compare particularly § 19 with Plato's Phædo, 105, C.) At last, the possibility of the soul's dying with the body is left an open question, but in either case death is stated to be the end of all evils.

[5] He actually says in *Plato*, Apol. 29, A. (Conf. 37, B.): death is feared as the greatest evil, whilst it may be the greatest good: ἐγὼ δὲ . . . οὐκ εἰδὼς ἱκανῶς περὶ τῶν ἐν Ἀΐδου οὕτω καὶ οἴομαι οὐκ εἰδέναι.

[6] The above description of the philosophy of Socrates rests on the exclusive authority of Xenophon, Plato, and Aristotle. What later writers say is for the most part taken from these sources, and whenever it goes beyond them, there is no guarantee for its accuracy. It is, however, just possible that some genuine utterances of Socrates may have been preserved in the writings of Æschines and others, which are omitted by our authorities. In that category place the statement of Cleanthes quoted by *Clement* (Strom. ii. 417, D.), and repeated by *Cicero* (Off. iii. 3, 11), that Socrates taught the identity of justice and happiness, cursing the man who first made a distinction between them: the statements in *Cic.* Off. ii. 12, 43 (taken from *Xen.* Mem. ii. 6, 39; conf. Cyrop. i. 6, 22); in *Seneca*, Epist. 28, 2; 104, 7 (travelling is of no good to fools); 71, 16 (truth and virtue are identical); in *Plut.*

Ed. Pu. c. 7, p. 4, on education (the passage in c. 9 is an inaccurate reference to *Plato*, Gorg. 470, D.); Cons. ad Apoll. c. 9, p. 106, that if all sufferings had to be equally divided, every one would gladly preserve his own; Conj. Præc. c. 25, p. 140 (*Diog.* ii. 33; Exc. e Floril. Joan. Damasc. ii. B. 98; *Stob.* Floril. ed. Mein. iv. 202), on the moral use of the looking-glass; Ser. Num. Vind. c. 5, p 550, deprecating anger; in *Demet.* Byz. quoted by *Diog.* ii. 21 (*Gell.* N. A. xiv. 6, 5), *Muson.* in the Exc. e Floril. Jo. Dam. ii. 13, 126, p. 221, Mein, that philosophy ought to confine itself to *ὅ, ττι τοι ἐν μεγάροισι, κακόν τ' ἀγαθόν τε τέτυκται* (others attribute the words to Diogenes or Aristippus); *Cic.* de Orat. i. 47, 204: Socrates said that his only wish was to stimulate to virtue; where this succeeded the rest followed of itself (a statement thoroughly agreeing with the views of the Stoic Aristo, and probably coming from him. Conf. *Zeller*, Stoics, Epicureans, &c., p. 60); in *Diog.* ii. 30, blaming the sophistry of Euclid; in *Diog.* ii. 31 (undoubtedly from some Cynic or Stoic treatise) that intelligence is the only good, ignorance the only evil, and that riches and noble birth do more harm than good; in *Diog.* ii. 32, that to marry or to abstain from marriage is equally bad; in *Gell.* xix. 2, 7 (*Athen.* iv. 158; *Plut.* And. Poet. 4, p. 21), that most men live to eat, whilst he eats to live; in *Stob.* Ekl. i. 54, giving a definition of God; Ibid. ii. 356, Floril. 48, 26 (conf. *Plato*, Legg. i. 626, E.), that self-restraint is the best form of government; in Teles. apud *Stob.* Floril. 40, 8, blaming the Athenians for banishing their best, and honouring their worst men, and the apophthegmata in *Valer. Max.* vii. 2, Ext. 1. A large number of sayings, purporting to come from Socrates, are quoted by Plutarch in his treatises and by Stobæus in his Florilegium; some, too, by Seneca. Most of them, however, are colourless, or else they aim at being epigrammatic, which is a poor substitute for being genuine. Altogether their number makes them very suspicious. Probably they were taken from a collection of proverbs which some later writer published under the name of Socratic proverbs.

CHAPTER IX.

RETROSPECT. XENOPHON AND PLATO. SOCRATES AND THE SOPHISTS.

CHAP. IX.

A. Truthfulness of Xenophon's description.

LOOKING back from the point now reached to the question before raised, as to which of his biographers we must look to for an historically accurate account of Socrates and his teaching, we are fain to admit, that no one of them is so satisfactory an authority as any original writings or verbal reports of the utterances of the great teacher would have been.[1] It is, however, patent at once that the personal character of Socrates, as pourtrayed by both Xenophon and Plato, is, in all essential points, one and the same. Their descriptions supplement one another in some few points, contradicting each other in none. The supplementary portions may be easily inserted in the general picture, present before the eyes of both.

(1) Xenophon's view in harmony with that of Plato and Aristotle.

Moreover the philosophy of Socrates as represented by Plato and Aristotle is not in the main different from what it appears in Xenophon, provided those parts only in the writings of Plato be taken into account which undoubtedly belong to Socrates, and a distinction be drawn between the underlying thought

[1] Conf. p. 99.

and the commonplace language of the Socrates of Xenophon. Even in Xenophon, Socrates expresses the opinion that true knowledge is the highest thing, and that this knowledge consists in a knowledge of conceptions only. In Xenophon, too, may be observed all the characteristics of that method by means of which Socrates strove to produce knowledge. In his pages, likewise, virtue is reduced to knowledge, and this position is supported by the same arguments, and therefrom are deduced the same conclusions, as in Aristotle and Plato. In short, all the leading features of the philosophy of Socrates are preserved by Xenophon; granting as we always must that he did not understand the deeper meaning of many a saying, and therefore failed to give to it the prominence it deserved. Now and then for the same reason he used a commonplace expression instead of a philosophical one; substituting for the accurate definition, 'All virtue is a knowing,' with less accuracy, 'All virtue is knowledge.' Nor need we feel surprise that the faults of the Socratic philosophy, its rough and ready way of treating things, the want of system in its method, the selfish foundation of its moral teaching, should appear more prominently in Xenophon than in Plato and Aristotle, considering the brevity with which Aristotle speaks of Socrates, and the liberty with which Plato expands the Socratic teaching both in point of substance and form. In favour of Xenophon's description sundry admissions of Plato tell,[1] likewise its consistency

[1] See above, pp. 81; 151, 1.

and conformity to the picture which we must make to ourselves of the first appearance of Socrates' newly discovered principle. No greater concession can be made to the detractors of Xenophon than this, that failing to understand the philosophical importance of his teacher, he failed to make it prominent in his description, and that in so far Plato and Aristotle are most welcome as supplementary authorities. It cannot for one moment be allowed that Xenophon has in any respect given a false account of Socrates, or that it is impossible to gather from his sketch the true character and importance of his master's teaching.

(2) *Schleiermacher's objection answered.*

It may indeed be said that this estimate of Xenophon is at variance with the position which Socrates is known to have held in history. As Schleiermacher observes:[1] 'Had Socrates confined his discourse to the matter and range never exceeded in the Memorabilia of Xenophon, although that discourse had been more attractive and brilliant, it is incomprehensible that in so many years he should not have emptied marketplace and workshop, public walks and schools, from fear of his presence; that he should so long have satisfied Alcibiades and Critias, Plato and Euclid; that he should have played the part he does in the dialogues of Plato; in short, that he should have become the founder and type of Attic philosophy.' Fortunately in Plato himself we have a valuable testimony to the accuracy of Xenophon's description. To what does

[1] Werke, iii. 2, 259, 287.

his Alcibiades appeal when anxious to disclose the divine element concealed under the Silenus-like appearance of the Socratic discourses? On what does his admirable description of the impression produced on him by Socrates fall back?[1] What is it which to his mind has been the cause of the revolution and change in the inner life of Greece? What but the moral considerations, which in Xenophon form the substance of the Socratic dialogues? These, and these only, are dwelt upon by Socrates,

[1] Symp. 215, E.: ὅταν γὰρ ἀκούω [Σωκράτους] πολύ μοι μᾶλλον ἢ τῶν κορυβαντιώντων ἥ τε καρδία πηδᾷ καὶ δάκρυα ἐκχεῖται ὑπὸ τῶν λόγων τῶν τούτου. ὁρῶ δὲ καὶ ἄλλους παμπόλλους τὰ αὐτὰ πάσχοντας: this was not the case with other speakers, οὐδὲ τεθορύβητό μου ἡ ψυχὴ οὐδ' ἠγανάκτει ὡς ἀνδραποδωδῶς διακειμένου (similarly Euthydemus in *Xen.* Mem. iv. 2, 39), ἀλλ' ὑπὸ τουτουῒ τοῦ Μαρσύου πολλάκις δὴ οὕτω διετέθην, ὥστε μοι δόξαι μὴ βιωτὸν εἶναι ἔχοντι ὡς ἔχω . . . ἀναγκάζει γάρ με ὁμολογεῖν ὅτι πολλοῦ ἐνδεὴς ὢν αὐτὸς ἔτι ἐμαυτοῦ μὲν ἀμελῶ τὰ δ' Ἀθηναίων πράττω . . . (conf. Mem. iv. 2; iii. 6) πέπονθα δὲ πρὸς τοῦτον μόνον ἀνθρώπων, ὃ οὐκ ἄν τις οἴοιτο ἐν ἐμοὶ ἐνεῖναι, τὸ αἰσχύνεσθαι ὀντινοῦν . . . . δραπετεύω οὖν αὐτὸν καὶ φεύγω, καὶ ὅταν ἴδω αἰσχύνομαι τὰ ὡμολογημένα· καὶ πολλάκις μὲν ἡδέως ἂν ἴδοιμι αὐτὸν μὴ ὄντα ἐν ἀνθρώποις· εἰ δ' αὖ τοῦτο γένοιτο, εὖ οἶδ' ὅτι πολὺ μεῖζον ἂν ἀχθοίμην, ὥστε οὐκ ἔχω, ὅ τι χρήσομαι τούτῳ τῷ ἀνθρώπῳ. Ibid. 221, D.: καὶ οἱ λόγοι αὐτοῦ ὁμοιότατοί εἰσι τοῖς Σειληνοῖς τοῖς διοιγομένοις . . . διοιγομένους δὲ ἰδὼν ἄν τις καὶ ἐντὸς αὐτῶν γιγνόμενος πρῶτον μὲν νοῦν ἔχοντας ἔνδον μούνους εὑρήσει τῶν λόγων, ἔπειτα θειοτάτους καὶ πλεῖστ' ἀγάλματ' ἀρετῆς ἐν αὐτοῖς ἔχοντας, καὶ ἐπὶ πλεῖστον τείνοντας, μᾶλλον δὲ ἐπὶ πᾶν ὅσον προσήκει σκοπεῖν τῷ μέλλοντι καλῷ κἀγαθῷ ἔσεσθαι. *Alberti's* (p. 78) objections to the above use of these passages resolve themselves into this, that those 'elements of conversation which rivet the soul,' which are not altogether wanting in Xenophon, are more frequent and noticeable in Plato, that therefore the spirit of the Socratic philosophy comes out more clearly in Plato. We grant this readily. The above remarks are not directed against the statement that Plato gives a deeper insight than Xenophon into the spirit of the Socratic teaching, but against Schleiermacher's statement that the discourses of Socrates were essentially different in substance and subject-matter from those reported by Xenophon.

speaking in Plato's Apology[1] of his higher calling and his services to his country; it is his business to exhort others to virtue; and if he considers the charm of his conversation to consist in its attempts at analysis,[2] the reference is to a process of which many examples are to be found in Xenophon, that of convincing people of ignorance in the affairs of their calling.

B. *Importance of the Socratic teaching for the age in which he lived.*

The effect produced by the discourses of Socrates need not surprise us, were they only of the kind reported by Xenophon. The investigations of Socrates, as he gives them, may often appear trivial and tedious; and looking at the result with reference to the particular case, they may really be so. That the forger of armour must suit the armour to him who has to wear it;[3] that the care of the body is attended with many advantages;[4] that friends must be secured by kind acts and attention:[5] these and such-like maxims, which are often lengthily discussed by Socrates, neither contain for us, nor can they have contained for his cotemporaries, anything new. The important element in these inquiries, however, does not consist in their substance, but in their method, in the fact that what was formerly unexplored hypothesis and unconscious guesswork,

[1] 29, B.; 38, A.; 41, E.

[2] Apol. 23, C.: *πρὸς δὲ τούτοις οἱ νέοι μοι ἐπακολουθοῦντες οἷς μάλιστα σχολή ἐστιν οἱ τῶν πλουσιωτάτων αὐτόματοι χαίρουσιν ἀκούοντες ἐξεταζομένων τῶν ἀνθρώπων, καὶ αὐτοὶ πολλάκις ἐμὲ μιμοῦνται εἶτα ἐπιχειροῦσιν ἄλλους ἐξετάζειν.* Conf. 33, B. An example of such sifting is to be found in the conversation of Alcibiades with Pericles, Mem. i. 1, 40.

[3] Mem. iii. 10, 9.

[4] Ibid. iii. 12, 4.

[5] Ibid. ii. 10, 6, 9.

was now arrived at by a process of thinking. In making a too minute or over-careful application of this method, Socrates would not give the same offence to his cotemporaries as to us, who have not as they to learn for the first time the art of conscious thinking and emancipation from the authority of blind custom.[1] For the most part the researches of the Sophists contain much less, which, notwithstanding their empty cavils, imparted an almost electrical shock to their age, simply and solely because in this partial application a new power and method of reasoning had dawned upon the Greek mind. Had therefore Socrates only dealt with those unimportant topics, upon which so many of his dialogues exclusively turn, his direct influence, at least on his cotemporaries, would not be unintelligible.

These unimportant topics really hold a subordinate position in Xenophon's dialogues. The main thing even in these are the philosophical investigations into the necessity of knowledge, into the nature of morality, into the conceptions of the various virtues, into moral and intellectual self-analysis; practical directions for the formation of conceptions; critical discussions obliging the speakers to consider what their notions implied, and at what their actions aimed. Can we wonder that such investigations should have produced a deep impression on the cotemporaries of Socrates, and an entire change in the Greek mode of thought, according to the

[1] Comp. *Hegel*, Gesch. d. Phil. ii. 59.

CHAP. IX.

unanimous testimony of historians?[1] or that a keener sight should have caught a glimpse of a newly discovered world behind the apparently commonplace and trivial expressions of Socrates which his biographers unanimously record? It was reserved for Plato and Aristotle to conquer this new world; yet Socrates was the first to discover it, and to point the way thereto. Frankly as we may admit the shortcomings of his productions, and the limits which his individual nature imposed on him, what remains will ever stamp him as the originator of the philosophy of conceptions, as the reformer of method, and as the first founder of a scientific doctrine of morals.

C. *His relation to the Sophists.*

The relation, too, of the Socratic philosophy to Sophistry will become clear by considering the imperfect and unsatisfactory element in its process and results as well as its greatness and importance. This relation, as is well known, has, during the last thirty years, been examined in several ways. Before that time there was a general agreement in accepting Plato's view, and looking on Socrates as the opponent of the Sophists. Hegel first obtained currency for the contrary opinion, that Socrates shared with the Sophists the same platform in attaching importance to the person and to introspection.[2] In a somewhat different way, Grote[3] has still more recently exploded the traditional view that the Socratic philosophy is opposed to Sophistry. If Sophist implies what the

[1] Conf. p. 81, 1 and 2; 121; 123, 2.

[2] See p. 117.

[3] Hist. of Greece, viii. 479, 606.

word from its derivation alone can mean, a public teacher educating youth for practical life, Socrates is himself the true type of a Sophist. If it is used to express the character of certain individuals and their teaching, it is an abuse to appropriate the term Sophistry to this purpose, or to group together in one class all the different individuals who came forward as Sophists. The Sophists were not a sect or a school, but a profession, men of the most varied opinions, for the most part highly deserving and meritorious people, with whose views we have not the least reason to quarrel. If, then, Hegel and his followers attacked the common notion of the disagreement of Socrates and the Sophists, because Socrates, in one respect, agreed with the Sophists, Grote attacks it for the very opposite reason, because the most distinguished of the so-called Sophists are at one with Socrates.

Previous inquiries will have shown that both views have their justification, neither being altogether right. It is a false view of history to contrast Socrates with the Sophists, in the same way that true philosophy is contrasted with false or good with evil; in this respect it is noteworthy that the contrast between Socrates and the Sophists is not so great in Xenophon as in Plato,[1] nor yet in Plato nearly so great as in several modern writers.[2] Still

[1] Compare *Xen.* Mem. iv. 4, besides p. 61, 1; and *Zeller's* Phil. d. Griech. Part I. p. 873, 1, 2.

[2] Proofs in Protagoras and Gorgias, Theætet. 151, D.; 162, D.; 164, D.; 165, E.; Rep. i. 354, A.; vi. 498, C.

CHAP. IX.

the results of previous inquiries [1] forbid our bringing Socrates into so close a connection, as Grote does in his valuable work, with men who are habitually grouped together under the name of Sophists, and who really in their whole tone and method bear so much resemblance to him. The scepticism of a Protagoras and Gorgias cannot for a moment be placed on the same level with the Socratic philosophy of conceptions, nor the Sophistic controversial skill with the Socratic sifting of men; the maxim that man is the measure of all things cannot be compared with the Socratic demand for action based on personal conviction,[2] nor can the rhetorical displays of the

[1] *Zeller*, Part I. 882, 938.

[2] As is done by *Grote*, Plato, I. 305. Respecting Socrates' explanation in Plato's Crito, 49, D., that he was convinced that under no circumstances is wrong-doing allowed, it is there observed; here we have the Protagorean dogma *Homo Mensura* . . . which Socrates will be found combating in the Theætetus . . . proclaimed by Socrates himself. How unlike the two are will, however, be seen at once by a moment's reflection on Protagoras' saying, Conf. Part I. 899 . . . p. 259, 535; iii. 479. Grote even asserts that not the Sophists but Socrates was the chief quibbler in Greece; he was the first to destroy the beliefs of ordinary minds by his negative criticism, whereas Protagoras, Prodicus and Hippias used previous authorities as they found them, leaving untouched the moral notions current. II. 410 and 428 he observes respecting Plato's statement (Soph. 232, B.) that the Sophists talk themselves and teach others to talk of things which they do not know, which Socrates did all his life long. In so saying, he forgets that Socrates in examining into the opinions of men neither pretends to better knowledge himself nor is content with the negative purpose of perplexing others. His aim was to substitute permanent conceptions for unscientific notions. He forgets, also, that in the case of the Sophists, owing to their want of true intellectual feeling, their shallowness of method, their denial of absolute truth, together with an incapacity for real intellectual productions, those practical consequences were sure to result which soon enough came to view. See Part I. 920.

older Sophists, or the dangerous and unscientific character of their latter ethics be lost sight of. Hegel's view, grouping Socrates with the Sophists, has called forth greater opposition than it deserves. The first propounders of this view do not deny that the relative truth of Socrates differed materially from that of the Sophists.[1] Neither they nor their opponents deny that the Sophists were the first to turn philosophy away from nature to morals and the human mind, that they first looked to knowledge for a foundation for practical conduct requiring a sifting of existing customs and laws, that they first referred to personal conviction the settling of truth and falsehood, right and wrong. So that the dispute with them ultimately resolves itself into the question: Shall we say that Socrates and the Sophists *resembled* one another, both taking personal truth as their ground, but differing in their views of personal truth? or that they *differed*, the nature of their treatment being different whilst they agreed in making it relative? Or, to put the question in another shape: There being both points of agreement and difference between them, which of the two elements is the more important and decisive? Here, for the reasons already explained, only one reply can be given,[2] which is this, that the difference between the Socratic and Sophistic philosophies far exceeds their points of resemblance. The Sophists are wanting in that very thing which is the root of the philosophical greatness of Socrates—the quest of an absolutely true and uni-

[1] See p. 119, 1. [2] See p. 111, and Part I. 135, 938.

CHAP. IX.

versally valid knowledge and a method for attaining it. They could question all that had previously passed for truth, but they could not strike out a new and surer road to truth. Agreeing as they do with Socrates in not busying themselves with the study of nature so much as with training for practical life, with them this training has a different character and a different importance from what it bears with Socrates. The ultimate end of their instruction is formal dexterity, the employment of which must consistently be left to individual caprice, since absolute truth is impossible. With Socrates, on the other hand, the acquisition of truth is an ultimate end, wherein alone the rule for the conduct of the individual is to be found. Hence the Sophistic teaching in its progress could not fail to break away from the philosophy which preceded it, and indeed from every intellectual inquiry. Had it succeeded in gaining undisputed sway, it would have dealt the death-stroke to Greek philosophy. Socrates alone bore in himself the germ of a new life for thought. He alone by his philosophical principles was qualified to be the reformer of philosophy.[1]

[1] *Hermann* admits this, when he says (Plato, i. 232) that the value of Socrates for the history of philosophy lies more in his contrast with the Sophists than in his general resemblance to them. Sophistry differed from the wisdom of Socrates only in the want of a fruit-bearing germ. But how is this admission consistent with making the second period of philosophy commence with the Sophists instead of with Socrates? On the other hand, a late treatise on the question before us (*Siebeck*, Untersuchung zur Philos. d. Griech. p. 1, Ueber Socr. Verhältniss zur Sophistik) shares the opinion here expressed; and likewise most of the later edi-

tors of the history of Greek philosophy. To the same effect writes *Strümpell* (Gesch. d. Pralit. Phil. d. Griech. p. 26), although his view of the Sophists differs from ours in that he denies a connection between their scepticism and their ethics. He regards as the distinctive peculiarity of Socrates the desire to reform ethics by a thorough and methodical intellectual treatment, whereas the Sophists aspiring indeed to be teachers of virtue, accommodated themselves in their instruction to the tendencies and notions of the time.

CHAPTER X.

THE DEATH OF SOCRATES.

CHAP. X.

A. *Details of the accusation, his defence, sentence, and death.*

(1) *The accusation.*

We are now at last in a position to pass a correct judgment on the circumstances which led to the tragic end of Socrates. The actual course of events is well known. A whole lifetime had been spent by Socrates in activity at Athens, during which he had been often attacked,[1] but never judicially impeached,[2] when in the year 399 B.C.,[3] an accusation was preferred against him charging him with falling away from the religion of his country, with introducing new Gods, and with exercising a harmful influence on youth.[4] The chief accuser[5] was Meletus,[6] with

[1] Compare besides the Clouds of Aristophanes, *Xen.* Mem. i. 2, 31; iv. 4, 3; *Plato*, Apol. 32, C.; 22, E.

[2] *Plato*, Apol. 17, D.

[3] See p. 54, 1.

[4] The indictment according to Favorinus in *Diog.* ii. 40, *Xen.* Mem. (Begin.), *Plato*, Apol. 24, B., was: τάδε ἐγράψατο καὶ ἀντωμόσατο Μέλητος Μελήτου Πιτθεὺς Σωκράτει Σωφρονίσκου Ἀλωπεκῆθεν· ἀδικεῖ Σωκράτης, οὓς μὲν ἡ πόλις νομίζει θεοὺς οὐ νομίζων, ἕτερα δὲ καινὰ δαιμόνια εἰσηγήμενος· ἀδικεῖ δὲ καὶ τοὺς νέους διαφθείρων· τίμημα θάνατος. It is clearly an oversight on the part of *Grote*, Plato i. 283, to consider the parody of the indictment which Socrates puts into the mouth of his first accusers as another version of the judicial γραφή.

[5] See *Plato*, Apol. 19, B.; 24, B.; 28, A.; Euthyphro, 2, B. *Max.* Tyr. ix. 2, proves nothing against this, as *Hermann* has shown, De Socratis Accusatoribus.

[6] For the way in which this name is written, instead of Μέλιτος, as was formerly the custom, see Hermann. It ap-

whom were associated Anytus, one of the leaders and abettors of the Athenian democracy,[1] and Lyco,[2] an orator otherwise unknown. The friends of Socrates appear at first to have considered his condemnation impossible;[3] still he was himself under no misap-

pears by a comparison of various passages, that the accuser of Socrates is neither the politician as Forchhammer supposes, nor the opponent of Andocides, with whom others have identified him, nor yet the poet mentioned by Aristophanes (Frogs, 1302), but some younger man, perhaps the son of the poet.

[1] Further particulars about him are given by *Forchhammer*, 79; and *Hermann*, 9. They are gathered from *Plato*, Meno, 90, A.; Schol. in Plat. Apol. 18, B.; *Lysias* adv. Dard. 8; adv. Agorat. 78; *Isoc.* adv. Callim, 23; *Plut.* Herod. malign. 26, 6, p. 862; Coriol. c. 14; Aristotle in *Harpokrates* v. δεκάζων; Schol. in Æschin. adv. Tim. § 87; *Diod.* xiii. 64. He is mentioned by *Xenoph.* Hell. ii. 3, 42, 44, as well as by *Isocrates*, l. c., as a leader of the Democratic party, together with Thrasybulus.

[2] For the various conjectures about him consult *Hermann*, p. 12. Besides the above-named persons a certain Polyeuctus, according to Favorinus in *Diog.* ii. 38, took part in assisting the accuser. Probably Ἄνυτος ought to be written in this passage instead of Πολύευκτος, and in the following passage Πολύευκτος instead of Ἄνυτος, Πολύευκτος being here probably a transcriber's mistake for Πολυκράτης. See *Hermann*, p. 14. The words as they stand must be incorrect. The celebrated orator Polycrates is said to have composed the speech of Anytus, *Diog.* l. c. according to Hermippus; *Themist.* Or. xxiii. 296, 6; *Quintil.* ii. 17, 4; Hypoth. in Isoc. Busir.; *Æsch.* Socrat. Epist. 14, p. 84 Or.; *Suidas*, Πολυκράτης, knows of two speeches; and it is proved beyond doubt by *Isocr.* Bus. 4; *Ælian*, V. H. xi. 10, that he drew up an indictment against Socrates. But it is also clear from Favorinus, that this indictment was not used at the trial. Indeed it would appear from Favorinus that it was not written till some time after the death of Socrates. Conf. *Ueberweg*, Gesch. d. Phil. i. 94.

[3] This is proved by the Euthyphro, allowing, as *Schleiermacher*, Pl. Werke, i. a, 52, and *Steinhart*, Plato's Werke, ii. 191 and 199 do., that this dialogue was hastily penned after the beginning of the trial, its object being to prove that Socrates, though accused of impiety, had a deeper piety and a keener appreciation of the nature of piety, than one who had incurred ridicule by his extravagances, but had nevertheless brought himself into the odour

CHAP. X.

prehension as to the impending danger.[1] To get up a defence, however, went contrary to his nature.[2] Partly considering it wrong and undignified to attempt anything except by simple truth; partly finding it impossible to move out of his accustomed groove, and to wear a form of artificial oratory strange to his nature, he thought trustfully to leave the issue in the hands of God, convinced that all would turn out for the best; and in this conviction getting more familiar with the thought that death would probably bring him more good than harm, and that an unjust condemnation would only save him the pressure of the weakness of age, leaving his fair name unsullied.[3]

of sanctity; a view which, notwithstanding Ueberweg's (Unters. d. Platon. Schrift, 250) and Grote's (Plato i. 316) objections, appears most probable. The treatment of the question is too light and satirical for the dialogue to belong to a time when the full seriousness of his position was felt.

[1] Comp. *Xen.* Mem. iv. 8, 6; *Plato*, Apol. 19, A.; 24, A.; 28, A.; 36, A.

[2] In *Xen.* Mem. iv. 8, 5, Socrates says that when he wished to think about his defence, the δαιμόνιον opposed him; and according to *Diog.* ii. 40; *Cic.* de Orat. i. 54; *Quintil.* Inst. ii. 15, 30; xi. 1, 11; *Val. Max.* vi. 4, 2; *Stob.* Floril. 7, 56, he declined a speech which Lysias offered him. It is asserted by *Plato*, Apol. 17, B., that he spoke without preparation. The story in Xenophon's Apology, 22, to the effect that some of his friends spoke for him, has as little claim to truth in face of Plato's description as that in *Diog.* ii. 41.

[3] As to the motives of Socrates, the above seems to follow with certainty from passages in *Plato*, Apol. 17, B.; 19, A.; 29, A.; 30, C; 34, C., and *Xen.* Mem. iv. 8, 4–10. Cousin and Grote, however, give him credit for a great deal more calculation than can be reconciled with the testimony of history or with the rest of his character. Cousin (Œuvres de Platon, i. 58) seems to think that Socrates was aware that he must perish in the conflict with his age, but he forgets that the explanation given in *Plato's* Apology, 29, B., is only a conditional one, and that the passage in that treatise 37, C., was written after the judicial

CHAP. X.

(2) *Socrates' defence of himself.*

Such was the tone of mind which dictated his defence.[1] The language is not that of a criminal,

sentence. Similarly *Volquardsen* (Dämon. d. Sokr. 15), in attempting to prove from Mem. iv. 4, 4; Apol. 19, A., that Socrates had predicted his condemnation, forgets that in these passages the question is only as to probable guesses. Even Grote goes too far in asserting, in his excellent description of the trial (Hist. of Greece, viii. 654), that Socrates was hardly anxious to be acquitted, and that his speech was addressed far more to posterity than to his judges. History only warrants the belief, that with magnanimous devotion to a cause Socrates was indifferent to the result of his words, and endeavoured from the first to reconcile himself to a probably unfavourable result. It does not, however, follow that he was anxious to be condemned; nor have we reason to suppose so, since he could have wished for nothing which he considered to be wrong. and his modesty kept him uncertain as to what was the best for himself See *Plato*, Apol. 19, A.; 29, A.; 30, D.; 35, D. We cannot, therefore, believe with Grote, p. 668, that Socrates had well considered his line of defence, and chosen it with a full consciousness of the result; that in his conduct before the court he was actuated only by a wish to display his personal greatness and the greatness of his mission in the most emphatic manner; and that by departing this life when at the summit of his greatness he desired to give a lesson to youth the most impressive which it was in the power of man to give. To presuppose such calculation on the part of Socrates is not only contradictory to the statement that he delivered his defence without preparation, but it appears to be opposed to the picture which we are accustomed to see of his character. As far as we can judge, his conduct does not appear to be the outcome of calculation, but the outcome of spontaneous conviction, a consequence of that uprightness of character which would not allow him to go one step beyond his principles. His principles, however, did not allow him to consider results, since he could not know what result would be beneficial to him. It was his concern to speak only the truth, and to despise anything like corrupting the judges by eloquence. This may appear a narrow-minded view, but no other course of conduct would so well have corresponded with the bearing and character of Socrates; and herein consists his greatness, that he chose what was in harmony with himself in the face of extreme danger, with classic composure and brow unruffled.

[1] We possess two accounts of the speech of Socrates before his judges, a shorter one in Xenophon and a longer one in Plato's Apology. Xenophon's

CHAP. X.

wishing to save his life, but that of an impartial arbiter, who would dispel erroneous notions by a

Apology is certainly spurious, and with it disappears any value attaching to the testimony of Hermogenes, to whom the compiler, imitating the Mem. iv. 8, 4, professes to owe his information. Touching Plato's, the current view seems well established, that this Apology is not a mere creation of his own, but that in all substantial points it faithfully records what Socrates said; and the attempt of Georgii, in the introduction to his translation of the Apology (conf. *Steinhart*, Platon. Werke, ii. 235) to prove the contrary will not hold water. Georgii complains that in the Socrates of Plato that μεγαληγορία is wanting which Xenophon commends in him—a judgment with which few will agree, not even the writer of the Apology attributed to Xenophon. He also considers the sophism with which the charge of atheism was met improbable in the mouth of Socrates, though it may just as likely have come from him as from one of his disciples. He doubts whether Socrates could have maintained a composure so perfect; although all that we know of Socrates shows unruffled calm as a main trait in his character. He sees in the prominent features of that character a diplomatic calculation, which others will look for in vain. He considers it incredible that Socrates should have begun with a studied quotation from the Clouds of Aristophanes, aiming at nothing else than the refutation of prejudices, which lasted undeniably (according to the testimony of *Xenophon*, Mem. i. 1, 11; Œc. 12, 3; Symp. 6, 6) till after his own death, and perhaps contributed much to his condemnation. He misses, with Steinhart, many things in Plato, which Socrates might have said in his defence, and did actually say according to the Apology of Xenophon. This statement again is valueless, and it is probable that in an unprepared speech Socrates omitted much which might have told in his favour. He can hardly believe that Socrates cross-questioned Miletus so searchingly as Plato describes. Such cross-questioning agrees with the usual character of the discourse of Socrates, and the sophism by which Socrates proved that he did not corrupt youth is quite his own. See p. 142. That Socrates should have met the charge of atheism by quibbles, instead of appealing to the fact of his reverence for the Gods of the state, he can only understand, by supposing that we have here an expression of Plato's religious views: although Plato would have had no reason for suppressing the fact, supposing Socrates had really made such an appeal: he even describes the devotion of his master to the Gods of his country, and is himself anxious to continue that service. Touching the simple setting forth of the truth, or of a patriot warning against wrong-doing and overhaste. He seeks to convince the accuser of his ignorance, to refute the accusation by criticism. At the same time dignity and principle are never so far forgotten as to address the judges in terms of entreaty. Their sentence is not feared, whatever it may be. He stands in the service of God, and is determined to keep his post in the face of every danger. No commands shall make him faithless to his higher calling, or prevent him from obeying God rather than the Athenians.

(3) *His condemnation.*

The result of his speech was what might have been expected. The majority of the judges would most unmistakeably have been disposed to pronounce him not guilty,[1] had not the proud bearing of the accused brought him into collision with the members of a popular tribunal, accustomed to a very different deportment from the most eminent statesmen.[2] Many who would otherwise have been

sophisms, even *Aristotle*, Rhet. ii. 23; iii. 18; 1398, a, 15; 1419, a, 8, has no fault to find. The rest of the reasoning of Georgii is of the same kind. The difference in style between the Apology and Plato's usual writings, would rather seem to prove that the Apology was not drawn up with his usual artistic freedom. Georgii's notion referring it to the same time as the Phædo appears altogether inconceivable considering the great difference between the two in regard to their philosophical contents and their artistic form. It certainly was not Plato's intention to record literally the words of Socrates, and we may be satisfied by comparing his Apology with the speeches in Thucydides, as Steinhart does, bearing in mind what Thucydides, i. 22, says of himself,—that he had kept as close as possible to the sense and substance of what was said — and applying it equally to Plato. Conf. *Ueberweg*, Unters. d. Plat. Schr. 237.

[1] *Xen.* Mem. iv. 4, 4.

[2] Let the attitude of Pericles be remembered on the occasion

CHAP. X.

on his side were set against him, and by a small majority[1] a verdict of Guilty was brought in.[2] Ac-

of the accusation of Aspasia, and that depicted by Plato in the Apology, 34, C. It is a well-known fact that sitting in judgment was a special hobby of the Athenian people (conf. Aristophanes in the Wasps, Clouds, 207), and that they were peculiarly jealous of this attribute of sovereignty. How *Volquardsen*, Dämon. d. Sokr. 15, can conclude from the above words that Hegel's judgment respecting Socrates' rebellion against the people's power is shared here, is inconceivable.

[1] According to *Plato*, Apol. 36, A., he would have been acquitted if three, or as another reading has it, if thirty of his judges had been of a different mind. But how can this be reconciled with the statement of *Diog.* ii. 41: κατεδικάσθη διακοσίαις ὀγδοήκοντα μιᾷ πλείοσι ψήφοις τῶν ἀπολυουσῶν? Either the text here must be corrupt, or a true statement of Diogenes must have been strangely perverted. Which is really the case it is difficult to say. It is generally believed that the whole number of judges who condemned him was 281. But since the Heliæa always consisted of so many hundreds, most probably with the addition of one deciding voice (400, 500, 600, or 401, 501, 601), on this hypothesis no proportion of votes can be made out which is compatible with Plato's assertion; whichever reading is adopted. We should have then to suppose with Böck, in *Süvern* on Aristoph. Clouds, 87, that a number of the judges had abstained from voting, a course which may be possible. Out of 600 Heliasts, 281 may have voted against and 275 or 276 for him. It is, however, possible, as Böck suggests, that in Diogenes, 251 may have been the original reading instead of 281. In this case there might have been 251 against and 245 or 246 for the accused, making together nearly 500; and some few, supposing the board to have been complete at first, may have absented themselves during the proceedings, or have refrained from voting. Or, if the reading τριάκοντα, which has many of the best MSS. in its favour, is established in Plato, we may suppose that the original text in Diogenes was as follows: κατεδικάσθη διακοσίαις ὀγδοήκοντα ψήφοις, ξʹ πλείοσι τῶν ἀπολυουσῶν. We should then have 280 against 220, together 500, and if 30 more had declared for the accused, he would have been acquitted, the votes being equal.

[2] This course of events is not only in itself probable, taking into account the character of the speech of Socrates and the nature of the circumstances, but Xenophon (Mem. iv. 4, 4) distinctly asserts that he would certainly have been acquitted if he had in any way condescended to the usual attitude of deference to his judges. See also *Plato*, Apol. 38, D.

cording to the Athenian mode of procedure, the next thing was to treat of the amount of the penalty. Socrates spoke out here with undaunted courage: were he to move for what he had deserved, he could only move for a public entertainment in the Prytaneum. He repeated the assurance that he could not on any account renounce his previous course of life. At length, yielding to the entreaties of his friends, he was willing to consent to a fine of thirty minæ, because he could pay this without owning himself to be guilty.[1] It may be readily understood that to the majority of the judges such language in the accused could only appear in the light of incorrigible obstinacy and contempt for the judicial office;[2] hence the penalty claimed by the accusers was awarded—a sentence of death.[3]

(4) *His death.*

The sentence was received by Socrates with a composure corresponding with his previous conduct. Not in any way repenting of his conduct, he frequently expressed before the judges his conviction that for him death would be no misfortune.[4] The execution of the sentence being delayed pending the

[1] The above is stated on the authority of Plato's Apology, against which the less accurate assertion of Xenophon, that he rejected any pecuniary composition, and that of *Diog.* ii. 41, cannot be allowed to weigh.

[2] How distinctly Socrates foresaw this effect of his conduct is unknown. It may have appeared probable to him; but he may also have anticipated all the more readily a contrary effect, if he thought such conduct imperative. Nietzsche's idea (Sokrates Bas. 1871, p. 17) that Socrates, with full consciousness, carried through his condemnation to death, appears untenable for the same reasons as the above.

[3] According to *Diog.* ii. 42, it was carried by eighty more votes than his condemnation.

[4] *Plato*, Apol. 38, C.

CHAP. X.

return of the sacred-ship from Delos,[1] he continued in prison thirty days, holding his accustomed intercourse with his friends, and retaining during the whole period his unclouded brightness of disposition.[2] Flight from prison, for which his friends had made every preparation, was scorned as wrong and undignified.[3] His last day was spent in quiet intellectual conversation, and when the evening came the hemlock draught was drunk with a strength of mind so unshaken, and a resignation so entire, that a feeling of wonder and admiration overcame the feeling of grief, even in his nearest relatives.[4] Among the Athenians, too, no long time after his death, discontent with the troublesome preacher of morals is said to have given way to remorse, in consequence of which his accusers were visited with severe penalties;[5] these statements, however, are

[1] Mem. iv. 8, 2; *Plato*, Phædo, 58, A.

[2] Phædo, 59, D.; Mem. l. c.

[3] See p. 77, 1. According to *Plato*, Crito urged him to flight. The Epicurean Idomeneus, who says it was Æschines (*Diog.* ii. 60; iii. 36) is not a trustworthy authority.

[4] Compare the Phædo, the account in which appears to be true in the main. See 58, E.; 116, A.; *Xen.* Mem. iv. 8, 2. Whether the statements in *Xen.* Apol. 28; *Diog.* ii. 35; *Ælian*, V. H. i. 16 are historical, is a moot point. Those in *Stob.* Floril. 5, 67 are certainly exaggerations.

[5] *Diodor.* xiv. 37 says that the people repented of having put Socrates to death, and attacked his accusers, putting them to death without a judicial sentence. *Suidas* makes Μέλητος (Meletus) die by stoning. *Plut.* de Invid. c. 6, p. 538 says that the slanderous accusers of Socrates became so hated at Athens that the citizens would not light their fires, or answer their questions, or bathe in the same water with them, and that at last they were driven in despair to hang themselves. *Diog.* ii 43, conf. vi. 9 says that the Athenians soon after, overcome with compunction, condemned Meletus to death, banished the other accusers, and erected a brazen statue to Socrates, and that

not to be trusted, and appear on the whole improbable.[1]

CHAP. X.

B. *The cause of this sentence of condemnation.*

(1) *It was not the work of the Sophists.*

The circumstances which brought about the death of Socrates are among the clearest facts of history. Nevertheless the greatest difference of opinion prevails as to the causes which led thereto and the justice of his condemnation. In former

Anytus was forbidden to set foot in their city. *Themist.* Or. xx. 239, says: The Athenians soon repented of this deed; Meletus was punished, Anytus fled, and was stoned at Heraclea, where his grave may be seen to this day. *Tertullian*, Apologet. 14, states that the Athenians punished the accusers of Socrates, and erected to him a golden statue in a temple. *Aug.* De Civ. Dei, viii. 3 reports that one of the accusers was slain by the people and the other banished for life.

[1] This view, already expressed by Forchhammer (l. c. 66) and Grote, viii. 683, appears to be the correct one notwithstanding Hermann's (l. c. 8, 11) arguments to the contrary. For though it is possible that political or personal opponents of Anytus and his fellow accusers may have turned against them the part they took against Socrates, and so procured their condemnation, yet (1) The authorities are by no means so ancient or so unimpeachable that we can trust them. (2) They contradict one another in all their details, not to mention Diogenes' anachronism respecting Lysippus. And (3) the main point is that neither Plato, nor Xenophon, nor the writer of Xenophon's Apology ever mention this occurrence, which they could not have failed to regard with great satisfaction. On the contrary, five years after the death of Socrates Xenophon thought it necessary to defend him against the attacks of his accusers, while Æschines appealed to the sentence on Socrates without dreading the very obvious retort, that his accusers had met with their deserts. That Isocrates is referring to this occurrence rather than to any other (περὶ ἀντιδόσ. 19) is not clear, nor need the passage contain a reference to any event in particular. Lastly, no value can be attached to the apocryphal story coming from some editor of Isocrates, that the Athenians, ashamed of having put Socrates to death, forbad any public mention of him, and that when Euripides (who died seven years before Socrates) alluded to him in the Palamedes, all the audience burst into tears. It is only lost labour to suggest that these scenes took place at some later time, when the play was being performed.

CHAP. X.

times it was thought most reasonable to attribute it to an accidental outburst of passion. Were Socrates the cold ideal of virtue he is represented to have been by those lacking a deeper insight into his position in history, it would indeed be inconceivable that any vested interests could have been sufficiently injured by him to warrant a serious attack. If he was nevertheless accused and condemned, what else can have been the cause but the lowest of motives —personal hatred? Who can have had so much reason for hatred as the Sophists, whose schemes Socrates was so effective in thwarting, and who were otherwise supposed to be capable of any crime? It must have been at their instigation that Anytus and Meletus induced Aristophanes to write his play of the Clouds, and afterwards themselves brought Socrates to trial.

This was the general view of the learned in former times.[1] Nevertheless its erroneousness was already pointed out by Fréret.[2] He proved that Meletus was a child when the Clouds was acted, and that at a much later period Anytus was on good terms with Socrates; that neither Anytus can have had anything to do with the Sophists—Plato always representing him as their inveterate enemy and despiser[3]—nor Meletus with Aristophanes;[4] and he

[1] Reference to *Brucker*, i. 549, in preference to any others.

[2] In the admirable treatise: Observations sur les Causes et sur quelques Circonstances de la Condamnation de Socrate, in the Mém. de l'Académie des Inscript. i. 47, 6, 209.

[3] Meno, 92, A.

[4] Aristophanes often amuses himself at the expense of the

showed, that no writer of credit knows anything of the part taken by the Sophists in the accusation of Socrates.[1] Besides, the Sophists, having little or no political influence in Athens,[2] could never have procured the condemnation of Socrates. Least of all would they have preferred against him charges which immediately recoiled on their own heads.[3] These arguments of Fréret's, after long passing unnoticed,[4] have latterly met with general reception.[5] Opinions are otherwise still much divided, and it is an open question whether the condemnation of Socrates was a work of private revenge, or whether it resulted from more general motives; if the latter, whether these motives were political, or moral, or religious; and lastly, whether the sentence was, according to the popular view, a crying wrong, or whether it may

poet Meletus, but, as has been remarked, this Meletus was probably an older man than the accuser of Socrates. See *Hermann*, De Socr. Accus. 5.

[1] *Ælian* (V. H. ii. 13), the chief authority for the previous hypothesis, knows nothing about a suborning of Anytus by the Sophists.

[2] The political career of Damon, who according to the use of the Greek language can be called a Sophist, establishes nothing to the contrary.

[3] Protagoras had been indicted for atheism before Socrates, and on the same plea Socrates was attacked by Aristophanes, who never spared any partisans of sophistry.

[4] The treatise of Fréret was written as early as 1786, but not published till 1809, when it appeared together with several other of his writings. See Mém. de l'Acad. i. 47, 6, 1. It was therefore unknown to the German writers of the last century, who for the most part follow the old view; for instance, *Meiners*, Gesch. d. Wissenschaft, ii. 476; *Tiedemann*, Geist. d. spek. Phil. ii. 21. Others, such as *Buhle*, Gesch. d. Phil. i. 372; *Tenneman*, Gesch. d. Phil. ii. 40, confine themselves to stating generally that Socrates made many enemies by his zeal for morality, without mentioning the Sophists.

[5] There are a few exceptions, such as *Heinsius*, p. 26.

CHAP. X.

admit of partial justification. One writer[1] has even gone the length of asserting with Cato,[2] that of all sentences ever passed, this was the most strictly legal.

(2) *It did not proceed from personal animosity.*

(*a*) *Anytus may have borne him a grudge.*

Among these views the one lying nearest to hand is that of the older writers, which attributes the execution of Socrates to personal animosity; always giving up the unfounded notion that the Sophists had in any way to do with it.[3] A great deal may be said in favour of this aspect of the case. In Plato,[4] Socrates expressly declares that he is not the victim of Anytus or Meletus, but of the ill-will which he incurred by his criticism of men. Even Anytus, it is said, owed him a personal grudge. Plato hints[5] at his being aggrieved with the judg-

[1] *Forchhammer*: Die Athener und Socrates, die Gesetzlichen und der Revolutionär.

[2] *Plut.* Cato, c. 23.

[3] This is found in *Fries*, Gesch. d. Phil. i. 249, who speaks of the 'hatred and envy of a great portion of the people,' as the motives which brought on the trial. *Sigwart*, Gesch. d. Phil. i. 89, gives prominence to this motive, and *Brandis*, Gr.-Röm. Phil. ii. 1, 26, who distinguishes two kinds of opponents to Socrates, those who considered his philosophy incompatible with ancient discipline and morality, and those who could not endure his moral earnestness, attributing the accusation to the latter. *Grote*, viii. 637 inclines to the same view. He proves how unpopular Socrates must have made himself by his sifting of men. He remarks that Athens was the only place where it would have been possible to carry it on so long, and that it is by no means a matter for wonder that Socrates was accused and condemned, but only that this did not happen sooner. If he had been tolerated so long, there must have been special reasons, however, for the accusation; and these he is inclined to find partly in his relations to Critias and Alcibiades, and partly in the hatred of Anytus.

[4] Apol. 28, A.; 22, E.; 23, C.

[5] Meno, 94; in reference to which Diog. ii. 38 says of Anytus: οὗτος γὰρ οὐ φέρων τὸν ὑπὸ Σωκράτους χλευασμόν.

CHAP. X.

ments passed by Socrates on Athenian statesmen, and, according to Xenophon's Apology,[1] took it amiss that Socrates advised him to bring up his son, a promising youth, to a higher business than that of a dealer in leather, thereby encouraging in the young man discontent with his trade.[2] Anytus is said to have first instigated Aristophanes to write his comedy, and afterwards in common with Meletus to have brought against Socrates the formal accusation.[3] That such motives came into play in the attack on Socrates, and contributed in no small degree to the success of this attack is antecedently probable.[4] To convince men of their ignorance is the most thankless task you can choose. Anyone who can persevere in it for a lifetime so regardless of consequences as Socrates, must make many enemies; dangerous enemies too, if he takes for his mark men of distinguished position or talents.

(b) But there must have been other causes at work to lead to his condemnation.

For all that personal animosity cannot have been the sole cause of his condemnation. Plato's statements cannot pass without gainsaying. Indeed, the more Socrates and his pupils became convinced of the justice of his cause, the less were they able

[1] Compare with this *Hegel*, Gesch. d. Phil. ii. 92; *Grote*, Hist. of Greece, viii. 641.

[2] Later writers give more details. According to *Plut.* Alc. c. 4; Amator. 17, 27, p. 762; and Satyrus in *Athenæus*, xii. 534, e, Anytus was a lover of Alcibiades, but was rejected by him, whilst Alcibiades showed every attention to Socrates, and hence the enmity of Anytus to Socrates. Such an improbable story ought not to have deceived *Luzac* (De Socr. Cive, 133); especially since Xenophon and Plato would never have passed over in silence such a reason for the accusation.

[3] *Ælian*, V. H. ii. 13. *Diog.* l. c.

[4] Compare *Grote*, l. c. 638.

CHAP. X.

to discover any grounds in fact for the accusation. The one wish of Socrates being to will and to do what was best, what reason could anyone possibly have had for opposing him, except wounded pride? The story as told in Xenophon's Apology would at most only explain the hatred of Anytus; it would not account for the widely spread prejudice against Socrates. Whether it is true at all is a question; and whether, granting its truth, personal injury was the only cause which arrayed Anytus as accuser against him.[1] Allowing, what was undoubtedly a fact, that Socrates made enemies of many influential people, is it not strange that their personal animosity should only have attained its object after the re-establishment of order in Athens? In the most unsettled and corrupt times no serious persecution had been set on foot against him. At the time of the mutilation of the Hermæ, neither his relations with Alcibiades, nor after the battle of Arginusæ[2] the incensed state of popular feeling, had been used against him. Plato, too, says[3] that what told against Socrates at the trial, was the general conviction that his teaching was of a dangerous cha-

[1] This is just possible. That the character of Anytus was not unimpeachable we gather from the story (Aristot. in *Harpokration* δεκάζων; *Diodor*. xiii. 64; *Plut*. Coriol. 14), that when he was first charged with treason he corrupted the judges. On the other hand, *Isocr*. (in Callim. 23) praises him for being together with Thrasybulus faithful to the treaties, and not abusing his political power to make amends for his losses during the oligarchical government.

[2] The astonishment expressed by Tenneman at this is natural from his point of view. Only his solution of the difficulty is hardly satisfactory.

[3] Apol. 18, B.; 19, B.; 23, D.

racter; and he states that, as matters then stood, it was impossible for any one to speak the truth in political matters without being persecuted as a vain babbler and corrupter of youth.[1] On this point the testimony of writers so opposite as Xenophon and Aristophanes proves that the prejudice against Socrates was not merely a passing prejudice, at least not in Athens, but that it lasted a whole life-time, not confined to the masses only, but shared also by men of high importance and influence in the state. Very deeply, indeed, must the feeling against Socrates have been rooted in Athens, if Xenophon found it necessary six years after his death to defend him against the charges on which the indictment was framed.

With regard to Aristophanes, it was an obvious blot in his plays to allow here and there such a prominence to political motives as to forget the claims of art, and for a comedian who in his mad way holds up to ridicule all authorities divine and human, to clothe himself with the tragic seriousness of a political prophet.[2] Yet it is no less an error to lose sight of the serious vein which underlies the comic license of his plays, and to mistake his occasional pathos for thoughtless by-play. Were this all, the

[1] Polit. 299, B.; Rep. vi. 488. 496, C.; Apol. 32, E.; Gorg. 473, E.; 521, D.

[2] Rötscher's spirited description suffers from this one-sidedness, and even Hegel, in his passage on the fate of Socrates, Gesch. d. Phil. ii. 82, is not quite free from it, although both of them justly recognise (*Hegel*, Phänomenol. 560; Æsthetik, 537, 562; *Rötscher*, p. 365), that there is an element subversive of Greek life, quite as much in the comedies of Aristophanes as in the state of things of which he complains.

hollowness of the sentiment would soon show itself in artistic defects. Instead whereof, a sincerely patriotic sentiment may be observed in Aristophanes, not only in the unsullied beauty of many individual passages;[1] but the same patriotic interest is the keynote sounding through all his plays, in some of the earlier ones even disturbing the harmony of the poetic chord,[2] but showing most conclusively how near to his heart lay the love of his country.

It was this patriotism which led him to give to his comedies that political turn, by means of which, as he justly takes credit to himself,[3] comedy gained a far higher ground than had been allowed to it by his predecessors. At the same time it must be granted that Aristophanes is as much deficient as others in the morality and the faith of an earlier age;[4] men and circumstances having so thoroughly changed, it was preposterous to try to recall the olden time. Only it does not follow herefrom that he was not sincere in the attempt. His was one of those cases so frequently met with in history, in which a man attacks a principle in others to which he has himself fallen a victim, without being aware of it. Aristophanes combats innovations in morals, politics, religion, and art. Being, however, in his inmost soul the offspring of his age, he can only

[1] See p. 30.

[2] Compare *Schnitzer*, translation of the Clouds, p. 24, and the passages quoted by him from Welcker, Süvern and Rötscher.

[3] Peace, 732; Wasps, 1022; Clouds, 537.

[4] Compare *Droysen*, Aristoph. Werke, 2 Aufl. i. 174, which seems to go too far.

combat them with the weapons and in the spirit of this age. With the thorough dislike of a narrow practical man unable to grasp anything new or going beyond the needs of to-day, he proscribes every attempt to analyse moral and political motives, or to test their reasonableness or the reverse. As a poet he thinks nothing of trifling with truth and good manners, provided the desired end is reached. He thus becomes entangled in an inconsistency, at once recalling, and by one and the same act destroying, the old morality. That he was guilty of this inconsistency cannot be denied.—And how short-sighted it was to attempt to charm back a form of culture which had been irretrievably lost!—That he was conscious of it cannot be believed. Hardly would a thoughtless scoffer—which is what some would make of him—have ventured upon the dangerous path of attacking Cleon. Hardly would Plato have brought him into the society of Socrates in the Symposium, putting into his mouth words full of spirited humour, had he seen in him only a despicable character. If, however, Aristophanes was in earnest in attacking Socrates, and really thought him a Sophist dangerous alike to religion and morality—with which character he clothes him in the Clouds—then the charges preferred at the trial were not merely trumped-up charges, and motives other than personal motives led to the condemnation of Socrates.

If we ask what those motives were, all that is known of the trial and the personal character of the

CHAP. X.

(3) *Political feeling only partially the cause.*

accusers leaves us a choice between two alternatives only: Either the attack on Socrates was directed against his political creed [1] in particular, or generally against his whole habit of thought and teaching in respect to morals, religion, and politics.[2] Both alternatives are somewhat alike; not so alike, however, that we can dispense with distinguishing them.

Much may be said in favour of the view that the attack on Socrates was in the first place set on foot in the interest of the democratic party. Amongst the accusers, Anytus is known as one of the leading democrats of the time.[3] The judges, too, are described as men who had been banished and had returned with Thrasybulus.[4] We know, moreover, that one of the charges brought against Socrates was, that he was the educator of Critias, the most unscrupulous and the most hated of the oligarchical party.[5] Æschines [6] tells the Athenians plainly: You have put to death the Sophist Socrates, because he was the teacher of Critias. Among the friends and pupils of Socrates others, too, are found who must

[1] This is the view of Fréret, l. c. p. 233, of *Dresig* in the dissertation De Socrate juste damnato (Lips. 1738), of *Süvern* (notes to Clouds, p. 86), of *Ritter*, Gesch. d. Phil. ii. 30, and of *Forchhammer* (Die Athener und Socrates, p. 39). More indefinite is *Hermann*, Plat. i. 35, and *Wiggers*, Socr. p. 123.

[2] *Hegel*, Gesch. d. Phil. ii. 81; *Rötscher*, p. 256, 268, with special reference to the Clouds of Aristophanes; *Henning*, Princ. der Ethik, p. 44. Compare *Baur*, Socrates und Christus, Tüb. Zeitschrift, 1837, 3, 128–144.

[3] See p. 195, 1.

[4] *Plato*, Apol. 21, A.

[5] *Xen.* Mem. i. 2, 12; *Plato*, Apol. 33, A.

[6] Adv. Tim. 173. This authority is of no great value, as the context shows. Æschines is talking as an orator, not as an historian.

have been hated by the democrats because of their aristocratic sympathies. Such were Charmides,[1] and Xenophon, who was banished from Athens[2] about the time of the trial of Socrates, perhaps in connection therewith, because of his friendship for Sparta and the Spartans' friend, the younger Cyrus. One of the formal indictments, it is stated, charges Socrates with speaking disparagingly of the democratic form of election by lot,[3] and with teaching his audience to treat the poor with insolence,[4] by so frequently quoting the words—

> Each prince of name or chief in arms approved,
> He fired with praise, or with persuasion moved.
> . . . .
> But if a clamorous vile plebeian rose,
> Him with reproof he check'd, or tamed with blows.[5]

[1] Charmides, the uncle of Plato, one of the thirty, was, according to *Xen.* Hell. ii. 4, 19, one of the ten commanders at the Peiræus, and fell on the same day with Critias in conflict with the exiled Athenians.

[2] *Forchhammer*, p. 84: he also mentions Theramenes, the supporter of the thirty tyrants, who may have been a pupil of Socrates without, as Forchhammer will have it, adopting the political opinions of his teacher. But *Diodor.* xiv. 5, from whom the story comes, is a very uncertain authority. For Diodorus combines with it the quite improbable story that Socrates tried to rescue Theramenes from the clutches of the thirty, and could only be dissuaded from this audacious attempt by many entreaties. Neither Xenophon nor Plato mentions Theramenes among the pupils of Socrates. Neither of them mentions an intervention of Socrates on his behalf, as *Plato*, Apol. 32, C, does in another case. In the accusation brought against the victors at Arginusæ, it was Socrates who espoused their cause, and Theramenes who by his intrigues brought about their condemnation. *Pseudoplut.* Vit. Dec. rhet. iv. 3, tells a similar and more credible story of Socrates. Probably it was first told of him and then transferred to Socrates.

[3] Mem. i. 2, 9.

[4] Ibid. i. 2, 58.

[5] Iliad, ii. 188. *Forchhammer*, p. 52, detects a great deal more in these verses. He

CHAP. X.

Taking all these facts into account, there can be no doubt that, in the trial of Socrates, the interests of the democratic party did come into play.

(4) His teaching generally regarded as dangerous.

These motives were not all. The indictment does not place the anti-republican sentiments of Socrates in the foreground. What it urges against him is his rejection of the Gods of his country, and his corruption of youth.[1] Those Gods were not only

thinks that Socrates was here expressing his conviction of the necessity of an oligarchical constitution, and was using the words of Hesiod ἔργον δ' οὐδὲν ὄνειδος (which the accusers also took advantage of), as a plea for not delaying, but for striking when the time for action came. The importance of the quotation from Homer lies, he contends, not in the verses quoted by Xenophon, but in those omitted (Il. ii. 192–197, 203–205): the charge was not brought against Socrates for spreading anti-democratic sentiments, which Xenophon alone mentions, but for promoting the establishment of an oligarchical form of government. This is, however, the very opposite of historical criticism. If Forchhammer relies upon the statements of Xenophon, how can he at the same time assert that they are false in most important points? And if on the other hand he wishes to strengthen these statements, how can he use them to uphold the view by which he condemns them? He has, however, detected oligarchical tendencies elsewhere, where no traces of them exist. For instance, he enumerates not only Critias but Alcibiades among the anti-democratical pupils of Socrates; and he speaks of the political activity of Socrates after the battle of Arginusæ by remarking that the oligarchs elected on the council board their brethren in political sentiments. It is true the levity of Alcibiades made him dangerous to the democratic party, but in his own time he never passed for an oligarch, but for a democrat. See *Xen.* Mem. i. 2, 12; *Thuc.* viii. 63, 48 and 68. With regard to the condemnation of the victors of Arginusæ, Athens had then not only partially, as Forchhammer says, but altogether shaken off the oligarchical constitution of Pisander. This may be gathered from *Fréret's* remark, l. c. p. 243, from the account of the trial (*Xen.* Hell. i. 7), as well as from the distinct statement of *Plato* (Apol. 32, C.: καὶ ταῦτα μὲν ἦν ἔτι δημοκρατουμένης τῆς πόλεως); not to mention the fact that these generals were decided democrats, and hence could not have been elected by oligarchs.

[1] *Plato*, Apol. 24, B. p. 194, 4.

the Gods of the republican party, but the Gods of Athens. If in some few instances, as in the trial for the mutilation of the Hermæ, insult to the Gods was connected with attacks on a republican form of government, the connection was neither a necessary one, nor was it named in the indictment of Socrates. Touching the charge of corrupting youth,[1] this count was certainly supported by the plea that Socrates instilled into the young contempt for republican forms of government and aristocratic insolence, and also that he was the teacher of Critias. But the training of Alcibiades was also laid to his charge, who had injured the city by republican rather than by aristocratic opinions. A further count was, that he taught sons to despise their fathers,[2] and said that no wrong or base action need be shunned if only it were of advantage.[3]

Herefrom it would appear that the moral and religious character of his teaching was the subject of attack rather than its political character. These aspects exclusively drew down the wrath of Aristophanes. After all the ancient and modern discussions as to the scope of the Clouds,[4] it might be taken for established that the Socrates of this comedy is not a representative—drawn with a poet's license —of a mode of thought which Aristophanes knew to

[1] Mem. i. 2, 9.

[2] *Xen.* Mem. i. 2, 49; Apol. 20 and 29.

[3] Mem. i. 2, 56.

[4] *Rötscher* (Aristophanes, p. 272) gives a review of previous opinions. Since then, Droysen and Schnitzer, Forchhammer, p. 25, and Köchly, Akad. Vortr. 1, have further gone into the question.

CHAP. X.

be foreign to the real man;[1] nor was it his intention only to attack the fondness for metaphysical subtleties, and the absurdity of sophistry and useless learning in general; but the play was distinctly aimed at the philosophic tendency of Socrates. There is no reason for supposing, after what has been said, that this attack proceeded only from malice or from personal animosity; Plato's description in the Symposium puts this out of the question. Reisig's[2] and Wolf's[3] opinions are also untenable. Reisig distributes the traits which Aristophanes assigns to Socrates between himself and the whole body of his pupils, including Euripides[4] more particularly. The spectators would refer them all to Socrates; hence Aristophanes must have intended this reference. Wolf supposes that the portrait drawn in the Clouds is of Socrates in his younger years, when he was given to natural philosophy. But the very same charges were repeated against him eighteen years later in the Frogs;[5] and we gather from Plato's Apology[6] that the current view of Socrates and his teaching up to the time of his death agreed substantially with that of Aristophanes; not to mention the fact that Socrates probably never was a student of

[1] As is assumed by *G. Hermann*, Præf. ad Nubes, p. 33, 11, and by others. Compare, on the other hand, *Rötscher*, p. 294, 273, 307, 311; *Süvern*, p. 3.

[2] Præf. ad Nubes; Rhein. Mus. ii. (1828) i. K. S. 191.

[3] In his translation of the Clouds, see *Rötscher*, 297. Similarly *Van Heusde*, Characterismi, p. 19, 24. Conf. *Wiggers*' Sokr. p. 20.

[4] Who was ten years older than Socrates, and certainly not his pupil, although possibly an acquaintance.

[5] Frogs, 1491.

[6] See p. 18.

natural philosophy, and that in the Clouds he is attacked as a Sophist[1] rather than as a natural philosopher.

Aristophanes must, then, really have thought to discern in the Socrates whom the history of philosophy sketches features deserving attack. Saying this, however, is, of course, not saying that he did not caricature the historical figure, conseiously attributing to it many really foreign features. For all that, we may suppose that the main features in his picture agreed with the idea he had formed to himself of Socrates, and also with common opinion. Süvern, in supposing[2] that the Socrates of the Clouds is not meant for an individual, but for a symbol, and that the poet's attack was not aimed at Socrates, but at the sophistic and rhetorical school in general,[3] cannot be right. So far is it otherwise, that Socrates was made to be the champion of sophistry, because in Aristophanes' mind he really was that. The poet believed that, taken in his public capacity, he was the dangerous innovator he was represented to be. Not a single line of his picture has an exclusively political colour. Independently of some things which are obviously not seriously meant,[4] the charges against him are threefold, his being occupied with useless physical and intellectual subtleties,[5] his re-

[1] Clouds, 98.

[2] In the treatise already referred to, pp, 19, 26, 30, 55.

[3] Not to mention the false opinion, which however is supported by *Hertzberg* (Alcibiades, p. 67), that the play was aimed at Alcibiades, who is concealed under the name of Phidippides. See, on the contrary, *Droysen*, p. 180; *Schnitzer*, p. 34.

[4] Such as the calculation of flea-jumps.

[5] 143–234, 636.

CHAP. X.

jecting the Gods of the city,[1] and, what is the corner-point of the whole play, his sophistic facility of speech, which can gain for the wrong side the victory over the right, and make the weaker argument the stronger.[2] In other words, the unpractical, irreligious, and sophistical elements in the Socratic teaching are attacked; there is not a word about his anti-republican tendency, which Aristophanes, we may suppose, would before all things have exposed had he observed. Even at a later time,[3] Aristophanes brings no other complaints against Socrates than these. Only these points, too, according to Plato, constituted the standing charges against Socrates, causing him special danger.[4] And there is every reason for believing his assurance.

If then the impeachment of Socrates has, nevertheless, been set down to political motives, how can this admission be made to agree with the previous statement? The true answer to this question has been already suggested by other writers.[5] The con-

[1] 365–410.

[2] Clouds, 889. *Droysen*, Clouds, p. 177, unfairly blames this play for making a stronger argument into a right one. The λόγος κρείττων is the really stronger case in point of justice, according to the original meaning of the word (*Xenoph.* Œc. ii. 25; *Arist.* Rhet. ii. 24), which is however thrown into the shade by the λόγος ἥττων; and what is meant by τὸν ἥττω λόγον κρείττω ποιεῖν is, making the case which in point of justice is weaker, to be the stronger as to the actual result—giving to an unjust act the colour of justice.

[3] Frogs, 1491.

[4] Apol. 23, D.: λέγουσιν, ὡς Σωκράτης τίς ἐστι μιαρώτατος καὶ διαφθείρει τοὺς νέους · καὶ ἐπειδάν τις αὐτοὺς ἐρωτᾷ, ὅ τι ποιῶν καὶ ὅ τι διδάσκων, ἔχουσι μὲν οὐδὲν εἰπεῖν, ἀλλ' ἀγνοοῦσιν, ἵνα δὲ μὴ δοκῶσιν ἀπορεῖν, τὰ κατὰ πάντων τῶν φιλοσοφούντων πρόχειρα ταῦτα λέγουσιν, ὅτι τὰ μετέωρα καὶ τὰ ὑπὸ γῆς, καὶ θεοὺς μὴ νομίζειν καὶ τὸν ἥττω λόγον κρείττω ποιεῖν. Ibid. 18, B.

[5] *Ritter*, p. 31. *Marbach*, Gesch. d. Phil. i. 185, 9; and

viction of the guilt of Socrates rested on the assumedly dangerous character of his teaching for morality and religion; the reason that this offence was judicially prosecuted lay without doubt in the special political circumstances of the time. The rationalism of the Sophists being neither the sole nor the chief cause of the fall of Athens in the Peloponnesian war nevertheless contributed unmistakeably to that result; and the opponents of the new culture were not disposed to make out its guilt to be less than it really was. For had not the schools of the Sophists sent forth not a few of the modern statesmen, who either as the leaders of oligarchy or democracy had torn the state to pieces? Was not in those schools a corrupt form of morality publicly taught, substituting the wishes and caprice of the individual in place of existing custom and religion, putting gain in the place of right, and teaching men to desire absolute sovereignty as the summit of human happiness? Were not those schools the cradle of an unscrupulous eloquence, which employed a variety of technical tricks for any purpose, no matter what, considering it the highest triumph to make the wrong side the winning side? Can we then wonder that Aristophanes thought the new-fangled education responsible for all the misfortunes of the commonwealth;[1] that Anytus in Plato cannot find terms strong enough to express his horror of the pernicious

Schwegler, Gesch. d. Phil. 30. Further details in *Süvern*,

[1] Clouds, 910; Knights, 1373. Clouds, 24.

influence of the Sophists;[1] that all friends of the good old time believed that in Sophistry lay the chief malady of the state; and that this feeling was intensified during the last years of the Peloponnesian war, and under the oligarchical reign of force? Was it then unnatural that those who had rescued Athens from the oligarchy, re-establishing with the old constitution her political independence, should wish by suppressing the education of the Sophists to stop the evil at its source? Now Socrates passed not only for a teacher of the modern Sophistic school, but the evil effects of his teaching were thought to be seen in several of his pupils, among whom Critias and Alcibiades were prominent.[2] What more intelligible under such circumstances, than that just those who were bent upon restoring a popular form of government, and the ancient glory of Athens, should see in him a corrupter of youth, and a dangerous citizen? Thus he certainly fell a victim to the republican reaction which set in after the overthrow of the thirty tyrants. For all that, his political views were not in themselves the principal motives which provoked the attack. His guilt was rather supposed to consist in the subversion of ancestral customs and piety of which the anti-republican tendency of his teaching was partly an indirect consequence, partly an isolated manifestation.

How then does it really stand touching the jus-

[1] Meno, 91, C.

[2] How largely this circumstance contributed towards the condemnation of Socrates is proved by *Xen.* Mem. i. 2, 12, as well as by the above-mentioned authority, Æschines.

CHAP. X.

C. *Justice of the sentence.*

(1) *Unfounded charges.*

(*a*) *In relation to his teaching, life, and influence.*

tice of the accusation[1] and of the sentence to which it led? And what must be thought of the modern attempts to defend it? Most of the charges which were preferred against Socrates rest undeniably on misunderstandings, perversions, or false inferences. Socrates is said to have rejected the Gods of the state. We have already seen this statement contradicted by all trustworthy authorities.[2] He is said to have substituted his δαιμόνιον in their place. We likewise know that he neither put it in the place of the Gods, nor sought thereby to encroach on the ground of oracles.[3] It was a private oracle in addition to those publicly recognised; and in a

[1] It is well known that Hegel has defended it on the side of Greek law, and Dresig, a hundred years earlier, maintained, in a very offhand treatise, that Socrates, as an opponent of a republican government, had been justly condemned. Forchhammer goes a great deal further in his treatise, and so does Dénis. See p. 179, 3. Köchly, on the other hand, confines himself, in Acad. Vortr. i. 382, to the assertion that in the indictment of Socrates guilt was equally divided and reduced to a minimum on either side. The answer of Heinsius to Forchhammer (Socrates nach dem Grade seiner Schuld. Lips. 1839) is unimportant, and the learned Apologia Socratis contra Meliti redivivi Calumniam, by P. van Limburg Brouwer (Grön. 1838), is deficient in apprehension of the general questions involved, and is inferior to the treatise of Preller (Haller, A. L. Z. 1838, No. 87), although many of its details are valuable. *Luzac.* De Socrate cive 1796, despite his usual learning, does little for the question. Grote's remarks, on the other hand, touching the extenuating circumstances, which, without altogether justifying, excuse the condemnation of Socrates, are deserving of all attention. *Grote*, Hist. of Greece, viii. 678, 653.

[2] Forchhammer repeats the charge without proof, as if its truth were obvious of itself, and he speaks of orthodoxy and heresy like a modern theologian. But a Greek thought far less of belief than of outward service, and hence *Xenophon*, Mem. i. 12, refutes the charge by an appeal to the fact that he had sacrificed to the Gods.

[3] Compare p. 77, 7; 90; 150, 1; 179.

CHAP. X.

country where divine revelations were not the exclusive property of the priesthood, a private oracle could be refused to no one.[1] He is said to have been devoted to the atheistic, higher wisdom of Anaxagoras,[2] although he expressly declared it to be absurd.[3] He is said according to Aristophanes to have given instruction in the Sophistic art of oratory—a charge so untrue, that to all appearances even Meletus did not venture to prefer it. He is blamed for having been the teacher of Critias and Alcibiades, to which charge even Xenophon justly replied[4] that these men did not learn their vices from Socrates, nor degenerate, until after being separated from him. Allowing, too, that a teacher must instil into his pupils a lasting turn for the good,[5] is it necessarily his fault if he does not succeed in some few cases? The value of any instruction can only be estimated by its collective effects, and these bear as bright a testimony to the value of the instruction of Socrates as can be wished. A man whose beneficial influence

[1] Xenophon therefore appeals to the *δαιμόνιον* (Mem. i. 1, 2) in good faith as a proof of Socrates' belief in the Gods, and Plato compares his revelations with the prophecies of Euthyphro (Euthyphro, 3, B). It is known, from other sources, that private divination was much practised, besides the appeals to public oracles.

[2] Not only Aristophanes but Meletus brings this charge against him in Plato, Apol. 26, C., p. 10, like Ast (Platon's Leben und Schriften, p. 480). If Forchhammer considers it incredible that Meletus should have given such a careless reply to Socrates, he forgets that it is always the way of the world to confound relative with positive atheism, doubts about particular religious notions with the denial of all religion. This is quite universal in the nations of antiquity, and therefore the early Christians were called ἄθεοι.

[3] See p. 136, 1.

[4] Mem. i. 2, 12.

[5] *Forchhammer*, p. 43.

not only reached to many individuals,[1] but by whom a new foundation for morals was laid which served his people for centuries, was, as a matter of course, no corrupter of youth. If, further, the verses of Hesiod, by which Socrates sought to promote useful activity, are quoted against him;[2] Xenophon has conclusively proved that an ill use has been made of these verses. If, lastly, he has been accused of teaching men to despise parents and relations, because he maintained that only knowledge constituted worth;[3] surely this is a most unfair inference from principles which had a simple meaning in his mouth. Any teacher who makes his pupil understand that he must learn something in order to become a useful and estimable man, is surely quite in order. Only the rabble can bear the teacher a grudge for making sons wiser than their fathers. Very different would it have been had Socrates spoken disparagingly of the ignorance of parents, or set lightly by the duty of children; but from so doing he was far removed.[4]

[1] *Plato's* Apol. 33, D., mentions a whole string; also *Xen.* Mem. i. 2, 48.

[2] Mem. i. 2, 56; *Plato*, Char. 163, B. Conf. p. 212, 4.

[3] Mem. i. 2, 49.

[4] Conf. Mem. ii. 2, 3. A further charge is connected with the above, viz., that he induced many young men to follow his training rather than that of their parents. This fact Xenophon's Apology allows and attempts to justify. But in order to decide whether it is an established fact, and whether Socrates is here to blame, it is indeed quite possible we need a more trustworthy authority, and we ought to know the circumstances better. In the single case there mentioned, that of the son of Anytus, the truth of which appears doubtful, Socrates probably did not set the son against his father, but urged the father to give him a better education, or else expressed himself to a third party to that effect.

CHAP. X.

It might be replied that one who judged the value of a man simply and solely by his knowledge, and who at the same time found all wanting in true knowledge, was making his pupils self-conceited, and teaching them to consider themselves above all authority by their own imaginary knowledge. But whilst with partial eye overrating the importance of knowledge, Socrates avoided this practically harmful inference by above all endeavouring to make his friends conscious of their own want of knowledge, and laying no claim to knowledge himself, but only professing to pursue it. No fear that any one imbued with this spirit of humility and modesty, would misuse the Socratic teaching. For its misconstruction and for the consequences of a superficial and defective conception of it Socrates is as little responsible as any other teacher.

(b) Charges affecting his position towards the state.

Of more moment is another point touched upon in the judicial proceedings—the relation of Socrates himself to the Athenian democracy. As is well known, Socrates considered the existing constitution a complete failure.[1] He would not have the power in the state awarded by lot or by election, but by the qualification of the individuals ; and he occasionally expressed opinions respecting the masses who thronged the Pnyx and filled the theatre at assemblies of the people containing no doubt a great deal of truth, but coming very near to treason against the sovereignty of the people.[2] It was natural that his

[1] See p. 168.

[2] In Mem. iii. 7 Socrates attempts to relieve Charmides of his dread of appearing in pub-

accusers should make use of such expressions, and that they should not be without influence on the judges. Still a free censure of existing institutions is by no means treason. Some Greek states may have confined the liberty of speech within very narrow limits, but at Athens the freedom of thought and of speech was unlimited; it formed an integral portion of the republican constitution; the Athenian regarded it as an inalienable right and was proud to be herein distinguished from every other state.[1] In the time of the most violent party quarrels there is no instance of interference with either political views or political teaching. The outspoken friends of a Spartan aristocracy could openly stick to their colours, so long as they refrained from actual attacks on the existing state of things; and was Socrates not to be allowed the same privilege?[2]

In the shape of actual deeds nothing, however, could be laid to his charge. He had never transgressed the laws of the state. His duties as a citizen had been conscientiously fulfilled. His avowed

lic by reminding him, that the people whom he is afraid of consist of peasants, shoemakers, pedlars, &c., and therefore do not deserve such consideration. The charge preferred by the accuser, Mem. i. 2, 58, that Socrates thought it was reasonable for the rich to abuse the poor, is clearly a misrepresentation.

[1] Compare *Plato*, Gorg. 461, E.; *Demosth.* in Androt. p. 603; Funebr. 1396.

[2] Grote's reference to the Platonic state, l. c. p. 679, in which no freedom of individual opinion was allowed, is not altogether to the point. The fundamental ideas of Plato's state differ from those prevailing at the time in Athens. *Plato*, Rep. viii. 557, B., reckons freedom of speech among the evils of a democracy, a type of which was the Athenian form of government.

opinion was that man must live for the state and obey its laws. He was no partisan of the oligarchical faction. Quite the reverse, he had twice hazarded his life,[1] once to rescue the victors at Arginusæ—good democrats—from the extrajudicial mercies of an infuriated populace, the other time to prevent an unjust command of the thirty tyrants from being carried out.[2] His school, too, in as far as it can be called a school, had no decided political bias. If the greater number of his pupils were taken from the upper classes,[3] and hence probably belonged to the aristocratic party, one of his most intimate friends[4] was amongst the companions of Thrasybulus; most of his adherents however seem to have taken no decided line in politics. A charge of political inactivity has been brought against him in modern times. On this head, different judgments may be passed on him from different points of view. From our side we can only praise him for continuing faithful to his higher calling, not wasting his powers and his life on a career, in which he would have attained no success, and for which he was unfitted. But whatever view may be taken, it is certainly not a punishable offence to avoid a statesman's career; least of all to avoid it under the conviction that you can do more good to the state in other ways. To help the state in his own way was to Socrates an object of the highest and deepest interest.[5] His

[1] *Xen.* i. 1, 17.

[2] See pp. 67; 68; 149; 167.

[3] *Plato*, Apol. 23, C. See p. 177.

[4] Chærephon, ibid. 21, A

[5] Compare p. 66.

political theories may not have been in harmony with existing institutions, but his character as a citizen must be admitted to be pure; and, according to the laws of Athens, he was guilty of no crime against the state.[1]

(2) Relation borne by his theory to the ancient morality.

The political views of Socrates were not the only things which gave offence. His whole position was, as Hegel has so well indicated,[2] at variance with the ground occupied by the old Greek morality. The moral life of Greece, like every national form of life, rested originally on authority. It relied partly on the unquestioned authority of the laws of the state, and partly on the all-powerful influence of custom and training, which raised general convictions to the rank of written laws of God, traceable by no one to a definite origin. To oppose this traditional morality was regarded as a crime and conceit, an offence against God and the commonweal. To doubt its rightfulness never occurred to any one, nor was indeed permitted; and for this reason, the need of an enquiry into its foundations, of proving its necessity, or even of supporting it by personal introspection, was never felt.

[1] At an earlier period it might have given offence, that Socrates appeared to hold aloof from the political questions of his time, and an appeal might have been made to the old law of Solon, *Plut.* Sol. c. 20; Arist. in *Gell.* N. A. ii. 12, 1, threatening neutrals in case of an internal quarrel with loss of civil rights. But this law had long fallen into disuse, if indeed it had ever been in force; and who can blame Socrates for remaining neutral when he could conscientiously side with none of the conflicting parties? Perhaps it was a political narrowness, but it was not a crime.

[2] Gesch. d. Phil. ii. 81.

CHAP. X.

(a) Personal conviction substituted for deference to authority.

Socrates, however, demanded such an enquiry. He would have nothing accepted, and nothing done, until men were first fully convinced of its truth or expediency. For him it was not enough to have a rule, universally recognised and legally established, but the individual must think out each subject for himself, and discover its reasons: true virtue and right action are only possible when they spring from personal conviction. Hence his whole life was spent in examining the prevailing notions touching morals, in testing their truth, and seeking for their reasons. This examination brought him in nearly all points to the same results as those which were established by custom and opinion. If his notions were in many respects clearer and more sharply defined, this advantage was one which he shared in common with the best and wisest of his cotemporaries. Tried by the standard of the old Greek morality, his position seems very critical. The value of conventional morality, and the received rules of conduct resting on authority and tradition, was denied. In comparison with knowledge, and conscious virtue, they were so much depreciated, that not only was the self-love of individuals injured, but the actual validity of the laws of the state was called in question. If man has but to follow his own convictions, he will agree with the popular will only when, and in as far as, it agrees with his convictions. If the two come into collision, there can be no doubt as to which he will prefer. This is candidly admitted by Socrates in his defence, in the well-known declaration

CHAP. X.

that he would obey God rather than the Athenians.[1] Thus his views stand, even in theory, in sharp and irreconcilable contradiction to the older view. It was impossible therefore to guarantee, indeed it was highly improbable that there would be, a perfect agreement between the two in their results; and as a matter of fact, by his political views Socrates was undeniably opposed to the existing form of government.[2]

(b) Less importance attached to politics.

Nor can there be any mistaking the fact, that the whole character of the Socratic philosophy is at variance with the preponderance given to political interests by the Greeks, without which, considering their limited range, these states could never have achieved greatness. The duty of the individual towards the community was indeed fully recognised by Socrates. Even his friends he urged to devote their attention to public affairs when any of them showed ability for the task;[3] and in keeping back from public life those who were young[4] and unformed, he acted meritoriously from the point of view of ancient Greece. Still the maxim that man must attend to himself first, and be sure of his own moral well-being before meddling with that of others and with the community;[5] his conviction that a political career was not only alien to his own character, but impossible, in the then state of things, for a man of integrity;[6] the whole inward turn given to thought and pursuits, the demand for self-knowledge, for moral knowledge,

[1] *Plat.* Apol. 29, C.
[2] See p. 168 and 224.
[3] See p. 168, 3.
[4] Mem. iii. 6; iv. 2; *Plato,* Symp. 216, A.
[5] *Plato,* l. c.
[6] *Plato,* Apol. 31, C.

CHAP. X.

for self-training—what effect could all these have but to weaken in himself and his pupils the desire for political life, making the moral perfection of the individual the main thing, while reducing activity for the state—that highest and most immediate duty of a citizen according to the ancient view—to a subordinate and derivative rank?

(c) His position subversive of religion.

If the charge of rejecting his country's Gods was, to his mind, wrongfully preferred against Socrates, still his theory, it must be admitted, went perilously near doing so. In the case of Antisthenes this was seen so soon as the Socratic demand for knowledge was consistently applied, and religious notions were dealt with in a like manner in order to discover what people understood thereby. This is true also of his *δαιμόνιον*. As a kind of oracle there was room for it on the platform of the Greek faith, but as being an inward oracle it removed the decision within the subject instead of leaving it dependent on external portents. And yet how dangerous was this proceeding in a country in which oracles were not only a religious but a political institution! How easily might others be led to imitate the example of Socrates, taking counsel, however, with their own understanding instead of with an undefined inward feeling, and thus thinking little of belief in the Gods or of their utterances! We may be convinced that Socrates was in all these points right in the main, and it is quite true that he was the precursor and founder of our moral view of the world; but how could this new idea of right be admitted by any one who shared the traditions of the ancient Greek world? How could a state built upon these traditions allow such an idea to spread, without committing an act of suicide? Remembering, then, that Socrates worked and taught in the manner he did, not in the Sparta of Lycurgus, but in Athens and amongst the generation that had fought at Marathon, we shall find it most natural for the state to endeavour to restrain his action. For Athens was absolutely ignorant of that freedom of personal conviction, which Socrates required, nor could she endure it.[1] In such a community the punishment of an innovator causes no surprise. For was not a dangerous doctrine, according to old notions, a crime against the state? And if the criminal resolutely refused to obey the sentence of the judges, as Socrates actually did, how could the penalty of death fail to follow? To one therefore starting from the old Greek view of right and the state, the condemnation of Socrates cannot appear to be unjust.[2]

(3) ***Relation borne by his theory to the times in which he lived.***

A very different question is it whether Athens at that time had a right to this opinion, and this is a point which the defenders of Athens assume far too readily.[3] To us the question appears to deserve

[1] To say that the line adopted by Socrates was not opposed to the constitution of Solon, but was a return to old Greek custom, as *Georgii* (Uebersetzung d. Plat. Apologie, p. 129) asserts, is not correct. For not only did he express disapproval of appointing to public offices by lot, which was, it is true, an institution later than Solon's time, but he disliked the popular elections of Solon; and his principle of free investigation is widely removed from the spirit of Solon's times.

[2] Compare the remarks of *Kock* on Aristophanes, i. 7.

[3] *Hegel*, l. c. p. 100, is here

CHAP. X.

(a) The old morality was already in a state of decay.

an unqualified negation. Had Socrates appeared in the time of Miltiades and Aristides, and had he been condemned then, the sentence might be regarded as a simple act of defence on the part of the old morality against the spirit of innovation. In the period after the Peloponnesian war such a view can no longer be entertained. For where was the solid morality which Anytus and Meletus were supposed to defend? Had not all kinds of relations, views, and modes of life long since been penetrated by an individualising tendency far more dangerous than that of Socrates? Had not men been long accustomed in place of the great statesmen of old to see demagogues and aristocrats in feud with each other on every other point, agreeing only in the thoughtless play of rivalry and ambition? Had not all the cultivated men of the time passed through a

most nearly right, although he regards the Athenians exclusively as the representatives of the old Greek morality. Forchhammer is prejudiced in calling the Athenians conservative, and Socrates revolutionary, and attributing to Socrates the extreme consequences of those principles, notwithstanding his protest. Nietzsche, too (Sokr. u. d. Griech. Tragödie, p. 29), forgets the difference of times in thinking that, when Socrates had once been impeached, his condemnation was quite just. If this were allowed, not a word could be said against the sentence of death. For, according to Athenian custom, when a verdict of guilty had been brought in, the judges could only choose between the penalty demanded by the plaintiff and that asked for by the defendant; in the present case between death and an illusory fine. But the question really is whether Socrates deserved punishment at all, and to this question a negative answer must be given both from our point of view and from that of his cotemporaries; from ours, because we take liberty of judgment to be something sacred and inviolable; from theirs, because the Athenians had long left the ancient state of things.

school of rationalism which had entirely pulled to pieces the beliefs and the morals of their ancestors? Had not men for a generation lived themselves into the belief that laws are the creations of caprice, and that natural right and positive right are very different things?[1] What had become of the olden chastity when Aristophanes could tell his hearers in the midst of his attacks on Socrates, half in joke, half in derision, that they were one and all adulterers?[2] What had become of ancient piety at a time when the sceptical verses of Euripides were in every one's mouth, when every year the happy sallies of Aristophanes and other comedians in successful derision of the inhabitants of Olympus were clapped, when the most unprejudiced complained that fear of God, trust, and faith had vanished,[3] and when the stories of future retribution were universally ridiculed?[4]

(b) Socrates only fell in with what he found existing.

This state of things Socrates did not make; he found it existing. What he is blamed for consists in this, that he entered into the spirit of his age, trying to reform it by means of itself, instead of making the useless and silly attempt to bring it back to a type of culture which was gone for ever. It was an obviously wrong move of his opponents to hold him responsible for the corruption of faith and morals, which he was trying to stem in the only possible way. It was a clumsy self-deception on their part to imagine themselves men of the good

[1] Conf. p. 29.
[2] Clouds, 1083.
[3] *Thuc.* iii. 82; ii. 53.
[4] *Plato*, Rep. i. 330, D.

CHAP. X.

old time. His condemnation is not only a great injustice according to our conception of right, but it is so also according to the standard of his own time. It was a crying political anachronism, one of those unfortunate measures, by which a policy of restoring the past is ever sure to expose its incompetence and shortsightedness. Socrates certainly left the original ground of Greek thought, and transported it beyond the bounds, within which this particular form of national life was alone possible. But he did not do so before it was time, nor before the untenableness of the old position had been amply demonstrated. The revolution which was going forward in the whole spirit of the Greeks, was not the fault of one individual, but it was the fault of destiny, or rather it was the general fault of the time. The Athenians in punishing him condemned themselves and committed the injustice of making him pay the penalty of what was historically the fault of all. The condemnation was not of the least use; instead of being banished, thereby the spirit of innovation was aroused all the more. Here is not a simple clashing of two moral powers equally justified and equally limited. Guilt and innocence are not equally divided between the parties. Socrates has on his side the unquestioned right to a principle historically necessary and of higher importance; one far more limited is represented by his opponents to which they have no longer a just right, since they do not faithfully adhere to it. This constitutes the peculiar tragic turn in the fate of Socrates. A truly conservative reformer is attacked by nominal and imaginary champions of old times. In punishing him the Athenians broke the rod on their own backs; for it was not for destroying morals and belief that he was punished, but for his attempts in the way of restoring them, and that by the very party most anxious to preserve them.

(c) A breach between Socrates and his countrymen was absolutely necessary

To form a correct judgment on the whole incident, we must not forget that Socrates was condemned by only a very small majority, that to all appearances it lay in his own power to secure his acquittal, and that he would have escaped with a far less punishment than death, had he not challenged his judges by the appearance of pride. These circumstances may make us doubtful of regarding his ruin as an unavoidable consequence of his rebellion against the spirit of his nation. As they place the guilt of the Athenians in a milder light by laying it in part on the head of the accused, so too they prove that accidental events, in no way connected with the leading character of his teaching, had weight in the final decision. No doubt Socrates was at variance with the position and the demands of the ancient morality in essential points; but it was not necessary in the then state of opinion at Athens, that it should come to a breach between him and his nation. Although the political reaction after the expulsion of the thirty tyrants was sufficiently powerful to bring about an attack on him, the conviction of his guilt was not so universal but that it might have been possible for him to escape the punishment of death.

For his honour and his cause it was a happy

CHAP. X.

(4) *The result of his death.*

thing that he did not escape. What Socrates in pious faith expressed after his condemnation—that to die would be better for him than to live—has been fully realised in his work. The picture of the dying Socrates must have afforded to his pupils, in the highest degree, what it now after centuries affords to us—a simple testimony to the greatness of the human mind, to the power of philosophy, and to the victory of a spirit pious and pure, resting on clear conviction. It must have stood before them in glory, as the guiding-star of their inner life, as it is depicted by Plato's master hand. It must have increased their admiration for their teacher, their zeal to imitate him, their devotion to his teaching. By his death the stamp of higher truth was impressed on his life and words. The sublime repose and happy cheerfulness with which he met death was the strongest corroboration of all his convictions, the zenith of a long life devoted to knowledge and virtue. Death did not add to the substance of his teaching, but it greatly strengthened its influence. A life had been spent in sowing the seeds of knowledge with a zeal unequalled by any other philosopher either before or after; his death accelerated the harvest, so that fruit was brought forth abundantly in the Socratic schools.

PART III.

THE IMPERFECT FOLLOWERS OF SOCRATES.

CHAPTER XI.

THE SCHOOL OF SOCRATES: HIS POPULAR PHILOSOPHY. XENOPHON: ÆSCHINES.

CHAP. XI.

A. *School of Socrates.*

A MIND in every way so great and active as that of Socrates could not fail to make a lasting impression on every kind of character with which it came into contact. If the most perfect systems are often not understood by all their adherents in the same sense, might not a much greater divergence and variety of apprehension be expected, in a case where no system lay ready to hand, but only the fragments and germs of what might be one—a person, a principle, a method, a mass of individual utterances and of desultory discussions? The greater part of the followers of Socrates confined their attention to what was most obvious and lay nearest to an ordinary intelligence—the originality, the purity of character, the intelligent view of life, the deep piety and the beautiful moral maxims of their teacher. Only a smaller number gave more careful attention to the

CHAP. XI.

deeper thoughts, which often appeared under so unpretending an outside, and of these nearly all took a very narrow view of the subjects which interested Socrates. Combining older theories with the teaching of their master, which it is true needed to be thus supplemented, they mostly managed to lose the distinctive merits of his philosophy. One only with a deeper insight into the spirit of Socrates has succeeded in building up a system which presents in a most brilliant and extended form what Socrates had otherwise attempted and on a more limited scale.

In the first of these classes must be placed without doubt by far the greater number of those who are known to us as the pupils of Socrates.[1] The

[1] Besides the followers of Socrates who will be presently mentioned, include here Crito (*Xen.* Mem. ii. 9; *Plato*, Crito, Phædo, 59, B., 60, A., 63, D., 115, A; Euthydemus; *Diog.* ii. 121, who makes him the author of seventeen books, with which, however, he has as little to do as with his supposed children Hermogenes, and the rest, and Clitobulus his son (*Xen.* Mem. i. 3, 8; ii. 6; Œc. 1–6; Symp. 4, 10; *Plato*, Apol. 33, D., 38, B.; Phædo, 59, B.; Æsch. in *Athenæus* v. 220, a.); Chærephon (Mem. i. 2, 48, ii. 3; *Plato*, Apol. 20, E.; Charm. 153, B.; Gorgias, Aristophanes, Clouds, Birds, 1296) and his brother Chærecrates (Mem. l. c.); also Apollodorus (Mem. iii. 11, 17; *Plato*, Apol. 34, A., 38, B.; Phædo, 59, B., 117, D.; Symp.); Aristodemus (Mem. i. 4; *Plato*, Symp. 173, B., 174, A., 223, B.); Euthydemus (Mem. iv. 2; 3; 5; 6; *Pl.*, Sym. 222 B.); Theages (*Pl.* Apol. 33, E.; Rep. vi. 496, B.); Hermogenes (*Xen.* Mem. ii. 10, 3, iv. 8, 4; Sym. 4, 46; Apol. 2, *Pl.* Phædo, 59, B. In Mem. i. 2, 48, perhaps Ἑρμογένης should be read for Hermocrates; but at any rate this Hermocrates must not be confounded with the Hermocrates mentioned *Pl.* Tim. 19, C., 20, A. Krit. 108, A; the latter being a stranger making a short stay at Athens. Compare *Steinhart*, Pl. W. vi. 39 and 235; Phædonides (Mem. i. 2, 48; *Pl.* Phædo, 59, C.); Theodotus (*Pl.* Apol. 33, E.); Epigenes (Phædo, 59, B.; Mem. iii. 12); Menexenus (Phædo, 59, B.; Lysis, 206, D.); Ctesippus (Phædo, Euthydemus, and Lysis); Theætetus (Theætet. Soph. Pol. *Procl.* in Euclid. 19, m. 20); the younger So-

writings too which are attributed to many of these followers of Socrates—amongst which, however, there is much that is spurious—were, on an average, little more than summaries of popular moral maxims.[1] One of the best illustrations of this mode of understanding and applying the doctrines of Socrates may be found in Xenophon.[2]

crates (*Plat.* Theæt. 147, E.; Soph. 218, 8; Polit. 257, C.; *Arist.* Metaph. vii. 11, 1036, 6, 25; conf. *Hermann*, Plat. i. 661); Terpsion (*Pl.* Theæt.; Phædo, 59, C.); Charmides (*Xen.* Mem. iii. 7; 6, 14; Symp. 4, 29; Hellen. ii. 4, 19; *Plato*, Charm. Sym. 222, B.; Prot. 315, A.); Glaucon the brother of Plato (Mem. iii. 6; the same individual to whom *Diog.* ii. 124, attributes nine genuine and thirty-two spurious dialogues, and who is identified with the Glauco of Plato's Republic and the Parmenides, as we assume following *Böckh*; conf. Abhandlung d. Berliner Acad. 1873, Hist. Philos. Kl. p. 86); Cleombrotus (Phæd. 59, C.; perhaps the same who is said by Callim. in *Cic.* Tusc. i. 34, 84, and *Sext.* Math. i. 48; *David*, Proleg. in Cat. 9; Schol. in Arist. 13, b, 35; Ammon in *Porphyr.* Isag. 2, b. to have committed suicide over the Phædo, probably not from misunderstanding the exhortation to a philosophic death, but from shame for his conduct there blamed); Diodorus (Mem. ii. 10); Critias whom *Dionys.* Jud. de Thuc. c. 31, p. 941, reckons among the followers of Socrates and Alcibiades in their younger years (Mem. i. 2, 12, Plato); not to mention others who were acquainted with Socrates, but did not join his way of thinking, such as Phædrus the friend of Sophistry (*Plato*, Phæd., Symp.); Callias (*Xen.* Symp., *Plato*, Phot.); the younger Pericles (Mem. iv. 5); Aristarchus (Mem. ii. 7); Eutherus (Mem. ii. 8); and many more.

[1] Crito and Glaucon.

[2] Xenophon, the son of the Athenian Gryllus, died according to a statement in *Diog.* ii. 56, 363–359 B.C. From Hellen. vi. 4, 35, however, it appears that he survived the murder of Alexander of Pheræ 357. If the treatise respecting the public revenues of Athens belongs to the year 355, he must also have outlived that year. On the authority of *Ps. Lucian.* Macrob. 21, his birth was formerly placed in 450, or, on account of the participation in the battle of Delium, p. 67, 2, in 445 B.C. The first of these passages is, however, extremely untrustworthy, as giving information depending on the date of his death, which is quite uncertain. The latter is so much at variance with what *Plato*, Symp. 220, D. says, that

CHAP. XI.

B. *Xenophon.*

It is impossible in reading the works of this author not to be struck with the purity and loftiness of the sentiment, with his chivalrous character, and

it is a most unstable foundation on which to build. Neither passage agrees with what Xenophon himself says (Anab. iii. 1, 4 and 25, οὐδὲν προφασίζομαι τὴν ἡλικίαν) 2, 37, where he mentions himself and Timasion as the two youngest amongst the generals. These passages place it beyond dispute, that at the time of the expedition he is describing, 401–400 B.C., he was about 45 years of age and not much older than his friend Proxenus, who fell in it at about the age of 30. (So *Grote*, Plato iii. 563; *Cobet*, Novæ Lect. 535; *Bergk* in Ersch. u. Gruber's Encyl. i. 81, 392; *Curtius*, Griech. Gesch. iii. 772, 31.) The circumstances of his life we only know imperfectly. He speaks himself in the Anabasis iii. 1, 4, Memorabilia and Œconomicus of his relations with Socrates, as to the origin of which *Diog.* ii. 48 tells a doubtful story, and in the Anabasis of his activity and experience in the retreat of the 10,000. After his return he entered the Spartan army in Asia Minor, and fought under Agesilaus at Coronea against his own countrymen. Banished for this from Athens, he settled in the Elean Scillus, colonised by Spartans (*Xen.* Anab. v. 3, 6; *Diog.* ii. 51; *Pausan.* v. 6, 4; *Plut.* Agesil. 18; De Exil. 10, p. 603). According to an ill-accredited story in Pausanias he died there. More credible authorities state that he was banished by the Eleans (probably in 370 B.C., when they joined the Thebans after the battle of Leuctra *Diodor.* xv. 62), and spent the rest of his life at Corinth (*Diog.* 53). His banishment appears to have ended, when Athens joined Sparta against Thebes, as the treatise on the revenues indicates, either before or after the battle of Mantinæa, in which his two sons fought among the Athenian cavalry, and the elder one, Gryllus, fell (*Diog.* 54; *Plut.* Consol. ad Apoll. 33, p. 118). Xenophon's writings are distinguished for purity and grace of language, and the unadorned clearness of the description. They appear to have been preserved entire. The Apology, however, the Agesilaus, and the treatise on the Athenian constitution are certainly spurious, and several others of the smaller treatises are either spurious or have large interpolations. *Steinhart*, Plat. l. 95, 300, wrongly doubts the Symposium. For his life and writings consult *Krüger*, De Xenoph. Vita, Halle, 1832, also in 2nd vol. of Historisch. philol. Studien, *Ranke*, De Xenoph. Vita et Scriptis, Berlin, 1851. *Grote*, Plato iii. 562; *Bergk*, l. c.; *Bähr* in Pauly's Realencyclop. vi. 6, 2791. For other literature on the subject Ibid. and *Ueberweg*, Gesch. d. Phil. i. 95.

the healthy tone of his mind. His philosophical capacities cannot be estimated very high. His description of Socrates is full of admiration for the greatness of his character; his philosophical merit and his intellectual activity he has only imperfectly understood. Not only does he share the narrowness of the position of Socrates—as for instance when he quotes the derogatory opinions of his master respecting natural science in proof of his piety and intelligence,[1]—but he misunderstands the true intellectual value of the discussions he reports. The formation of conceptions, constituting the germ of the whole teaching of Socrates, is only accidentally mentioned by him in order to show what care his master devoted to the critical culture of his friends.[2] All that he sees in Socrates' peculiar habit of asking every one whom he came across, in his thirst for knowledge, as to his mode of life, is that he tried to make himself useful to people of every class, craftsmen included.[3] The importance of those tenets, too, relative to virtue, in which the whole peculiarity of the Socratic ethics consists, can only be gathered from his account with so much difficulty that it is obvious how little Xenophon himself[4] understood it. Many echoes and reminiscences of the Socratic mode of teaching are indeed to be found in his independent sketches; but he is too exclusively occupied with their practical application to engage in any really scientific re-

[1] Mem. i. 1, 11; iv. 7.
[2] Ibid. iv. 6.
[3] Ibid. iii. 10, 1; i. 1; conf, 107, 2.
[4] Mem. iii. 9, and p. 141.

CHAP. XI.

searches. He describes the catechetical mode of teaching,[1] in which he seems to have been somewhat skilled; but his dialogues do not aim, like those of the genuine Socratic type, at the formation of conceptions, and are often far too slipshod in their proofs and deductions. He recommends self-knowledge,[2] but primarily only in the popular sense, meaning that no one ought to attempt what is beyond his powers. He insists on piety, self-restraint,[3] and so forth, but he appears not to hold the maxim of Socrates,[4] that all these virtues consist in knowledge. Following the method used by Socrates, he proves that nothing is a good of which you do not make a right use;[5] that every one readily submits to the wise,[6] that right and law are synonymous terms,[7] and that the rich are not more happy than the poor,[8] that the true measure of riches and poverty is not possession as such, but possession proportionate to the needs of the possessor.[9] He repeats what Socrates had said about truth and error,[10] yet not without hinting that these principles are liable to be abused. With the same decision as his master, he declares against the sensual and unnatural abuses of love;[11] and, following out this train

[1] Œc. 19, 14.

[2] Cyrop. vii. 2, 20.

[3] Ibid. viii. 1, 23.

[4] Compare the conversation between Cyrus and Tigranes, Cyrop. iii. 1, 16, and Mem. i. 2, 19, in which the ordinary view is given rather than the Socratic, although the language allows the latter.

[5] See above, p. 142, 2.

[6] Cyrop. i. 6, 21. See above, p. 169, 2.

[7] Ibid. i. 3, 17. See p. 149, 1.

[8] Ibid. viii. 3, 40; Symp. 4, 29; Mem. i. 6, 4.

[9] Œc. 2, 2.

[10] Cyrop. i. 6, 31; Mem. iv. 2, 13.

[11] Symp. 8, 7, p. 161.

of thought, he requires that woman should have a recognised social position, have more care spent on her education, and that her union should be made into a real companionship for life, and should be based on a reciprocity of capacities and performances.[1] He exhorts to work, without, however, like his teacher condemning the Greek prejudice against manual labour.[2] By many expressions he gives an insight into his ideal of a beautiful and happy life;[3] but he neither attempts to give a philosophic reason for that ideal, nor does he place it outside the platform of traditional Greek ethics. Touching the knowledge and omnipotence of the Gods, their care for mankind, the blessing consequent upon piety,[4] he expresses himself with warmth; but at the same time he fully shares the belief of his nation[5] in regard to predictions and sacrifices, himself understanding their interpretation. He makes Cyrus express the hope of a higher life after death, confirming that hope by several considerations, without, however, venturing to assert it with full assurance. He reminds us that the soul is invisible; that vengeance surely comes on the murderers of the innocent, and that honour is due to the dead. He cannot believe that the soul which gives life to the body should be

[1] Œc. 313, c. 7; see p. 167, 4.

[2] Œc. 4, 2; 6, 5; 20, 15; conf. p. 171, 1.

[3] Mem. iv. 8, 11; Cyrop. viii. 7, 6; Œc. 11, 8.

[4] Symp. 4, 46; Cyrop. i. 6, 2; Œc. 7, 18.

[5] Compare amongst other passages, Cyrop. i. 6, 2; 23; 44; Œc. 5, 19; 7, 7; 11, 8; Hipparch. i. 1; 5, 14; 7, 1; 9, 8; Anab. iii. 1, 11; v. 9, 22 and 6, 28, and also pp. 66, 5; 148; Cyrop. i. 6, 23 agrees fully with Mem. i. 1, 6.

CHAP. XI.

itself mortal, or that reason should not survive in greater purity after its separation from the body, seeing a sign thereof in prophesying in sleep.[1] In all these explanations we discern the faithful and thoughtful follower of Socrates, but there is not a trace of original thought. Indeed it is doubtful whether the few passages in which Xenophon seems to have somewhat amplified the teaching of his master, ought not really to be attributed to Socrates.

His larger work on politics, the Cyropædeia, is, as a book of political philosophy, unimportant. Xenophon here proposes to portray the Socratic ideal of a ruler who understands his business,[2] and who cares for his people as a shepherd cares for his flock;[3] but what he really gives, is a description of a valiant and prudent general,[4] of an upright man, of a chivalrous conqueror. No attempt is made to define clearly the province of government, to give a higher meaning to the state, or to fulfil its object by fixed institutions. The demand for careful education[5] may reveal the follower of Socrates, but there is so little reference in that education to knowledge,[6] that it might more readily pass for a Spartan than for a Socratic education. Everything centres in the person of the prince. The state is an Asiatic kingdom. The end at which

[1] Cyrop. viii. 7, 17. See p. 171.

[2] Ibid. i. 1, 3. See p. 168.

[3] Ibid. viii. 2, 14; Mem. i. 2, 32.

[4] Ibid. 6, 12 speaks of these duties in language similar to Mem. iii. 1. Perhaps Xenophon may be the nameless friend referred to in this passage.

[5] Cyrop. i. 2, 2; viii. 8, 13; vii. 5, 72.

[6] A weak echo of the principle of Socrates is found i. 4, 3.

all its institutions aim [1] is the strength and wealth of the sovereign and his courtiers. Even this view is very imperfectly carried out, many important departments of government being altogether omitted.[2] The same remarks apply to the Hiero. In this dialogue Xenophon shows plainly enough how little the supposed good fortune of an absolute sovereign is to be envied. His remarks touching the means whereby such a sovereign can make himself and his people happy—allowing that many of his proposals are expedient—do not advance beyond a benevolent despotism. More successful is his smaller treatise on family life. It bears witness to an intelligent mind and a benevolent heart, which comes out particularly in the passages respecting the position assigned to woman [3] and the treatment of slaves.[4] But it makes no pretensions to be a philosophical treatise, though it may contain many individual Socratic thoughts.[5] From Xenophon, then, the history of philosophy can gain but little.[6]

[1] Compare viii. 1. The treaty between Cyrus and the Persians, viii. 5, 24, has for its object, security by the advantages of government.

[2] Compare the spirited remarks of *Mohl*, Gesch. d. Staatswissenschaft, i. 204.

[3] C. 3, 13, c. 7.

[4] 12, 3; 14, 9; c. 21; 7, 37 and 41; 9, 11.

[5] See p. 243, 2.

[6] A more favourable view of Xenophon by *Strümpell*, Gesch. d. Prakt. Phil. d. Gr. 466–509. He sees in him the development of Socratic thought from the point of applied ethics, and a supplement to Plato's pure speculations. Yet he too says that excepting in the Œconomica there can be no trace of a systematic development in Xenophon (p. 481); his ethical teaching is extremely simple, almost entirely devoid of philosophic language (p. 484); he never really proves anything, nor employs any form for deduction, not even the favourite method with Socrates, that of definition (p. 467). In what, then, does his importance for philosophy and history consist? The application of the thoughts of others,

CHAP. XI.

C. *Æschines.*

Æschines [1] would appear to have treated the teaching of Socrates in the same way. The writings of this disciple[2] are reckoned among the best models of Attic prose,[3] and are by some preferred to those of Xenophon.[4] It is, moreover, asserted that they reproduce the spirit of Socrates with wonderful fidelity,[5]

without verifying their contents or observing their method, may in many respects be very meritorious, but it cannot be regarded as a service rendered to philosophy.

[1] Æschines, son of Lysanias (*Plato*, Apol. 33 E), against whom *Diog.* ii. 60, cannot have weight, is praised for his adherence to Socrates (*Diog.* ii. 31; *Senec.* Benef. i. 8). Plato mentions him (Phædo, 59, R.) among those who were present at the death of Socrates. Idomeneus, however (*Diog.* ii. 60, 35; iii. 36), transferred to him the part played by Crito in Plato, probably only from spite to Plato. We afterwards meet him in the company of the younger Dionysius (*Diog.* ii. 61; 63; *Plut.* Adul. et Am. c. 26, p. 67; *Philost.* v. Apollon. i. 35, p. 43; *Lucian*, Paras. c. 32, conf. *Diodor.* xv. 76), to whom he had been recommended by Plato according to *Plutarch*, by Aristippus according to *Diogenes.* Aristippus appears as his friend in *Diog.* ii. 82; *Plut.* Coh. Ira, 14. Poor to begin with (*Diog.* ii. 34, 62), he was poor in after-life on his return to Athens. He did not venture, it is said, to found a school, but delivered a few speeches and treatises for money (*Diog.* ii. 62; what *Athen.* xi. 507, c. and *Diog.* ii. 20, say is not credible). Whether the dirty stories are true which Lysias in *Athen.* xiii. 611, tells of him is a moot point. His writings, according to *Athen.*, give the impression of an honourable man. The time of his death is not known.

[2] According to *Diog.* ii. 61, 64, *Phrynichus* in *Phot.* Bibliothek, c. 151, p. 101, seven of these were considered to be genuine. The few remains of them existing have been collected by *Hermann*, De Æschin. Socr. Reliquiis, Gött. 1850. See Ibid. p. 8.

[3] *Longin.* περὶ εὑρές.; Rhet. Gr. ix. 559 (ed. Walz).

[4] *Phrynich.* in *Phot.* Cod. 61, Schl. 158, g. E; *Hermogenes*, Form. Orat. ii. 3; Rhet. Gr. iii. 394. M. *Psellos* in Con. Catal. of Bodl. MSS. p. 743, quoted by *Grote*, Plato, iii. 469, against which authority Timon in *Diog.* ii. 55; 62, carries no weight. He is said to have imitated Gorgias in speech, *Diog.* ii. 63.

[5] *Aristid.* Or. xlv. p. 35. Conf. *Demetr.* De Interpret. 297. Hence the story (*Diog.* ii. 60, 62; *Athen.* xiii. 611), that his speeches had been composed by Socrates, and given to him by Xanthippe. *Diog.* ii. 47

and the few fragments which remain confirm this view. Nevertheless they appear to have been singularly poor in real philosophic thought. Their strength consists far more in the grace and elegance of their language than in an independent treatment of the Socratic teaching.

D. *Simmias and Cebes.*

More philosophic characters were the two Thebans, Simmias[1] and Cebes.[2] Both were pupils of Philolaus;[3] both are described by Plato[4] as thoughtful men. Still nothing certain is known of their philosophical opinions and performances. The writings attributed to them[5] were already rejected by Panætius[6] as far as he knew them, and the single one extant, known as the 'Mirror' of Cebes, is certainly spurious.[7] Still less can any dependence be placed

ranks him among the most distinguished followers of Socrates.

[1] *Xen.* Mem. i. 2, 48; iii. 11, 17; *Plato*, Phædo, 59, C., 63 A.

[2] Mem.; Phædo, 59, C., 60, C.

[3] Phædo, 61, D.

[4] It is said (Phædo, 242, B.) that Simmias delivered and composed more philosophical speeches than any one else. In the Phædo, 85, C., he is made to express the sentiment, that every question should be pursued as far as possible. Of Cebes it is said (Phædo, 63, A., 77, A.) that he could always raise objections, and was the most inveterate wrangler; and the part which he and Simmias play in the Phædo corresponds with this description.

[5] *Diog.* ii. 124, mentions twenty-three lectures of Simmias and three of Cebes, including the Mirror. Other testimonies for the latter in *Schweighäuser*, Epicteti Enchiridion et Cebetis Tabula, p. 261.

[6] *Diog.* ii. 64: πάντων μέντοι τῶν Σωκρατικῶν διαλόγων Παναίτιος ἀληθεῖς εἶναι δοκεῖ τοὺς Πλάτωνος, Ξενοφῶντος, Ἀντισθένους, Αἰσχίνου· διστάζει δὲ περὶ τῶν Φαίδωνος καὶ Εὐκλείδου, τοὺς δὲ ἄλλους ἀναιρεῖ πάντας.

[7] In modern times its genuineness has been maintained by *Bähr* (*Pauly's* Real-Encyclop. 2 vol. art. Cebes) and Schweighäuser, c. 13, 33; but their assumption is refuted by two passages in it, one of which mentions a Peripatetic, and the other quotes from Plato's Laws. In other respects,

CHAP. XI.

in the genuineness of the writings which were circulated at a later time under the name of the shoemaker Simon.[1] Probably he is altogether an imaginary person.[2]

In addition to Plato, four founders of Socratic schools are known to us: Euclid, Phædo, Antisthenes, and Aristippus. Of these the two former are much alike; the two others follow courses peculiar to themselves. There arose thus three distinct Socratic schools: the Megarian-Elean, the Cynic, and the Cyrenaic. All these are derived from Socrates. One-sided in their aims, and dependent themselves on earlier theories, they only imperfectly catch the spirit of the teaching of Socrates, and diverge from him and from one another in the most opposite directions. Socrates made it the highest business of man to know the good. What that good was he could not mark out more accurately, being partly satisfied with a

too, notwithstanding its general colourlessness, traces appear of later times, e.g. in its Stoic morality and attacks on false culture.

[1] See *Diog.* ii. 122; *Suid.* Σωκράτης· Epist. Socrat. 12, 13; *Plut.* c. Prin. Philos. c. 1, p. 776; *Böckh*, in Plat. Minoëm. 42. Simonis Socrat. Dialogi iv. *Hermann*, Plat. i. 419, 585.

[2] What Diogenes says of him is unsatisfactory, and the story that Pericles asked him for shelter which he refused, besides being chronologically suspicious, is hardly likely to be true. Of the dialogues attributed to him a great part are found in writings belonging to other people (*Hermann*, l. c.). It is suspicious that he is not mentioned by any ancient authority, and that both Plato and Xenophon are silent about an old and very remarkable pupil of Socrates. In addition to the above, *Suidas* (Σωκράτ. p. 843) mentions also Bryso of Heraclea as a pupil of Socrates. Others, however, as Suidas remarks, called him a pupil of Euclid's, and the comedian Ephippus in *Athen.* xi. 509, c. calls him an Academician. Theopompus' statement (l. c. 508, D.) that Plato copied some of his writings, would harmonise with either view; but it is in any case false.

practical description of it, and partly restricted to a theory of relative pleasure. These various sides of the Socratic philosophy now diverge, and are rounded off into systems. One party confines itself to the general burden of the teaching of Socrates—the abstract idea of the good. Others starting from pleasure which is its result make that the gauge of the good, and the good itself something relative. Again, of those confining themselves to the good some attach importance to the theoretical, others to the practical, carrying out and treatment of the good. Thus the Socratic teaching gave rise to the three schools just named, which in so far as they bring into prominence individual elements in the spirit of Socrates to the detriment of the rest, revert to older lines of thought long since left behind in the historical development of philosophy. The Megarians and Cynics go back to the Eleatic doctrine of the One and All, and to the Sophistry of Gorgias; the Cyrenaics to the negative teaching of Protagoras, and to the early scepticism of Heraclitus.

CHAPTER XII.

THE MEGARIAN AND THE ELEAN-ERETRIAN SCHOOLS.

CHAP. XII.

I. *The Megarians.* A. *History of the School.*

THE founder of the Megarian school [1] is Euclid.[2] A

[1] *Deycks*, De Megaricorum Doctrina, Bonn, 1827, whose careful work has not been added to by *Mallet's* Histoire de l'Ecole de Mégare, Par. 1845. More independent, but sometimes too diffuse, is *Henne*, Ecole de Mégare, Par. 1843. *Ritter*, Ueber die Philosophie der Meg. Schule in Rhein. Mus. ii. (1828), p. 295; *Hartenstein*, Ueber die Bedeutung der Meg. Schule für die Gesch. d. Metaphys. Probleme, Verhandl. der Sächs. Gesellschaft der Wissensch. 1848, p. 190; *Prantl*, Gesch. d. Logik, i. 33, which enters most deeply into the logical teaching of the Megarians.

[2] Euclid's home was Megara (*Plato*, Theætet.; Phædo, 59, C.); that it was his birthplace is asserted by *Cic.* Acad. iv. 42, 129; *Strabo*, ix. 1, 8, p. 393; *Diog.* ii. 106. The statement that he came from Gela (τινὲς in *Diog.*) doubtless rests on a misunderstanding. *Deycks*, p. 4, imagines it arose from confounding him with Euclid the jester, γελοῖος, to whom, however, *Athen.* vi. 242, b, 250, e, does not give this epithet. *Henne*, p. 32, conjectures, but without sufficient reason, that he was educated at Gela. That he also possessed property in Attica, *Grote*, Plat. iii. 471, concludes, but without sufficient reason, from *Dionys.* Judic. de Isæo, c. 14; *Karpocrat.* ὅτι τὰ ἐπικηρυττ. *Poll.* viii. 48. Dionysius only refers to a judicial speech of Isæus πρὸς Εὐκλείδην *apropos* of a piece of land, but that this Euclid was the follower of Socrates is pure conjecture. The time of his birth cannot be accurately determined, nor does the anecdote in *Gell.* vi. 10 help towards determining it. He was, however, probably older than Plato. This seems to be proved by the fact that on the death of Socrates he served for some time as a centre to his disciples. The time of his death is also uncertain. If Stilpo and Pasicles were his personal pupils, he must have lived at least till 360 B.C.; but this is very uncertain On the whole little is known of him. A celebrated saying of his to his brother, bearing witness to a gentle character, is quoted by *Plut.* de Ira, 14, p. 462; Frat. Am. 18, p. 489; *Stob.* Flor. 84, 15; *Diog.* ii. 108, mentions six discourses of his.

faithful friend and admirer of Socrates,[1] but at the same time familiar with the Eleatic doctrine,[2] Euclid made use of this doctrine to develop the Socratic philosophy as he understood it. He thus established a separate branch of the Socratic School,[3] which continued to exist until the early part of the third century.[4] Ichthyas[5] is named as his pupil

[1] The story told by *Gell.*, N. A. vi. 10, of his nightly visits to Athens is well known. It cannot, however, go for much, though not in itself improbable. On the contrary, it may be gathered from *Plato's* Theætet. 142, C. that Euclid constantly visited Socrates from Megara, and from the Phædo, 59, C. that he was present at his death. A further proof of his close connection with the followers of Socrates will be found in the fact (*Diog.* ii. 106; iii. 6) that Plato and other followers of Socrates stayed with him for a considerable time after the death of their master. He is usually spoken of as a disciple of Socrates, and has a place amongst his most distinguished disciples.

[2] As may be gathered from his system with greater certainty than from *Cic.* and *Diog.* When Euclid became acquainted with the Eleatic Philosophy is uncertain. It is most probable that he was under its influence before he came under that of Socrates, although the story in *Diog.* ii. 30, is too uncertain to prove much.

[3] The σχολὴ Εὐκλείδου (for which the Cynic Diogenes in *Diog.* N. 34, substitutes Εὐκλείδου χολὴ), called Megarian or Eristic or Dialectic, *Diog.* ii. 106. Consult *Deycks* as to these names. He proves that the terms Eristic and Dialectic were not confined to the Megarian School. Compare *Sextus* Empiricus, who generally understands by Dialecticians, Stoics, for instance, Pyrrh. ii. 146, 166, 229, 235.

[4] How early Euclid was at the head of a special circle of pupils, and whether he appeared formally as a Sophist, or like Socrates, only gradually gathered about him men desirous to learn, we are not told. Perhaps the emigration of many followers of Socrates to Megara gave occasion for the establishment of this school—i.e., for the formation of a society, which at first moved about Euclid's house and person, busying itself with discussions. There is no ground for supposing that Plato and his friends removed to Megara, attracted by the fame of the School of Euclid, as *Henne* maintains, pp. 27 and 30.

[5] *Suid.* Εὐκλείδης—*Diog.* ii. 112, only makes the general remark, that he belonged to the School of Euclid.

CHAP. XII.

and successor, respecting whom, however, nothing further is known.[1] Of greater note was Eubulides,[2] the celebrated dialectician,[3] who wrote against Aristotle,[4] and who is mentioned as the teacher of Demosthenes.[5] Cotemporary with him were Thrasymachus[6] of Corinth, and Dioclides,[7] perhaps also Clinomachus.[8] Pasicles,[9] however, would appear to be younger. A pupil of Eubulides was Apollonius of Cyrene, surnamed Cronus,[10] the teacher of the

[1] His name is still found in *Diog.* ii. 112; vi. 80 (Diogenes dedicated to him a dialogue called Ichthyas). *Athen.* viii. 335, a.

[2] Of Miletus according to *Diog.* ii. 108. Whether he was the head of a school, or whether he was an immediate disciple of Euclid, we do not know. Diogenes only says, τῆς δ' Εὐκλείδου διαδοχῆς ἐστι καὶ Εὐβ.

[3] Compare *Diog.* ii. 108; *Sext.* Math. vii 13.

[4] *Diog.* ii. 109; Aristocles in *Eus.* Pr. Ev. xv. 2, 5; *Athen.* viii. 354, b. *Themist.* Or. xxiii. 285, c. From these passages it is seen that the attack of Eubulides was very violent, and not free from personal abuse. We also hear from *Athen.* x. 437 of a comedy of Eubulides. But he can hardly be the individual whose work on the Cynic Diogenes is quoted by *Diog.* vi. 20, 30.

[5] The fact seems pretty well established (although it is conspicuously omitted by Plutarch in his life of Demosthenes), being not only attested by *Diog.* ii. 108; *Pseudoplut.* v. Dec. Orat. viii. 21; *Apulei.* De Mag. c. 15, p. 478; *Suid.* Δημοσθένης, and *Phot.* Cod. 265, but being also alluded to by the Comedian in Diog., who can hardly have called a bare acquaintance a disciple.

[6] According to *Diog.* ii. 121, a friend of Ichthyas, and a teacher of Stilpo's.

[7] *Suid.* Στίλπων, a pupil of Euclid, and the teacher of Pasicles.

[8] A Thurian (according to *Diog.* ii. 112), and a teacher of Stilpo's son Bryso, *Suid.* Πύῤῥων, Diog. says he was the first to write on predicates, sentences, and such like.

[9] According to *Suid.* Στίλπων, a brother of the Cynic Crates, who had also Dioclides, a pupil of Euclid's, for teacher, and Stilpo for pupil. *Diog.* vi. 89, in calling Crates his brother and Euclid his teacher, probably confounded Euclid with Dioclides, unless this be the work of a transcriber and Διοκλείδου should be read for Εὐκλείδου.

[10] *Diog.* ii. 111; *Strabo* xiv. 2, 21, p. 658; xvii. 3, 22, p. 838.

sharp-witted Diodorus Cronus,[1] and another of his pupils was Euphantus, known only to us as a poet and historian.[2]

All other members of this school were, however, thrown into the shade by Stilpo,[3] a pupil of Thrasy-

[1] Diodorus, a native of Iasos in Caria, belongs to the most distinguished dialecticians of the Megarian School. *Cic.* De Fato, 6, 12, calls him 'valens dialecticus'; *Sext.* Math. i. 309, διαλεκτικώτατος. *Sext.* and *Diog.* ii. 111, quote two epigrams of Callimachus. His fallacies and his researches into motion, and into hypothetical sentences, will be mentioned hereafter. Pique at a dialectical defeat inflicted by Stilpo at the table of Ptolemy Soter, is said to have killed him (*Diog.*; *Plin.* Hist. Nat. vii. 53, 180). He bequeathed his dialectic to his five daughters; *Clem. Al.* Strom. iv. 523, A.; *Hieron.* adv. Jovin. i. t. iv. 186. His nickname, Kronos, is differently explained by Strabo and Diog., and in modern times by *Panzerbieter* in Jahn's Jahrb. f. Philol. Supplement b. V. 223, f., who, however, does not explain it altogether satisfactorily. Consult, also, *Steinhart* in Ersch. und Gruber's Encyclop. Sec. i. B., 25, p. 286.

[2] All we know of him is from *Diog.* ii. 110, who calls him the tutor of King Antigonus, and says that to Antigonus he addressed a book, περὶ βασιλείας. *Athen.* vi. 251 quotes an extract from the fourth book of his history, in which, if he has not made a gross mistake, πρώτου must be read for τρίτου. See *Mallet*, p. 96. Callicrates, also mentioned by Athenæus, is known from *Diodor.* xx. 21, as a favourite of Ptolemy Soter.

[3] Stilpo of Megara (*Diog.* ii. 113) must have lived until the end of the fourth century. At least he survived the capture of Megara by Ptolemy Lagi, and his defeat by Demetrius Poliorcetes, two events which happened 307 and 306 B.C. respectively, *Diodor.* xx. 37 and 45. On the former occasion the interview with Diodorus Cronus may have happened; for Stilpo never visited Egypt (*Diog.* 115). Since he died at an advanced age, we may approximately place his birth in 380, and his death in 300 B.C. Probably we ought to place the date of both later, for the notices about his pupils in *Diog.* ii. 113–120, *Senec.* Epist. 10, 1, lead us to believe that his active life was cotemporary with that of Theophrastus; and accordingly it cannot have begun long before the death of Aristotle. *Suid.* Εὐκλείδ. calls him successor to Ichthyas. Some of the pupils of Euclid are mentioned as his teachers, and (*Diog.* ii. 113) in particular Thrasymachus. (*Suid.* Εὐκλείδ. and Στίλπο.) Even Euclid himself is named by some, but none of these statements are probable. His

CHAP. XII.

machus. His spirited lectures made him an object of wonder to his cotemporaries, and the crowds who flocked from all sides to listen to them gained for the Megarian School a lustre such as it had not hitherto enjoyed.[1] With him the development of the Megarian doctrine took a new turn, the principles of the Cynic School which he had learnt from Diogenes[2] being incorporated with his own to such an extent, that doubts may be felt whether Stilpo rather belongs to the Cynics or to the Megarians.[3] Thereby he became the immediate precursor of the Stoa, into which these two branches of the Socratic philosophy were resolved by his pupil Zeno.[4] Other Megarians, however, continued faithful to the exclusively critical character of this school. Alexinus of Elis, partly a

character, as to which more will be said hereafter, is commended as upright, gentle, persevering, open, generous, and unselfish, *Diog.* ii. 117; *Plut.* Vit. Pud. c. 18, p. 536; adv. Col. 22, 1, p. 111, a. In early life dissipated, he entirely mastered this tendency by strength of will (*Cic.* De Fato, 5, 10). He also took part in public business, *Diog.* 114. Nine of his dialogues are mentioned by *Diog.* ii. 120.

[1] *Diog.* ii. 113, exaggerates in saying, τοσοῦτον δ' εὑρεσιλογίᾳ καὶ σοφιστείᾳ προῆγε τοὺς ἄλλους, ὥστε μικροῦ δεῆσαι πᾶσαν τὴν Ἑλλάδα ἀφορῶσαν εἰς αὐτὸν μεγαρίσαι. He also mentions (119 and 115) the pupils, who came over to him from other philosophers, and the universal admiration bestowed on him at Athens and by several princes. It is all the more striking that *Diog.* 120 calls his speeches ψυχροί.

[2] *Diog.* vi. 76.

[3] The proof of this will be given later.

[4] That Zeno was a pupil of Stilpo is stated by *Diog.* ii. 120; vii. 2, 24, on the authority of Heraclides. The same person is no doubt referred to in *Diog.* ii. 116, as Zeno the Phœnician. The founder of the Stoa is frequently called a Phœnician, *Diog.* vii. 15, 25, 30. In no case can it be Zeno of Sidon, the pupil of Apollodorus, as *Mallet*, p. 62, supposes, who was himself a pupil of Epicurus, and who, according to *Diog.* x. 25, vii. 35, continued faithful to Epicureanism.

cotemporary of Stilpo[1] but somewhat younger, is notorious for his captiousness; and logical subtleties are recorded[2] of Philo, the pupil of Diodorus.[3] Other Megarians of this and the following age are only known to us by name.[4] With the verbal criti-

[1] *Diog.* ii. 109, speaks of him as a pupil of Eubulides (*μεταξὺ δὲ ἄλλων ὄντων τῆς Εὐβουλίδου διαδοχῆς Ἀλεξῖνος ἐγένετο Ἠλεῖος*). The age in which he lived can be approximately determined by his disputes with Stilpo (*Plut.* Vit. Pud. c. 18, p. 536); with Menedemus (*Diog.* ii. 135), and with Zeno, whose strongest opponent he was, *Diog.* ii. 109; *Sext.* Math. ix. 108; *Plut.* Comm. Not. 10, 3, p. 1063. He must have been younger than Stilpo, and have flourished in the first ten years of the third century. His love of contention and his malicious ways gained for him the nickname Ἐλεγξῖνος, *Diog. Plut.* Vit. Pud. 18; Aristotle in *Eus.* Pr. Ev. xv. 2, 4. We also learn from Hermippus in *Diog.* that he retired to Olympia in his last years, in order to establish a new school there. This place of abode not suiting his pupils, he remained there alone, but soon died of an injury. For his writings consult *Diog.* ii. 110; vii. 163; *Athen.* xv. 696; Aristotle in *Eus.* l. c.

[2] *Diog.* vii. 16, a passage which does not appear so ambiguous as *Ritter*, Rh. Mus. ii. 30; Gesch. d. Phil. ii. 145, would make it, particularly when the subsequent accounts are taken into consideration. Diog. related that Zeno of Cittium was fond of his society; *Clemens*, Stromat. iv. 523, and *Jerome* adv. Jov. i., quote from his 'Menexenus' the information already given respecting the daughters of Diodorus, whom he must then have spoken of in terms of praise. It is a clear mistake on the part of Jerome to make him the teacher of Carneades. Still stranger is Mallet's mistake, confounding the disputant Philo with Philo of Larissa, the founder of the fourth Academy. The latter lived some 150 to 200 years later. Nor can Philo be reckoned among the Stoics, although this has been done by Fabricius in Sext. Pyrrh. ii. 110, and by *Prantl.* Gesch. d. Logik, i. 404.

[3] *Diog.* vii. 191, 194, mentions Philo's writings *περὶ σημασιῶν*, and *περὶ τρόπων*, against which Chrysippus wrote, without doubt meaning this Philo. To the same individual must be referred what *Cic.* Acad. ii. 47, 143, and *Sext.* Math. viii. 113, Pyrrh. ii. 110, say as to his views of hypothetical sentences differing from those of Diodorus, and what *Alex.* Aphi. in Anal. pr. 59, b, says respecting their differences in respect of the possible. By *Diog.* vii. 16, and Clemens he is surnamed *ὁ διαλεκτικός*.

[4] A dialectician Panthoides, doubtless the same person as

CHAP. XII.

cism of the Megarians is connected Pyrrho's philosophy of doubt exactly as the scepticism of Gorgias is connected with the critical subtleties of the Eleatics; the connecting links being Pyrrho, whom Bryso is said to have taught,[1] and Timon, who studied under Stilpo himself.[2]

B. *Their doctrine.*

The Megarian philosophy is only imperfectly known to us from the fragmentary notices of the ancients; frequently it is impossible to decide whether their statements refer to the founder and the older members, or only to the later followers of the

Sext. Math. vii. 13, mentions, and whose disagreement with Diodorus in respect of the possible (see p. 233, 1, 2) *Epictet.* Diss. ii. 19, 5, speaks of, is mentioned by *Diog.* v. 68, as the teacher of the Peripatetic Lyco, and must therefore have flourished 280 to 270 B.C. A dialectician Aristides is also mentioned by *Diog.* ii. 113, among the cotemporaries of Stilpo, and an Aristotle living in Sicyon about 255 B.C. *Plut.* Arat. 3. Dinias who is there named with him appears also to have been a Megarian. Somewhat younger must have been Artemidorus, who wrote against Chrysippus, *Diog.* ix. 53.

[1] *Diog.* ix. 61: Πύῤῥων ἤκουσε Βρύσωνος τοῦ Στίλπωνος, ὥς Ἀλέξανδρος ἐν Διαδοχαῖς. *Suid.* Πύῤῥων: διεήκουσε Βρύσωνος, τοῦ Κλεινομάχου μαθητοῦ. Instead of Bryso, Δρύσων was formerly read in *Diog. Sext.* Math. vii. 13, however also calls him Bryso. Suid. Πύῤῥων. These statements are not without their difficulties. Allowing it to be possible that Clinomachus and not Stilpo instructed Bryso, or that he enjoyed the instruction of both, the chronology is still troublesome. For how can Pyrrho, before Alexander's expedition to Asia, as Diog. expressly says, have studied under the son of a man, whose own professional career probably comes after that expedition? It seems as though the relation of Pyrrho and Bryso as pupil and teacher were an imaginary combination, designed to connect the school of Pyrrho with the Megarian. Possible it also is that Bryso, the teacher of Pyrrho, has been wrongly identified with the son of this Stilpo. *Suid.* Σωκράτ. calls Bryso the teacher of Pyrrho, a pupil of Socrates, or according to others a pupil of Euclid. *Röper*, Philol. xxx. 462, proposes to read in the passage of Diog. instead of Βρύσωνος τοῦ Στίλπωνος, Βρύσ. ἢ Στίλπ.

[2] *Diog.* ix. 109.

School. It is therefore very satisfactory to have from Plato [1] particulars respecting a theory in which Schleiermacher [2] first recognised Megarian views, and which, in common with most writers,[3] we feel justi-

[1] Soph. 242, B. Plato defined Sophistry as the art of deception. The difficulty immediately arises, that deception is only then possible, when not-being, to which all deception refers, admits a certain kind of being. It may then be asked, how is the being of the not-being possible? To answer this question Plato reviews various opinions respecting being. In the first place he examines the two most opposite statements, that being is the many, and that it is the one, and after having shown that neither a manifoldness of original substances without a substratum of unity, nor the unity of the Eleatics excluding the many, can be admitted, he continues, p. 245, E.: *τοὺς μὲν τοίνυν διακριβολογουμένους ὄντος τε πέρι καὶ μὴ πάντας μὲν οὐ διεληλύθαμεν, ὅμως δὲ ἱκανῶς ἐχέτω· τοὺς δὲ ἄλλως λέγοντας αὖ θεατέον.* These are again divided into classes, those who only allow reality to what is material, and others who are called 248, A., *οἱ τῶν εἰδῶν φίλοι.* Of the latter it is stated 246, B.: *τοιγαροῦν οἱ πρὸς αὐτοὺς* (the materialists) *ἀμφισβητοῦντες μάλα εὐλαβῶς ἄνωθεν ἐξ ἀοράτου ποθὲν ἀμύνονται νοητὰ ἄττα καὶ ἀσώματα εἴδη βιαζόμενοι τὴν ἀληθινὴν οὐσίαν εἶναι· τὰ δὲ ἐκείνων σώματα καὶ τὴν λεγομένην ὑπ' αὐτῶν ἀλήθειαν κατὰ σμικρὰ διαθραύοντες ἐν τοῖς λόγοις γένεσιν ἀντ' οὐσίας φερομένην τινὰ προσαγορεύουσιν.*

[2] Platon's Werke, ii. 2.

[3] *Ast*, Platon's Leben u. Schreiben, 201; *Deycks*, 37; *Heindorf* on Soph. 246, B.; *Brandis*, ii. a., 114; *Hermann*, Plat. 339; Ges. Abh. 246; *Stallbaum*, Plat. Parm. 60; Soph. f. Polit. 61; *Susemihl*, Genet. Entw. i. 298; *Steinhart*, Allg. Encyk. i. 29, 53; Platon's Werke, iii. 204, 423, 554; *Henne*, Ecole de Mégare, 84–158; *Prantl*, Gesch. d. Log. i. 37. Against Schleiermacher are Ritter, Rhein. Mus. von Niebuhr und Brandis ii. 305; *Petersen*, Zeitschrift f. Alterthümer, 1836, 892, *Henne*, p. 49, and *Mallet*, p. xxx., refers the description in Theætet. 185, C. of the formation of conceptions, to the Megarians, on the ground that it does not agree with Plato's own method. But it would seem that he is wrong in so doing, since we have no reason to think of others besides Plato and Socrates. The passage in Parm. 131, B. cannot be rightly referred to the Megarians, as has been done by *Schleiermacher*, Pl. Werke, i. 2, 409, and *Deycks*, p. 42. The question whether things participate in Ideas, is one which the Megarians did not examine, and it is widely remote from the view discussed in the Sophistes.

CHAP. XII.

fied in applying to them.[1] By making use of the testimony of Plato, and by considering the inward

[1] The following are the reasons. It is clear and generally allowed that Plato's description is too minute to be without reference to some philosophic School then existing. Even *Deussen*, De Plat. Sophiste, Marb. 1869, p. 44, is reduced to admit this. There is also definite reference to a Socratic School in the passage where an opinion is attributed to certain philosophers, to the effect that true existence only belongs to immaterial things. A philosophy of conceptions was unknown before the time of Socrates, and the description agrees with no one of the pre-Socratic Schools. The philosophers of conceptions are clearly distinguished from the Eleatics, and are manifestly quite different from them. Still less can the Pythagoreans be thought of, as *Mallet* has done, p. liii.; for they had neither a philosophy of conceptions, nor did they indulge in that subtle refutation of opponents, which Plato attributes to these philosophers. Nor can the language of *Plato*, 246, C., be quoted to prove the contrary, where speaking of the dispute between the idealists and the materialists he says that: ἐν μέσῳ δὲ περὶ ταῦτα ἄπλετος ἀμφοτέρων μάχη τις ἀεὶ ξυνέστηκεν. This does not mean that this dispute has always existed, but that it was as old as the Schools themselves, or that, every time the point was touched upon, a violent altercation ensued between the parties. We are not obliged by this statement to refer this view to an earlier period than that of Socrates. And among the Socratic Schools there is none to which it can be attributed with so much probability as to the Megarian. Some think that the passage refers to Plato (as *Socher*, Plat. Schriften, 265, and *Schaarschmidt*, Die Sammlung der Plat. Sch., 210, do); and this reference commends itself most to those who with them declare that the Sophistes is not the work of Plato. The reference would of course be to an earlier form of Plato's teaching or to such Platonists as had failed to advance with their school. This is the view of *Ueberweg*, Unters. Plat. Schrift. 277; *Pilger*, Ueber d. Athetese d. Plat. Soph. Berlin, 1869, 21; *Grote*, Plato, i. 458; iii. 482; *Campbell*, the Sophistes and Politicus of Plato, Soph. lxxiv. f. 125. But is it likely that Plato can have treated a theory of his own with so much irony as he lavishes, p. 246, A. B., on these εἰδῶν φίλοι? Is it Plato's teaching, or have we reason for thinking that it ever was Plato's teaching, that the δύναμις τοῦ ποιεῖν does not belong to Being but to the Becoming? In his system, as far as it is known to us, it does belong to the idea of the good, to the creative νοῦς of Timæus, to the αἰτία of Philebus, which must at any rate be reckoned as οὐσία

connection of the several doctrines, we hope a picture will be produced of the Megarian doctrine,

and not as γένεσις, and in Phædo 95, E., it belongs to ideas in general. Moreover, if the contested theory only belonged to a small portion of Plato's scholars, how could the little fraction be opposed to the materialists as the chief supporters of the idealistic point of view? Does not the whole description create the impression that the contrast was one which the writer saw before him, and not one made from different conceptions of his own metaphysic? It might seem that by friends of εἴδη in this passage Euclid cannot have been meant, because (1) according to Aristotle's definite assertion (Metaph. i. 6, 987, b, 7; xiii. 4, 1078, b, 9; Eth. N. 1. 4, 1096, a, 13) Plato first introduced the doctrine of ideas, and (2) the Megarians held one and not many primary substances. The first reason is not very cogent. Doubtless Plato first brought into notice the doctrine of ideas to which Aristotle refers, allowing that Euclid agreed with him in declaring the εἶδος to be the only real element in things. The second argument is not more conclusive. Euclid may well have insisted, that in every object the incorporeal form was the only real thing, and yet have gathered all these forms together under the one substance—the good. If the latter assertion involved him in contradiction with his original premises, the contradiction is not greater than that involved in denying every change, and yet speaking of an action as an ἐνεργεῖν of being. Indeed, how otherwise can he have advanced from the Socratic philosophy of conceptions to his doctrine of unity? And does not the language of the Sophistes, 246, B., telling how that the friends of ideas destroy matter by resolving it into its smallest particles, best correspond with Euclid and his school? Does it not best harmonise with the statement of Aristocles respecting the Megarians, that the latter should have refused to being the capacity to act or to suffer? whereas this would not at all harmonise with Plato. That these philosophers are included 245, E., among those ἄλλως λέγοντες is not true, ἄλλως λέγοντες meaning literally those who speak differently, with whom all does not turn (as with the philosophers mentioned 243, D.) upon the antithesis of being and not-being. With the philosophers to whom Plato comes 245, E., the question is not whether there is one or more than one form of being, everything else being not-being, but whether there is only the corporeal or the incorporeal. Conf. p. 243, D., with 246, A. Compare *Henne*, 105; *Bonitz*, Plat. Stud. ii. 49. In the explanation of διακριβολογουμένους, no one appears to have exactly hit the mark.

CHAP. XII.

which shall, in the main, faithfully represent the facts.

(1) *Conception of being and becoming.*

The starting-point of the Megarian philosophy must be looked for in Socrates' demand for a knowledge of conceptions. With this demand Euclid combined the Eleatic doctrine of a contrast between sensational and rational knowledge. Distinguishing these two kinds of knowledge by their objects far more than by their form, he arrived at the conviction that the senses show us what is capable of change and becoming, and that thought only can supply us with the knowledge of what is unchangeable and really existing.[1] He stood, therefore, in general, on the same footing as Plato, and it is possible that this view was simultaneously arrived at by both philosophers in their intellectual intercourse, and that owing to Plato Euclid was influenced by Heraclitus' view of the world of sense. Socrates had indeed made the immediate business of thought to be the acquisition of a knowledge of conceptions. Conceptions, accordingly, represent that part of a thing which never changes. Not material things, but only incorporeal species, taught Euclid, admit of true being.[2] The same view Stilpo expressed, when

[1] *Plato*, 248, A.: *Γένεσιν, τὴν δὲ οὐσίαν χωρίς που διελόμενοι λέγετε; ἦ γάρ;*—Ναί.—*Καὶ σώματι μὲν ἡμᾶς γενέσει δι' αἰσθήσεως κοινωνεῖν, διὰ λογισμοῦ δὲ ψυχῇ πρὸς τὴν ὄντως οὐσίαν, ἣν ἀεὶ κατὰ ταὐτὰ ὡσαύτως ἔχειν φατέ, γένεσιν δὲ ἄλλοτε ἄλλως.* For this reason Aristoc. in *Eus.* Pr. Ev. xiv. 17, 1, says of the Megarians and Eleatics together: *οἴονται γὰρ δεῖν τὰς μὲν αἰσθήσεις καὶ φαντασίας καταβάλλειν, αὐτῷ δὲ μόνον τῷ λόγῳ πιστεύειν.*

[2] In the passage of the Soph. 246, B., quoted at p. 257, 1, in which the words *τὰ δὲ ἐκείνων σώματα* must not be taken to mean 'the bodies of those

he refused to allow the general conception to apply to individual things, on the ground that a general conception implies something quite different from every individual thing, and not like these having its origin in time.[1] In this respect the Megarians again agree with Plato.[2] Whilst Plato, however, regarded species as living spiritual forces, Euclid, following in the steps of Parmenides, denied every kind of motion to being. He, therefore, reduced action and passion to the sphere of the becoming. Of being, he asserted, you can neither predicate action, nor passion, nor yet motion.[3]

conceptions,' εἴδη ἀσώματα, but 'the bodies of the materialists,' in which they look for all real being.

[1] *Diog.* ii. 119, says of him: ἔλεγε, τὸν λέγοντα ἄνθρωπον εἶναι μηδένα (in which we suggest εἰπεῖν instead of εἶναι), οὔτε γὰρ τόνδε λέγειν οὔτε τόνδε. τί γὰρ μᾶλλον τόνδε ἢ τόνδε; οὔτε ἄρα τόνδε. καὶ πάλιν· τὸ λάχανον οὐκ ἔστι τὸ δεικνύμενον. λάχανον μὲν γὰρ ἦν πρὸ μυρίων ἐτῶν· οὐκ ἄρα ἐστὶ τοῦτο λάχανον. Diogenes introduces this with the remark: δεινὸς δὲ ἄγαν ὢν ἐν τοῖς ἐριστικοῖς ἀνῄρει καὶ τὰ εἴδη, and it would in itself be possible, that Stilpo and others had derived their hostility to general conceptions, and especially to the Platonic ideas, from the Cynic School. But the above examples are not directed against the reality of groups expressed by a general conception, but against the reality of particular things. Stilpo denies that the individual is a man, because the expression man means something universal and different from any particular man. He denies that what is shown to him is cabbage, because there was cabbage 10,000 years ago; in other words, because the general conception of cabbage means something unchangeable, not something which has come into being. We may then believe with *Hegel*, Gesch. d. Phil. ii. 123, and *Stallbaum*, Plat. Parm. 65, that either Diogenes or his authority must have made some mistake here.

[2] Probably expressions like 'Hi quoque multa in Platone,' said of the Megarians by *Cic.* Acad. iv. 42, 129, refer to such points of similarity.

[3] *Plato*, Soph. 248, C.: λέγουσιν, ὅτι γενέσει μὲν μέτεστι τοῦ πάσχειν καὶ ποιεῖν δυνάμεως, πρὸς δὲ οὐσίαν τούτων οὐδετέρου τὴν δύναμιν ἁρμόττειν φασίν. It is accordingly afterwards repeatedly stated as their view:

CHAP. XII.

Connected with this denial of the becoming is the assertion, probably coming from Euclid, certainly from his school, that capacity does not exist beyond the time of its exercise; and that thus what is actual is alone possible.[1] What is simply possible but not actual, would at the same time be and not be. Here would be the very contradiction which Parmenides thought to discover in the becoming, and the change from the possible to the actual would be one of those changes which Euclid could not harmonise with the conception of being.[2] Hence,

[τὸ παντελῶς ὂν] ἀκίνητον ἑστὸς εἶναι. ἀκίνητον τὸ παράπαν ἑστάναι, and in opposition to this view Plato requires: καὶ τὸ κινούμενον δὴ καὶ κίνησιν συγχωρητέον ὡς ὄντα . . . . μήτε τῶν ἓν ἢ καὶ πολλὰ εἴδη λεγόντων τὸ πᾶν ἑστηκὸς ἀποδέχεσθαι.—Aristocl. in *Eus.* Pr. Ev. xiv. 17, 1. The proofs by which the Megarians denied motion will be described hereafter. It does not, however, seem likely that the objections raised to the theory of ideas in the first part of Plato's Parmenides are of Megarian origin, as *Stallbaum*, Pl. Parm. 57 and 65, supposes.

[1] *Arist.* Metaph. ix. 3: εἰσὶ δέ τινες οἵ φασιν, οἷον οἱ Μεγαρικοί, ὅταν ἐνεργῇ μόνον δύνασθαι, ὅταν δὲ μὴ ἐνεργῇ οὐ δύνασθαι. οἷον τὸν μὴ οἰκοδομοῦντα οὐ δύνασθαι οἰκοδομεῖν, ἀλλὰ τὸν οἰκοδομοῦντα ὅταν οἰκοδομῇ· ὁμοίως δὲ καὶ ἐπὶ τῶν ἄλλων. In refuting this statement Aristotle observes that it would make all motion and becoming impossible; which was just what the Megarians wanted. Further particulars on this point will be quoted from Diodorus in the sequel. The passage in the Sophistes, 248, C., which *Henne*, p. 133, connects with that of Aristotle, refers to something different.

[2] *Hartenstein*, p. 205, is of opinion that the above statement is made in direct contradiction to Aristotle. It would in this case belong to Eubulides. But the Aristotelian technical terms δύνασθαι, ἐνεργεῖν, do not prove much. Aristotle often expressed the statements of others in his own terminology. The Megarian doctrine already quoted, even if it comes from Euclid, can have no very great importance for Aristotle's system. It is only a peculiar way of stating the Eleatic hostility to becoming and motion. Nor can we defend the Megarians against Aristotle as *Grote*, Plato, iii. 491, does: because a builder without materials, tools and intentions, cannot build, and when these and

only what is immaterial and unchangeable is allowed by him to be actual, and regarded as the subject matter of science.

(2) *The Good.*

Socrates had described the good as the highest object of knowledge.[1] In this he was followed by Euclid.[2] Regarding that which is most essentially real as the highest object of knowledge, Euclid, in accordance with his principles, thought himself justified in transferring to the good all the attributes which Parmenides had assigned to real being. One only real good is there, unchangeable, ever the same, of which our highest conceptions are only different names. Whether we speak of God, or of Intelligence, or of Reason, we always mean one and the

other conditions are there, must build. For this is not at all the point on which the dispute between Aristotle and the Megarians turns. Aristotle on the contrary says in the connection of the above enquiry (Metaph. iv. 5, c. 7; 1049, a. 5), that if the necessary conditions for the exercise of a capacity are given (among which besides the δυνάμεις λογικαὶ the intention must be included), its exercise always follows. This, according to Grote, is likewise the meaning of the Megarian sentence, which he disputes. Its real meaning—that a capacity until it shows itself by action is not only kept in abeyance by the absence of the necessary means and conditions, but is not even existing—may be gathered from the objections urged by Aristotle, c. 3, and from the quotations, 268, 2. Grote to defend the Megarians attributes to them arguments which we have no right to attribute to them.

[1] See p. 134 and 148.

[2] That his assertions about the good should have nothing to do with the Socratic knowledge (*Hermann*, Ges. Abhandlung, 242) could only be accepted on the supposition that that knowledge was not knowledge about the good, and that Euclid was not a pupil of Socrates. A pure Eleatic philosopher, if he had only moved in an ethical sphere of ideas, would hardly have treated this part of philosophy in the same way as Euclid. As long as he remained a pure Eleatic philosopher, he could not have taken this ethical direction and have placed the conception of the good at the head of his system.

CHAP. XII.

same thing, the Good.[1] For the same reason the moral aim, as Socrates had already shown, is always one—the knowledge of the Good,—and if we speak of many virtues, all these are but varying names for one and the same virtue.[2]

What, however, is the relation of other things to this one Good? Even Euclid, as accounts tell us, denied any existence to what is not good;[3] from which it follows immediately, that besides the Good nothing real exists. On better authority this statement is attributed to the later Megarian School.[4] Therewith many conceptions, the reality of which had been originally assumed, were destroyed as such, and reduced, in as far as any reality was admitted about them, to mere names of the Good.[5] Here,

[1] *Cic.* Acad. iv. 42, 129: Megarici qui id bonum solum esse dicebant, quod esset unum et simile et idem semper (οἷον, ὅμοιον ταὐτόν). *Diog.* ii. 106, says of Euclid: οὗτος ἓν τὸ ἀγαθὸν ἀπεφαίνετο πολλοῖς ὀνόμασι καλούμενον· ὅτε μὲν γὰρ φρόνησιν, ὅτε δὲ θεόν, καὶ ἄλλοτε νοῦν καὶ τὰ λοιπά.

[2] *Diog.* vii. 161, says of the Stoic Aristo: ἀρετάς τ' οὔτε πολλὰς εἰσῆγεν, ὡς ὁ Ζήνων, οὔτε μίαν πολλοῖς ὀνόμασι καλουμένην, ὡς οἱ Μεγαρικοί. That this one virtue was the knowledge of the good, appears not only from the internal connection of the system and its external relation to Socrates, but also from Cicero l. c. who asserts: a Menedemo autem . . . Eretriaci appellati; quorum omne bonum in mente positum et mentis acie, qua verum cerneretur. Illi (the Megarians) similia, sed, opinor, explicata uberius et ornatius. Conf. *Plato*, Rep. vi. 505, B., in which Antisthenes is mentioned in addition to Euclid.

[3] *Diog.* ii. 106: τὰ δὲ ἀντικείμενα τῷ ἀγαθῷ ἀνῄρει μὴ εἶναι φάσκων.

[4] Arist. in *Eus.* Pr. Ev. xiv. 17, 1: ὅθεν ἠξίουν οὗτοί γε [οἱ περὶ Στίλπωνα καὶ τοὺς Μεγαρικοὺς] τὸ ὂν ἓν εἶναι καὶ τὸ μὴ ὂν ἕτερον εἶναι, μηδὲ γεννᾶσθαί τι μηδὲ φθείρεσθαι μηδὲ κινεῖσθαι τοπαράπαν. *Arist.* Metaph. xiv. 4; 1091, b, 13, refers to Plato, and can hardly be applied to the Megarians.

[5] *Prantl's* view, p. 35, that the conceptions of the Megarians must invariably have a nominalistic meaning, does

probably, traces of gradual development in the Megarian doctrine are to be found. Euclid apparently first spoke of a plurality of essential conceptions in contrast to objects of sense, and this form of teaching belongs primarily to a time in which his system was being developed out of this contrast.[1] At a later period the Megarians appear to have used the manifoldness of conceptions for the purpose of attacking popular notions,[2] otherwise keeping it in the background, and confining themselves to the essential oneness of being and the Good. Inconsistent, no doubt, they were; yet we can understand how they became involved in this contradiction by gradually pushing the Socratic theory of conceptions to the abstract doctrine of the Eleatic One.[3]

C. *Eristic.*

The sharper the contrast which they presented

not agree with the statements of Plato. If the Megarians declared conceptions and conceptions only to be ἀληθινὴ οὐσία, surely they were Realists, not Nominalists. Not even Stilpo can, accordingly, be called a Nominalist. He had, moreover, absorbed too much of the Cynic doctrines for us to be able to form from him any conclusion respecting the original Megarian views.

[1] Plato, at least in the passage before quoted, does not mention a good which is One. On the contrary, he speaks of his philosophers of conceptions differing from the Eleatics in assuming many conceptions.

[2] See p. 261, 1.

[3] *Henne*, p. 121, tries to get over the difficulty in another way. The Megarians, he believes, attributed being to each particular idea, in as far as it was a unity, and various conceptions were used by them to express various kinds of the good. But this very point—the existence of various kinds of good—was what the Megarians denied. Starting with the oneness of being, they cannot have arrived at the notion of a manifoldness of conceptions, since this oneness excludes in its abstract form any development or subordinate distinction. But it is quite possible that the Socratic conceptions may gradually have been lost in the Eleatic unity.

CHAP. XII.

to the prevailing mode of thought, the greater became the necessity for fortifying their own position against assault. Here again they had only to follow the example of the Eleatics. To prove the soundness of their position directly, as Parmenides had done, was no easy matter. More important results might be expected, if their opponents' ground were assailed by the criticism of Zeno and Gorgias. From Zeno the founder of the School had appropriated the Eleatic doctrine precisely in this its critical function, Zeno and the Sophists being the principal persons to draw attention hereto in central Greece. This path of criticism the Megarians now struck out with such preference, that the whole school herefrom derived its name.[1] We are assured by Diogenes,[2] that it was the practice even of Euclid, to attack conclusions and not premises—in other words, to refute by a reductio ad absurdum. It is also said that Euclid[3] rejected explanation by analogy—a form much used by Socrates—because a similar case when cited makes nothing clearer, and a dissimilar case is irrelevant. The most telling description of Euclid's method will probably be found in Plato, who, speak-

(1) *That of Euclid.*

[1] See p. 251, 3.

[2] ii. 107: *ταῖς τε ἀποδείξεσιν ἐνίστατο οὐ κατὰ λήμματα ἀλλὰ κατ' ἐπιφοράν.* Since in Stoical terminology—which we are of course not justified in ascribing to Euclid on the strength of this passage—*λῆμμα* means the major premiss, or more often both premises, and *ἐπιφορὰ* the conclusion (*Deycks*, 34; *Prantl*, 470), it is most probable that the meaning given above is the real meaning of these words.

[3] *Ibid.*: *καὶ τὸν διὰ παραβολῆς λόγον ἀνῄρει, λέγων ἤτοι ἐξ ὁμοίων αὐτὸν ἢ ἐξ ἀνομοίων συνίστασθαι· καὶ εἰ μὲν ἐξ ὁμοίων, περὶ αὐτὰ δεῖν μᾶλλον ἢ οἷς ὅμοιά ἐστιν ἀναστρέφεσθαι· εἰ δ' ἐξ ἀνομοίων, παρέλκειν τὴν παράθεσιν.*

ing in the Sophistes of the philosophers of conceptions, says that in their discourses they destroy matter piecemeal, in order to prove that it has no real being, but is subject to flux and change.[1] This is exactly the line which Zeno adopted, in order to prove the uncertainty of the perceptions of the senses;[2] and which we notice also in the Sorites of the later Megarians: the apparently substantial bodily mass is divided into its component parts, and there being no limit to the division, and no ultimate atom on which contemplation can rest, it is argued that matter must be itself unreal, and a mere passing phenomenon. Euclid is accordingly rightly regarded as the founder of the Megarian criticism. Still, with him criticism does not seem to have attained the character of formal captiousness, although objection may be taken to his controversial tone:[3] it would appear that, like Zeno before him, he was primarily anxious to maintain his positive principles, and that he only used the subtleties of argument as a means to this end. Nothing, at least, is known of him which would lead to an opposite conclusion, nor is any one of the quibbling fallacies laid to his charge, for which the Megarian school was afterwards notorious.

[1] See p. 257, 1; 260, 2.

[2] See *Zeller*, G. d. Griech. Part I., 496.

[3] According to *Diog.* ii. 30, Socrates had already observed, that because of his captiousness, he might associate possibly with Sophists, but not with human beings. But this statement proves but little, since it uses the term Sophist in a way peculiar to post-Socratic times. It is more worthy of belief (*Diog.* ii. 107) that Timon called him a quarrelsome person, who introduced amongst the Megarians a rage for disputes.

CHAP XII.

Among the immediate successors of Euclid, however, the element of captiousness prevailed over positive teaching. Such teaching as they had was too scanty to command attention for long, and too abstract to admit of further development. On the other hand a polemic against prevailing opinions presented to the sharp-witted, to the contentious, and to those ambitious of intellectual distinction, an unexplored field, over which the Megarians eagerly ranged.[1] Not seldom their metaphysical assumptions served only as occasions for hard fighting with words. Among the fallacies which are attributed to Eubulides,[2] though they probably belong

[1] The ordinary form of these captious proofs is that of asking questions. Hence the regular expression: λόγον ἐρωτᾶν (to raise a point) in *Diog.* ii. 108; 116; *Sext.* Math. x. 87; and the Μεγαρικὰ ἐρωτήματα in the fragment of Chrysippus; in *Plut.* Sto. Rep. 10, 9, p. 1036. Conf. *Arist.* Phys. viii. 8, 263, a, 4, 7; Anal. Pr. ii. 19, 66, a, 26; 36; i. 32, 47, a, 21. But like the Sophists, they refused every answer but Yes or No. *Diog.* ii. 135.

[2] *Diog.* ii. 108, enumerates 7: that called ψευδόμενος, that called διαλανθάνων, the Electra, the ἐγκεκαλυμμένος, the σωρίτης, the κερατίνης, the φαλακρός. The first of them is given as follows in *Arist.* Soph. El. 25, 180, a, 34, b, 2; *Alex.* ad loc. *Cic.* Acad. ii. 29, 95: If a man says he is at the moment telling a lie, is he telling a lie, or is he speaking truth? The διαλανθάνων, the ἐγκεκαλυμμένος, and the Electra are only different forms of the same fallacy. Do you know who is concealed? Do you know who is behind the veil? Did Electra know her brother before he announced himself to her? and the solution of them all consists in the fact, that he who was concealed, or behind the veil, or had not yet announced himself respectively, was known to, but not immediately recognised by the lookers on. See *Arist.* S. El. c. 24, 179, a, 33; *Alex.* in loc. and 49; *Lucian*, Vit. Auct. 22, and *Prantl.* The κερατίνης is as follows: Have you lost your horns? If you say Yes, you allow that you had horns. If you say No, you allow that you have them still. *Diog.* vii. 187; vi. 38; *Seneca*, Ep. 45, 8; *Gell.* xvi. 2, 9; *Prantl*, p. 53. The Sorites consists in the question: How

CHAP. XII.

(2) *Eristic of Eubulides.*

to an earlier time,[1] one only, the Sorites, has any intelligible relation to their metaphysics. By means of this form of argument it could be proved that no enduring being belongs to objects of sense, but that every such object passes into its opposite, and represents what is changing, and not what is real and unchangeable.[2] The rest appear to be simple sophisms, having no other object than to involve opponents in difficulties,[3] critical works of art, which made indeed the need felt of an accurate investigation into the laws of thought, but in the handling of which the aim of leading to a right intellectual method, by pointing out difficulties and refuting untenable opinions, is altogether lost sight of.

(3) *That of Alexinus.*

The powers of Alexinus in argument seem to

many grains make a heap? or more generally: With what number does Many begin? Of course it is impossible to assign a number. See *Cic.* Acad. ii. 28, 92; 16, 49; *Diog.* vii. 82; *Pers.* Sat. vi. 78; *Prantl*, p. 54. The φαλακρὸς is another form of the same: How many hairs must you lose to become a bald-head? See *Hor.* Ep. ii. 1, 45; *Prantl*, l. c.; *Deycks*, 51.

[1] There are, for instance, indications of the Sorites in Zeno and Euclid. In general it is difficult to say who are the discoverers of quibbles, which are taken seriously at the time they are produced, but are after all only bad jokes. *Seneca*, Ep. 45, 10, says that many books had been written on the ψευδόμενος, among which those of Theophrastus and Chrysippus are known to us from *Diog.* vii. 196; v. 49. Chrysippus, according to *Diog.* vii. 198, 192, also wrote on the διαλανθάνων, the ἐγκεκαλυμμένος, and the σωρίτης. Philetus of Cos is said to have worked himself to death in writing about the ψευδόμενος, *Athen.* ix. 401, e. The κερατίνης and ἐγκεκαλυμμένος were also attributed to Diodorus (*Diog.* ii. 111), and the former (*Diog.* vii. 187) as also the Sorites (*Diog.* vii. 82) to Chrysippus, certainly without reason to Chrysippus.

[2] Compare what will be later said about Diodorus' proofs in denying motions.

[3] The motion which *Prantl*, p. 52, sees in the ἐγκεκαλυμμένος is not so patent, and the assumptions of *Brandis*, p. 122, do not seem accurate.

CHAP. XII.

have been of a similar kind. He, at least, is only known to us as a captious disputant.[1] Beyond an argument in which he vainly attempted to entangle Menedemus in what is called the 'horned' fallacy, and a refutation of Xenophon's proofs of the reason able arrangement of the world,[3] which was subsequently repeated by the Academicians, nothing further is known of him.[4] In close connection with the Megarian doctrines may be placed the discussions of Diodorus on motion and destruction, on the possible and on hypothetical sentences.

(4) *That of Diodorus.*

(*a*) *On Motion.*

Tradition has preserved four arguments, by which Diodorus attempted to support the fundamental teaching of his school on the impossibility of motion. The first,[5] which in the main is the same as that of Zeno, is as follows. Supposing anything to move, it must either move in the space in which it is, or in the space in which it is not. In the former it has not room to move, because it entirely fills it; in the latter it can neither act nor be acted upon; hence motion is inconceivable.[6] The second is a less

[1] See p. 255, 1.

[2] In *Diog.* ii. 135.

[3] *Sext.* Math. ix. 107: Zeno had concluded, because the world is the best possible, and reason is higher than the absence of reason, that the world must have reason. See *Cic.* De N. D. ii. 8, 21; iii. 9, 22. To this Alexinus replied: τὸ ποιητικὸν τοῦ μὴ ποιητικοῦ καὶ τὸ γραμματικὸν τοῦ μὴ γραμματικοῦ κρεῖττόν ἐστι· καὶ τὸ κατὰ τὰς ἄλλας τέχνας θεωρούμενον κρεῖττόν ἐστι τοῦ μὴ τοιούτου. οὐδὲ ἓν δὲ κόσμου κρεῖττόν ἐστι· ποιητικὸν ἄρα καὶ γραμματικόν· ἐστιν ὁ κόσμος.

[4] *Cic.* N. D. iii. 8, 21; 10, 26; 11, 27.

[5] *Sext.* Pyrrh. ii. 242; iii. 71; Math. x. 85; i. 311.

[6] *Sext.* Pyrrh. iii. 243, mentions a similar argument against becoming in general, in immediate connection with the proof given above: Neither can what is come into being, for it exists already; nor can what is not, for nothing can happen to it;

accurate form of the same proof.[1] All that moves is in space: What *is* in space reposes: Therefore what is moved reposes. A third proof[2] is based on the assumption of infinitesimal atoms and particles. It is generally attributed to Diodorus.[3] Probably he only used it hypothetically, as Zeno did his argument, to refute ordinary notions.[4] It is this: As long as the particle A is in the corresponding space A, it does not move, because it completely fills it. Just as little does it move when it is in the next following space, B; for no sooner is it there than its motion has ceased. Accordingly it does not move at all. In this conclusion one cannot fail to discover the note of Zeno's inferences, and of that critical process which had been already described by Plato.[5] The fourth proof,[6] besides assuming the existence of atoms, distinguishes between partial and complete motion.[7] Every moving body must first have the

consequently nothing at all is. It is possible that this argument also belongs to Diodorus. But *Steinhart* is wrong in attributing to him (Allg. Encykl. Sect. i. vol. xxv. p. 288) the distinction between space in the wider and in the narrower sense, which is found in *Sext.* Pyrrh. iii. 75; Math. x. 95, since it would appear from these passages that the distinction was made with a view to meet Diodorus' objections.

[1] *Sext.* Math. x. 112.

[2] *Id.* x. 143 and 119. *Alexander*, too, De Sensu, 125, b, mentions Diodorus, λόγος περὶ τῶν ἀμερῶν.

[3] *Id.* ix. 362; Pyrrh. iii. 32; Dionys. in *Eus.* Pr. Ev. xiv. 23, 4; *Stob.* Ekl. i. 103; *Pseudo-clement*, Recogn. viii. 15, all of which point to one common source. *Simpl.* Phys. 216, b; Schol. in Arist. 405, a, 21. Diodorus called these atoms ἀμερῆ.

[4] Even the first proof, according to *Sext.* Math. x. 85, was put in such a shape as to prove that every atom fully occupied its space; but this is unimportant here.

[5] See p. 266.

[6] *Sext.* Math. x. 113.

[7] κίνησις κατ' ἐπικράτειαν an κίνησις κατ' εἰλικρίνειαν.

CHAP. XII.

majority of its particles moved, before it can move as a whole; that it should move with the majority is, however, not conceivable. For supposing a body to consist of three atoms, two of which move whilst the third is at rest, such a body must move because the majority of its particles move. The same applies, when a fourth atom at rest is added; for the body being moved κατ' ἐπικράτειαν, the three atoms of which it consists are moved, consequently the fourth at rest is added to the three moving atoms. Why not equally when a fifth and a sixth atom is added? So that a body consisting of 10,000 particles must be moved, if only two of these first move. If this however is absurd, a movement of the majority of particles is inconceivable, and therefore a movement of the whole body. The inconclusiveness of this argument Sextus already noticed.[1] Diodorus, however, appears to have considered it unanswerable, and hence, he concludes all his researches by saying that it never can be said of a thing, It is moving, but only, It has moved.[2] He was, in other words, prepared to allow what the senses seemed to prove,[3] that a body is now in one place and now in another, but he declared the transition from the one to the other to be impossible. This is indeed a contradiction, and as such it was laid to his charge by the

[1] *Sext.* Math. x. 112, 118. A further argument, the first argument of Zeno's, is not attributed to Diodorus by *Sext.* Math. x. 47. He only says as to its result, that Diodorus agreed therein with the Eleatics.

[2] *Sext.* Math. x. 48; 85; 91; 97–102.

[3] This reason is specially mentioned by *Sext.* Math. x. 86.

ancients, and by him very inadequately answered.[1] At the same time it is a deviation from the original teaching of his school. Euclid denied motion absolutely, and would just as little have allowed a completed motion as a transition in the present.

(b) On Destruction.

With the third of these arguments agrees substantially the argument of Diodorus that nothing perishes. It is as follows. A wall, he says, does not perish; so long as the stones keep together, it stands; but when the stones are separated it no longer exists.[2] That it may however *have* perished, he appears to have likewise allowed.

(c) On the Possible.

Closely related to the enquiry into motion, are his discussions on what is possible. In both cases the conceivability of change is the point raised, but in one case it is raised in reference to something, in the other abstractedly. In both cases, Diodorus stands on the same footing with regard to his School. The older Megarians allowed as possible only what actually is, understanding by actual what was before them in the present.[3] To this Diodorus added what might be in the future, by saying: Possible is what either is actual or what will be actual.[4]

[1] See *Sext.* 91, 97. Diodorus nere proves the assertion that anything predicated of the past may be true, whilst it is not true predicated of the present, by such irrelevant statements as that it can be said of Helen that she *had* three husbands (one after another), but never that she *has* three (cotemporaneously). This example is sufficient to show how erroneous Grote's view (Plato iii. 501) is, that Diodorus only intended to assert that present motion is the transition-point between the past and the present.

[2] *Sext.* Math. x. 347.

[3] See p. 262.

[4] *Cic.* De Fato, 6, 12; 7, 13; 9, 17; Ep. ad Fam. ix. 4; *Plut.* Sto. Rep. 46, p. 1055; *Alex.*

CHAP. XII.

In proof of this statement he used an argument, which goes by the name of *κυριεύων*, and is still admired after centuries [1] as a masterpiece of subtle ingenuity. It is in the main as follows: From anything possible nothing impossible can result; [2] but it is impossible that the past can be different from what it is; for had this been possible at a past moment, something impossible would have resulted from something possible. It was therefore never possible. And speaking generally it is impossible that anything should happen differently from what has happened.[3]

(5) *That of Philo.*

(*a*) *On the Possible.*

Far less exacting was Philo, a pupil of Diodorus, when he declared everything to be possible, even should outward circumstances prevent it from being

Aph. in Anal. Pr. 59, b; Schol. in Arist. 163, b. 29; *Simpl.* ibid. 65, b, 7; *Philip*, ibid. 163, b, 19; *Boeks*, de Interpret. Op. ed. Basil, 364; *Prantl*, Gesch. d. Log. i. 19. The above sentence is expressed here thus: Possible is ὅπερ ἢ ἔστιν ἀληθὲς ἢ ἔσται.

[1] Comp. *Epict.* Diss. ii. 18, 18: we ought to be proud of moral actions, οὐκ ἐπὶ τῷ τὸν κυριεύοντα ἐρωτῆσαι, and just before: κομψὸν σοφισμάτιον ἔλυσας, πολὺ κομψότερον τοῦ κυριεύοντος. He also mentions, ii. 19, 9, treatises of Cleanthes, Chrysippus, Antipater, and Archidemus on the κυριεύων. Chrysippus could only meet it (according to *Alex.* in Anal. Pr. 57, b, in Schol. in Arist. 163, a, 8) by asserting that possibly the impossible might result from the possible. Other passages are quoted by *Prantl*, p. 40, 36.

[2] So ἀκολουθεῖν is rendered, thus keeping up the ambiguity of the original, where ἀκολουθεῖν means not only sequence in time, but causal sequence.

[3] *Epict.* Diss. ii. 19, 1: ὁ κυριεύων λόγος ἀπὸ τοιούτων τινῶν ἀφορμῶν ἠρωτῆσθαι φαίνεται· κοινῆς γὰρ οὔσης μάχης τοῖς τρισὶ τούτοις πρὸς ἄλληλα, τῷ ‘πᾶν παρεληλυθὸς ἀληθὲς ἀναγκαῖον εἶναι,’ καὶ τῷ ‘δυνατῷ ἀδύνατον μὴ ἀκολουθεῖν,’ καὶ τῷ ‘δυνατὸν εἶναι ὃ οὔτ’ ἔστιν ἀληθὲς οὔτ’ ἔσται.’ συνιδὼν τὴν μάχην ταύτην ὁ Διόδωρος τῇ τῶν πρώτων δυοῖν πιθανότητι συνεχρήσετο πρὸς παράστασιν τοῦ μηδὲν εἶναι δυνατὸν ὃ οὔτ’ ἔστιν ἀληθὲς οὔτ’ ἔσται. Conf. *Cic.* De Fato, 6.

realised,[1] provided a thing has only the capacity therefor. This was undeniably a departure from the Megarian teaching.

(b) On hypothetical sentences.

In regard, too, to the truth of hypothetical sentences, Philo laid down criteria different from those of his teacher.[2] Diodorus declared those conditional sentences to be true, in which the apodosis neither can be false, nor ever could be false if only the protasis be true. Philo says more vaguely, those are true in which there is not a true protasis and a false apodosis. The question here appears, however, to have been one of formal correctness in expressing logical rules.[3]

(c) On the meaning of words.

With Diodorus' view of the possible the assertion appears to be connected, that no words are meaningless or ambiguous, every one always meaning something, and always requiring to be understood according to this meaning:[4] he will only allow that meaning of a word to be possible which is actually present to the speaker's mind. Respecting Diodorus, however, and the whole Megarian School, our infor-

[1] *Alex.*-Simpl. in Categ.-Schol. in Arist. 65, a, 39, b, 6; *Boeks*, l. c. *Panthoides*, according to *Epict.* Diss. ii. 19, 5, attempted by another turn to avoid Diodorus' argument, by disputing the sentence that everything past must be of necessity.

[2] See *Sext.* Pyrrh. ii. 110; Math. viii. 113; i. 309; *Cic.* Acad. iv. 47, 143.

[3] The inferences by which *Sextus*, M. viii. 115, refutes Philo do not affect his real meaning at all, however much they may follow from the words of his definition. Hence *Prantl*, p. 454, can hardly have quite grasped the meaning of Philo.

[4] *Gell.* xi. 12; *Ammon.* De Interpret. 32, a; Schol. in Arist. 1103, b, 15; *Simpl.* Categ. f. 6, h. In order to show that every word has a meaning, Diodorus, according to Ammon., gave the name ἀλλαμὴν to one of his slaves.

CHAP. XII.

mation is far too scanty to enable us to bring the fragments of their teaching into a perfectly satisfactory composition,[1] although enough is known to evince one and the same tendency in all these thinkers. It may then be assumed as probable, that the Megarians did not confine themselves to those logical subtleties which are known to us; our notices are, however, too deficient for us to be able to attribute others to them with anything like certainty.[2]

(6) That of Stilpo, which adopted much from the Cynics. (a) Every combination of subject and predicate re-

A peculiar position in the Megarian philosophy is that occupied by Stilpo. Ever ready to defend the teaching of the School at the head of which he stood, clinging to universal conceptions, maintaining the impossibility of becoming, the unity of being,[3] and the difference between sensuous and rational perceptions,[4] he at the same time combines with his Megarian views theories and aims which originally

[1] *Ritter's* (Rh. Mus. ii. 310, Gesch. der Phil. ii. 140) conjectures seem in many respects to go beyond historical probability, and beyond the spirit of the Megarian teaching. To illustrate this here would take too long.

[2] *Prantl*, p. 43, believes that the majority of the sophisms enumerated by Aristotle really belong to the Megarians. Most of them, however, would appear to come from the Sophists; in proof of which a reference may be made to Plato's Euthydemus, which can hardly have the Megarians in view. Towards Euclid Plato would not have used such language, as may be gathered from the Sophistes, 246, C., and the introduction to the Theætetus; and Eubulides had not appeared when Plato composed the Euthydemus. That the Megarians made use of many of the Sophistic fallacies is of course not denied. Only nothing for certain is known of such use.

[3] See pp. 261, 3; 264, 4.

[4] Compare the passage in Aristocles quoted p. 260, 1, in which οἱ περὶ Στίλπωνα καὶ τοὺς Μεγαρικοὺς are spoken of in addition to the Eleatics.

jected as impossible.

belonged to the Cynics. In the first place he rejected, as did Antisthenes, every combination of subject and predicate, since the conception of the one is different from the conception of the other, and two things with different conceptions can never be declared to be the same.[1] The doctrine of the unity of being,[2] in as far as it can be shown to have originated with Stilpo, may be deduced as a corollary from this view; for if nothing can be predicated of anything else, it follows that being can alone be predicated of itself.

Truly cynical are also Stilpo's moral principles. The captious logic to which other Megarians devoted themselves with speculative onesidedness, to the entire neglect of the ethical element,[3] was also a

[1] In *Plut.* adv. Col. 22, 1, p. 1119, the *Epicurean* Stilpo raises the objection: τὸν θεὸν ἀναιρεῖσθαι ὑπ' αὐτοῦ, λέγοντος ἕτερον ἑτέρου μὴ κατηγορεῖσθαι. πῶς γὰρ βιωσόμεθα, μὴ λέγοντες ἄνθρωπον ἀγαθὸν . . . ἀλλ' ἄνθρωπον ἄνθρωπον καὶ χωρὶς ἀγαθὸν ἀγαθόν; . . . and again, c. 23: οὐ μὴν ἀλλὰ τὸ ἐπὶ Στίλπωνος τοιοῦτόν ἐστιν. εἰ περὶ ἵππου τὸ τρέχειν κατηγοροῦμεν, οὔ φησι ταὐτὸν εἶναι τῷ περὶ οὗ κατηγορεῖται τὸ κατηγορούμενον, ἀλλ' ἕτερον μὲν ἀνθρώπῳ τοῦ τί ἦν εἶναι τὸν λόγον, ἕτερον δὲ τῷ ἀγαθῷ· καὶ πάλιν τὸ ἵππον εἶναι τοῦ τρέχοντα εἶναι διαφέρειν· ἑκατέρου γὰρ ἀπαιτούμενοι τὸν λόγον οὐ τὸν αὐτὸν ἀποδίδομεν ὑπὲρ ἀμφοῖν. ὅθεν ἁμαρτάνειν τοὺς ἕτερον ἑτέρου κατηγοροῦντας. The very same thing will be found in the case of Antisthenes. All the less reason has Plutarch to regard Stilpo's assertion as a mere joke. The same proof is given by *Simpl.* Phys. 26, a.: διὰ δὲ τὴν περὶ ταῦτα (the distinction between the different categories and the ambiguity of words) ἄγνοιαν καὶ οἱ Μεγαρικοὶ κληθέντες φιλόσοφοι λαβόντες ὡς ἐναργῆ πρότασιν, ὅτι ὧν οἱ λόγοι ἕτεροι ταῦτα ἕτερά ἐστι καὶ ὅτι τὰ ἕτερα κεχώρισται ἀλλήλων, ἐδόκουν δεικνύναι αὐτὸν αὑτοῦ κεχωρισμένον ἕκαστον: i.e. since the conception of Σωκράτης μουσικὸς is a different one from that of Σωκράτης λευκός, the one according to Megarian hypothesis must be a different person from the other.

[2] See p. 264.

[3] Excepting Euclid's doctrine of the oneness of virtue, nothing bearing on Ethics is

CHAP. XII.

characteristic of Stilpo;[1] and perhaps it is only an accident that no subtle assertion or discovery of his is on record. His character, however, is not always mentioned by biographers with the greatest respect;[2] many traits being recorded of him, which identify his morality with that of the Cynics.

(b) The highest good placed in apathy.

The highest good he placed in that apathy, which forbids the feeling of pain even to exist. The wise man is required to be in himself independent, not even standing in need of friends to secure happiness.[3] When Demetrius Poliorcetes enquired after his losses by the plunder of Megara, he gave for answer that he had seen no one carrying off his knowledge.[4] When reminded of the immoral life of his daughter, he rejoined, that if he could not bring honour on her, she could not bring disgrace on him.[5] Banish-

known as belonging to the Megarians.

[1] See Chrysipp. in *Plut.* Sto. Rep. 10, 11, p. 1036, and pp. 212, 2; 211, 6.

[2] See p. 252, note 3.

[3] *Sen.* Ep. 9, 1: 'An merito reprehendat in quadam epistola Epicurus eos, qui dicunt sapientem se ipso esse contentum et propter hoc amico non indigere, desideras scire. Hoc objicitur Stilboni ab Epicuro et iis, quibus summum bonum visum est animus impatiens.' And a little further on: Hoc inter nos et illos interest: noster sapiens vincit quidem incommodum omne sed sentit; illorum ne sentit quidem.' Connected herewith is the observation of Stilpo in Teles. in *Stob.* Floril. 103, 83, in order to warn from excessive grief at the death of relatives. What *Alex.* Aphr. De An. 103, a, remarks, also probably applies to Stilpo, that the Megarians look on ἀσχλησία as πρῶτον οἰκεῖον.

[4] *Plutarch,* Demet. c. 9; Tranquil. An. c. 17, p. 475; Puer. Ed. c. 8, p. 6; *Sen.* de Const. 5, 6; Epis. 9, 18; *Diog.* ii. 115; Floril. *Joan.* Damasc. ii. 13, 153 (*Stob.* Floril. ed. Mein. iv. 227). That Stilpo thereby lost his wife and daughter is probably a rhetorical exaggeration of Seneca. The well-known 'omnia mea mecum porto,' attributed by Seneca to Stilpo, is by Cicero referred to Bias of Prisne.

[5] *Plut.* An. Tran. c. 6; *Diog* ii. 114.

CHAP. XII.

ment he would not allow to be an evil.[1] To be independent of everything external and to be absolutely free from wants—this highest standard of Cynicism for the wise man—was also his ideal. And lastly, the free attitude towards religion adopted by the Cynics was shared by him, and finds expression in many of his utterances.[2]

(c) The Cynic and Megarian theories not logically harmonised by him.

Whether, and if so, in what way, he attempted to set up a logical connection between the Cynic and Megarian theories, we are not told. In itself, such a task was not difficult. With the assertion that no subject can admit a predicate, Euclid's hostile attitude towards proof by analogy is closely related; this too rests on the general proposition that things dissimilar cannot be compared. It is also quite in harmony with the negative criticism of the Megarians; and if Euclid denied to the good any form of manifoldness, others might add, as Antisthenes really did, that the one and not the manifold could alone exist. Moreover, from the oneness of the good the apathy of the wise man might be deduced, considering that all else besides the good is unreal and indifferent.[3] The denial of the popular faith was also involved in the doctrine of the one, even as

[1] In the fragment in *Stob.* Flor. 40, 8.

[2] According to *Diog.* ii. 116, he proved that the Athene of Phidias was not a God, and then before the Areopagus evasively replied that she was not a θεὸς but a θεά, and when Crates asked him as to prayers and sacrifices, replied that these subjects could not be discussed in the street. The story in *Plut.* Prof. in Virt. 12, p. 83, of the dream in which he conversed with Poseidon is apparently invented to justify his omission to sacrifice.

[3] Conf. *Diog.* ii. 106, and p. 263, 3.

CHAP. XII.

it was first taught by Xenophanes. In the Cynic element as adopted by Stilpo, there were not wanting, it is true, points of approach to the Megarians, but to allow knowingly such an element to exist was a departure from the original form of the Megarian teaching.

II. *Elean-Eretrian School.*

A. *Its history.*

Closely connected with the Megarian school is the Elean-Eretrian, respecting which very little information has reached us. Its founder was Phædo of Elis,[1] the well-known favourite of So-

[1] See *Preller's* Phædo's Life and Writings, Rhein. Mus. für Philol. iv. 391. Phædo, the scion of a noble Elean family, had been taken captive not long before the death of Socrates, probably 400 or 401 B.C. Preller concludes from Phædo, 89, B., that he was not eighteen years of age at the time of the death of Socrates; it may, however, be asked whether Phædo followed Athenian customs in his dress. He was employed as a slave in most humiliating services at Athens, until one of Socrates' friends (besides Crito, Cebes and Alcibiades are both mentioned, the latter certainly not being at Athens at the time, and probably not being alive) redeemed him at the intercession of Socrates. See *Diog.* ii. 31, 105; *Suid.* under Φαίδων; and *Hesych.* Vir Illustr. Φαίδων. *Gell.* N. A. ii. 18; *Macrob.* Sat. i. 11; *Lact.* Inst. iii. 25, 15; *Orig.* c. Cels. iii. 67; *Cic.* N. D. i. 33, 93; *Athen.* xi. 507, c. Preller not improbably finds the source of the story in *Hermippus*, περὶ τῶν διαπρεψάνεων ἐν παιδείᾳ δούλων. *Grote* (Plato, iii. 503) objects to this story, that no conquest of Elis took place at that time, whereas Diog. says of Phædo: συνεάλω τῇ πατρίδι. He therefore infers that Μήλιος should be read for Ἠλεῖος in *Diog.* ii. 105. Yet Phædo is called an Elean by both *Gell.* l. c. and *Strabo*, ix. 1, 8, p. 393, and his school called Elean. If Elis itself did not fall into an enemy's hand, its suburbs were occupied by the Spartan army in the Elean-Spartan war, probably in the spring of 408 B.C. (*Xen.* Hell. iii. 2, 21, and *Preller*, on the passage, *Curtius*, Gr. Gesch. iii. 149, 757.) Phædo appears to have been taken captive at that time. Most probably Phædo left Athens on the death of Socrates. But whether he at once returned home, or repaired with others to Euclid at Megara, is unknown. *Diog.* ii. 105, mentions two genuine and four spurious dialogues of his. His Zopyrus is even quoted by *Pollux*, iii. 18, and the Antiatheista in *Bekker's* Anecdot. i. 107. Panætius seems to have had doubts as to all the treatises passing

crates.[1] On the death of his teacher, Phædo collected a circle of disciples in his native town, who thence received the name of the Elean philosophers.[2] Plistanus is named as his successor,[3] and Archipylus and Moschus as his pupils.[4] Beyond the names, we know nothing of any one of them. By Menedemus and Asclepiades,[5] the school was removed to Eretria, and it was then called the Eretrian.[6] Flourishing

under his name, *Diog.* ii. 64. He is called by Gellius 'philosophus illustris,' and his writings are spoken of as 'admodum elegantes.' Even *Diog.* ii. 47, enumerates him among the most distinguished Socraticists.

[1] Compare for his relations to Socrates the Phædo, 58, D. 89, H.

[2] Ἠλειακοί, *Strabo*, ix. 1, 8, p. 393; *Diog.* ii. 105, 126.

[3] *Diog.* ii. 105.

[4] 126. Perhaps these men were not immediate pupils of his. Since nothing is said of Menedemus' studying under Plistanus, the latter, we may suppose, was no longer alive.

[5] The account given by *Diog.* ii. 125 of these philosophers in his life of Menedemus (probably taken from Antigonus of Carystus and Heraclides Lembus) is as follows: Menedemus of Eretria, originally a tradesman, had been sent as a soldier to Megara. There he became acquainted with the school of Plato (so Diog. says with Plato; but this is chronologically impossible) and joined it together with his friend Asclepiades, both of them (according to *Athen.* iv. 168, a) earning a living by working at night. Soon, however, they joined Stilpo at Megara, and thence went to Moschus and Archipylus at Elis, by whom they were introduced to the Elean doctrines. Returning to their native city and becoming connected by marriage, they continued together in faithful friendship until the death of Asclepiades, even after Menedemus had risen to highest rank in the state, and had attained wealth and influence with the Macedonian princes. The sympathetic, noble and firm character of Menedemus, his pungent wit (on which *Plut.* Prof. in Virt. 10, p. 81; Vit. Pud. 18, p. 536), his moderation (*Diag.* ii. 129; *Athen.* x. 419, e), his liberality and his merits towards his country, are a subject of frequent panegyric. Soon after the battle of Lysimachia, which took place 278 B.C., he died, possibly by suicide—the result of a grief which is differently stated—at the age of seventy-four. According to Antigonus in *Diog.* ii. 136, he left no writings.

[6] *Strabo*, ix. 1, 8; *Diog.* ii. 105, 126; *Cic.* Acad. iv. 42, 129.

CHAP. XII.

as its condition here was for a time, it appears soon to have died out.[1]

B. *Remains of their teaching.*

Among its adherents[2] Phædo and Menedemus are the only two respecting whose opinions any information is forthcoming, and that is little enough. By Timon[3] Phædo is classed with Euclid as a babbler, which points to an argumentative tendency.[4] Perhaps, however, he devoted himself to Ethics[5] more than Euclid did. Menedemus at least appears to have been distinguished from his cotemporary quibblers by having devoted his attention to life and to moral questions. He is, however, spoken of as a sharp and skilful disputant.[6] Hardly going the length of Antisthenes in declaring every combination of subject and predicate impossible,[7] he still was captious enough to allow only affirmative judgments to be valid, rejecting negative and hypothetical ones.[8]

[1] *Plut.* Tranqu. An. 13, p. 472.

[2] *Athen.* iv. 162, e, mentions a certain Ctesibius as a pupil of Menedemus, but what he says of him has nothing to do with philosophy. A treatise of the Stoic Sphærus against the Eretrian School in 260 B.C. is the last trace of the existence of the Eretrian School. *Diog.* vii. 178.

[3] *Diog.* ii. 107.

[4] The Platonic Phædo does not give the slightest ground for thinking, as *Steinhart*, Plat. W. iv. 397, does, that Phædo was inclined to a sceptical withholding of judgment.

[5] Compare the short but clever fragment on the subject of morals, which *Sen.* Ep. 94, 41, quotes from Phædo.

[6] *Diog.* ii. 134: ἦν δὲ δυσκατανόητος ὁ Μ. καὶ ἐν τῷ συνθέσθαι δυσανταγώνιστος. ἐστρέφετό τε πρὸς πάντα καὶ εὑρεσιλόγει· ἐριστικώτατός τε, καθά φησιν Ἀντισθένης ἐν διαδοχαῖς, ἦν. The verses of Epicrates in *Athen.* ii. 59, cannot well refer to this Menedemus, since they are also directed against Plato, who was then still living.

[7] Even this is asserted. According to Phys. 20, a (Schol. in Arist. 330, a, 3), the Eretrians asserted μηδὲν κατὰ μηδενὸς κατηγορεῖσθαι. They appear in this passage to be confounded with the Cynics and the later Megarians.

[8] *Diog.* ii. 135.

Chrysippus [1] blames his exploded fallacies [2] as well as Stilpo's. It may also be true that he disputed the view that properties exist apart from particular objects, in the spirit of Cynic nominalism.[3] It is asserted that in positive opinions he was a Platonist and only employed argument for amusement.[4] From what has been already stated, this seems incredible; it does not follow from his disputes with Alexinus,[5] and is in itself most improbable.[6] So much seems to be ascertained, that, together with Stilpo, he attributed to ethical doctrines a value above criticism. For we not only hear that he admired Stilpo, who was his teacher, more than any other philosopher,[7] and that he was himself often

[1] *Plut.* Sto. Rep. 10, 11, p. 1036.

[2] *Hermann*, Ges. Abh. 253, refers to Menedemus the verses of John Salisbury (Enthet. ed. Peters, p. 41), in which a certain Endymion is mentioned, who called fides, opinio vera, and error, opinio fallax, and who denied that you could know what was false, for no knowledge could be deceptive. The allusion does not, however, appear probable. The continuation, that the sun corresponds to truth, and the moon to falsehood, that error and change bear rule under the moon, but truth and immutability in the domain of the sun, certainly does not come from Menedemus.

[3] *Simpl.* Categ. Schol. in Arist. 68, a, 24: οἱ ἀπὸ τῆς Ἐρετρίας ἀνῄρουν τὰς ποιότητας ὡς οὐδαμῶς ἐχούσας τι κοινὸν οὐσιῶδες ἐν δὲ τοῖς καθέκαστα καὶ συνθέτοις ὑπαρχούσας.

[4] Heraclides in *Diog.* ii. 135. *Ritter's* conjecture, Gesch. d. Phil. ii. 155, that this Menedemus is confounded with Menedemus the Pyrrhæan, whom we know from *Plut.* adv. Col. 32, p. 1126, 8, and *Athen.*, is hardly to be trusted. For Heraclides Lembus had treated the Eretrians in detail, as we learn from *Diog.*, so that it is difficult to imagine such a confusion. The context also tells against that view.

[5] *Diog.* 135, 136, says that he was constantly attacking Alexinus with violent derision, but yet did him some service.

[6] *Diog.* 134: τῶν δὲ διδασκάλων τῶν περὶ Πλάτωνα καὶ Ξενοκράτην . . . κατεφρόνει.

[7] *Diog.* 134.

CHAP. XII.

laughed at for being a Cynic,[1] but we know that he occupied himself with enquiring after the chief good in a practical way. He affirmed that there was only one good intelligence,[2] which, to his mind, was identical with a rational direction of the will.[3] What are commonly spoken of as distinct virtues, are, he maintained, only different names of this one virtue;[4] by his activity as a statesman,[5] he proved that his aim was not dead knowledge. In his free views of religion he likewise reminds us of Stilpo and the Cynics.[6] About this time Zeno having united the most valuable and lasting parts of the Megarian and Cynic teaching in the more comprehensive Stoic system, stragglers, such as the Eretrians, soon found themselves unable to exercise any important influence.

[1] *Diog.* 140: τὰ μὲν οὖν πρῶτα κατεφρονεῖτο, κύων καὶ λῆρος ὑπὸ τῶν Ἐρετρείων ἀκούων.

[2] *Cic.* Acad. ii. 42: *Diog.* 123: πρὸς δὲ τὸν εἰπόντα πολλὰ τὰ ἀγαθὰ ἐπύθετο πόσα τὸν ἀριθμὸν καὶ εἰ νομίζοι πλείω τῶν ἑκατόν· and in 134 are some questions to prove that the useful is not the good.

[3] *Diog.* 136: καί ποτέ τινος ἀκούσας, ὡς μέγιστον ἀγαθὸν εἴη τὸ πάντων ἐπιτυγχάνειν ὧν τις ἐπιθυμεῖ, εἶπε· πολὺ δὲ μεῖζον τὸ ἐπιθυμεῖν ὧν δεῖ.

[4] *Plut.* Virt. Mor. 2: Μενέδημος μὲν ὁ ἐξ Ἐρετρίας ἀνῄρει τῶν ἀρετῶν καὶ τὸ πλῆθος καὶ τὰς διαφορὰς, ὡς μιᾶς οὔσης καὶ χρωμένης πολλοῖς ὀνόμασι· τὸ γὰρ αὐτὸ σωφροσύνην καὶ ἀνδρείαν καὶ δικαιοσύνην λέγεσθαι, καθάπερ βροτὸν καὶ ἄνθρωπον.

[5] That he exercised a considerable influence on his friends by his teaching and his personality is shown by *Plutarch*, Adul. et. Am. c. 11, p. 55; *Diog.* ii. 127–129.

[6] *Diog.* 125: Βίωνός τε ἐπιμελῶς κατατρέχοντος τῶν μάντεων, νεκροὺς αὐτὸν ἐπισφάττειν ἔλεγε· against which a trait of personal fear, such as is described by *Diog.* 132, proves nothing. *Josephus*, Antiquit. Jud. xii. 2, 12. *Tertullian's* (Apologet. 18) language on Menedemus and his belief in Providence, is probably as worthless as the whole fable of Aristeas.

CHAPTER XIII.

THE CYNICS.

CHAP. XIII.

A. History of the Cynics.

THE Cynic, like the Megarian School, arose from a fusion of the teaching of Socrates with the doctrines of the Eleatics and Sophists. Both schools, as has been already remarked, were united by Stilpo, and passed over into the Stoa in Zeno.[1] The founder of Cynicism, Antisthenes, a native of Athens,[2] appears

[1] It is accordingly not compatible with an insight into the historical connection of these schools to insert the Cyrenaics between the Cynics and the Megarians, as Tennemann, Hegel. Marbach, Braniss, Brandis, and Strümpell have done. Otherwise it is of no moment whether we advance from the Megarians to Antisthenes and thence to Aristippus, or *vice versâ*: for these three schools were not developed from one another, but grew up side by side from the same origin. The order followed above appears to be the more natural one; the Megarians confining themselves more closely to the fundamental position of Socrates: Antisthenes considering its practical consequences: and Aristippus its effects on happiness, according to his own imperfect conception of happiness.

[2] Antisthenes was the son of an Athenian and a Thracian slave (*Diog.* vi. 1; ii. 31; *Sen.* De Const. 18, 5; *Plut.* De Exil. 17, p. 607, calling his mother, and *Clemens*, Strom. i. 302, C. in calling himself a Phrygian, are confounding him with Diogenes, or else must have been thinking of the anecdote in *Diog.* vi. 1; *Sen.* and *Plut.* l. c. For further particulars consult *Winckelmann*, Antisth Fr. p. 7; *Müller*, De Antisth. vita et scriptis, Marb. 1860, p. 3). He lived, according to *Xen.* Mem. ii. 5; Sym. 3, 8; 4, 34, in extreme poverty. The time of his birth and death is not further known to us. *Diodor.* xv. 76, mentions him as one of the men living about 366 B.C.

CHAP. XIII.

to have become acquainted with Socrates only late in life,[1] but ever afterwards to have clung to him[2] with enthusiastic devotion,[3] imitating his critical reasoning, though not always without an element of captiousness and quibbling. Early in life he had enjoyed the instruction of Gorgias,[4] and included other Sophists likewise among his friends.[5] Indeed he had himself appeared Sophist-like as a pleader and teacher, before he made the acquaintance of Socrates.[6] It was therefore only a going back to his old mode of life, when on the death of Socrates he opened a School.[7] At the same time he did not

and *Plut.* Lycurg. 30, Sch., quotes a remark of his on the battle of Leuctra. According to Eudocia (*Villoison's* Anecd. i. 56), he attained the age of 70, which would place his birth in 436 B.C., but the fact is uncertain.

[1] We have every reason to refer Plato's *γερόντων τοῖς ὀψιμάθεσι*, Soph. 251, B., to him, as will be subsequently seen. The only thing against it is the account in *Diog.* vi. 1, that Antisthenes was praised by Socrates for his valour in the battle of Tanagra. This objection applies even if the battle referred to was not the victory of the Athenians in the year 456 B.C. (in which it is impossible that Antisthenes can have taken part), but the battle mentioned by *Thucyd.* iii. 91 in 426 B.C., or that which was fought late in the autumn of 423 B.C. between Delium and Tanagra (*Thuc.* iv. 91), which is usually called the battle of Delium. The story, however, is not authentic, for *Diog.* ii. 31, quotes the same words of Socrates in a different way.

[2] *Xen.* Mem. iii. 11, 17; Sym. 4, 44; 8, 4–6. *Plato*, Phædo, 59, B.; *Diog.* vi. 2; Ibid. 9.

[3] This at least is the description given of him by *Xen.* Symp. 2, 10; 3, 4; 6; 4, 2; 6; 6, 5; 8.

[4] *Diog.* vi. 1, referring to the rhetorical school of Gorgias; nor does Antisthenes deny his teaching. At a later period Antisthenes wrote against Gorgias, *Athen.* v. 220, d.

[5] According to *Xen.* Symp. 4, 62, he introduced Prodicus and Hippias to Callias and recommended to Socrates an unknown Sophist from Heraclea.

[6] Hermippus in *Diog.* vi. 2; *Hieron.* c. Jovin. ii. 14.

[7] In the *γυμνάσιον* of Cynosarges, *Diog.* vi. 13; *Göttling*, Ges. Abh. i. 253, which was intended for those who, like himself, were of mixed Athenian

neglect to commit his views to writing in numerous treatises,[1] the language and style of which are most highly praised.[2]

Among the pupils[3] of Antisthenes, Diogenes[4] of

blood, *Plut.* Themist. c. 1. According to *Diog.* vi. 4, he had but few pupils because of his harsh and severe treatment of them. It is not reported that he required payment, but he appears to have received voluntary presents. *Diog.* vi. 9.

[1] *Diog.* vi. 15 (comp. *Müller*, l. c. p. 25) gives a list of these writings, which, according to *Diog.* ii. 64, was in the main approved of by Panætius. They are by him divided into 10 volumes. Excepting a few fragments, the only ones which are preserved are the two small and comparatively worthless declamations, Ajax and Ulysses, the genuineness of which is fully ascertained. *Winckelmann* (Antisthenis Fragmenta, Zur. 1842) has collected all the fragments. Because of his many writings, Timon called him παντοφυῆ φλεδόνα, *Diog.* vi. 18.

[2] See Theopomp. in *Diog.* vi. 14 and 15, and vii. 19; *Dionys.* Jud. de Thuc. c. 31, p. 941; *Epictet.* Diss. ii. 17, 35; Phrynich. in *Phot.* Cod. 158, p. 101, b; *Fronto*, De Orat. i. p. 218; *Longin.* De Invent. Rhet. Gr. ix. 559; *Cic.* ad Att. xii. 38; and *Lucian* adv. Indoct. c. 27; Theopompus passes the same opinion on his spoken addresses.

[3] Called by *Aristotle*, Metaph. viii. 3; 1043, b, 24, Ἀντισθένειοι, but in later times universally, and probably even in the time of Antisthenes, called Κυνικοί, partly from their place of meeting, partly because of their mode of life. Conf. *Diog.* vi. 13; *Lact.* Inst. iii. 15, g, E. Schol. in Arist. 23; a, 42; 35; a, 5. Antisthenes was already called ἁπλοκύων (*Diog.* l. c.), and Brutus speaks disparagingly of a Cynic (*Plut.* Brut. 34). Diogenes boasted of the name (*Diog.* 33; 40; 45; 55–60: *Stob.* Ecl. ii. 348, u, a), and the Corinthians placed a marble dog on his grave (*Diog.* 78).

[4] *Steinhart*, Diogenes, Allg. Encyc. sect. i. bd. xxx. 301; *Göttling*, Diogenes der Cyniker. Ges. Abh. i. 251; *Bayle*, Dict., art. Diogène, is always worth reading. Diogenes was the son of the money-changer Kikosios at Sinope. In his youth he had been engaged with his father in issuing counterfeit coin, and in consequence was obliged to leave his country. *Diog.* vi. 20, quoting authorities, gives further particulars, but is not always faithfully explained by *Göttling*, 251. Conf. Ibid. 49, 56; *Plut.* Inimic. Util. c. 2; De Exil. c. 7, p. 602; Musonius in *Stob.* Floril. 40, 9; *Lucian*, Bis Accus. 24; *Dio Chrys.* Or. viii. We have no reason to doubt this fact, as *Steinhart* does, p. 302, although the accounts may disagree in a few details. In Athens he became

CHAP. XIII.

Sinope is alone known to fame, that witty and eccentric individual, whose imperturbable originality,

acquainted with Antisthenes, who, for some reason or other, drove him away with a stick, but was at length overcome by his perseverance. (*Diog.* 21; *Ælian*, V. H. x. 16; *Hieron.* adv. Jovin. ii. 206.) When this took place is unknown, and Bayle's conjecture that the condemnation of Socrates was the cause of Antisthenes' hatred of mankind, is not to be depended upon for chronological reasons. Diogenes now devoted himself to philosophy in the Cynic sense of the term, and soon surpassed his master in self-denial and abstemiousness. He himself mentions Antisthenes as his teacher, in the verses in *Plut.* Qu. Conv. ii. 1, 7, 1. He appears to have lived a very long time at Athens, at least if the account of his meeting with Philip before the battle of Chæronea may be trusted (*Diog.* 43; *Plut.* de Adulat. c. 30, p. 70; De Exil. c. 16, p. 606; *Epict.* Diss. iii. 22, 24; it is not, however, stated that Diogenes fought at Chæronea, as *Göttling*, p. 265, says, nor is this probable of a Cynic), according to which he was then still living at Athens. But it is also possible—and this agrees with his principle of having no home—that he may have visited other places as a wandering preacher of morals, particularly Corinth. (*Diog.* 44; 63; *Plut.* Prof. in Virt. 6, p. 78; *Dio Chrys.* Or. vi.; *Val. Max.* iv. 3; *Diog.* ii. 66; vi. 50.) According to Diogenes, he met Aristippus in Syracuse. On some such journey he fell into the hands of pirates, who sold him to Xeniades, a Corinthian. For this event see *Diog.* vi. 29; 74; *Plut.* Tran. An. 4, p. 466; An Vitios. s. 3, p. 499; *Stob.* Floril. 3, 63; 40, 9; *Epict.* Diss. iii. 24, 66; *Philo*, Qu. Omnis Prob. Lib. 883, C.; *Julian*, Or. vii. 212, d. Xeniades appointed him the instructor of his sons, and he is said to have discharged this duty admirably. Highly esteemed by his pupils and by their parents, he remained with them till his death. At this time occurred the meeting with the younger Dionysius, mentioned by *Plut.* Timol. 15, and the conversation with Alexander, so greatly exaggerated by tradition. (*Diog.* 32; 38; 60; 68; *Sen.* Benef. v. 4, 3; *Juvenal*, xiv. 311; *Theo.* Progym. c. 5; *Julian*, Or. vii. 212.) The most simple version of it is that found in *Plut.* Alex. c. 14; De Alex. Virt. c. 10, p. 331; ad Princ. Inerud. c. 5, p. 702. Diogenes died at Corinth, on the same day, it is said, as Alexander (*Plut.* Qu. Conv. viii. 1, 4, p. 717; *Demetr.* in *Diog.* 79), i.e. 323 B.C., at an advanced age (*Diog.* 76, says almost ninety, *Cens.* Di. Nat. 15, 2, says eighty-one). The story of his death is differently told. (*Diog.* 76; 31; *Plut.* Consol. ad Apoll. c. 12, p. 107; *Ælian*, V. H. viii. 14; *Cens.* l. c.; *Tatian*, adv. Gr. c. 2; *Hieron.* adv. Jovin. ii.

coarse humour, strength of character, admirable even in its excesses, fresh and vigorous mind, have made him the most typical figure of ancient Greece.[1]

Of the pupils of Diogenes,[2] Crates is the most celebrated.[3] By his influence, his wife Hippar-

207, m; *Lucian*, Dial. Mort. 21, 2; *Cic.* Tusc. i. 34, 104; *Stob.* Floril. 123, 11.) Most probably he succumbed to old age. The Corinthians honoured him with a solemn burial and a tomb, and Sinope erected a monument to his memory (*Diog.* 78; *Pausan.* ii. 2, 4; Anth. Gr. iii. 558). *Diog.* 80, mentions many writings which bear his name. A portion of them were, however, rejected by Sotion. Others denied that he left any writings. Theophrastus' treatise: τῶν Διογένους συναγωγὴ (in *Diog.* v. 43), attributed by *Grote*, Plato, iii. 508, to the Cynic Diogenes, certainly refers to Diogenes of Apollonia.

[1] That he exercised an irresistible charm over many persons by his manners and words is attested by *Diog.* 75, and confirmed by examples like that of Xeniades, Onesicritus, and his sons.

[2] Amongst them are known, besides Crates and Stilpo: Onesicritus, the companion and biographer of Alexander, with his sons Androsthenes and Philiscus (*Diog.* vi. 75; 73; 80; 84; *Plut.* Alex. 65; for particulars respecting Onesicritus in *Müller*, Script. Rer. Alex. M. p. 47); Monimus of Syracuse, the slave of a Corinthian money-changer, who was driven away by his master for throwing money out of the window in Cynic fanaticism, one of the most distinguished Cynics, and the author of several treatises, amongst them of παίγνια σπουδῇ λαληθυίᾳ μεμιγμένα (*Diog.* vi. 82); Menander and Hegesias (*Diog.* vi. 84), and perhaps Bryson the Achæan (Ibid. 85). Phocion is also said to have been a pupil of his (*Diog.* 76; Phoc. c. 9); but Plutarch was not aware of it; and as Phocion adhered to the Academy, there is probably no truth in the story beyond the fact of a passing acquaintance.

[3] The Theban Crates, generally called a pupil of Diogenes, but by Hippobotus, a pupil of Bryson the Achæan (*Diog.* vi. 78), flourished about 328–324 B.C. (*Diog.* vi. 87). Since, however, stories are current not only of his tilting with Stilpo (*Diog.* ii. 117), but also of his quarrelling with Menedemus in his later years (*Diog.* ii. 131; vi. 91), his life must have lasted to the third century. Another Crates, a pupil of Stilpo, who is mentioned *Diog.* ii. 114, must not be confounded with the Cynic Crates. He is probably the same as the Peripatetic of that name in *Diog.* iv. 23. In zeal for the Cynic philosophy, Crates gave away his considerable property. For the different and very conflicting accounts

CHAP. XIII.

chia[1] and her brother Metrocles[2] were gained for the Cynic School. The names of several immediate and remote pupils of Metrocles[3] are known, through whom the School may be traced down to the end of the third century. Yet all its nobler features were cultivated by the Stoics from the beginning of the third century, toned down and supplemented by the addition of other elements also. Henceforth Cynicism was useless as a special branch of the Socratic philosophy. Subsequent attempts which were made to preserve its distinct character only resulted in

see *Diog.* vi. 87; *Plut.* Vit. Aer. Al. 8, 7, p. 831; *Apul.* De Mag. 22; Floril. ii. 14; *Simpl.* in Epict. Enchir. p. 64; *Philostr.* v. Apoll. i. 13, 2; *Hieron.* adv. Jovin. ii. 203. He died at an advanced age (*Diog.* 92, 98). Diog. 98 mentions some letters of his, the style of which resembled Plato's, and some tragedies, and *Demetr.* De Elocut. 170, 259, also mentions moral and satirical poems. According to *Julian,* Or. vi. 200, b, Plutarch also wrote an account of his life. From *Diog.* 91; *Apul.* Floril. 14, we learn that he was ugly and deformed.

[1] The daughter of an opulent family from Maronea in Thrace, who from love to Crates renounced her prospects and habits of comfort, and followed him in his beggar's life, *Diog.* 96; *Apul.* Floril. ii. 14.

[2] Formerly a pupil of Theophrastus and Xenocrates, but won over to Cynicism by Crates (Telos. in *Stob.* Floril. 97, 31, vol. iii. 214, Mein.), after having been cured by him of his childish idea of suicide. At a later period, however, he hung himself to escape the burdens of age, *Diog.* 94. Respecting his apathy, see *Plut.* An. Vitios. Ad. Infelic. c. 3, p. 499; for a conversation of his with Stilpo see *Plut.* Tranqu. An. 6, p. 468.

[3] *Diog.* 95. His pupils were Theombrotus and Cleomenes; the former was the teacher of Demetrius, the latter of Timarchus, and both of them of Echecles. Cotemporary with Echecles was Colotes, *Diog.* vi. 102. Cotemporary with Metrocles was Diodorus of Aspendus, mentioned in *Zeller's* Phil d. Griech. vol. i. 289. At an earlier period, under Antigonus the Great, lived the Cynic Thrasylus (*Plut.* Reg. Apophtheg. Antig. 15, p. 182; Vit. Pud. 7, p. 531); under one of the Ptolemies, Sotades, whose Cynical abstinence *Nonnus,* Exeg. Histor. Greg. Naz. 26 (Greg. in *Julian,* Invect. ed. Eton. 1610, p. 136), mentions.

caricatures. Two of the basest of its later representatives are known to us in the persons of Menedemus[1] and Menippus.[2] Soon after it became extinct

[1] A pupil of Echecles, and previously, as it would seem, of the Epicurean Colotes (*Diog.* vi. 95, 102), of whom we only hear that he occasionally appeared in the mask of a fury, to add greater force to his philippics. A pupil of his is Ktesibius, whom *Athen.* i. 15, c. iv. 162, e, names as a cotemporary of Antigonus (Gonatas).

[2] Menippus was, according to *Diog.* vi. 99 (conf. *Gell.* N. A. ii 18, 6), originally a Phœnician slave. He is said to have amassed a considerable fortune by money-lending (Hermippus in *Diog.* l. c.), the loss of which he took so much to heart that he hung himself. His career must fall in the first half of the third century. Diogenes indicates that, placing him between Metrocles and Menedemus, it being his habit to mention the philosophers of this school in chronological order; also the story that he was the author of a treatise respecting the festivities of Epicurus' birthday (*Diog.* vi. 101), and of an Arcesilaus (*Athen.* xiv. 664, c.; the Academician of this name died at a great age in 240 B.C.); also the circumstance that a portion of his writings was attributed to a Zopyrus (*Diog.* vi. 100), probably the friend of the Sillograph Timon (Ibid. ix. 114); also Probus who (Virg. Ecl. vi. 31) calls Menippus much earlier than Varro; also *Lucian* Ikaromen. 15, who makes Menippus an eye-witness of a number of things, all of which happened about 280 B.C. In the face of so many clear proofs, the language of *Diog.* vi. 99, who, speaking of Meleager living about 100 B.C. says, τοῦ κατ' αὐτὸν γενομένου, cannot count for much. There is probably here a mistake in the text; perhaps κατ' is written for μετ', or as *Nitsche*, p. 32, proposes, we ought to read τοῦ καὶ αὐτοῦ γενομένου κυνικοῦ. Probably this Menippus is the same person as Menippus of Sinope, called by *Diog.* vi. 95, one of the most distinguished men of the school of Metrocles; for *Diog.* vi. 101 in counting up the various Menippuses does not mention him as well as this Menippus, but calls him as *Athen.* xiv. 629, e, 664, e, likewise does Μένιππος ὁ κυνικός. The name Σινωπεὺς is thus explained: his master was a certain Baton of Pontus (Achaicus in *Diog.* vi. 99), with whom he probably lived at Sinope. (Compare also *Nietzsche's* Beitr. z. Quellenkunde u. Kritik des Laërt. Diogenes. Basel, 1870, p. 28.) According to Diog. 13, treatises of Menippus were in circulation, of which he gives the titles of seven, and *Athen.* the titles of two more. That they were not his own production is probably only an enemy's slander. All these writings appear to have been satires. His proficiency as a

CHAP. XIII.

as a School, and only reappeared at a very much later time as an offshoot of Stoicism.[1]

B. Cynic teaching. (1) Depreciation of theoretical knowledge.

The Cynic philosophy claims to be the genuine teaching of Socrates.[2] The many-sidedness, however, of Socrates, whereby the intellectual and the moral elements were completely fused and the foundations of a more thorough and comprehensive science laid, was above the powers of Antisthenes. Naturally narrow and dull,[3] but fortified with singular strength of will, Antisthenes admired[4] above all things the independence of his master's character, the strictness of his principles, his self-control, and his cheerful contentment in every position in life. That these moral traits were in a great measure the result of free inquiry on the part of Socrates, which thus preserved them from narrowness, he did

satirist may be gathered from the fact that he was not only imitated in ancient times by Meleager (*Diog.* vi. 99), but also by Varro in his Satiræ Menippeæ (*Cic.* Acad. i. 2, 8; *Gell.* N. A. ii. 18, 6, also *Macrob.* Saturn. i. 11; conf. *Probus,* l. c.), and that even Lucian gives him a prominent place in his dialogues. Conf. *Riese,* Varr. Sat. Rel. p. 7.

[1] Besides the above, Meleager of Gadara should be mentioned, could we be sure that he was a member of the Cynic School. But the mere fact that *Athen.* iv. 157, 6, in addressing a Cynic calls him ὁ πρόγονος ὑμῶν, and that he is perhaps mentioned by Diogenes as a Cynic, does not prove the continuance of the Cynic School. His attaching himself as a writer to Menippus would fully explain these statements.

[2] See p. 286, 2, and *Diog.* vi. 11.

[3] This fact is established by his teaching, independently of the opinions of opponents, such as *Plato,* Theætet. 155, E., in which the words σκληροὺς καὶ ἀντιτύπους ἀνθρώπους and μάλ' εὖ ἄμουσοι refer without doubt to Antisthenes and not to the Atomists; Soph. 251, B, γερόντων τοῖς ὀψιμάθεσι . . . ὑπὸ πενίας τῆς περὶ φρόνησιν κτήσεως τὰ τοιαῦτα τεθαυμακόσι. *Arist.* Metaph. v. 29, 1024, b, 33, viii. 3; 1043, b, 23.

[4] As *Cic.* De Orat. iii. 17, 62, and *Diog.* vi. 2, remark, apparently on the same authority.

not understand, nor discern that the principle of a knowledge of conceptions reached far beyond the range of the Socratic platform. All knowledge not immediately subservient to ethical purposes he accordingly rejected as unnecessary, or even as injurious, as the offspring of vanity and love of pleasure. Virtue, he maintained, is an affair of action, and can dispense with words and with wisdom. All that it needs is the strength of will of a Socrates.[1] Thus he and his School not only regarded logical and physical inquiries as worthless, but passed the same opinion on all arts and sciences which have not the moral improvement of mankind[2] for their

[1] *Diog.* 11, Antisthenes teaches αὐτάρκη δὲ τὴν ἀρετὴν πρὸς εὐδαιμονίαν, μηδενὸς προσδεομένην ὅτι μὴ Σωκρατικῆς ἰσχύος. τήν τ' ἀρετὴν τῶν ἔργων εἶναι, μήτε λόγων πλείστων δεομένην μήτε μαθημάτων.

[2] *Diog.* 103: ἀρέσκει οὖν αὐτοῖς τὸν λογικὸν καὶ τὸν φυσικὸν τόπον περιαιρεῖν, ἐμφερῶς Ἀρίστωνι τῷ Χίῳ, μόνῳ δὲ προσέχειν τῷ ἠθικῷ. According to Diocles, Diogenes said — what others attribute to Socrates or Aristippus (see p. 151, and *Plut.* in Eus. Pr. Ev. i. 8, 9)—that we ought to learn ὅττι τοι ἐν μεγάροισι κακόν τ' ἀγαθόν τε τέτυκται. παραιτοῦνται δὲ καὶ τὰ ἐγκύκλια . . . περιαιροῦσι δὲ καὶ γεωμετρίαν καὶ μουσικὴν καὶ πάντα τὰ τοιαῦτα. When a dial was shown him, Diogenes replied, that it was not a bad instrument to avoid being late for meals. Ibid. 27: τοὺς δὲ γραμματικοὺς ἐθαύμαζε [Diog.] τὰ μὲν τοῦ Ὀδυσσέως κακὰ ἀναζητοῦντας τὰ δ' ἴδια ἀγνοοῦντας· καὶ μὴν καὶ τοὺς μουσικοὺς τὰς μὲν ἐν τῇ λύρᾳ χορδὰς ἁρμόττεσθαι, ἀνάρμοστα δ' ἔχειν τῆς ψυχῆς τὰ ἤθη· τοὺς μαθηματικοὺς ἀποβλέπειν μὲν πρὸς τὸν ἥλιον καὶ τὴν σελήνην, τὰ δ' ἐν ποσὶ πράγματα παρορᾶν. τοὺς ῥήτορας λέγειν μὲν ἐσπουδακέναι τὰ δίκαια, πράττειν δὲ μηδαμῶς. The passage on astronomers may possibly have been supported by the story of Thales falling into a well whilst contemplating the heavens. An answer thereto is the passage in the Theætetus 174, A, 175, D, on the Thracian maiden who upbraided him for so doing. The mother of Antisthenes was a Thracian slave, and the words which Plato puts into the mouth of the Thracian girl closely resemble those quoted by Diogenes. It would also tally with the character of Antisthenes, that he as an ἀπαίδευτος should be charged

CHAP. XIII.

immediate object; for, said Diogenes,[1] as soon as any other object intervenes, self is neglected. Even reading and writing Antisthenes declared could be dispensed with.[2]

The last statement must be taken with considerable limitation;[3] for the Cynic School as a whole cannot be regarded as so hostile to culture as this language would seem to imply. In fact, very decided remarks made by Antisthenes,[4] Diogenes,[5] Crates,[6]

with not troubling himself about the general conception of things. *Diog.* 73 says of Diogenes: μουσικῆς τε καὶ γεωμετρικῆς καὶ ἀστρολογίας καὶ τῶν τοιούτων ἀμελεῖν ὡς ἀχρήστων καὶ οὐκ ἀναγκαίων. Conf. *Diog.* 24; 39; *Julian*, Or. vi. 190, a; *Seneca*, Ep. 88, particularly § 7, 32; *Stob.* Floril. 33, 14; *id.* 80, 6; an astronomer pointing to a map of the heavens says: οὗτοί εἰσιν οἱ πλανώμενοι τῶν ἀστέρων· upon which Diogenes replies, pointing to those present: μὴ ψεύδου· οὐ γὰρ οὗτοί εἰσιν οἱ πλανώμενοι, ἀλλ' οὗτοι. The saying of Diogenes in *Simpl.* De Cœlo, 33, b, Schol. in Arist. 476, b, 35, that even an ass takes the shortest cut to his food and to the water, was probably meant as a hit at geometry and its axiom of the straight line.

[1] Excerp. e Joan. Damasc. ii. 13, 61. (*Stob.* Floril. ed. Mein.)

[2] *Diog.* 103: γράμματα γοῦν μὴ μανθάνειν ἔφασκεν ὁ Ἀντισθένης τοὺς σώφρονας γενομένους, ἵνα μὴ διαστρέφοιντο τοῖς ἀλλοτρίοις.

[3] It would be hardly credible in a man so fond of writing. If it is not altogether a fancy, it may either rest upon some individual expression, such as, that it would be better not to read at all than to read such nonsense, or it is based upon more general statements, such as that quoted by *Diog.* 5, that wisdom must not be written in books, but in the soul.

[4] Exc. e Floril. Jo. Damasc. ii. 13, 68: δεῖ τοὺς μέλλοντας ἀγαθοὺς ἄνδρας γενήσεσθαι τὸ μὲν σῶμα γυμνασίοις ἀσκεῖν, τὴν δὲ ψυχὴν παιδεύειν. Ibid. 33, in answer to the question ποῖος στέφανος κάλλιστός ἐστιν, he replied: ὁ ἀπὸ παιδείας.

[5] *Diog.* 68: τὴν παιδείαν εἶπε τοῖς μὲν νέοις σωφροσύνην, τοῖς δὲ πρεσβυτέροις παραμυθίαν, τοῖς δὲ πένησι πλοῦτον, τοῖς δὲ πλουσίοις κόσμον εἶναι.—Exc. e Floril. Jo. Damasc. 13, 29; ἡ παιδεία ὁμοία ἐστὶ χρυσῷ στεφάνῳ· καὶ γὰρ τιμὴν ἔχει καὶ πολυτέλειαν. Ibid. 74, 75.

[6] *Diog.* 86: ταῦτ' ἔχω ὅσσ' ἔμαθον καὶ ἐφρόντισα καὶ μετὰ Μουσῶν σέμν' ἐδάην· τὰ δὲ πολλὰ καὶ ὄλβια τῦφος ἔμαρψε. A parody of this verse is the epitaph on Sardanapalus in *Clem.* Stromat. ii. 411, D.

and Monimus,[1] in favour of culture are on record. Diogenes is said to have zealously impressed on his pupils the sayings of poets and of prose writers.[2] Besides, it is on general grounds inconceivable that men, who wrote so much and so well, should have declared war against all culture. One thing we may however take for established, that the value of culture was exclusively estimated by its efficacy in producing the Cynic type of virtue. Hence this School depreciated all speculative knowledge, only studying logic and physics, in as far as these sciences seemed necessary for ethical purposes.[3] From this judgment we are not justified in exempting even the founder.[4] The statements of Anti-

[1] Floril. Jo. Damasc. ii. 13, 88: Μόνιμος . . . ἔφη κρεῖττον εἶναι τυφλὸν ἢ ἀπαίδευτον· τὸν μὲν γὰρ εἰς τὸν βάθρον, τὸν δ' εἰς τὸ βάραθρον ἐμπίπτειν.

[2] *Diog.* 31, according to Eubulus; κατεῖχον δὲ οἱ παῖδες πολλὰ ποιητῶν καὶ συγγραφέων καὶ τῶν αὐτοῦ Διογενοῦς, πᾶσάν τ' ἔφοδον σύντομον πρὸς τὸ εὐμνημόνευστον ἐπήσκει.

[3] *Krische*, Forschungen, 237. See *Ritter*, ii. 120.

[4] Although the division of philosophy into Logic, Ethics, and Physics can have been hardly introduced in the time of Antisthenes, and hence the words in *Diog.* 103 cannot be his, it does not follow that the statement there made is false. Amongst the writings of Antisthenes some are known to us, which would be called logical writings, to use a later division; others are on physical subjects. To the first class belong Περὶ λέξεως, Ἀλήθεια, Περὶ τοῦ διαλέγεσθαι, Σάθων ἢ περὶ τοῦ ἀντιλέγειν, Περὶ διαλέκτου, Περὶ ὀνομάτων, Περὶ ὀνομάτων χρήσεως, Περὶ ἐρωτήσεως καὶ ἀποκρίσεως, Περὶ δόξης καὶ ἐπιστήμης, Δόξαι ἢ ἐριστικὸς, Περὶ τοῦ μανθάνειν προβλήματα. To the second, Περὶ ζώων φύσεως, Περὶ φύσεως (perhaps the same which *Cicero* mentions N. D. i. 13, 32), Ἐρώτημα περὶ φύσεως. A commentary on the writings of Heraclitus, which *Diog.* ix. 15 mentions, does not belong to him. See *Zeller*, Phil. d. Griech. i. 527, and *Krische*, p. 238. So little, however, is known of these writings, that no conclusions can be arrived at which contradict the above assumptions. His logical writings, to judge by their titles, appear to have contained those polemical dissertations on con-

CHAP. XIII.

sthenes on logic, so far as they are known to us, consist in a polemic against the philosophy of conceptions, the object of which is to prove the impossibility of speculative knowledge. His remarks upon nature have for their object to show what is natural for man. For this no deep research seemed necessary to him or his followers;[1] a healthy intelligence can tell everyone what he ought to know; all beyond is useless subtlety.

(2) *Logic.*

In support of these views Antisthenes put forward a theory, based it is true on a leading position of Socrates,[2] but one, nevertheless, which in its expanded form and in its sceptical results plainly shows the disciple of Gorgias. Socrates having required the essence and conception of every object to be investigated before anything could be predicated of it, Antisthenes likewise required the conception of things what they are or were to be determined.[3]

ceptions, judgments, and expressions, which were required as a foundation for critical researches. Of the writings on Physics, it is not known whether they treat of other than those natural subjects, which Antisthenes required immediately for his Ethics, in order to bring out the difference between nature and custom and the conditions of a life of nature. Even the treatise περί ζώων φύσεως may have had this object. Probably *Plato*, Phileb. 44, C., reckoned Antisthenes among the μάλα δείνους λεγομένους τὰ περὶ φύσιν, only because in all questions about morals and prevailing customs, he invariably referred to the requirements of nature.

[1] Even *Cicero* ad Attic. xii. 38, calls Antisthenes 'homo acutus magis quam eruditus.'

[2] Compare the relation of this theory to the doctrine of ideas, and what *Diog.* 39, *Simpl.* 236, b, m, 278, b, u, says of Diogenes, with what the Scholiast on Arist. Categor. p. 22, b, 40 says of Antisthenes. *Sext.* Pyrrh. iii. 66, only asserts of a Cynic in general that he refutes the arguments against motion by walking up and down. Similarly Diogenes in *Diog.* 38.

[3] *Diog.* vi. 3: πρῶτός τε ὡρι-

Confining himself, however, exclusively to this point of view, he arrived at the conclusion of the Sophists,[1] that every object can only be called by its own peculiar name, and consequently that no subject can admit a predicate differing from the conception of the subject. Thus it cannot be said that a man is good, but only that a man is human, or that the Good is good.[2] Moreover, every explanation of a conception consisting in making one conception clearer

σατο λόγον εἰπών· λόγος ἐστὶν ὁ τὸ τί ἦν ἢ ἔστι δηλῶν. *Alexander* in Top. 24, m, Schol. in Arist. 256, b. 12, on the Aristotelian τί ἦν εἶναι, says that the simple τί ἦν, which Antisthenes wanted, is not sufficient.

[1] See *Zeller*, Phil. d. Griech. 904.

[2] *Arist.* Metaph. v. 29; 1024, b, 33: Ἀντισθένης ᾤετο εὐήθως μηδὲν ἀξιῶν λέγεσθαι πλὴν τῷ οἰκείῳ λόγῳ ἓν ἐφ' ἑνός· ἐξ ὧν συνέβαινε, μὴ εἶναι ἀντιλέγειν, σχεδὸν δὲ μηδὲ ψεύδεσθαι. Alexander on the passage. *Plato* Soph. 251, B.: ὅθεν γε, οἶμαι, τοῖς τε νέοις καὶ τῶν γερόντων τοῖς ὀψιμαθέσι θοίνην παρεσχήκαμεν· εὐθὺς γὰρ ἀντιλαβέσθαι παντὶ πρόχειρον ὡς ἀδύνατον τά τε πολλὰ ἓν καὶ τὸ ἓν πολλὰ εἶναι, καὶ δή που χαίρουσιν οὐκ ἐῶντες ἀγαθὸν λέγειν ἄνθρωπον, ἀλλὰ τὸ μὲν ἀγαθὸν ἀγαθόν, τὸν δὲ ἄνθρωπον ἄνθρωπον.—Cf. Philebus 14, C.; *Arist.* Soph. El. c. 17, 175, b, 15; Phys. i. 2, 185, b, 25; *Simpl.* in loc. p. 20; *Isokr.* Hel. i. 1, and particularly what is said p. 277, 1, respecting Stilpo. Hermann, Sokr. Syst. p. 30, once thought to discern in these sentences of Antisthenes a great advancement as proving that Antisthenes recognised all analytical judgments *à priori* as such to be true, but has since been obliged to modify his opinion (*Plat.* i. 217, Ges. Abh. 239), on being reminded by *Ritter* (Gesch. d. Phil ii. 133) that Antisthenes could only be speaking of identical judgments. Still he adheres to it so far as to state that by the teaching of Antisthenes, philosophy for the first time gave to identical judgments an independent value. In what this value consists, it is hard to say, for nothing is gained by recognising identical judgments, nor has it ever occurred to any philosopher to deny them, as Hermann, Ges. Abh. asserted, though without quoting a single instance in support. Indeed, how can it be a forward step in philosophy to deny all but identical judgments. Such a denial is the result of an imperfect view of things, and is destructive of all knowledge.

by means of another, he rejected all definitions, on the ground that they are language which does not touch the thing itself. Allowing with regard to composite things, that their component parts could be enumerated, and that they could in this way be themselves explained, with regard to simple ones, he insisted all the more strongly that this was impossible: compared they might be with others, but not defined: names there might be of them, but not conceptions of qualities, a correct notion but no knowledge.[1] The characteristic of a thing, however,

[1] *Arist.* Metaph. viii. 3; 1043, b, 23: *ὥστε ἡ ἀπορία, ἣν οἱ Ἀντισθένειοι καὶ οἱ οὕτως ἀπαίδευτοι ἠπόρουν, ἔχει τινὰ καιρὸν, ὅτι οὐκ ἔστι τὸ τί ἔστιν ὁρίσασθαι, τὸν γὰρ ὅρον λόγον εἶναι μακρόν*—see Metaph. xiv. 3; 1091, a, 7; and Schwegler on this passage—*ἀλλὰ ποῖον μέν τί ἐστιν ἐνδέχεται καὶ διδάξαι, ὥσπερ ἄργυρον τί μέν ἐστιν, οὔ, ὅτι δ' οἷον καττίτερος. ὥστ' οὐσίας ἔστι μὲν ἧς ἐνδέχεται εἶναι ὅρον καὶ λόγον, οἷον τῆς συνθέτου, ἐάν τε αἰσθητὴ ἐάν τε νοητὴ ᾖ· ἐξ ὧν δ' αὕτη πρώτων οὐκ ἔστιν.* That this, too, belongs to the description of the teaching of Antisthenes, appears from *Plato*, Theætet. 201, E., and is wrongly denied by *Brandis*, ii. b, 503; the expressions are indeed Aristotelian. Alexander, on the passage, explains it more fully, but without adding anything fresh. That this view was not first put forward by the disciples of Antisthenes, appears from *Plato's* Theætet. 201, E.: *ἐγὼ γὰρ αὖ ἐδόκουν ἀκούειν τινῶν ὅτι τὰ μὲν πρῶτα ὡσπερεὶ στοιχεῖα, ἐξ ὧν ἡμεῖς τε συγκείμεθα καὶ τἆλλα, λόγον οὐκ ἔχοι. αὐτὸ γὰρ καθ' αὑτὸ ἕκαστον ὀνομάσαι μόνον εἴη, προσειπεῖν δὲ οὐδὲν ἄλλο δυνατόν, οὐθ' ὡς ἔστιν οὔθ' ὡς οὐκ ἔστιν . . . . ἐπεὶ οὐδὲ τὸ αὐτὸ οὐδὲ τὸ ἐκεῖνο οὐδὲ τὸ ἕκαστον οὐδε τὸ μόνον προσοιστέον, οὐδ' ἄλλα πολλὰ τοιαῦτα· ταῦτα μὲν γὰρ περιτρέχοντα πᾶσι προσφέρεσθαι, ἕτερα ὄντα ἐκείνων οἷς προστίθεται. δεῖν δὲ, εἴπερ ἦν δυνατὸν αὐτὸ λέγεσθαι καὶ εἶχεν οἰκεῖον αὑτοῦ λόγον, ἄνευ τῶν ἄλλων ἁπάντων λέγεσθαι. νῦν δὲ ἀδύνατον εἶναι ὁτιοῦν τῶν πρώτων ῥηθῆναι λόγῳ· οὐ γὰρ εἶναι αὐτῷ ἀλλ' ἢ ὀνομάζεσθαι μόνον· ὄνομα γὰρ μόνον ἔχειν· τὰ δὲ ἐκ τούτων ἤδη συγκείμενα, ὥσπερ αὐτὰ πέπλεκται, οὕτω καὶ τὰ ὀνόματα αὐτῶν συμπλακέντα λόγον γεγονέναι· ὀνομάτων γὰρ συμπλοκὴν εἶναι λόγου οὐσίαν.* And 201, C: *ἔφη δὲ τὴν μὲν μετὰ λόγου δόξαν ἀληθῆ ἐπιστήμην εἶναι, τὴν δὲ ἄλογον ἐκτὸς ἐπιστήμης· καὶ ὧν μὲν μή ἐστι λόγος, οὐκ ἐπιστητὰ εἶναι, οὑτωσὶ καὶ ὀνομάζων, ἃ δ' ἔχει,*

the name which can never be defined, the conception of the subject which is borrowed from nothing else, and therefore can never be a predicate, consists only in its proper name. By this it is known when it can be explained by nothing else. All that is real is strictly individual. General conceptions do not express the nature of things, but they express men's thoughts about them. Plato having derived from the Socratic demand for knowledge of conceptions a system of the most decided Realism, Antisthenes derives therefrom a Nominalism quite as decided.

ἐπιστητά. This whole description agrees with what has been quoted from Aristotle so entirely, trait for trait, that we cannot possibly refer it to any one else but Antisthenes. It is all the more remarkable that *Plato* repeatedly (201, C.; 202, C.) affirms the truth of his description. In modern times, *Schleiermacher*, Pl. W. ii. 1 and 184, was the first to observe the reference to Antisthenes. His opinion is shared by *Brandis*, Gr.-Röm. Phil. ii. a, 202, f: *Susemihl*, Genet. Entw. d. Plat. Phil. i. 200; *Schwegler* and *Bonitz* on Arist. l. c., but denied by *Hermann* (Plat. 499, 659) and *Stallbaum* (De Arg. Theætet. ii. f). *Steinhart* (Plat. W. iii. 16, 204, 20) finds that the explanation of knowledge, as here given, corresponds with the mind of Antisthenes, but refuses notwithstanding to accept it as his. Schleiermacher (as *Brandis*, ii. a, 203; *Susemihl*, pp. 200, 341, remark) has not the slightest right to think the reference is to the Megarians in Theæt. 201, D. What is there stated agrees most fully with the statements of Aristotle touching Antisthenes, whereas no such principle is known of the School of Megara. We may, therefore, endorse Schleiermacher's conjecture (Pl. W. ii. b, 19) that the Cratylus was in great part directed against Antisthenes — a conjecture which appears to harmonise with the view that Antisthenes was the expounder of Heraclitus. It is opposed by *Brandis*, ii. a, 285, f. We cannot attribute to Antisthenes a theory of monads connecting it with the theory of ideas (*Susemihl*, i. 202, in connection with *Hermann*, Ges. Abh. 240). What we know of him does not go beyond the principle, that the simple elements of things cannot be defined; what he understood by simple elements may be gathered from the example quoted from *Arist.* Metaph. vii. 3, of the silver and the tin.

CHAP. XIII.

General conceptions are only fictions of thought. Horses and men are seen; not, however, the conception of a horse or a man.[1] From this position he opened a campaign against his fellow pupil, with whom he was for other reasons not on good terms,[2] but his fire was met with corresponding spirit.[3]

[1] *Simpl.* in Categ. Schol. in Arist. 66, b, 45, says: τῶν δὲ παλαιῶν οἱ μὲν ἀνῄρουν τὰς ποιότητας τελέως, τὸ ποιὸν συγχωροῦντες εἶναι (the terminology of course belongs to the Stoics) ὥσπερ Ἀντισθένης, ὅς ποτε Πλάτωνι διαμφισβητῶν, 'ὦ Πλάτων,' ἔφη, 'ἵππον μὲν ὁρῶ, ἱππότητα δὲ οὐχ ὁρῶ,' to which Plato gave the excellent answer: True, for you have the eye with which you see a horse, but you are deficient in the eye with which you see the idea of horse. Ibid. 67, b, 18; Ibid. 68, b, 26: Ἀντισθένην καὶ τοὺς περὶ αὐτὸν λέγοντας, ἄνθρωπον ὁρῶ ἀνθρωπότητα δὲ οὐχ ὁρῶ. Quite the same, Ibid. 20, 2, a. *Diog.* vi. 53, tells the same story of Diogenes and Plato, with this difference, that he uses τραπεζότης and κυαθότης instead of ἀνθρωπότης. *Ammon.* in Porph. Isag. 22, b, says: Ἀντισθένης ἔλεγε τὰ γένη καὶ τὰ εἴδη ἐν εἰλαῖς ἐπινοίαις εἶναι, and then he mentions ἀνθρωπότης and ἱππότης as examples. The same language, almost word for word, is found in *Tzetz.* Chil. vii. 605, f. Plato is no doubt referring to this assertion of Antisthenes, when in the Parm. 132, B., he quotes an objection to the theory of ideas, μὴ τῶν εἰδῶν ἕκαστον ᾖ τούτων νόημα καὶ οὐδαμοῦ αὐτῷ προσήκῃ ἐγγίγνεσθαι ἄλλοθι ἢ ἐν ψυχαῖς.

[2] The character and position in life of the two men was widely different. Plato must have felt himself as much repelled by the plebeian roughness of a proletarian philosopher as Antisthenes would have been annoyed by the refined delicacy of Plato.

[3] Compare (besides what has been said, p. 293, 2) *Plato*, Soph. 251, C., and the anecdotes in *Diog.* iii. 35, vi. 7; also the corresponding ones about Plato and Diogenes, which are partially fictions, in vi. 25; 40; 54; 58; *Ælian*, V. H. xiv. 33; Theo. Progym. p. 205; *Stob.* Floril. 13, 37. As to the picked fowl story in *Diog.* 40, compare *Plato*, Polit. 266, B.; *Göttling*, p. 264. For the Cynical attack which Antisthenes made on Plato in his Σάθων, see *Diog.* iii. 35, vi. 16; *Athen.* v. 220, d, xi. 507, a. A trace of Antisthenes' polemic against the doctrine of ideas is found in the Euthydemus of Plato, 301, A. Plato there meets the assertion of the Sophist that the beautiful is only beautiful by the presence of beauty, by saying: ἐὰν οὖν παραγένηταί σοι βοῦς, βοῦς εἶ, καὶ ὅτι νῦν ἐγώ σοι πάρειμι Διονυσόδωρος εἶ; We may

Such being his views, it is only natural that Antisthenes should have attached the greatest importance to inquiries respecting names.[1] Stopping at names and refusing to allow any further remarks respecting things, he in truth made all scientific inquiry impossible. This fact he partially admitted, drawing from his premises the conclusion that it is impossible to contradict yourself.[2] Taken strictly, the inference

suppose that Antisthenes really made use of the illustration of the ox, to which Plato then replied by making use of the same illustration in the person of Dionysodorus. *Steinhart* (Plato's Leben, 14, 266) considers the Σάθων spurious. He will not credit Antisthenes with such a scurrilous production.

[1] Antisth. in *Epict.* Diss. i. 17, 12: ἀρχὴ παιδεύσεως ἡ τῶν ὀνομάτων ἐπίσκεψις. It is a pity that we do not know more accurately the sense and the connection of this saying. As it is, we cannot judge whether it required an individual inquiry into the most important names, or only a general inquiry into the nature and the meaning of names, which the principles contained in the above should develop. Respecting the theory that Antisthenes held to the etymologies of Heraclitus, see p. 298, 1.

[2] *Arist.* Metaph. v. 29; see 296, 1; Top. i. 11; 104, b, 20: οὐκ ἔστιν ἀντιλέγειν, καθάπερ ἔφη Ἀντισθένης, which *Alex.* (Schol. in Arist. 732, a, 30; similarly as the passage in the Topics, Ibid. 259, b, 13) thus explains: ᾤετο δὲ ὁ Ἀντισθένης ἕκαστον τῶν ὄντων λέγεσθαι τῷ οἰκείῳ λόγῳ μόνῳ καὶ ἕνα ἑκάστου λόγον εἶναι . . . ἐξ ὧν καὶ συνάγειν ἐπείρατο ὅτι μὴ ἔστιν ἀντιλέγειν· τοὺς μὲν γὰρ ἀντιλέγοντας περί τινος διάφορα λέγειν ὀφείλειν, μὴ δύνασθαι δὲ περὶ αὐτοῦ διαφόρους τοὺς λόγους φέρεσθαι τῷ ἕνα τὸν οἰκεῖον ἑκάστου εἶναι· ἕνα γὰρ ἑνὸς εἶναι καὶ τὸν λέγοντα περὶ αὐτοῦ λέγειν μόνον· ὥστε εἰ μὲν περὶ τοῦ πράγματος τοῦ αὐτοῦ λέγοιεν, τὰ αὐτὰ ἂν λέγοιεν ἀλλήλοις (εἷς γὰρ ὁ περὶ ἑνὸς λόγος) λέγοντες δὲ ταὐτὰ οὐκ ἂν ἀντιλέγοιεν ἀλλήλοις· εἰ δὲ διαφέροντα λέγοιεν, οὐκέτι λέξειν αὐτοὺς περὶ τοῦ αὐτοῦ. *Prantl*, Gesch. d. Log. i. 33, mentions later writers, who, however, only repeat Aristotle's sayings. In exactly the same way Plato's Dionysodorus (Euthyd. 285, E) establishes his assertion, that it is impossible to contradict: εἰσὶν ἑκάστῳ τῶν ὄντων λόγοι; Πάνυ γε. Οὐκοῦν ὡς ἔστιν ἕκαστον ἢ ὡς οὐκ ἔστιν; Ὡς ἔστιν. Εἰ γὰρ μέμνησαι, ἔφη, ὦ Κτήσιππε, καὶ ἄρτι ἐπεδείξαμεν μηδένα λέγοντα ὡς οὐκ ἔστι. τὸ γὰρ μὴ ὂν οὐδεὶς ἐφάνη λέγων. Πότερον οὖν . . . ἀντιλέγοιμεν ἂν τοῦ αὐτοῦ πράγματος λόγον ἀμφότεροι λε-

CHAP. XIII.

from these premises is not only that drawn by Aristotle[1] that no false propositions, but also that no propositions of any kind, are possible. The doctrine of Antisthenes was logically destructive of all knowledge and every kind of judgment.

C. Theory of Morals. Good and evil.

Not that the Cynics were themselves disposed to renounce knowledge in consequence. Four books came from the pen of Antisthenes, respecting the difference between knowledge and opinion.[2] In fact, the whole School prided itself in no small degree on having advanced beyond the deceptive sphere of opinions,[3] and being in full possession of truth.

γοντες, ἢ οὕτω μὲν ἂν δήπου ταὐτὰ λέγοιμεν; Συνεχώρει. 'Αλλ' ὅταν μηδέτερος, ἔφη, τὸν τοῦ πράγματος λόγον λέγῃ, τότε ἀντιλέγοιμεν ἄν; ἢ οὕτω γε τὸ παράπαν οὐδ' ἂν μεμνημένος εἴη τοῦ πράγματος οὐδέτερος ἡμῶν; Καὶ τοῦτο συνωμολόγει. 'Αλλ' ἄρα, ὅταν ἐγὼ λέγω μὲν τὸ πρᾶγμα, σὺ δὲ οὐδὲ λέγεις τὸ παράπαν· ὁ δὲ μὴ λέγων τῷ λέγοντι πῶς ἂν ἀντιλέγοι; Plato probably had Antisthenes in his eye, although this kind of argument had not come from him. Conf. *Zeller*, l. c. i. 905, and *Diog*. ix. 53: τὸν 'Αντισθένους λόγον τὸν πειρώμενον ἀποδεικνύειν ὡς οὐκ ἔστιν ἀντιλέγειν, οὗτος (Protagoras) πρῶτος διείλεκται κατά φησι Πλάτων ἐν Εὐθυδήμῳ (286, c). Here, too, belongs the saying of Antisthenes in *Stob*. Flor. 82, 8, that contradiction ought never to be used, but only persuasion. A madman will not be brought to his senses by another's raving. Contradiction is madness; for he who contradicts does what is in the nature of things impossible. Of this subject the Σάθων ἢ περὶ τοῦ ἀντιλέγειν treated.

[1] See p. 297, 1 *Procl.* in Crat. 37: 'Αντισθένης ἔλεγεν μὴ δεῖν ἀντιλέγειν· πᾶς γάρ, φησί, λόγος ἀληθεύει· ὁ γὰρ λέγων τὶ λέγει· ὁ δὲ τὶ λέγων τὸ ὂν λέγει· ὁ δὲ τὸ ὂν λέγων ἀληθεύει. Conf. *Plato*, Crat. 429, D.

[2] Περὶ δόξης καὶ ἐπιστήμης, *Diog*. 17. Doubtless this treatise contained the explanation given p. 254, 1.

[3] *Diog*. 83 says of Monimus οὗτος μὲν ἐμβριθέστατος ἐγένετο, ὥστε δόξης μὲν καταφρονεῖν, πρὸς δ' ἀλήθειαν παρορμᾷν. *Menander*, Ibid. says of the same Cynic: τὸ γὰρ ὑποληφθὲν τῦφον εἶναι πᾶν ἔφη, and *Sext*. Math. viii. 5: Μόνιμος ὁ κύων τῦφον εἰπὼν τὰ πάντα, ὅπερ οἴησίς ἐστ τῶν οὐκ ὄντων ὡς ὄντων. Conf. *M. Aurel*. πο. ἑαυτ. ii. 15; ὅτι πᾶν ὑπόληψις· δῆλα μεν γα: τὸ πο∂s τοῦ κυνικοῦ Μονιμοι λε[illegible]μενα. On this ground the later

With them, knowledge is directed entirely to a practical end, that of making men virtuous, and happy in being virtuous.[1] As the highest object in life the Cynics, herein agreeing with all other moral philosophers, regarded happiness.[2] Happiness being usually distinguished from virtue, or, at least, not united to virtue, they regard the two as absolutely identical. Nothing is good but virtue, nothing an evil but vice; what is neither the one nor the other is for man indifferent.[3] For each thing that only can be a good which belongs to it.[4] The only real

Sceptics wished to reckon Monimus one of themselves, but wrongly so. What he says has only reference to the worthlessness of common opinion and what it considers a good. In Lucian v. Auct. 8, Diogenes calls himself a prophet of truth and freedom.

[1] See p. 293.

[2] Diog. ii.: αὐτάρκη τὴν ἀρετὴν πρὸς εὐδαιμονίαν, so that happiness is the end, and virtue the means. *Stob.* Ecl. 103, 20, 21

[3] *Diog.* vi. 104: ἀρέσκει δ' αὐτοῖς καὶ τέλος εἶναι τὸ κατ' ἀρετὴν ζῆν ὡς Ἀντισθένης φησὶν ἐν τῷ Ἡρακλεῖ, ὁμοίως τοῖς στωικοῖς. Ibid. 105: τὰ δὲ μεταξὺ ἀρετῆς καὶ κακίας ἀδιάφορα λέγουσιν ὁμοίως Ἀρίστωνι τῷ Χίῳ. *Diocles.* in Diog. vi. 12 says of Antisthenes: τἀγαθὰ καλὰ τὰ κακὰ αἰσχρά. *Epiph.* Exp. Fid. 1089, C: ἔφησε [Diogenes] τὸ ἀγαθὸν οἰστὸν τοἰκεῖον παντὶ σοφῷ εἶναι, τὰ δ' ἄλλα πάντα οὐδὲν ἢ φλυαοιας ὑπάρχειν. Whether the epigram of Athen. in *Diog.* vi. 14, refers to the Cynics or the Stoics is not quite clear.

> Ὦ στοϊκῶν μύθων εἰδήμονες, ὦ πανάριστα
> δόγματα ταῖς ἱεραῖς ἐνθέμενοι σελίσιν·
> τὰν ἀρετὰν ψυχᾶς ἀγαθὸν μόνον· ἅδε γὰρ ἀνδρῶν
> μούνα καὶ βιοτὰν ῥύσατο καὶ πολιάς.

According to Diogenes it would appear as though the Stoic doctrine that virtue is the only good were therein attributed to the Cynics.

[4] This maxim follows from *Diog.* 12, who states as the teaching of Antisthenes: τὰ πονηρὰ νόμιζε πάντα ξενικά. Compare *Plato*, Symp. 205 E: οὐ γὰρ τὸ ἑαυτῶν, οἶμαι, ἕκαστοι ἀσπάζονται, εἰ μὴ εἴ τις τὸ μὲν ἀγαθὸν οἰκεῖον καλοῖ καὶ ἑαυτοῦ, τὸ δὲ κακὸν ἀλλότριον. In the Charm. 163, C. Critias says only the useful and good is οἰκεῖον. Although Antisthenes is not here named, yet the passage in Diogenes makes it

CHAP. XIII.

thing which belongs to man is mind.[1] Everything else is a matter of chance. In mental and moral powers only is he independent. Intelligence and virtue constitute the armour from which all the attacks of fortune recoil;[2] that man only is free who is bound by no external ties and has no desires for things without.[3]

Thus man requires nothing to make him happy save virtue.[4] All else he may learn to despise, in

probable that the antithesis of ἀγαθὸν and οἰκεῖον belongs to him, even if he was not the first to introduce it.

[1] Compare p. 294, 6; *Xen.* Symp. 4, 34, puts words to the same effect in the mouth of Antisthenes: νομίζω, ὦ ἄνδρες, τοὺς ἀνθρώπους οὐκ ἐν τῷ οἴκῳ τὸν πλοῦτον καὶ τὴν πενίαν ἔχειν, ἀλλ' ἐν ταῖς ψυχαῖς· this is then further expanded; and *Epictet.* Diss. iii. 24, 68, makes Diogenes say of Antisthenes: ἐδίδαξέ με τὰ ἐμὰ καὶ τὰ οὐκ ἐμά· κτῆσις οὐκ ἐμή· συγγενεῖς, οἰκεῖοι, φίλοι, φήμη, συνήθεις, τόποι, διατριβή, πάντα ταῦτα ὅτι ἀλλότρια. σὸν οὖν τί; χρῆσις φαντασιῶν. ταύτην ἔδειξέ μοι ὅτι ἀκώλυτον ἔχω, ἀνανάγκαστον, κ.τ.λ. We have, however, certainly not got the very words of Diogenes or Antisthenes.

[2] Diog. 12 (teaching of Antisthenes): ἀναφαίρετον ὅπλον ἀρετή . . . τεῖχος ἀσφαλέστατον φρόνησιν· μήτε γὰρ καταῤῥεῖν μήτε προδίδοσθαι. The same is a little differently expressed by *Epiph.* Exp. Fid. 1089, C. *Diog.* 63 says of Diogenes: ἐρωτηθεὶς τί αὐτῷ περιγέγονεν ἐκ φιλοσοφίας, ἔφη· εἰ καὶ μηδὲν ἄλλο, τὸ γοῦν πρὸς πᾶσαν τύχην παρεσκευάσθαι—and 105: ἀρέσκει αὐτοῖς τύχῃ μηδὲν ἐπιτρέπειν. *Stob.* Ekl. ii. 348: Διογένης ἔφη ὁρᾶν τὴν Τύχην ἐνορῶσαν αὐτῷ καὶ λέγουσαν· τοῦτον δ' οὐ δύναμαι βαλέειν κύνα λυσσητῆρα. (The same verse is applied by *David*, Schol. in Arist. 23, to Antisthenes.) Conf. *Stob.* Floril. 108, 71.

[3] This is what Diogenes says of himself in *Epict.* Diss. iii. 24, 67: ἐξ οὗ μ' Ἀντισθένης ἠλευθέρωσεν, οὐκέτι ἐδούλευσα, and he also asserts in *Diog.* 71 that he led the life of a Hercules, μηδὲν ἐλευθερίας προκρίνων. Crates in *Clem.* Strom. ii. 413, A. (*Theod.* Cur. Gr. Aff. xii. 49, p. 172) praises the Cynics:

ἡδονῇ ἀνδραποδώδει ἀδούλωτοι καὶ ἄκαμπτοι
ἀθάνατον βασιλείαν ἐλευθερίαν τ' ἀγαπῶσιν,

and he exhorts his Hipparchia

τῶνδε κράτει ψυχῆς ἤθει ἀγαλλομένη,
οὔθ' ὑπὸ χρυσίων δουλουμένη
οὔθ' ὑπ' ἐρώτων θηξιπόθων.

[4] See note 2.

order to content himself with virtue alone.[1] For what is wealth without virtue? A prey for flatterers and venal menials, a temptation for avarice, a root of all evil, a fountain of untold crimes and deeds of shame, a possession for ants and dung-beetles, a thing bringing neither glory nor enjoyment.[2] Indeed what else can wealth be, if it be true that wealth and virtue can never dwell together,[3] the Cynic's beggar-life being the only straight way to wisdom?[4] What are honour and shame? The talk of fools, about which no child of reason will trouble himself? For in truth facts are the very opposite of what we think. Honour amongst men is an evil. To be despised by them is a good, since it keeps us back from vain attempts. Glory only falls to his lot, who seeks it not.[5] What is death? Clearly

[1] See *Diog.* 105: ἀρέσκει δ' αὐτοῖς καὶ λιτῶς βιοῦν, πλούτου καὶ δόξης καὶ εὐγενείας καταφρονοῦσι. *Diog.* 24. *Epict.* Diss. i. 24, 6.

[2] Antisth. in *Stob.* Floril. i. 30; 10, 42; *Xen.* Sym. 4, 35; Diog. in *Diog.* 47; 50; 60; *Galen.* Exhort. c. 7, i. 10, K. Metrocles in *Diog.* 95; Crates in *Stob.* 97, 27; 15, 10; the same in *Julian*, Or. vi. 199, D.

[3] *Stob.* Floril. 93, 35: Διογένης ἔλεγε, μήτε ἐν πόλει πλουσίᾳ μήτε ἐν οἰκίᾳ ἀρετὴν οἰκεῖν δύνασθαι. Crates therefore disposed of his property, and is said to have settled that it should only be restored to his children when they ceased to be philosophers (*Diog.* 88, on the authority of Demetrius Magnes). Unfortunately, however, Crates can at that time have neither had wife nor children.

[4] *Diog.* 104; Diog. in *Stob.* Floril. 95, 11; 19. See *Lucian* V. Auct. 11; Crates in *Epiph.* Exp. Fid. 1089, C.: ἐλευθερίας εἶναι τὴν ἀκτημοσύνην.

[5] *Epict* Diss. i. 24, 6: (Διογένης) λέγει, ὅτι εὐδοξία (Winckelmann, p. 47, suggests ἀδοξία, which certainly might be expected from what preceded) ψόφος ἐστὶ μαινομένων ἀνθρώπων. *Diog.* 11 says of Antisth.: τήν τ' ἀδοξίαν ἀγαθὸν καὶ ἴσον τῷ πόνῳ, and 72: εὐγενείας δὲ καὶ δόξας καὶ τὰ τοιαῦτα πάντα διέπαιζε (Diogenes), προκοσμήματα κακίας εἶναι λέγων. In 41 he speaks of δόξης ἐξανθήματα. In 92: ἔλεγε δὲ (Crates) μέχρι τού-

CHAP. XIII.

not an evil. For only what is bad[1] is an evil: and death we do not experience to be an evil, since we have no further experience when we are dead.[2] All these things are then only empty fancies,[3] nothing more. Wisdom consists in keeping the mind free from them.[4] The most worthless and the most harmful thing is—what men most covet—pleasure. Pleasure the Cynics not only deny to be a good,[5] but they declare it to be the greatest evil; and a saying is preserved of Antisthenes, that he would rather be mad than pleased.[6] Where the desire of pleasure

του δεῖν φιλοσοφεῖν, μέχρι ἂν δόξωσιν οἱ στρατηγοὶ εἶναι ὀνηλάται. Compare also 93. *Doxopater* in Aphthon. c. 2, Rhet. Gr. i. 192, says that Diogenes, in answer to the question, How is honour to be gained? replied 'By not troubling yourself at all about honour.'

[1] *Epict.* l. c.: λέγει, ὅτι ὁ θάνατος οὐκ ἔστι κακόν, οὐδὲ γὰρ αἰσχρόν. See p. 303, 3.

[2] Diogenes in *Diog.* 68. Conf. *Cic.* Tusc. i. 43, 104. Evidently the Cynic here is not thinking of immortality, nor does it follow from the remark of Antisthenes on Il. xxiii. 15 (Schol. Venet. in *Winckelmann*, p. 28) to the effect that the souls have the same forms as bodies.

[3] Or as the Cynics technically call it, mere smoke, τῦφος. See *Diog.* 26, 83, 86, and p. 301, 3.

[4] *Clemens*, Strom. ii. 417, B. (*Theod.* Cur. Gr. Aff. xi. 8, p. 152): Ἀντισθένης μὲν τὴν ἀτυχίαν (τέλος ἀπέφηνει).

[5] As Crates—probably the Cynic—proves in *Teles.* in *Stob.* Floril. 98, 72, by the consideration, that the human life from beginning to end brings far more unhappiness than pleasure; if therefore the πλεονάζουσαι ἡδοναὶ were the measure of happiness, a happy man could not be found.

[6] *Diog.* vi. 3: ἔλεγέ τε συνεχές· μανείην μᾶλλον ἢ ἡσθείην. Ib. ix. 101, Conf. *Sext.* Math. xi. 741: [ἡ ἡδονὴ δοξάζεται] κακὸν ὑπ' Ἀντισθένους. The same in *Gell.* ix. 5, 3: *Clemens*, Stromat. ii. 412, D.; *Eus.* Pr. Ev. xv. 13, 7 (*Theod.* Cur. Gr. Aff. xii. 47, p. 172). Conf. *Diog.* vi. 8, 14, and p. 259, 4. Plato is no doubt referring to this Cynical dictum, Phileb. 44. C.: λίαν μεμισηκότων τὴν τῆς ἡδονῆς δύναμιν καὶ νενομικότων οὐδὲν ὑγιές, ὥστε καὶ αὐτὸ τοῦτο αὐτῆς τὸ ἐπαγωγὸν γοήτευμα οὐχ ἡδονὴν εἶναι: and Arist. Eth. x. 1, 1172, a, 27: οἱ μὲν γὰρ τἀγαθὸν ἡδονὴν λέγουσιν, οἱ δ' ἐξ ἐναντίας κομιδῇ φαῦλον. Ib. vii. 12, 1152, b, 8: τοῖς μὲν οὖν δοκεῖ οὐδεμία ἡδονὴ εἶναι ἀγαθὸν οὔτε καθ' αὑτὸ οὔτε

CHAP. XIII.

becomes unbridled passion, as in love, where man lowers himself to be the slave of his desires, there no means can be too violent to eradicate it.[1] Conversely, what most men fear, labour and toil, are good, because they only bring man to that state in which he can be independent.[2] Hercules [3] is therefore the patron-saint and pattern for the Cynic,[4] no one else having fought his way through so arduous and toilsome a life for the good of mankind, with so much courage and vigour. In support of this tenet,

κατὰ συμβεβηκός· οὐ γὰρ εἶναι ταὐτὸν ἀγαθὸν καὶ ἡδονήν. Compare p. 297.

[1] *Clemens*, l. c. 406, C.: ἐγὼ δὲ ἀποδέχομαι τὸν Ἀντισθένην, τὴν Ἀφροδίτην, λέγοντα, κἂν κατατοξεύσαιμι, εἰ λάβοιμι· ὅτι πολλὰς ἡμῶν καλὰς καὶ ἀγαθὰς γυναῖκας διέφθειρεν. τόν τε ἔρωτα κακίαν φησὶ φύσεως· ἧς ἥττους ὄντες οἱ κακοδαίμονες θεὸν τὴν νόσον καλοῦσιν. Crates in *Diog.* vi. 86 (*Clemens*, Strom. ii. 412, D.; *Theod.* l. c. xii. 49; *Julian*, Or. vi. 198, D.):

ἔρωτα παύει λιμός, εἰ δὲ μή, χρόνος
ἐὰν δὲ τούτοις μὴ δύνῃ χρῆσθαι, βρόχος.

On the same subject compare also *Diog.* vi. 38; 51; 67; *Stob.* Floril. 64, 1; 6, 2; 18, 27; *Diog.* 66: τοὺς μὲν οἰκέτας ἔφη τοῖς δεσπόταις. τοὺς δὲ φαύλους ταῖς ἐπιθυμίαις δουλεύειν. See p. 304, 3.

[2] *Diog.* vi. 2, says of Antisthenes: καὶ ὅτι ὁ πόνος ἀγαθὸν συνέστησε διὰ τοῦ μεγάλου Ἡρακλέους καὶ τοῦ Κύρου. Diogenes says in Exc. e Floril. Jo. Damasc. ii. 13, 87 (*Stob.* Floril. ed. Mein. iv. 200) that boys, if they are to come to any good, ought to be educated by abstemiousness, as early as they are susceptible of culture.

[3] Who had also a temple near Cynosarges.

[4] Antisthenes speaks of two Herculeses, *Diog.* 2, 18. Winckelmann, p. 15. Diogenes says of himself in *Diog.* 71: τὸν αὐτὸν χαρακτῆρα τοῦ βίου διεξάγειν ὅνπερ καὶ Ἡρακλῆς, μηδὲν ἐλευθερίας προκρίνων. Therefore *Eus.* Pr. Ev. xv. 13, 7, calls Antisthenes Ἡρακλεωτικός τις ἀνὴρ τὸ φρόνημα: and in *Lucian*, V. Auct. 8, Diogenes replies to the query as to whom he was imitating: τὸν Ἡρακλέα, at the same time showing his stick for a club, and his philosopher's cloak for a lion's skin, with the addition, which probably comes from a Cynic writing: στρατεύομαι δὲ ὥσπερ ἐκεῖνος ἐπὶ τὰς ἡδονὰς . . . ἐκκαθᾶραι τὸν βίον προαιρούμενος, . . . ἐλευθερωτὴς εἰμι τῶν ἀνθρώπων καὶ ἰατρὸς τῶν παθῶν. See Dens. Cyn. 13, *Julian*, Or. vi. 187, C.

CHAP. XIII.

Antisthenes appears to have argued that pleasure is nothing but the pause after pain.[1] On this supposition it will appear absurd to pursue pleasure; which can only be attained by having previously experienced a corresponding amount of pain.

From this rigid development of their principles to which Antisthenes had been brought, partly by

[1] *Plato*, Phileb. 44, B. (Conf. 51, A.; Rep. ix. 583, B.) speaks of people, as μάλα δεινοὺς λεγομένους τὰ περὶ φύσιν, οἳ τοπαράπαν ἡδονὰς οὔ φασιν εἶναι, for they maintain λυπῶν ταύτας εἶναι πάσας ἀποφυγὰς ἃς νῦν οἱ περὶ Φίληβον ἡδονὰς ἐπονομάζουσιν. This passage refers without doubt to Antisthenes. *Wendt* (Phil. Cyren. 17, 1) applies it to philosophers who declare freedom from pain to be the highest good. *Grote*, Plato ii. 609, thinks of the Pythagoreans, from whom he imagines Speusippus derived his theory of pleasure. Only no philosophers of Plato's age are known to us who made freedom from pain the highest good. As to the Pythagoreans, we know of their asceticism, but no ethical theory of theirs is known which altogether rejected pleasure. On the other hand, we know that Antisthenes did reject pleasure. The probability is, therefore, that Plato in writing this passage had Antisthenes in his eye. That the expression δεινοὶ τὰ περὶ φύσιν is no obstacle to this view, has been already indicated, p. 295, 4; the expression not referring to physical research, but to the practical inquiry as to what is conformable to nature, to which Antisthenes wanted to go back without excluding pleasure. If the further objection is raised, that the opponents of pleasure here referred to, hate (according to Phil. 46, A.) τὰς τῶν ἀσχημόνων ἡδονάς, whereas the Cynics allowed no difference between things seemly and unseemly, this rests on a misapprehension; for the ἡδοναὶ τῶν ἀσχημόνων are, as the context shows, condemned by the opponents of pleasure, not because of their unseemliness, but because they are always combined with unhappiness. Nor can we assert that Plato would not have spoken of Antisthenes with so much consideration as he here does (44, C.). If he at one time of life replied to his sallies with appropriate severity (see p. 293, 2; 300, 3), it does not follow that after the lapse of years, and in respect of a question on which their views more nearly approximated, he could not express himself more gently and appreciatingly. Yet even here he will not allow to him the properly scientific capacity, the τέχνη.

his own natural temperament,[1] partly from regard to it as a means of education,[2] the Cynics so far departed, as to admit a certain kind of pleasure to be legitimate. Pleasure which is not followed by remorse,[3] or, more accurately, pleasure resulting from labour and effort,[4] is said to have been called a good, even by Antisthenes. In Stobæus,[5] Diogenes recommends justice as the most useful and at the same time as the most pleasant thing, because it alone affords peace of mind, protects from trouble and sickness, and even secures bodily enjoyments. He also asserts,[6] that happiness consists in that true joy which can only be obtained by an unruffled cheerfulness of mind. Moreover, the Cynics, when wishing to set forth the advantages of their philosophy, did not fail to follow in the steps of Socrates, by asserting that life with them was far more pleasant and

[1] *Plato*, l. c. continues: τούτοις οὖν ἡμᾶς πότερα πείθεσθαι συμβουλεύεις, ἢ πῶς, ὦ Σώκρατες; —Οὔκ, ἀλλ' ὥσπερ μάντεσι προσχρῆσθαί τινι, μαντευομένοις οὐ τέχνῃ, ἀλλά τινι δυσχερείᾳ φύσεως οὐκ ἀγεννοῦς, λίαν, κ.τ.λ. See p. 306, 6.

[2] *Arist.* Eth. x. 1: Some hold pleasure to be altogether a mistake: οἱ μὲν ἴσως πεπεισμένοι οὕτω καὶ ἔχειν, οἱ δὲ οἰόμενοι βελτίον εἶναι πρὸς τὸν βίον ἡμῶν ἀποφαίνειν τὴν ἡδονὴν τῶν φαύλων, καὶ εἰ μὴ ἐστίν· ῥέπειν γὰρ τοὺς πολλοὺς πρὸς αὐτὴν καὶ δουλεύειν ταῖς ἡδοναῖς, διὸ δεῖν εἰς τοὐναντίον ἄγειν· ἐλθεῖν γὰρ ἂν οὕτως ἐπὶ τὸ μέσον. *Diog.* vi. 35: μιμεῖσθαι, ἔλεγε (Διογένης), τοὺς χοροδιδασκάλους καὶ γὰρ ἐκείνους ὑπὲρ τόνον ἐνδιδόναι ἕνεκα τοῦ τοὺς λοιποὺς ἅψασθαι τοῦ προσήκοντος τόνου.

[3] *Athen.* xii. 513, a: Ἀντισθένης δὲ τὴν ἡδονὴν ἀγαθὸν εἶναι φάσκων, προσέθηκε τὴν ἀμεταμέλητον, but we require to know the context in which Antisthenes said this.

[4] Antisth. in *Stob.* Flor. 29, 65: ἡδονὰς τὰς μετὰ τοὺς πόνους διωκτέον, ἀλλ' οὐχὶ τὰς πρὸ τῶν πόνων.

[5] Floril. 9, 49; 24, 14, where probably the Cynic Diogenes is meant. It is, however, a question whether the words are taken from a genuine writing of his.

[6] Ibid. 103, 20; 21.

CHAP. XIII.

independent than with other men, that their abstemiousness gave the right flavour to enjoyment, and that mental delights afforded a far higher pleasure than sensual ones.[1] All that this language proves is, that their theory was imperfectly developed, and that their mode of expression was inaccurate, their meaning being that pleasure as such ought in no case to be an end,[2] and that when it is anything

[1] Thus in *Xen.* Symp. 4, 34, where the description appears on the whole to be true, Antisthenes demonstrates that in his poverty he was the happiest of men. Food, drink, and sleep he enjoyed; better clothes he did not need; and from all these things he had more enjoyment than he liked; so little did he need that he was never embarrassed to think how he should find support; he had plenty of leisure to associate with Socrates, and if he wanted a pleasant day, there was no need to purchase the requisite materials in the market, but he had them ready in the soul. Diogenes in *Diog.* 71 speaks in a similar strain (not to mention *Dio Chrys.* Or. vi. 12; 33); he who has learned to despise pleasure, finds therein his highest pleasure; and in *Plut.* De Exil. 12, p. 605, he congratulates himself on not having, like Aristotle, to wait for Philip for breakfast; or like Callisthenes for Alexander (*Diog.* 45): to the virtuous man according to Diogenes (*Plut.* Tranq. An. 20, p. 477) every day is a festival. In like manner *Plut.* Tranquil. An. 4, says that Crates passed his life in jesting and joking, like one perpetual festival; and Metrocles (in *Plutarch*, An. Vitios. ad Infelic. 3, p. 499), like Diogenes (in *Lucian*, V. Auct. 9), blesses himself for being happier than the Persian king. See *Diog.* 44, 78.

[2] As *Ritter* ii. 121, has remarked, the difference between the teaching of Antisthenes and that of Aristippus might be thus expressed: Aristippus considered the result of the emotion of the soul to be the good: Antisthenes considered the emotion itself to be the end, and the value of the action to consist in the doing of it. Ritter, however, asks with justice whether Antisthenes ever went so far as this, since it is never distinctly imputed to him. And in the same way it will be found that Aristippus never regarded pleasure as a state of rest, but as a state of motion for the soul. The contrary is not established by what *Hermann*, Ges. Abh. 237, f, alleges. Hermann proves, it is true, that Antisthenes considered the good to be virtuous activity, and that Aristippus took it to

more than a natural consequence of action and of satisfying essential wants, it is a thing to be avoided.

From these considerations the conclusion followed, that everything excepting virtue and vice is indifferent for us, and that we in turn ought to be indifferent thereto. Only those who soar above poverty and wealth, shame and honour, ease and fatigue, life and death, and who are prepared to submit to any labour and condition in life, fearing no one, troubling themselves about nothing—only such as these offer no exposed places to fortune, and can therefore be free and happy.[1]

(1) *Virtue.*

As yet, here are only negative conditions of happiness. What is the positive side corresponding thereto? Virtue alone bringing happiness, and the goods of the soul being alone worth possessing, in what does virtue consist? Virtue, replies Antisthenes, herein following Socrates and Euclid, consists in wisdom or prudence;[2] and Reason is the

be pleasure, but he does not prove that Antisthenes and Aristippus spoke in explicit terms of the rest and the motion of the soul.

[1] Diog. in *Stob.* Floril. 86, 19 (89, 4), says the noblest men are οἱ καταφρονοῦντες πλούτου δόξης ἡδονῆς ζωῆς, τῶν δὲ ἐναντίων ὑπεράνω ὄντες, πενίας ἀδοξίας πόνου θανάτου. *Diog.* 29 says of the same: ἐπῄνει τοὺς μέλλοντας γαμεῖν καὶ μὴ γαμεῖν, καὶ τοὺς μέλλοντας καταπλεῖν καὶ μὴ καταπλεῖν, καὶ τοὺς μέλλοντας πολιτεύεσθαι καὶ μὴ πολιτεύεσθαι, καὶ τοὺς παιδοτροφεῖν καὶ μὴ παιδοτροφεῖν, καὶ τοὺς παρασκευαζομένους συμβιοῦν τοῖς δυνάσταις καὶ μὴ προσιόντας. Crates, Ibid. 86, says that what he had gained by philosophy was θέρμων τε χοῖνιξ καὶ τὸ μηδενὸς μέλειν. Antis. in *Stob.* Floril. 8, 14: ὅστις δὲ ἑτέρους δέδοικε δοῦλος ὢν λέληθεν ἑαυτόν. Diogenes in *Diog.* 75: δούλου τὸ φοβεῖσθαι. See pp. 303, 2; 304, 2 and 3; 305, 4.

[2] This follows from *Diog.* 13: τεῖχος ἀσφαλέστατον φρόνησιν . . . τείχη κατασκευαστέον ἐν τοῖς αὑτῶν ἀναλώτοις λογισμοῖς, if we connect with it his maxims about the oneness and the teachableness of virtue,

CHAP. XIII.

only thing which gives a value to life.[1] Hence, as his teacher had done before him, he concludes that virtue is one and indivisible,[2] that the same moral problem is presented to every class of men,[3] and that virtue is the result of teaching.[4] He further maintains that virtue is an inalienable possession; for what is once known can never be forgotten.[5] He thus bridges over a gulf[6] in the teaching of Socrates by a system in which Sophistical views[7] contributed no less than practical interests to make virtue in itself independent of everything external.[8] Wherein,

and his doctrine of the wise man.

[1] Compare the saying attributed to Antisthenes in *Plut.* Sto. Rep. 14, 7, p. 1040, and to Diogenes in *Diog.* 24: εἰς τὸν βίον παρεσκευάζεσθαι δεῖν λόγον ἢ βρόχον. Also *Diog.* 3.

[2] Schol. Lips. on Il. O. 123 (*Winckelmann*, p. 28): Ἀντισθένης φησίν, ὡς εἴ τι πράττει ὁ σοφὸς κατὰ πᾶσαν ἀρετὴν ἐνεργεῖ.

[3] *Diog.* 12 according to Diocles: ἀνδρὸς καὶ γυναικὸς ἡ αὐτὴ ἀρετή.

[4] *Diog.* 10: διδακτὴν ἀπεδείκνυε (Ἀντισθένης) τὴν ἀρετήν. 105: ἀρέσκει δ' αὐτοῖς καὶ τὴν ἀρετὴν διδακτὴν εἶναι, καθὰ φησὶν Ἀντισθένης ἐν τῷ Ἡρακλεῖ, καὶ ἀναπόβλητον ὑπάρχειν. Without doubt the reference in *Isocr.* Hel. i. 1 is also to Antisthenes. Isocrates quotes the passages just given, with the sentence of Antisthenes which was discussed, p. 301, 2, added: καταγεγηράκασιν· οἱ μὲν οὐ φάσκοντες οἷόν τ' εἶναι ψευδῆ λέγειν οὐδ' ἀντιλέγειν. . . . οἱ δὲ διεξιόντες ὡς ἀνδρία καὶ σοφία καὶ δικαιοσύνη ταὐτόν ἐστι· καὶ φύσει μὲν οὐδὲν αὐτῶν ἔχομεν, μία δ' ἐπιστήμη καθ' ἁπάντων ἐστίν· ἄλλοι δὲ περὶ τὰς ἔριδας διατρίβουσι κ.τ.λ. The expression οἱ μὲν . . . οἱ δὲ does not prove that the first of these statements belongs to a different school from that to which the second belongs.

[5] *Diog.* 12: ἀναφαίρετον ὅπλον ἡ ἀρετή. *Xen.* Mem. i. 2, 19: ἴσως οὖν εἴποιεν ἂν πολλοὶ τῶν φασκόντων φιλοσοφεῖν, ὅτι οὐκ ἄν ποτε ὁ δίκαιος ἄδικος γένοιτο, οὐδὲ ὁ σώφρων ὑβριστής, οὐδὲ ἄλλο οὐδέν, ὧν μάθησίς ἐστιν, ὁ μαθὼν ἀνεπιστήμων ἄν ποτε γένοιτο.

[6] The maxim that prudence is insuperable. See p. 143, 3.

[7] The maxim that you cannot forget what you know is only the converse of the Sophistic maxim that you cannot learn what you do not know.

[8] It is only independent of external circumstances, when it cannot be lost: for since the wise and virtuous man will never, as long as he continues

however, true prudence consisted the Cynics could not say more precisely. If it were described as knowledge concerning the good,[1] this, as Plato justly observed,[2] was simply a tautology. If, on the contrary, it were said to consist in unlearning what is bad,[3] this negative expression does not lead a single step further. So much only is clear, that the prudence of Antisthenes and his School invariably coincides with a right state of will, firmness, self-control and uprightness,[4] thus bringing us back to the Socratic doctrine of the oneness of virtue and knowledge. Hence by learning virtue they understood moral exercise rather than intellectual research.[5]

wise and virtuous, forego his wisdom and virtue, and since, according to the teaching of Socrates, no one intentionally does wrong, it follows that knowledge can only be taken away by a cause foreign to the will of the individual.

[1] *Plato*, Rep. vi. 505, B.: ἀλλὰ μὴν τόδε γε οἶσθα, ὅτι τοῖς μὲν πολλοῖς ἡδονὴ δοκεῖ εἶναι τὸ ἀγαθὸν, τοῖς δὲ κομψοτέροις φρόνησις . . . καὶ ὅτι γε, ὦ φίλε, οἱ τοῦτο ἡγούμενοι οὐκ ἔχουσι δεῖξαι ἥτις φρόνησις, ἀλλ' ἀναγκάζονται τελευτῶντες τὴν τοῦ ἀγαθοῦ φάναι. If the Cynics are not here exclusively meant, the passage at any rate refers to them.

[2] l. c.

[3] *Diog.* 8, according to Phanias: (Ἀντισθένης) ἐρωτηθεὶς ὑπὸ τοῦ . . . τί ποιῶν καλὸς κἀγαθὸς ἔσοιτο, ἔφη· εἰ τὰ κακὰ ἃ ἔχεις ὅτι φευκτά ἐστι μάθοις παρὰ τῶν εἰδότων. Ibid. 7: ἐρωτηθεὶς τί τῶν μαθημάτων ἀναγκαιότατον, ἔφη, τὸ κακὰ ἀπομαθεῖν. The same is found in Exc. e Floril. Joan. Damasc. ii. 13, 34 (*Stob.* Floril. ed. Mein. iv. 193).

[4] Compare pp. 293, 1; 304, 2 and 3.

[5] Here it may suffice to call to mind what has been said p. 293, 1, and what Diogenes in *Diog.* 70 says: διττὴν δ' ἔλεγεν εἶναι τὴν ἄσκησιν, τὴν μὲν ψυχικήν, τὴν δὲ σωματικήν· ταύτην . . . (the text here appears faulty) καθ' ἣν ἐν γυμνασίᾳ συνεχεῖς [συνεχεῖ]? γινόμεναι [αἱ] φαντασίαι εὐλυσίαν πρὸς τὰ τῆς ἀρετῆς ἔργα παρέχονται· εἶναι δ' ἀτελῆ τὴν ἑτέραν χωρὶς τῆς ἑτέρας . . . παρετίθετο δὲ τεκμήρια τοῦ ῥᾳδίως ἀπὸ τῆς γυμνασίας ἐν τῇ ἀρετῇ καταγίνεσθαι (to be at home in); for in every art practice makes perfect; 71: οὐδέν γε μὴν ἔλεγε τὸ παράπαν ἐν τῷ βίῳ χωρὶς ἀσκήσεως κατορθοῦσθαι, δυνατὴν δὲ ταύτην πᾶν ἐκνικῆσαι.

CHAP. XIII.

They would not have recognised the Platonic and Aristotelian distinction between a conventional and a philosophical, an ethical and an intellectual virtue; and in answer to Meno's[1] question whether virtue was produced by exercise or instruction, they would have replied, that practice was the best instruction.

(2) Wisdom and Folly.

He who has attained to virtue by the help of the Cynic teaching, is a wise man. Everyone else is lacking in wisdom. To tell the advantages of the one, and the misery of the other, no words are too strong for the Cynics. The wise man never suffers want, for all things are his. He is at home everywhere, and can accommodate himself to any circumstances. Faultless and love-inspiring, fortune cannot touch him.[2] An image of the divinity, he lives with the Gods. His whole life is a festival, and the Gods, whose friend he is, bestow on him everything.[3] The reverse is the case with the great bulk of mankind. Most of them are mentally cripples, slaves of fancy, only by a hair's breadth removed from madness.

[1] *Plato*, Meno, init.

[2] *Diog.* 11: αὐτάρκη τ' εἶναι τὸν σοφόν· πάντα γὰρ αὐτοῦ εἶναι τὰ τῶν ἄλλων. Ibid. 12 (according to Diocles): τῷ σοφῷ ξένον οὐδὲν οὐδ' ἄπορον. ἀξιέραστος ὁ ἀγαθός. Ibid. 105: ἀξιέραστόν τε τὸν σοφὸν καὶ ἀναμάρτητον καὶ φίλον τῷ ὁμοίῳ, τύχῃ τε μηδὲν ἐπιτρέπειν. See p. 304, 2. The passage in *Arist.* Eth. N. vii. 13, 1053, b, 19, probably also refers to the Cynics: οἱ δὲ τὸν τροχιζόμενον καὶ τὸν δυστυχίαις μεγάλαις περιπίπτοντα εὐδαίμονα φάσκοντες εἶναι, ἐὰν ᾖ ἀγαθός, ἢ ἑκόντες ἢ ἄκοντες οὐδὲν λέγουσιν. Yet Diogenes (in *Diog.* 89) allows that no one is perfectly free from faults.

[3] Diogenes, in *Diog.* 51: τοὺς ἀγαθοὺς ἄνδρας θεῶν εἰκόνας εἶναι. Ibid. 37, 72: τῶν θεῶν ἐστι πάντα· φίλοι δὲ οἱ σοφοὶ τοῖς θεοῖς· κοινὰ δὲ τὰ τῶν φίλων. πάντ' ἄρα ἐστὶ τῶν σοφῶν. Diog. in *Plut* Tran. An. 20: ἀνὴρ ἀγαθὸς οὐ πᾶσαν ἡμερὰν ἑορτὴν ἡγεῖται; Exc. e Floril. Joan. Damasc. ii. 13, 76: Ἀντισθένης ἐρωτηθεὶς ὑπό τινος τί διδάξει τὸν υἱόν, εἶπεν· εἰ μὲν θεοῖς μάλλει συμβιοῦν, φιλόσοφον, εἰ δὲ ἀνθρώποις, ῥήτορα.

To find a real man, you must look for him with a lantern in broad daylight. Misery and stupidity are the universal fate of mortals.[1] Accordingly all mankind are divided into two classes. Innumerable fools stand opposite to a small number of wise men. Only very few are happy through prudence and virtue. All the rest live in misfortune and folly, the fewest of all being aware of their deplorable state.

D. *The practical effects of their Teaching.*

Following out these principles, the Cynics conceived it to be their special mission to set an example of strict morality, of abstemiousness, of the independence of the wise man, and also to exercise a beneficial and strengthening influence on others. To this mission they devoted themselves with extraordinary self-denial, not, however, without falling into such extravagances and absurdities, such offensive coarseness, utter shamelessness, overbearing self-conceit, and empty boasting, that it is hard to say

[1] *Diog.* 33: ἀναπήρους ἔλεγε (Διογένης) οὐ τοὺς κωφοὺς καὶ τυφλούς, ἀλλὰ τοὺς μὴ ἔχοντας πήραν. Ibid. 35: τοὺς πλείστους ἔλεγε παρὰ δάκτυλον μαίνεσθαι. Compare what has been said of Socrates p. 122, 2, Ibid. 47: τοὺς ῥήτορας καὶ πάντας τοὺς ἐνδοξολογοῦντας τρισανθρώπους ἀπεκάλει ἀντὶ τοῦ τρισαθλίους. Ibid. 71: Instead of becoming happy by practice of virtue, men παρὰ τὴν ἄνοιαν κακοδαιμονοῦσι. Ibid. 33: πρὸς τὸν εἰπόντα, Πύθια νικῶ ἄνδρας, Ἐγὼ μὲν οὖν, εἶπεν, ἄνδρας, σὺ δ' ἀνδράποδα. Ibid. 27: men he had found nowhere, but boys he had found in Lacedæmon. Ibid. 41; the story of Diogenes with his lantern. Ibid. 86; verses of Crates on the stupidity of mankind. Compare also *Stob.* Floril. 4, 52. Diogenes in Exc. e Floril. Joan. Damasc. ii. 13, 75, says that the vilest thing upon earth is a man without culture. Either Diogenes or Philiscus asserts in *Stob.* Flor. 22, 41 (Conf. *Diog.* vi. 80): ὁ τῦφος ὥσπερ ποιμὴν οὗ θέλει [τοὺς πολλοὺς] ἄγει. Compare p. 293, 2.

CHAP. XIII.

whether their strength of mind rather calls for admiration, or their eccentricities for ridicule; and whether they rather command esteem, or dislike, or commiseration. Previous inquiries, however, make it possible for us to refer these various peculiarities to one common source.

(1) *Self-renunciation.*

The leading thought of Cynicism is the self-sufficiency of virtue.[1] Blunt and one-sided in their conception of this principle, the Cynics were not content with a mere *inward* independence of the enjoyments and wants of life. Their aim, they thought, could only be reached by entirely renouncing all enjoyment, by limiting wants to what is absolutely indispensable, by deadening feelings to outward impressions, and by cultivating indifference to all that is not in our own power. The Socratic independence of wants[2] became with them a renunciation of the world.[3] Poor to begin with,[4] or renouncing their property voluntarily,[5] they lived as beggars.[6] Possessing no

[1] See p. 303.

[2] According to *Diog.* vi. 105, conf. *Lucian*, Cyn. 12, Diogenes repeated the language which we saw Socrates used, p. 65, 3. To the same effect is the story that Diogenes, at the beginning of his Cynic career, refused to look for a runaway slave, because he could do without the slave as well as the slave could do without him. *Diog.* 55; *Stob.* Floril. 62, 47. Ibid. 97, 31, p. 215 Mein.

[3] See pp. 304; 311, 1.

[4] Such as Antisthenes, Diogenes, and Monimus.

[5] Such as Crates and Hipparchia.

[6] According to Diocles in *Diog.* vi. 13, Antisthenes already assumed the beggar's guise, the staff and scrip; nor is the truth of his account impugned by Sosicrates, in saying that Diodorus of Aspendus was the first to do so; for this statement is not very accurate, both Antisthenes and Diogenes being older than Diodorus. Nevertheless, in *Diog.* 22, Diogenes is described with great probability as the originator of the full mendicant garb,

houses of their own, they passed the day in the streets, or in other public places; the nights they spent in porticos, or wherever else chance might find them.[1] Furniture they had none.[2] A bed seemed superfluous.[3] The simple Greek dress was by them made still simpler, and they were content with the tribon[4]

and he is also said to have been the first to gain his living by begging. *Diog.* 38; 46; 49; Teles. in *Stob.* Flor. v. 67; *Hieron.* adv. Jovin. ii. 207. His followers Crates (see the verses in *Diog.* 85 and 90) and Monimus (Diog. 82) adopted the same course.

[1] Diogenes must have been the first to act thus. For Antisthenes in *Xen.* Symp. 4, 38, still speaks of having a house, although its furniture was confined to the bare walls. Diogenes, however, and the later Cynics lived as described. See *Diog.* 22; 38; 76; 105: *Teles.* l. c. and in *Stob.* Floril. 97, 31, p. 215 Mein. *Hieron. Lucian,* V. Auct. 9. Diogenes for a time took up his abode in a tub which stood in the entrance-court of Metroon, at Athens, as had been done by homeless folk before. *Diog.* 23; 43; 105; *Sen.* Ep. 90, 14. But it cannot have been, as *Juvenal,* xiv. 208, and *Lucian,* Consc. His. 3, state, that he spent his whole life there without any other home, even carrying his tub about with him, as a snail does its shell. Compare *Steinhart,* l. c. p. 302, *Göttling,* Ges. Abh. 258, and Brücker's report of the discussions between Hermann and Kasæus, Hist. Phil. i. 872. Equally fictitious is the romantic story that Crates and Hipparchia lived in a tub. Simpl. in *Epict.* Enchir. p. 270. All that Musonius in *Stob.* Floril. 67, 20, p. 4, Mein. says, is that they spent day and night in the open porticos. In southern countries the night is even now often spent in a portico.

[2] The story that Diogenes threw away his cup, when he had seen a boy drinking with the hollow of his hand, is well known. *Diog.* 37; *Plut.* Prof. in Virt. 8, p. 79; *Seneca,* Ep. 90, 14; Hier. l. c. He is also reported to have trampled on Plato's costly carpets with the words, πατῶ τὸν Πλάτωνος τῦφον, to which Plato replied, ἑτέρῳγε τύφῳ, Διογενές. *Diog.* 26.

[3] Antisthenes in *Xen.* Symp. 4, 38, boasts that he slept admirably on the simplest bed. And the fragment in *Demetr.* de Elocut. 249 (Winckelmann, p. 52), belongs here. As far as Diogenes (*Epict.* Dido. i. 24, 7, distinctly asserts this of Diogenes) and Crates are concerned, they slept, as a matter of course, on the bare ground.

[4] Compare the passages quoted p. 55, 4.

CHAP. XIII.

of Socrates, the ordinary dress of the lower orders,[1] without any underclothing.[2] In scantiness of diet they even surpassed the very limited requirements of their fellow-countrymen.[3] It is said that Diogenes tried to do without fire, by eating his meat raw,[4] and he is credited with saying that everything without exception, human flesh included, might be used for purposes of food.[5] In extreme age he refused to depart from his accustomed manner of living,[6] and, lest

[1] That is at Athens; at Sparta the τρίβων was universal (*Göttling*, 256; *Hermann*, Antiquit. iii. § 21, 14), from which it will be seen that the word did not originally mean something worn out, but a rough dress which rubbed the skin; an ἱμάτιον τρίβον not an ἱμάτιον τετριμμένον, and that ἱμάτιον τρίβων γενόμενον in *Stob.* Floril. 5, 67, means a covering which had grown rough.

[2] This was often done by the poor (*Hermann*, l. c.). Antisthenes, however, or Diogenes, according to others, made this dress the dress of his order, allowing the τρίβων to be doubled for better protection against the cold. *Diog.* 6; 13; 22; 76; 105. Teles. in *Stob.* Floril. 97, 31, p. 215 Mein. The Cynic ladies adopted the same dress, *Diog.* 93. This single article of dress was often in the most miserable condition. See the anecdotes about Crates, *Diog.* 90, and the verses on him, Ibid. 87. Because of the self-satisfaction with which Antisthenes exposed to view the holes in his cloak, Socrates is said to have observed that his vanity peeped through them. *Diog.* 8.

[3] Their ordinary food consisted of bread, figs, onions, garlic, linseed, but particularly of the θέρμοι, or beans. Their drink was cold water. *Diog.* 105; 25; 48; 85; 90; Teles. in *Stob.* Floril. 97, 31; Ibid. p. 215, M.; *Athen.* iv. 156 c; *Lucian*, V. Auct. 9; *Dio Chrys.* Or. vi. 12 and 21, and *Göttling*, p. 255. But, in order to prove their freedom, they occasionally allowed a pleasure to themselves and others. *Diog.* 55; *Aristid.* Or. xxv. 560 (*Winckelmann.* p. 28).

[4] *Diog.* 34; 76; *Pseudo-Plut.* de Esu Carn. i. 6, 995; *Dio Chrys.* Or. vi. 25.

[5] In *Diog.* 73, this principle is supported by the argument that everything is in everything else, even flesh in bread, &c. *Diog.* refers for this to a tragedy of Thyestes, the writer of which was not Diogenes, but Philiscus. A similar statement was subsequently made by the Stoics. See *Zeller's* Stoics, &c.

[6] See *Diog.* 34.

his friends should expend any unnecessary care on his corpse, he forbad their burying it at all.[1] A life in harmony with nature,[2] the suppression of everything artificial, the most simple satisfaction of all natural wants, is the watchword of his School.[3] They were never weary of lauding the good fortune and the independence which they owe to this freedom from wants.[4] To attain thereto, bodily and mental hardships are made a principle.[5] Diogenes, when his teacher did not appear to treat him with sufficient severity,[6] is said to have undertaken self-mortification in this behalf.[7] Even the scorn and contempt

[1] See the accounts which differ in details in *Diog.* 79; 52; *Cic.* Tusc. i. 43, 104; *Ælian.* V. H. viii. 14; *Stob.* Floril. 123, 11. The same is repeated by Chrysippus in *Sext.* Pyrrh. iii. 258; Math. xi. 194.

[2] Which Diogenes also required, witness for instance his saying in *Diog.* 71: *δέον οὖν ἀντὶ τῶν ἀχρήστων πόνων τοὺς κατὰ φύσιν ἑλομένους ζῆν εὐδαιμόνως, παρὰ τὴν ἄνοιαν κακοδαιμονοῦσι.*

[3] Compare on this subject the expressions of Diogenes in *Diog.* 44; 35; *Stob.* Floril. 5, 41; 67; the hymn of Crates on *εὐτέλεια*, and his prayer to the Muses in *Julian*, Or. vi. 199, in addition to what *Plut.* de Sanit. 7, p. 125, *Diog.* 85; 93, and *Stobæus* tell of him. Compare also *Lucian*, V. Auct. 9, and the anecdote of the mouse, the sight of which confirmed Diogenes in his renunciation of the world in *Plut.* Prof. in Virtut. 6; *Diog.* 22, 40.

[4] Compare the language used by Crates and Metrocles in Teles. in *Stob.* Floril. 97, 31 Mein. and the quotations p. 304 and 3.

[5] Compare p. 251, 1, and *Diog.* 30. Diogenes' training appears to have been described by Eubulus in the same glowing terms as that of Cyrus was by Xenophon. Exc. e Floril. Joan. Damasc. ii. 13, 68; 67. Diogenes in *Stob.* Floril. 7, 18, expresses the view that mental vigour is the only object of all exercise, even that of the body.

[6] *Dio Chrys.* Or. viii. 2 (*Stob.* Floril. 13, 19); conf. *Diog.* 18.

[7] According to *Diog.* 23; 34, he was in the habit of rolling in the summer in the burning sand, and in winter of walking barefoot in the snow, and embracing icy columns. On the other hand, Philemon's words about Crates in *Diog.* 87, that

CHAP. XIII.

necessarily incurred by this manner of life were borne by the Cynics with the greatest composure;[1] nay, they accustomed themselves thereto,[2] on the ground that the reproaches of enemies teach man to know himself,[3] and the best revenge you can take is to amend your faults.[4] Should life from any reason become insupportable, they reserved to themselves the right, as the Stoics did at a later time,[5] of securing their freedom by means of suicide.

(2) *Renunciation of social life.*

Among external things of which it is necessary to be independent, the Cynics included several matters which other men are in the habit of regarding

he went about wrapped up in summer and in rags in winter, are probably only a comedian's jest on his beggarly covering.

[1] Antisthenes in *Diog.* 7, requires: κακῶς ἀκούοντας καρτερεῖν μᾶλλον ἢ εἰ λίθοις τις βάλλοιτο. He also says in *Epict.* Diss. iv. 6, 20 (conf. *Diog.* 3): βασιλικόν, ὦ Κῦρε, πράττειν μὲν εὖ, κακῶς δ' ἀκούειν. It is said of Diogenes, *Diog.* 33, and also of Crates, *Diog.* 89, that when his body had been ill-treated, he only wrote by the side of his blains the names of those by whom they had been inflicted.

[2] *Diog.* 90 says of Crates, τὰς πόρνας ἐπίτηδες ἐλοιδόρει, συγγυμνάζων ἑαυτὸν πρὸς τὰς βλασφημίας.

[3] Antisthenes remarks, *Diog.* 12: προσέχειν τοῖς ἐχθροῖς· πρῶτοι γὰρ τῶν ἁμαρτημάτων αἰσθάνονται. He also says in *Plut.* Inim. Util. 6, p. 89, and the same saying is attributed to Diogenes in De Adul. 36, p. 74; Prof. in Virt. ii. p. 82: τοῖς μέλλουσι σώζεσθαι ἢ φίλων δεῖ γνησίων ἢ διαπύρων ἐχθρῶν.

[4] Diog. in *Plut.* Inimic. Util. 4, p. 88 and Poet. 4, p. 21.

[5] When Antisthenes in his last illness became impatient under his sufferings, Diogenes offered him a dagger (*Diog.* 18) to put an end to his life, but Antisthenes had not the courage to use it. That Diogenes made away with himself is indeed asserted in several of the accounts to which reference has been made, but cannot be proved. In *Ælian*, V. H. x. 11, he refuses the contemptuous challenge to put an end to his sufferings by suicide; for the wise man ought to live. Nevertheless, Metrocles put an end to himself (*Diog.* 95), not to mention Menedemus (Ibid. 100). So also Crates in *Diog.* 86; *Clemens*, Strom. ii. 412, D.

CHAP. XIII.

(a) *Of family life.*

as morally good and as duties. To be free in every respect, the wise man must be fettered and hampered by no relations to others. He must satisfy his social wants by himself alone,[1] or he will be dependent on others, and nothing which is out of his power ought to influence his happiness. To these matters belongs family life. Not that Antisthenes would do away with marriage, because he thought it useful to keep up the race of men;[2] but Diogenes early discovered that this object might be attained by a community of wives.[3] Deeply imbued with Grecian peculiarities, it never occurred to these philosophers to require, in the spirit of the later asceticism, the entire uprooting of all sexual desires. Natural impulses might, however, be satisfied in a far simpler way.[4] Their mendicant life, not affording them an

[1] In *Diog.* 6, Antisthenes in reply to the question, What good philosophy had done him, answers: τὸ δύνασθαι ἑαυτῷ ὁμιλεῖν. Out of this came the caricature of later Cynicism, described by *Lucian*, V. Auct. 10. Yet Diogenes and Crates were anything but haters of their fellow-men.

[2] *Diog.* 11: γαμήσειν τε [τὸν σόφον] τεκνοποιΐας χάριν ταῖς εὐφυεστάταις συνιόντα γυναιξί. The conjecture ἀφυεστάταις (*Winckelmann*, p. 29, according to Hermann) appears mistaken: Antisthenes might well require εὐφυέσταται πρὸς τεκνοποιΐαν, women most suited for child-bearing, whilst considering anyone good enough for a plaything.

[3] *Diog.* 72: ἔλεγε δὲ καὶ κοινὰς εἶναι δεῖν τὰς γυναῖκας, γάμον μηδένα νομίζων, ἀλλὰ τὸν πείσαντα τῇ πεισθείσῃ συνεῖναι· κοινοὺς δὲ διὰ τοῦτο καὶ τοὺς υἱέας. The correctness of this is supported by the fact that Zeno and Chrysippus, according to *Diog.* vii. 33, 131, projected the same state of things for their ideal state.

[4] Something of the same kind has been already observed in Socrates, p. 164, 1. With the Cynics this treatment of the relation between the sexes becomes an extravagance and a deformity. In *Xen.* Symp. 4, 38, Antisthenes boasts of his comforts, since he only associates with those fair dames to whom others would have nothing to say. That he did so on principle is stated in *Diog.* 3.

CHAP. XIII.

opportunity[1] for home pleasures, it is readily understood that they were in general averse to marriage,[2]

That he declared adultery permissible, as *Clemens*, Floril. v. 18 says, is by no means certain. He is even said to have satisfied his lusts in a coarser way, complaining that hunger could not be treated in the same way. *Brucker*, i. 880, *Steinhart*, p. 305, and *Göttling*, p. 275, doubt the truth of these and similar stories. Without vouching for their accuracy, it may be enough to say that they are not only quoted by *Diog.* 46, 49; *Dio Chrys.* Or. vi. 16, p. 203, R.; *Lucian*, V. Auct. 10; *Galen.* Loc. Affect. vi. 5; viii. 419, K.; *Athen.* iv. 158, f; *Dio Chrys.* 34 Hom. in Math. p. 398, C.; *S. Aug.* Civ. Dei, xiv. 20; but also, according to *Plut.* Stob. Rep. 21, 1, p. 1044, Chrysippus had on this score vindicated the Cynics, and according to *Sext.* Pyrrh. iii. 206, Zeno appears to have done the same. Dio probably borrowed his revolting extracts from Chrysippus. The things are, however, not so out of keeping with the ways of Antisthenes that we could call them impossible; and the very thing which to us appears so unintelligible, the public want of modesty, makes them very likely to be true of Diogenes. If true, they were an attempt on his part to expose the folly of mankind. It is from this point of view rather than on any moral grounds that the Cynics conduct their attacks on adulterers and stupid spendthrifts. To them it seemed foolish in the extreme to incur much toil, danger, and expense for an enjoyment which might be had much more easily. See *Diog.* 4; 51; 60; 66; 89; *Plut.* Ed. Pu. 7, Schl. p. 5; *Stob.* Floril. 6; 39; 52. Diogenes is also accused of having publicly practised unchastity, *Diog.* 69; *Theod.* Cur. Gr. Aff. xii. 48, p. 172. In Corinth the younger Lais, according to *Athen.* xiii. 588, b, or Phryne, according to *Tertull.* Apol. 46, is said to have had a whim to bestow on him her favours gratuitously, whereas the philosopher did not despise others. *Clemens* (Hom. V. 18) represents him as purchasing these attentions by scandalous conditions. In his tragedies (according to *Julian*, Or. vii. 210, c) stood things that one might believe ὑπερβολὴν ἀῤῥητουργίας οὐδὲ ταῖς ἑταίραις ἀπολελεῖφθαι. On the other hand his morality is commended, *Demetr.* de Eloc. 261.

[1] The case of Crates is an exception, and even Crates had not wooed Hipparchia. He only married her, when she would not renounce her affection for him, but was prepared to share his mode of life. He certainly married his children in a peculiar way, according to *Diog.* 88; 93.

[2] See the apophthegms in *Diog.* 3, and *Lucian*, V. Auct. 9: γάμου δὲ ἀμελήσεις καὶ παίδων καὶ πατρίδος. Far less objectionable is the maxim of Antisthenes in *Diog.* 12: τὸν δίκαιον

and to feminine society, treating family life as a thing indifferent.[1] Diogenes is said to have seen nothing revolting[2] in marriage between the nearest relations.

(b) Of civil life.

Another matter which they considered to be equally indifferent with family life for the wise man, was civil life. The sharp contrast between slavery and freedom does not affect the wise man. The man who is really free can never be a slave—for a slave is one who is afraid—and for the same reason a slave can never be free. The wise man is the natural ruler of others, although he may be called a slave, in the same way that the physician is the ruler of the sick. Thus it is said that Diogenes, when about to be sold, had the question asked: Who wants a master? declining the offer of his friends to buy him back.[3] Such conduct was not a vindication of slavery. Far from it, the Cynics seem to have been the first among Greeks to declare slavery an institution opposed to nature,[4] in obvious

περὶ πλείονος ποιεῖσθαι τοῦ συγγενοῦς.

[1] See pp. 311, 1, and 278.

[2] *Dio Chrys.* Or. x. 29, whose statement is confirmed by its agreeing with the universal doctrine of the Stoics. See *Zeller's* Stoics, &c., p. 4.

[3] *Diog.* 29; 74. Compare pp. 287, 4; 333, 4. According to *Diog.* 16, Antisthenes wrote περὶ ἐλευθερίας καὶ δουλείας, and perhaps this is the origin of the account in *Stob.* Flor. 8, 14.

[4] For this we have certainly no direct authority. Still (as has been already observed, p. 172, 4), it is probably in reference to the Cynics that *Arist.* Polit. i. 3; 1253, b, 20, says: τοῖς μὲν δοκεῖ ἐπιστήμη τέ τις εἶναι ἡ δεσποτεία . . . τοῖς δὲ παρὰ φύσιν τὸ δεσπόζειν· νόμῳ γὰρ τὸν μὲν δοῦλον εἶναι τὸν δ' ἐλεύθερον, φύσει δ' οὐθὲν διαφέρειν. διόπερ οὐδὲ δίκαιον, βίαιον γάρ. The contrast between νόμῳ and φύσει is not found so strongly drawn at that time except among the Sophists and Cynics. Nor is it only met with in their religious views.

CHAP. XIII.

conformity with their principle, that every difference between men other than that of virtue and vice is unimportant and has nothing to do with the law of nature and reason. Yet they did not go so far as to attempt even in a small circle (as the Essenes did at a later time) the abolition of slavery, regarding the outward condition as a thing indifferent, the wise man even in slavery being a free man. The same treatment was given to civil life. The wise man of the Cynics feels himself above the restraints which civil life imposes, without feeling any inclination to mix himself up in such matters; for where could a form of government be found which would satisfy his requirements? A popular form of government is severely censured by Antisthenes.[1] By an absolute monarch these freedom-

Their whole politics, and even their practical philosophy, are governed by the effort to bring human society from an artificial state recognised by law and custom to a pure state of nature. We should hardly look in sophistic circles for the opponents of slavery whom Aristotle mentions, where the rule of the stronger over the weaker was regarded as the most conformable to nature. But the view is most in keeping with a school which could never allow that one portion of mankind enjoy the right, independently of their moral state, to govern the rest; the claim of the wise man to govern the fool resting upon reason; and naturally all men being citizens of one state; between fellow-citizens the relation of master and slave cannot exist.

[1] *Arist.* Pol. iii. 13; 1284, a, 15, tells the fable—the application of which to a democracy is obvious—of the hares suggesting universal equality to the lions. The blame which he attaches to those states, which do not distinguish the good from the bad (*Diog.* 5; 6), must be intended for a hit at democracy. The saying in *Diog.* 8—that should the Athenians call their asses horses, it would be quite as good as choosing incompetent generals—must also be directed against a popular form of government. According to *Athen.* v. 220, d, Antisthenes had made a sharp attack on all the popular leaders at Athens.

loving philosophers understand a wretched and miserable man.[1] Aristocratical institutions fell far below their ideal, none being adapted for the rule of wise men: for what law or custom can fetter him whose life is regulated by the laws of virtue?[2] What country can be large enough for those who regard themselves as citizens of the world?[3] Allowing a conditional necessity for a state and laws,[4] the Cynics[5] refused in their homelessness to take any

Likewise in *Diog.* 24; 41, Diogenes calls them *ὄχλου διακόνους*. and he amuses himself at the expense of Demosthenes. Ibid. 34, on which see *Epict.* Diss. iii. 2, 11. See also what was said of Socrates, p. 167.

[1] Compare *Xen.* Symp. 4, 36; *Dio. Chrys.* Or. vi. 47; *Stob.* Floril. 49, 47; 97, 26; *Diog.* 50. Also *Plut.* Adul. et Am. c. 27, p. 68.

[2] Antisthenes, in *Diog.* 11 says: *τὸν σόφον οὐ κατὰ τοὺς κειμένους νόμους πολιτεύσεσθαι ἀλλὰ κατὰ τὸν τῆς ἀρετῆς.* Diogenes, ibid. 38: *ἔφασκε δ' ἀντιτιθέναι τύχῃ μὲν θάρσος, νόμῳ δὲ φύσιν, πάθει δὲ λόγον.* This antithesis of *νόμος* and *φύσις* seems to be what Plato has in view, Phil. 44, C. See p. 295, 4.

[3] *Diog.* 63 says of Diogenes: *ἐρωτηθεὶς πόθεν εἴη, κοσμοπολίτης, ἔφη.* See p. 168, 8. Ibid. 72: *μόνην τε ὀρθὴν πολίτειαν εἶναι τὴν ἐν κόσμῳ.* Antisthenes, ibid. 12: *τῷ σοφῷ ξένον οὐδὲν οὐδ' ἄπορον.* Crates, ibid. 98:

οὐχ εἷς πάτρας μοι πύργος, οὐ μία στέγη,
πάσης δὲ χέρσου καὶ πόλισμα καὶ δόμος
ἕτοιμος ἡμῖν ἐνδιαιτᾶσθαι πάρα.

The same individual in *Plut.* de Adul. 28, p. 69, shows that banishment is no evil, and according to *Diog.* 93 (conf. *Ael.* V. H. iii. 6) he is said to have given a negative answer to Alexander's question, whether he did not wish to see Thebes rebuilt: *ἔχειν δὲ πατρίδα ἀδοξίαν καὶ πενίαν ἀνάλωτα τῇ τύχῃ καὶ Διογένους εἶναι πολίτης ἀνεπιβουλεύτον φθόνῳ.* See also *Epict.* Diss. iii. 24, 66. *Lucian,* V. Auct. 8. Also the Stoic doctrine in *Zeller's* Stoics, &c., chapter on Stoics, and what has been said above, page 279, 1.

[4] The confused remarks of Diogenes in *Diog.* 72, support this statement.

[5] Antisthenes was not without a citizen's rights (see *Hermann,* Antiquit. 1, § 118), although a proletarian by birth and circumstances. Diogenes was banished from Sinope, and lived at Athens as a foreigner. Crates had chosen this life, after his native town had been destroyed. Monimus was a slave, whom his master had driven away.

CHAP. XIII.

part in civil life. They wished to be citizens of the world, not of any one state; their ideal state, as far as they do sketch it, is a destruction of all civil life.[1] All mankind are to live together like a flock. No nation may have its own special laws and boundaries severing it from others. Confining themselves to the barest necessaries of life, needing no gold, that source of so much mischief, abstaining from marriage and family life, they wished to return to the simplicity of a state of nature;[2] the leading

[1] *Stob.* Floril. 45, 28: 'Αντισθένης ἐρωτηθεὶς πῶς ἄν τις προσέλθοι πολιτείᾳ, εἶπε καθάπερ πυρὶ, μήτε λίαν ἐγγὺς ἵνα μὴ καῇς, μήτε πόῤῥω ἵνα μὴ ῥιγώσῃς.

[2] The above description rests only in part on direct testimony, but the combination which is the basis of it does not lack great probability. We know on authority that Diogenes in his πολιτεία (*Diog.* 80) demanded a community of wives and children, and that in the same treatise he proposed a coinage of bones or stones (ἀστραγάλοι) instead of gold and silver, *Athen.* iv. 159, e. We know further that Zeno's πολιτεία ran to this effect: ἵνα μὴ κατὰ πόλεις μηδὲ κατὰ δήμους οἰκῶμεν, ἰδίοις ἕκαστοι διωρισμένοι δικαίοις, ἀλλὰ πάντας ἀνθρώπους ἡγώμεθα δημότας καὶ πολίτας εἷς δὲ βίος ᾖ καὶ κόσμος, ὥσπερ ἀγέλης συννόμου νόμῳ κοινῷ τρεφομένης, *Plut.* Alex. Vit. i. 6, p. 329; and since this treatise of Zeno was always considered to express the opinions of the Cynic School, we have every reason to look to it for a Cynic's views. That such views were on the whole advocated by Antisthenes, probably in the treatise περὶ νόμου ἢ περὶ πολιτείας, which appears to be identical with the πολιτικὸς διάλογος mentioned by *Athen.* v. 220, d, is in itself probable, and is confirmed by Plato's Politicus. Rejecting, as this dialogue does, the analogy between statesmanship and the superintendence of a flock, we might naturally think that Plato was provoked to it by some such theory; and since we know from Plutarch's account of Zeno, that the Cynics reduced the idea of the state to that of a herd of men, it is most natural to think of them. Moreover, the description of the natural state, Rep. ii. 372, appears to refer to Antisthenes. Plato at first describes it as though from himself, but he afterwards clearly intimates that it belongs to another, when he calls it a state fit for pigs. We know of no one else to whom it could be better referred than to the founder of the Stoic School.

thought of their enlarged political sympathies being not so much the oneness and the union of all mankind, but the freedom of the individual from the bonds of social life and the limits of nationality. Here again may be seen the negative spirit of their morality, destitute of all creative power.

(c) Suppression of modesty.

The same tone may be recognised in a feature for us the most revolting in Cynicism—their deliberate suppression of the natural feeling of shame. This feeling they did not consider altogether unreasonable,[1] but they urged that you need only be ashamed of what is bad, and that what is in itself good may not only be unblushingly discussed, but done without reserve before the eyes of all.[2] They therefore permitted themselves what they considered natural, without regard to places, not shrinking even from doing in the public streets[3] what other

[1] It is expressly told of Diogenes, *Diog.* 37, 54, that he expostulated with a woman who lay in an indecent position in a temple, and that he called blushes the colour of virtue.

[2] See the following note, and *Cic.* Off. i. 35, 128: Nec vero audiendi sunt Cynici aut si qui fuerant Stoici pæne Cynici, qui reprehendunt et irrident, quod ea, quæ turpia non sint (for instance, the begetting of children) nominibus ac verbis flagitiosa dicamus (that we consider it unseemly to name them), illa autem quæ turpia sunt (stealing, &c.) nominibus appellemus suis.

[3] This is especially said of Diogenes, *Diog.* 22: παντὶ τρόπῳ ἐχρῆτο εἰς πάντα, ἀριστῶν τι καὶ καθεύδων καὶ διαλεγόμενος, and according to *Diog.* 69, he supported this by the argument, If it is at all allowable to breakfast, it must be allowable to breakfast in public. Following out this principle, he not only took his meals in public in the streets (*Diog.* 48; 58), but he also did many other eccentric and startling things, in the sight of all passers by (*Diog.* 35, 36). It is even asserted of him, *Diog.* 69: εἰώθει δὲ πάντα ποιεῖν ἐν τῷ μέσῳ, καὶ τὰ Δήμητρος καὶ τὰ Ἀφροδίτης. *Theod.* Cur. Gr. Aff. xii. 48, p. 172, says the same of him, mentioning an instance. We have already, p. 321, 4, observed

CHAP. XIII.

men prefer to do in secret. Lest he should in any way forego his independence, the Cynic puts out of sight all regard for others, and what is not shameful in itself he thinks he need not be ashamed of before others. Men's opinion is to him indifferent. He is neither hurt by their familiarity with his personal life, nor fears such familiarity.

(d) Renunciation of religion.

To the same source may be referred the Cynic attitude towards religion. No course of study under Antisthenes was required to make men doubt the truth of the popular faith. Such doubts were raised on all sides, and since the appearance of the Sophists, had permeated the educated classes. Not even the Socratic circle had passed unscathed.[1] From his intercourse with Gorgias and the other Sophists, Antisthenes in particular must have been familiar with freer views respecting the Gods and their worship, and specially with the principles of

that these statements can hardly be altogether inventions. But it is incredible that Crates and Hipparchia, as is said to have been the case, consummated their nuptials in the midst of numerous spectators. There are, however, not a few authorities for it: *Diog.* 97; *Sext.* Pyrrh. i. 153; iii. 200; *Clemens*, Stromat. iv. 523, A.; *Apul.* Floril. 14; *Lact.* Inst. iii. 15, who mentions it as the common practice of the Cynics; *S. Aug.* Civ. Dei, xiv. 20, who does not altogether credit it, but does not improve it by his interpretation. Yet all these are later authorities. The whole story may rest upon some such story as that this married couple once passed a night in the στοὰ ποικίλῃ, or else upon the theoretical assertion of some Cynic philosophers, that a public consummation of nuptials was permissible. On the other hand, we have no reason to doubt what *Diog.* 97 states, that Hipparchia went about in public dressed as a man.

[1] As we gather from the dialogues of Socrates with Aristodemus and Euthydemus, *Xen.* Mem. i. 4; iv. 3; not to mention Critias.

the Eleatics, whose teaching in other respects he also worked up into his own. For him, however, these views had a peculiar meaning. Hence may be explained the sharp and hostile attitude of the Cynics to the popular faith, in which they so distinctly departed from the example of Socrates. The wise man, independent of everything external, cannot possibly be dependent on a traditional faith. He cannot feel pledged to follow popular opinions, or to connect his well-being with customs and devotional practices, which have nothing to do with his moral state.[1] Thus in religious matters the Cynics are decidedly on the side of free thought. The existence of a God they do not deny, nor can their wise men do without one; but they object to a number of gods resembling men—popular gods, owing, as they say,[2] their existence to tradition: in reality there is but one God, who resembles nothing

[1] In this way we must explain the free thought of Aristodemus, Mem. i. 4, 2, 9–11; 14; who is also described by *Plato*, Symp. 173, B., as a kindred spirit to Antisthenes.

[2] *Cic.* N. D. i. 13, 32: 'Antisthenes in eo libro, qui physicus inscribitur, populares [νόμῳ] Deos multos, naturalem [φύσει] unum esse dicens,' which is repeated by *Minuc. Fel.* Oct. 19, 8, and *Lact* Inst. i. 5, epit. 4. *Clemens*, Protrept. 46, C., and also Stromat. v. 601, A., says: Ἀντισθένης . . . θεὸν οὐδενὶ ἐοικέναι φησίν· διόπερ αὐτὸν οὐδεὶς ἐκμαθεῖν ἐξ εἰκόνος δύναται. *Theod.* Cur. Gr. Affect. i. 75, p. 14: Ἀντισθένης . . . . περὶ τοῦ θεοῦ τῶν ὅλων βοᾷ· ἀπὸ εἰκόνος οὐ γνωρίζεται, ὀφθαλμοῖς οὐχ ὁρᾶται, οὐδενὶ ἔοικε διόπερ αὐτὸν οὐδεὶς ἐκμαθεῖν ἐξ εἰκόνος δύναται. *Tertull.* Ad Nat. ii. 2: In reply to the question, Quid in cœlis agatur? Diogenes replied: Nunquam ascendi; to the question, Whether there were any Gods? he answered: Nescio nisi ut sint expedire. No very great dependence can, it is true, be placed on Tertullian's sayings. Id. Apol. 14; Ad Nat. i. 10: Diogenes nescis quid in Herculem ludit, without, however, giving further particulars. Compare what was said of Socrates, p. 176.

CHAP. XIII.

visible, and cannot be represented by any symbol.[1] The same reasoning holds good of the worship of the gods. There is but one way of pleasing God—by virtue; everything else is superstition. Wisdom and uprightness make us followers and friends of the gods. What is generally done to secure their favour is worthless and unmeaning. The wise man honours God by virtue, not by sacrifice[2] which God does not require.[3] He knows that a temple is not more holy than any other place.[4] He does not pray for things which are considered goods by the unwise; not for riches, but for righteousness.[5]

Herewith the ordinary notion respecting prayer is abandoned; for everyone owes virtue to his own exertions. Hence it may be understood how Diogenes ridiculed prayers and vows.[6] Oracles, prophecy, and prophets,[7] all were included in the same sweeping condemnation. The mystic rites were assailed with

[1] The Cynics are therefore Atheists in the ancient sense of the term—*i.e.* they denied the Gods of the state, although from their point of view they were certainly right in rejecting the charge of atheism. Nothing follows from the anecdotes in *Diog.* 37; 42.

[2] *Julian,* Or. vi. 199, B., excusing Diogenes because of his poverty, says that he never entered a temple or offered sacrifice. Crates, ibid. 200, A., promises to honour Hermes and the Muses οὐ δαπάναις τρυφεραῖς, ἀλλ' ἀρεταῖς ὁσίαις.

[3] See p. 316, 2.

[4] See *Diog.* 73: μηδέν τι ἄτοπον εἶναι ἐξ ἱεροῦ τι λαβεῖν.

[5] See the prayer of Crates in *Julian* l. c. and *Diog.* 42.

[6] Compare the anecdotes in *Diog.* 37; 59.

[7] In *Diog.* 24 he says that, looking at pilots, physicians, and philosophers, he thinks man the most intelligent being; but looking at interpreters of dreams, or prophets, or credulous believers in them, he considers him the most foolish of creatures. Similar statements in *Diog.* 43; 48; *Theod.* Cur. Gr. Aff. vi. 20, p. 88; and *Dio.* Or. x. 2; 17. Antisthenes appears also in *Xen.* Sym. 8, 5, to have doubts upon the subject

withering sarcasm,[1] both by Diogenes and Antisthenes. As far as religious views are concerned, these philosophers hold a perfectly independent attitude towards the popular faith, gladly availing themselves of any foothold which mythology supplied for their own arguments, and doing so more readily in proportion to the earnestness of their desire to influence the masses. Antisthenes was even helped in so doing by the sophistical training which he had previously enjoyed.[2] Folklore had to be explained to fit in with this view. Hence we find Antisthenes to a large extent engaged in allegorical interpretations of the myths and the poets, and in a commentary on Homer, which he committed to writing in numerous volumes.[3] Looking for a hidden meaning[4] in legendary story, he everywhere discovered moral teaching, and tacked on moral reflections.[5] By laying down the further axiom, that the poet does not always express his own

of the δαιμόνιον of Socrates, but no conclusion can be formed from a passage so jocular.

[1] *Diog.* 4; 39; 42; *Plut.* Aud. Poet. 5, p. 21; *Clemens*, Protrept. 49, C.

[2] For the allegorical interpretations of that period consult *Krische*, Forsch. 234; *Xen.* Sym. 3, 6; *Plato*, Theætet. 153, C.; Rep. ii. 378, D.; Io, 530, C.; Phædrus, 229, C.; and *Zeller's* Phil. d. Griech. i. 930, 3; also pp. 755, 831; Stoics, &c.

[3] *Diog.* 17, mentions twelve or thirteen volumes of his on Homer and various portions of the Homeric poems, and one on Amphiaraus. Here, too, belong the treatises on Hercules. *Julian*, Or. vii. 209, A.; 215, C.; 217, A., also testifies to the fact of his frequently using myths. See *Krische*, 243.

[4] The ὑπόνοια or διάνοια. *Xen.* Symp. 3, 6; *Plato*, Rep. ii. 378, D.; Io, 530, C.

[5] Thus on Od. i. 1, he inquired in what sense πολυτροπία was meant for praise. On Od. v. 211; vii. 257, he remarked that no reliance could be placed upon lovers' promises. In Il. xv. 123, he found his doctrine of the oneness of virtue. See the passages in *Winckelmann*, pp. 23–28.

CHAP. XIII.

sentiments,[1] he had no difficulty in finding anything anywhere. Traces of this allegorical interpretation may also be found in Diogenes.[2] Yet the Cynics do not seem to have carried the process nearly so far as the Stoics;[3] as is also quite natural, Cynic teaching being very imperfectly expanded,[4] and the taste for learned activity being with them very small.

E. *Their influence on the world.*

From the above it will be seen in what sense the Cynics spoke of the self-sufficingness of virtue. The wise man must be absolutely and in every respect independent; independent of wants, of desires, of prejudices, and of after-thoughts. The devotion and strength of will with which they compassed this end has certainly something grand about it. Insensible to the limits of individual existence, and putting out of sight the conditions of a natural and a moral life, the Cynic grandeur borders on pride, and their strength of principle on self-will. A value out of all proportion is attached to the surroundings of life to such an extent that they again become dependent on external circumstances. The sublime becomes ridiculous, and every freak claims at last to be honoured as being higher wisdom. Plato, or who-

[1] *Dio Chrys.* Or. liii. 5, says that whereas the same had been previously said of Zeno, ὁ δὲ λόγος οὗτος Ἀντισθένους ἐστὶ πρότερον, ὅτι τὰ μὲν δόξῃ τὰ δὲ ἀληθείᾳ εἴρηται τῷ ποιητῇ· ἀλλ' ὁ μὲν οὐκ ἐξειργάσατο αὐτόν, ὁ δε καθ' ἕκαστον τῶν ἐπὶ μέρους ἐδήλωσεν.

[2] According to *Stob.* Floril. 29, 92, he explained the legend of Medea boiling the old into young to mean that, by bodily exercise, she made effeminate men young again.

[3] Dio says this expressly, and little has come down to us from Cynic interpretations.

[4] Even their Ethics are scanty enough, and their system gave no opportunity for those lengthy, physical discussions, on which the Stoics were so great.

ever it was who called Diogenes a Socrates gone mad, was not far wrong in what he said.[1]

Notwithstanding these pretensions, the independence of these philosophers was not so complete that they could dispense with every relation to others. That they should wish to see all virtuous persons united as friends was quite natural;[2] and, besides, they considered it the wise man's business to raise the rest of mankind to his own level. Anxious not to monopolise the blessings of virtue, but to share them with their fellows, they sought for work as educators of their people, desiring, if possible, to bring a lax and effeminate nation back to the days of moral strictness and simplicity. The mass of men are fools, slaves of pleasure, suffering from self-conceit and pride.[3] The Cynic is a physician to heal their disease,[4] a guide to lead them to what is good.[5]

[1] *Ælian*, V. H. xiv. 33; *Diog.* vi. 54.

[2] *Diog.* 11: καὶ ἐρασθήσεσθαι δὲ μόνον γὰρ εἰδέναι τὸν σοφόν, τίνων χρὴ ἐρᾶν. 12: ἀξιέραστος ὁ ἀγαθός· οἱ σπουδαῖοι φίλοι. Antisthenes wrote both an Ἐρωτικὸς and an Ἐρώμενος (*Diog.* 14; 18), and he had mentioned love in his Hercules (*Procl.* in Alc. 98, 6; *Winckelmann*, p. 16). An Ἐρωτικὸς of Diogenes is also mentioned, *Diog.* 80.

[3] See p. 315.

[4] *Diog.* 4: Ἀντισθένης ἐρωτηθεὶς διὰ τί πικρῶς τοῖς μαθηταῖς ἐπιπλήττει, καὶ οἱ ἰατροί, φησί, τοῖς κάμνουσιν· Ibid. 6: καὶ οἱ ἰατροί, φησί, μετὰ τῶν νοσούντων εἰσίν, ἀλλ' οὐ πυρέττουσιν. In *Stob.* Floril. 13, 25, Diogenes, when asked why he remained in Athens, whilst he was always praising the Spartans, replied: οὐδὲ γὰρ ἰατρὸς ὑγιείας ὢν ποιητικὸς ἐν τοῖς ὑγιαίνουσι τὴν διατριβὴν ποιεῖται. Accordingly, Diogenes calls himself in *Lucian*, V. Auct. 8, ἐλευθερωτὴς τῶν ἀνθρώπων καὶ ἰατρὸς τῶν παθῶν, and he expresses astonishment in *Dio.* Or. viii. 7, that men less frequently apply to him, the healer of souls, than they do to an oculist or dentist.

[5] When Diogenes was purchased by Xeniades, he is said to have told Xeniades that he would have to obey his slave, just as in another case he would have to obey a pilot or

CHAP. XIII.

Hence he considers it his mission to care for the outcast and despised, only the sick needing a physician,[1] and no more fears contamination from such intercourse than the sun fears impurity from shining in the dirtiest haunts.[2]

The improvement of mankind, however, is no easy task.[3] He who will be saved must hear the truth; nothing being more destructive than flattery.[4] Yet truth is always unpleasant;[5] none but a bitter enemy or a real friend dare tell it.[6] This friendly service the Cynics propose to render to mankind.[7] It matters not to them[8] if in so doing they give offence. A sound man is always hard to bear with;[9] he who annoys no one does no one any good.[10] It was moreover a principle of theirs to pitch their demands both in word and example above what they really wanted, because men only imperfectly conform to them.[11] Thus they pressed advice on friend and

physician. *Diog.* 30; 36; conf. 74; *Plut.* An. Vitios. c. 3, p. 499; *Stob.* Flor. 3, 63; *Philo*, Qu. Omn. Pr. Lib. 833, E.

[1] According to *Epict.* iii. 24, 66, Diogenes read a lesson to the pirates who captured him. It cannot, however, have done much good, for they sold him notwithstanding; and the story is altogether very unlikely.

[2] *Diog.* 63, and above, p. 333, 3.

[3] *Diog.* 4, and p. 333, 3.

[4] *Diog.* 4; 51; 92; *Stob.* Floril. 14, 16; Antisthenes in *Plut.* Vid. Pud. c. 18, g, E., p. 536.

[5] Diogenes in Exc. e Floril. Joan. Damasc. ii. 31, 22: τὸ ἀληθὲς πικρόν ἐστι καὶ ἀηδὲς τοῖς ἀνοητοῖς. It is like light to those who have weak eyes.

[6] See p. 320, 3.

[7] Diogenes in *Stob.* Flor. 13, 26: οἱ μὲν ἄλλοι κύνες τοὺς ἐχθροὺς δάκνουσιν, ἐγὼ δὲ τοὺς φίλους, ἵνα σώσω.

[8] See p. 319.

[9] δυσβάστακτον εἶναι τὸν ἀστεῖον.—Antisth. in *Philo*, Qu. Omn. Pr. Lib. 869, C.

[10] In *Plut.* Virt. Mort. c. 12, g, E., p. 452, Diogenes says of Plato: τί δ' ἐκεῖνος ἔχει σεμνόν, ὃς τοσοῦτον χρόνον φιλοσοφῶν οὐδένα λελύπηκεν;

[11] See p. 309, 1.

stranger alike without regard,[1] Diogenes not seldom imparting it in the coarsest manner,[2] although gentler features are not altogether unknown.[3] At the same time coarseness of manner was somewhat relieved by humour, in which Diogenes and Crates more particularly excelled. For they loved to clothe serious teaching in the garb of joke, or of poetry,[4] and to hurl epigrams [5] at the folly of mankind.[6] Like the Oriental prophets, Diogenes added force to his utterances by symbolical actions, seeking thus to win for them attention.[7]

Doubtless the position occupied by the Cynics in the Greek world is a peculiar one. Ridiculed because

[1] Compare what *Diog.* vi. 10, says of Antisthenes, and vi. 26; 46; 65 of Diogenes; also *Lucian* V. Auct. 10. Because of his importunity, Crates received the name of θυρεπανοίκτης.—*Diog.* 86; *Plut.* Qu. Conv. ii. 1, 7, 4, p. 632; *Apul.* Floril. iv. 22.

[2] *Diog.* 24; 32; 46; Ex. e Floril. Jo. Damasc. i. 7, 43.

[3] *Plut.* De Adul. 28, p. 69, relates that when Demetrius Phalerius, after his banishment, fell in with Crates, he was not a little surprised at being received with friendly words of warm comfort instead of the violent language he expected. The attractiveness of the conversation of Antisthenes and Diogenes is also commended, *Diog.* 14. Conf. *Xen.* Symp. 4, 61.

[4] See *Diog.* 27; 83; 85; *Demetr.* de Elocut. 170; 259; 261; *Plut.* Tranqu. An. 4, p. 466; *Julian*, Or. vii. 209, a; Antisth.: ἔνια διὰ τῶν μύθων ἀπήγγελλε. Similarly, Ibid. 215, c; 217, a.

[5] *Hermog.* Progym. c. 3; *Theo.* Progym. c. 5; *Nicol.* Progym. c. 3.

[6] Abundant examples of these ways of the Cynics are to be found in the ἀποφθέγματα of *Diogenes*, in his sixth book, and in *Stobæus*' Floril. See also *Winckelmann*, Antisth. Frag.; *Plut.* Prof. in Virt. c. 11, p. 82; Virt. Doc. c. 2, p. 439; Coh. Ira, c. 12, p. 460; Curios. c. 12, p. 521; Cup. Div. c. 7, p. 526; Exil. c. 7, p. 602; An. Seni. s. Ger. Rep. i. 5, p. 783; conf. Præc. c. 26, 141; De Alex. Virt. c. 3, p. 336; *Epict.* Diss. iii. 2, 11; *Gell.* xviii. 13, 7; *Tertullian*, Apol. 39; not to mention others.

[7] See *Diog.* 26; 31; 39; 64; 41 (the lantern); *Stob.* Flor. 4, 84. This eccentricity becomes a caricature in Menedemus, *Diog.* 102.

CHAP. XIII.

of their eccentricities,[1] and admired for their self-denial, despised as beggars, and feared as moralists, full of contempt for the follies, of pity for the moral miseries of their fellow men, they opposed alike to the intellect and the low tone of their time the rude vigour of a resolute will, hardened even to insensibility. Possessing the pungent, ever-ready wit of the plebeian, benevolent, with few wants, full of whims and jokes, and national even to their very dirtiness, they resemble in many points the friars of the Middle Ages;[2] and notwithstanding all their extravagances, their action was in many ways beneficial. For all that, philosophy could gain but little from this mendicant philosophy. When supplemented by other elements, regulated and connected with a wider view of the world in the Stoa, Cynicism was able to bear fruit on a large scale. The Cynic school, as such, appears to have had only a very narrow extension, nor is this to be wondered at considering the terrible severity of its demands. Besides, it was incapable of philosophic expansion, even its practical action being chiefly of a negative character. It attacked the vices and the follies of men. It required independence and self-denial, but it separated man from man. It isolated the individual, thus giving play to moral pride, vanity, and the most

[1] *Diog.* 83, 87, 93.

[2] The Cynics really have an historical connection with the monks of Christendom. The link between the two is the Cynicism of the time of the Cæsars, and the late Pythagorean asceticism, which exercised, partly directly and partly through the Essenes, so important an influence on Eastern monasticism.

capricious whims, of which full advantage was taken. The abstract sovereignty of the personal will resulted ultimately in individual caprice, and thus Cynicism trenched on the ground of the philosophy of pleasure, to which as a system it was diametrically opposed.

CHAPTER XIV.

THE CYRENAICS.[1]

CHAP. XIV.

A. *History of the Cyrenaics.*

RESPECTING the Cyrenaic branch of the Socratic school, the information we possess is quite as scanty, or even more so, than that which we have respecting the Cynics. Aristippus[2] of Cyrene,[3] the founder, had been brought to Athens[4] by a call from Socrates, whose extraordinary personal character exercised a strange fascination over him,[5] although it found in

[1] See *Wendt*, De Philosophia Cyrenaica, Gött. 1841.

[2] The accounts of ancient and the views of modern writers on the life of Aristippus are found in detail in *H. v. Stein's* De Philosophia Cyrenaica, Part. prior. de vita Aristippi (Gött. 1855), a work which might have been a little more critical. There even are references to the earlier literature.

[3] All authorities without exception state this. His father is called Aritadas by *Suid.* Ἀρίστιππος.

[4] Æschin. in *Diog.* ii. 65, says that he came to Athens κατὰ κλέος Σωκράτους, and *Plut.* Curios. 2, p. 516, gives full particulars how at the Olympic games he heard of Socrates and his teaching from Ischomachus, and was at once so taken by it that he did not rest till he had made his acquaintance. See *Diog.* ii. 78; 80.

[5] Aristippus is not only universally described as a follower of Socrates (*Diog.* ii. 47; 74; 80; *Strabo,* xvii. 3, 22, p. 837; *Eus.* Pr. Ev. xiv. 18, 31; *Stein.* p. 26), but he also regarded himself as such, and paid a tribute of most genuine respect to his teacher. According to *Diog.* ii. 76, he prayed that he might die like Socrates. Ibid. 71, he says that if anything good can be truly repeated of himself, he owes it to Socrates, and *Arist.* Rhet. ii. 23; 1398, b, 29, says, Ἀρίστιππος πρὸς Πλάτωνα ἐπαγγελτικώτερόν τι εἰπόντα, ὡς ᾤετο· ἀλλὰ μὴν ὅ

him one too weak to endure in the last trial.[1] From Cyrene, his luxurious home, then at the height of wealth and power,[2] he had brought habits far removed from the simplicity and abstemiousness of Socrates.[3] Perhaps he had been already touched by those Sophistical influences which may be observed in his subsequent career.[4] At any rate he had attained to a certain maturity of thought when he

ἑταῖρός γ' ἡμῶν, ἔφη, οὐδὲν τοιοῦτον, λέγων τὸν Σωκράτην (which *Steinhart*, Plat. Leben, 303, 17, contrary to the natural sense, refers to Plato's too sanguine expectations of the younger Dionysius). We also see from *Xen.* Mem. i. 2, iii. 8, that he was on intimate terms with Socrates; and Plato in blaming him, Phædo, 59, C., for being absent from the circle of friends who met on the day of Socrates' death, evidently reckons him as belonging to this circle. Conf. *Stein.* p. 25, who also, pp. 50 and 74, groups together the authorities respecting Aristippus' relations to the pupils of Socrates.

[1] *Plato*, l. c., who however only says that Aristippus and Cleombrotus had been in Ægina. That on this fertile island they caroused on the day of their master's death, as *Demetr.* de Elocut. 288, asserts, is barely possible. The accuracy of Plato's statement is indisputable, notwithstanding *Diog.* iii. 56; ii. 65; but whether Aristippus left Athens from excessive regard for his own safety, or whether his weakness led him to wish to escape the painful interval pending the death of Socrates, cannot be ascertained.

[2] See *Thrige*, Res Cyrenensium, 191.

[3] This may be gathered from *Xen.* Mem. ii. 1, 1, in addition to the proof afforded by his subsequent conduct. That Aristippus belonged to a wealthy family would seem to be established by his whole mode of living, and by the journey which he undertook to Athens.

[4] We might have imagined that a city so rich and cultivated as Cyrene (on this point see *Thrige*, l. c. p. 340, 354), would not have been neglected by the Sophists, even if there were no express evidence to prove it. It is, however, known from *Plato*, Theætet. 161, B.; 162, A., that the celebrated mathematician, Theodorus of Cyrene, was a friend of Protagoras, and the principles of Protagoras are afterwards met with in Aristippus. From the zeal with which Aristippus followed Socrates it may be further conjectured that the study of philosophy was to him no new thing.

CHAP. XIV.

first became acquainted with Socrates.[1] No wonder, therefore, that this youth of promise [2] met his teacher with a considerable amount of independence,[3] not following him on the whole so blindly as to sink his own peculiarities. He is even said to have come forward as a teacher before the death of Socrates;[4] it is better established that he did so afterwards, and also that, contrary to the principles of his greatest friend, but quite in harmony with the practice usual among the Sophists, he required payment for his instruction.[5] In another point he

[1] The chronology of his life is very uncertain. Neither the date of his birth nor of his death is known. According to *Diodorus*, xv. 76, he was living in 366 B.C., and *Plut.* Dio. 19, tells us that he met Plato on his third visit to Sicily, which is placed in 361 B.C. But Diodorus probably derived from Dionysius his anecdote about the interview with Plato. Its accuracy cannot therefore be trusted; and as we are ignorant how old Aristippus was at the time, these accounts are far from satisfactory. According to *Diog.* ii. 83, it would appear he was older by several years than Æschines; and it would also appear, from what has been said p. 338, 5, that at the time he followed Socrates he was independent in his civil relations, and, further, that his connection with Socrates continued for several years.

[2] This is what he appears to have been from all that is known. See *Stein.* p. 29.

[3] See *Xen.* Mem. ii. 1; iii. 8.

[4] According to *Diog.* ii. 80, Socrates censured his taking pay for his instruction. How little dependence can be placed upon this story will be seen from the fact that Aristippus says, in his reply, that Socrates did the same, only taking less. Another passage, *Diog.* ii. 65, seems to imply, on the authority of Phanias, that Aristippus offered to give Socrates some of the money he had gained in this way. Perhaps, however, all that Phanias said was, that Aristippus had taken pay, and offered it to his teacher, without however bringing the two facts into closer connection in point of time.

[5] Phanias in *Diog.* ii. 65; Ibid. 72; 74; 80, where it is also stated in what way he defended this conduct. Alexis in *Athen.* xii. 544, e; *Plut.* Edu. Pu. 7, p. 4; *Stob.* Exc. e Floril. Joan. Damasc. ii. 13, 145 (that Aristippus is here meant appears from 146; conf. *Diog.* ii.

followed the example of the Sophists, passing a great portion of his life moving from place to place without any fixed abode.[1] Subsequently he

68). Also *Xen.* Mem. i. 2, 60, appears to have an eye on him. The amount of these fees is estimated at 1,000 drachmæ by Plutarch, at 500 by *Diog.* 72.

[1] He says of himself in *Xen.* Mem. ii. 1, 13: οὐδ' εἰς πολίτειαν ἐμαυτὸν κατακλείω, ἀλλὰ ξένος πανταχοῦ εἰμί. In *Plut.* Virt. Doc. p. 2, p. 439, someone asks him: πανταχοῦ σὺ ἆρα εἶ; to which he replies with a bad joke. He is mentioned by later writers, often no doubt bad authorities, as having been in different places; in Megara, where he met with Æschines (*Diog.* ii. 62; conf. Ep. Socr. 29); in Asia Minor, where he was imprisoned by the Persians (*Diog.* ii. 79); in Corinth, where he revelled with Lais (Hermesianax in *Ath.* xiii. 599, b; *Diog.* ii. 71); in Ægina, where he not only lived for a time after the death of Socrates, but where, according to Athen. xiii. 588, e; conf. xii. 544, d, he every year took up his residence in company with Lais; and at Scillus, where Xenophon read to him his Memorabilia, Ep. Socr. 18. Much in particular is told of his stay at the court of Syracuse, of his hostile encounter with Plato, and of many other adventures which he there experienced. But in these notices there is great confusion, since at one time the elder Dionysius, at another the younger Dionysius, at another simply Dionysius, is spoken of. Conf. *Stein.* p. 57. It is asserted by the Scholiast on *Lucian*, Men. 13, that Aristippus was at Syracuse under the *elder* Dionysius. This statement is borne out by Hegesander in *Athen.* xii. 544, c; for the Antiphon there mentioned was (according to *Plut.* De Adulat. 27, p. 68) executed by command of the elder Dionysius. The anecdote of his shipwreck in *Galen*, Exhort. c. 5, must be referred to the same time. It can only belong to his first visit to Sicily, but by *Vitruv.* vi. Præfat. was transferred to the island of Rhodes. On this point see *Stein.* 61. On the other hand, *Plut.* Dio. 19, brings him into contact with Plato on Plato's third journey to Sicily, 361 B.C., in the time of the *younger* Dionysius. The notices in *Athen.* xi. 507, b; *Diog.* ii. 66, 69, 73, 75, 77–82, are indefinite, although the stories there told harmonise better with the court of the younger Dionysius than with that of his father. Nothing can however be stated with certainty respecting the visits of Aristippus to Sicily. That he visited Sicily may be believed on tradition. That he there met Plato is not impossible, though it is also possible that the account of this meeting was invented in order to bring out the contrast between both philosophers. In fact,

CHAP. XIV.

appears to have returned to his native city, and to have taken up his permanent residence there.[1] Here it is that we first hear of his family and his school.[2] The heiress to his principles was a daughter, Arete, a lady of sufficient education to instruct her son,[3] the younger Aristippus,[4] in his

Plato's journeys to Sicily were a favourite topic for later anecdote-tellers. But any one of the above stories, taken by itself, must be accepted with caution; it is not even certain that he visited both the Dionysiuses. When the younger one came to the throne (368 B.C.) he was at least sixty years of age, and yet most of the stories which are told appear to have reference to him. On the other hand, in those stories Aristippus presents a character better suited to his years of travel than to his later years. The supposed incidents of meeting between Aristippus and Plato probably went the round as anecdotes, without any attention being paid to their foundation in fact; and when this was done by subsequent biographers, it became impossible to find out what the facts were.

[1] Whether this stay was shortened by frequent travels, whether Aristippus died in Cyrene or elsewhere, and how long he lived, are points unknown. For the journey to Sicily in 361 B.C. is, as we have seen, uncertain. The twenty-ninth letter, which Socrates is supposed to have addressed to his daughter from Lipara after his return, and in expectation of death, is valueless as an historical testimony, not even rendering the existence of a corresponding tradition probable; and the hypothesis derived from *Diog.* ii. 62, that Aristippus flourished at Athens in 356, has been with justice refuted by *Stein.* p. 82. *Steinhart*, Plat. Leben, 305, 33, proposes to read 'Αριστοτέλη for 'Αρίστιππον in *Diog.* ii. 62, but the chronology is against this correction. Σπεύσιππον would be better.

[2] Generally called Cyrenaics, more rarely Hedonists, as in *Athen.* vii. 312, f; xiii. 588, a.

[3] Who was thence called μητροδίδακτος.

[4] *Strabo*, xvii. 3, 22, p. 837; *Clemens*, Strom. iv. 523, A.; *Eus.* Pr. Ev. xiv. 18, 32; *Theod.* Cur. Gr. Aff. xi. 1; *Diog.* ii. 72, 84, 86; *Suid.* 'Αρίστιππος; *Themist.* Or. xxi. 244. If, therefore, *Ælian*, H. Anim. iii. 40, calls Arete the Sister of Aristippus, it must be through an oversight. Besides this daughter he is said to have had another son, whom he did not own, *Diog.* 81; *Stob.* Floril. 76, 14. Most likely this was only the child of an ἑταῖρα, although Stobæus calls his mother a wife.

grandfather's philosophy. Besides this daughter, Æthiops and Antipater are also mentioned as pupils of the elder Aristippus.[1] His grandson, the younger Aristippus, is said to have instructed Theodorus, called the Atheist;[2] the fruits of Antipater's teaching[3] were Hegesias[4] and Anniceris.[5] These three men

[1] *Diog.* ii. 86. We know further from *Cic.* Tusc. v. 38, 112, that Antipater bore the loss of sight with resignation. Cicero tells a somewhat tame joke.

[2] *Diog.* 86. This Theodorus appears to have belonged to the Optimates, who were driven from Cyrene in the party-quarrels immediately after the death of Alexander, and took refuge with the Egyptian sovereigns. *Thrige*, Res. Cyren. 206. We hear of him as an exile in the last years of the fourth century (*Plut.* De Exil. 16, p. 606; *Diog.* 103; *Philo*, Qu. Omn. Pr. Lib. 884, C.), in Greece, and particularly at Athens (*Diog.* ii. 100, 116; iv. 52; vi. 97), where a friend of Ptolemy's, Demetrius Phalereus, helped him, between 316 and 306 B.C., and subsequently at the court of Ptolemy, on whose behalf he undertook an embassy to Lysimachus (*Diog.* 102; *Cic.* Tusc. i. 43, 102; *Valer.* vi. 2, 3; *Philo*, l. c.; *Plut.* An. Vittos. 3, p. 499; *Stob.* Floril. 2, 33). At last he returned to his own country, and was there held in great honour by Magus, the Egyptian governor, *Diog.* 103. What made him particularly notorious was his atheism. Indicted on this account at Athens, he was rescued by Demetrius, but obliged to leave the city (*Diog.* 101; *Philo*). The assertion of Amphicrates (in *Diog.* and *Athen.* xiii. 611, a), that he was put to death by a hemlock-draught, is contrary to all we know of him. According to Antisth. in *Diog.* 98, he was a pupil not only of Aristippus the younger, but also of Anniceris and of the dialectician Dionysius. It is however difficult to see how he can have been younger than Anniceris. *Suid.* Θεόδ. makes Zeno, Pyrrho, and Bryso (see p. 256, 1) his teachers, the first one probably with reason, the two others quite by mistake. Under Σώκρατ. he makes him a pupil of Socrates, at the same time confounding him with a mathematician from Cyrene of the same name (see p. 339, 4), who is known to us through Plato. In *Diog.* ii. 102, iv. 52, he is called a Sophist, i. e. one who took pay for his instruction.

[3] According to *Diog.* 86, through Epitimides of Cyrene and his pupil Paræbates, the latter of whom is said to have studied under Aristippus. *Suid.* Ἀννίκερις.

[4] A cotemporary of Ptolemy Lagi, who is said to have pro-

(For Note 5 see p. 344.)

CHAP. XIV.

established separate branches of the Cyrenaic School, which bore their respective names.[1] Amongst the pupils of Theodorus were Bio the Borysthenite,[2] and perhaps Euemerus, the well-known Greek rationalist,[3]

hibited him from lecturing, because he described the ills of life so graphically that many were led to commit suicide. *Cic.* Tusc. i. 34, 83; *Valer. Max.* viii. 9, 3; *Plut.* Am. Prol. 5, p. 497. Suicide was also the subject of his book Ἀποκαρτερῶν, *Cic.* loc. cit. Hence his name Πεισιθάνατος, *Diog.* 86, *Suid.* Ἀρίστ.

[5] Probably also under Ptolemy I., although Suidas, Ἀννικ., places him in the time of Alexander. Conf. Antisth. in *Diog.* ii. 88.

[1] For the Θεοδώρειοι and their teaching see *Diog.* 97; Callimachus in *Athen.* vi. 252, c; for the Ἡγησιακοί, *Diog.* 93; for the Ἀννικέρειοι, ibid. 96; *Strabo*, xvii. 3, 22, p. 837; *Clemens*, Strom. ii. 417, B.; *Suid.* Ἀννίκ. Strabo calls Anniceris ὁ δοκῶν ἐπανορθῶσαι τὴν Κυρηναϊκὴν αἵρεσιν καὶ παραγαγεῖν αὐτ' αὐτῆς τὴν Ἀννικερείαν. To the Annicereans belonged Posidonius the pupil, and probably also Nicoteles, the brother of Anniceris. *Suid.* l. c.

[2] This individual lived at Athens and elsewhere (*Diog.* iv. 46, 49, 53; ii. 135). According to *Diog.* iv. 10 (where, however, the Borysthenite appears to be meant), he was acquainted with Xenocrates. In *Diog.* iv. 46, 54, ii. 35; *Athen.* iv. 162, d, he appears as a cotemporary of Menedemus (see p. 282), and the Stoic Persæus (*Zeller's* Stoics, &c.). He appears, therefore, to have survived to the middle of the third century. According to *Diog.* iv. 51, he left the Academy, which he first frequented, and joined the Cynics (which reads in our text of Diogenes as if he had deserted the Academician Crates in order to become a Cynic, but this is not possible in point of time; perhaps the original text meant that by the agency of Crates he was brought over from the Academy to Cynicism). He then turned to Theodore, and at last to Theophrastus, *Diog.* iv. 151. His free thought and the instability of his moral principles (*Diog.* iv. 49, 53) recall the School of Theodore, in which Numenius in *Eus.* Pr. Ev. xiv. 6, 5, actually places him. In other respects he is rather a literary wit than a philosopher See *Diog.* iv. 46–57, various sayings of his in *Plutarch.*

[3] Euemerus of Messene, according to the most numerous and approved authorities, according to others of Agrigentum, Cos, or Tegea (see *Sieroka*, De Euhemero, Königsbg. 1869, p. 27), is often mentioned in connection with Theodorus, Diogoras, and other Atheists (*Sieroka*, 19, 31). The notion that Theodore was his teacher rests solely on hypothesis. For we have no business to write Εὐήμερον in *Diog.* ii. 97 instead of Ἐπίκουρον (with Nietzsche, Rhein. Mus. N. F.

while amongst his cotemporaries was Aristotle of Cyrene.[1]

B. *Teaching of the Cyrenaics.*

The Cyrenaic teaching, the leading traits of which undoubtedly belong to Aristippus,[2] takes up,

xxv. 231). Epicurus derived his views respecting the Gods mostly from Theodorus' treatise περὶ θεῶν. A connection with the Cyrenaic School is not in itself probable, since this was the only School which at that time busied itself with combating the popular belief. Doubtless, too, that tame resolution of myths into history, for which Euemerus is known, is quite after their taste; indeed, the Cynics who, together with the Cyrenaics, were at that time the representatives of free thought, did not resort to natural explanations, but to allegory. In point of time Euemerus may easily have been a pupil of Theodorus. He lived under the Macedonian Cassander (311 to 298 B.C.), the latter having sent him on that journey on which he visited the fabulous island of Panchæa, and pretended to have discovered in a temple there the history of the Gods, the account of which is given in his ἱερὰ ἀναγραφή. Diodor. in *Eus.* Pr. Ev. ii. 2, 55; *Plut.* De Is. 23, page 360. Copious extracts from this work are found in Diodorus, v. 41–46, and fragments of the translation undertaken by Ennius, or of a revision of this translation in *Lactant.* Inst. i. 11, 13 (see *Vahlen*, Ennian. Poës. Reliq. p. xciii. f); 17, 22, l. c. 169. Shorter notices of the contents of his treatise in *Cic.* N. D. i. 42, 119, followed by *Minuc. Fel.* Octav. 21, 2; also in *Strabo,* ii. 3, 5; 4, 2; p. 102, 104; vii. 3, 6, p. 299; *Plut.* l. c.; *Athen.* xiv. 658, e; *Sext.* Math. ix. 171, 34; *Aug.* C. D. vii. 26; Ep. 18; Serm. 273, 3; *Higgin.* Poet. Astron ii. 12, 13, 42, D. See also *Sieroka* and *Steinhart*, Allg. Encykl. v. Ersch. d. Gr. i. vol. 39, 50; *Müller*, Frag. Hist. Graec. ii. 100.

[1] According to *Diog.* ii. 113, president of a philosophical School in the time of Stilpo, apparently at Athens. Diogenes there calls him Κυρηναϊκός. *Ælian*, however, V. H. x. 3, in recording a saying of his, calls him Κυρηναῖος. He is probably the Cyrenaic, who, according to *Diog.* v. 35, wrote a treatise περὶ ποιητικῶν. A saying in *Stob.* Floril. 63, 32, belongs to him according to some MSS., but to Aristippus according to Cod. B.

[2] The thing is not altogether undisputed. *Eus.* Pr. Ev. xiv. 18, 31, f, says of the elder Aristippus, without doubt on the authority of Aristocles: ἀλλ' οὐδὲν μὲν οὕτως ἐν τῷ φανερῷ περὶ τέλους διελέξατο, δυνάμει δὲ τῆς εὐδαιμονίας τὴν ὑπόστασιν ἔλεγεν ἐν ἡδοναῖς κεῖσθαι. ἀεὶ γὰρ λόγους περὶ ἡδονῆς ποιουμένους εἰς ὑποψίαν ἦγε τοὺς προσιόντας αὐτῷ τοῦ λέγειν τέλος εἶναι τὸ ἡδέως ζῆν: and of the younger

CHAP. XIV.

like the Cynic, the practical side of the philosophy of Socrates. Of Aristippus too, and his pupils, it was

one, ὃς καὶ σαφῶς ὡρίσατο τέλος εἶναι τὸ ἡδέως ζῆν, ἡδονὴν ἐντάττων τὴν κατὰ κίνησιν. This testimony appears to be further corroborated by the fact that Aristotle, in refuting the doctrine of pleasure, Eth. x. 2, does not mention Aristippus, but Eudoxus, as its representative. To this must be added what Sosicrates and others, according to *Diog.* 84, maintained, that Aristippus left no writings; which would at least point to a lower development of his teaching. *Diog.* ii. 64 does not go quite so far: πάντων μέντοι τῶν Σωκρατικῶν διαλόγων Παναίτιος ἀληθεῖς εἶναι δοκεῖ τοὺς Πλάτωνος, Ξενοφῶντος, Αντισθένους, Αἰσχίνου: for, according to 84 in our text, Panætius is quoted as an authority for a number of dialogues of Aristippus. It may therefore be asked with *Brandis,* ii. a, 92, whether in 64, Aristippus' name has not been omitted by some oversight; on the other hand, Διατριβαὶ were hardly dialogues: cf. *Susemihl,* Rhein. Mus. N. F. xxvi. 338. For these reasons *Ritter*, ii. 93, supposes that the views of Aristippus were not reduced to a connected form till a later time. The assertion of Sosicrates however appears to be without foundation; for Diogenes gives two lists of the works of Aristippus, which agree in the main, and one of which was acknowledged by Sotion and Panætius. Theopompus knew of writings of his, for according to *Athen.* xi. 508, c, he accused Plato of plagiarism from the diatribes of Aristippus. Allowing then that subsequent additions were made to the writings of Aristippus, the whole collection cannot be supposed to be spurious. Perhaps in ancient times, and in Greece proper, these writings were less diffused than those of the other followers of Socrates. This fact may easily be explained, supposing the greater part of them not to have been written till Aristippus had returned to his native country. This may also account for Aristotle's never mentioning Aristippus; perhaps he omitted him because he included him among the Sophists, Metaph. iii. 2, 996, a, 32. The remarks of Eusebius can only be true in one sense, viz. that the elder Aristippus does not make use of the expression τέλος, and does not put his sentences in the form which subsequently prevailed in the Schools. That he recommended pleasure, that he declared it to be a good in the most decided manner, that thus the leading features of the Cyrenaic teaching are due to him, cannot be doubted, in face of the numerous witnesses who affirm it, nor would the unity of his School be otherwise comprehensible. Doubtless Plato wrote the Philebus with an eye to this philosopher, and Speusippus had written on Aristippus, *Diog.* iv. 5.

CHAP. XIV.

(1) *Their general position.*

asserted, as well as of the Cynics, that they neglected questions touching nature and logic, giving to the study of ethics[1] exclusive value. Nor is this assertion contradicted by the fact that they were themselves unable to keep clear of theory, since the sole object of their teaching was to establish ethics, and indeed their own exclusive pursuit of ethics.[2] The end to be secured by philosophy is the happiness of mankind. On this point Aristippus and Antisthenes agree. Antisthenes, however, knows of no happiness which does not immediately coincide with virtue, and thus

[1] *Diog.* ii. 92 : ἀφίσταντο δὲ καὶ τῶν φυσικῶν διὰ τὴν ἐμφαινομένην ἀκαταληψίαν, τῶν δὲ λογικῶν διὰ τὴν εὐχρηστίαν ἥπτοντο. Μελέαγρος δὲ . . . καὶ Κλειτόμαχος . . . φασὶν αὐτοὺς ἄχρηστα ἡγεῖσθαι τό τε φυσικὸν μέρος καὶ τὸ διαλεκτικόν. δύνασθαι γὰρ εὖ λέγειν καὶ δεισιδαιμονίας ἐκτὸς εἶναι καὶ τὸν περὶ θανάτου φόβον ἐκφεύγειν τὸν περὶ ἀγαθῶν καὶ κακῶν λόγον ἐκμεμαθηκότα. *Sext.* Math. vii. 11 : δοκοῦσι δὲ κατά τινας καὶ οἱ ἀπὸ τῆς Κυρήνης μόνον ἀσπάζεσθαι τὸ ἠθικὸν μέρος παραπέμπειν δὲ τὸ φυσικὸν καὶ τὸ λογικὸν ὡς μηδὲν πρὸς τὸ εὐδαιμόνως βιοῦν συνεργοῦντα. Plut. in *Eus.* Pr. Ev. i. 8, 9 : Ἀρίστιππος ὁ Κυρηναῖος τέλος ἀγαθῶν τὴν ἡδονήν, κακῶν δὲ τὴν ἀλγηδόνα, τὴν δὲ ἄλλην φυσιολογίαν περιγράφει, μόνον ὠφέλιμον εἶναι λέγων τὸ ζητεῖν· Ὅττι τοι ἐν μεγάροισι κακόν τ' ἀγαθόν τε τέτυκται, which is also told of Socrates and Diogenes. Arist. Met. ii. 2, 996, a, 32: ὥστε διὰ ταῦτα τῶν σοφιστῶν τινες οἷον Ἀρίστιππος προεπηλάκιζον αὐτὰς [τὰς μαθηματικὰς ἐπιστήμας]· ἐν μὲν γὰρ ταῖς ἄλλαις τέχναις, καὶ ταῖς βαναύσοις οἷον τεκτονικῇ καὶ σκυτικῇ, διότι βέλτιον ἢ χεῖρον λέγεσθαι πάντα, τὰς δὲ μαθηματικὰς οὐθένα ποιεῖσθαι λόγον περὶ ἀγαθῶν καὶ κακῶν. The same in *Alex.* on the passage Schol. in *Arist.* 609, b, 1 ; *Ps. Alex.* on Met. xiii. 3 ; 1078, a, 33; Ibid. 817, a, 11 ; *Syrian* in Metaph. Arist. T. V. 844, b, 6 ; 889, b, 19. Compare the language of Aristippus in *Diog.* ii. 71, 79 ; *Plut.* Ed. Pr. 10, 7.

[2] According to the sense in which it is understood, it is equally true to say that they set logic aside and that they made use of it. See p. 348, 2. Of what was afterwards called logic, they appropriated just as much as was necessary for their theory of knowledge, but they assigned no independent value to it, nor did they extend their study of it beyond what was wanted for their purposes. Conf. *Sen.* Ep. 89, 12: Cyrenaici naturalia cum rationalibus sustulerunt et contenti fuerunt moralibus, sed hi quoque, quæ removent, aliter inducunt.

CHAP. XIV.

makes virtue the only object in life. Aristippus, on the other hand, considers enjoyment an end in itself, and pleasure an unconditional good,[1] regarding all things else as good and desirable only in as far as they are a means to enjoyment.[2] Both Schools therefore at starting go off in opposite directions, this divergence, however, not preventing a subsequent approach to a greater extent than might seem at first sight to be possible.

(2) *Feelings the only object of knowledge.*

The ground thus occupied was worked out by Aristippus and his pupils as follows.[3] Perceptions,

[1] Aristippus in *Xen.* Mem. ii. 1, 9: ἐμαυτὸν τοίνυν τάττω εἰς τοὺς βουλομένους ᾗ ῥᾷστά τε καὶ ἥδιστα βιοτεύειν. *Cic.* Acad. iv. 42, 131: alii voluptatem summum bonum esse voluerunt: quorum princeps Aristippus. Ibid. Fin. ii. 6, 18; 13, 39; *Diog.* 87: ἡδονὴν . . . ἣν καὶ τέλος εἶναι, 88: ἡ ἡδονὴ δι' αὐτὴν αἱρετὴ καὶ ἀγαθόν. *Athen.* xii. 544, a: ['Αρίστιππος] ἀποδεξάμενος τὴν ἡδυπάθειαν ταύτην τέλος εἶναι ἔφη καὶ ἐν αὐτῇ τὴν εὐδαιμονίαν βεβλῆσθαι. *Euseb.* l. c. p. 296, 1. The same view is mentioned and attacked by *Plato*, Gorg. 491, E.; Rep. vi. 505, B. (See above p. 313, 1), and Philebus, 11, B., where it is thus described: Φίληβος μὲν τοίνυν ἀγαθὸν εἶναί φησι τὸ χαίρειν πᾶσι ζώοις καὶ τὴν ἡδονὴν καὶ τέρψιν καὶ ὅσα τοῦ γένους ἐστὶ τούτου σύμφωνα. Ibid. 66, D.: τἀγαθὸν ἐτίθετο ἡμῖν ἡδονὴν εἶναι πᾶσαν καὶ παντελῆ. That Plato had Aristippus in mind will be presently shown in respect of the Philebus, and it is therewith proved for the Republic, which refers to the Philebus.

[2] *Diog.* ii. 91: τὴν φρόνησιν ἀγαθὸν μὲν εἶναι λέγουσιν, οὐ δι' ἑαυτὴν δὲ αἱρετήν, ἀλλὰ διὰ τὰ ἐξ αὐτῆς περιγινόμενα. 92: καὶ τὸν πλοῦτον δὲ ποιητικὸν ἡδονῆς εἶναι, οὐ δι' αὐτόν αἱρετον ὄντα. *Cic.* Off. iii. 33, 116: Cyrenaici atque Annicerei philosophi nominati omne bonum in voluptate posuerunt; virtutemque censuerunt ob eam rem esse laudandam, quod efficiens esset voluptatis. To this sentence of Aristippus, *Wendt*, Phil. Cyr. 28, and Ast refer the passage of the Phædo, 68, E., but without reason. It refers to common unphilosophical virtue.

[3] The Cyrenaics divided their ethics into five parts. *Sext.* Math. vii. 11: καίτοι περιτρέπεσθαι τούτους ἔνιοι νενομίκασιν ἐξ ὧν τὸ ἠθικὸν διαιροῦσιν εἴς τε τὸν περὶ τῶν αἱρετῶν καὶ φευκτῶν τόπον καὶ εἰς τὸν περὶ τῶν παθῶν καὶ ἔτι εἰς τὸν περὶ τῶν πράξεων καὶ ἤδη τὸν περὶ τῶν αἰτίων, καὶ τελευταῖον εἰς τὸν περὶ τῶν πίσ-

being sensations of a change within ourselves, do not supply us with the least information as to things in themselves. We may indeed be conscious of having a sensation of sweetness, whiteness, and so forth; but whether the object which causes the sensation is sweet, or white, is unknown to us. One and the same thing often produces an entirely different effect upon different persons. How, then, can we be sure that in any given case, be it owing to the nature of our organism or to the circumstances under which we receive the impression, things may not appear to us entirely different from what they are in themselves? Knowledge, therefore, is limited to our own feelings; as to these we are never mistaken; but of things in themselves we know absolutely nothing.[1] We know quite as little of the feelings of

τεων· ἐν τούτοις γὰρ ὁ περὶ αἰτίων τόπος, φασίν, ἐκ τοῦ φυσικοῦ μέρους ἐτύγχανεν, ὁ δὲ περὶ πίστεων ἐκ τοῦ λογικοῦ. *Sen.* Ep. 89, 12 (according to what has been said, p. 347, 2): in quinque enim partes moralia dividunt, ut una sit de fugiendis et expetendis, altera de adfectibus, tertia de actionibus, quarta de causis, quinta de argumentis; causæ rerum ex naturali parte sunt, argumenta ex rationali, actiones ex morali. We cannot, however, tie our faith to this account, not knowing how the subject was divided among these several parts, nor how old and universal the division is. That it was not made by Aristippus may be gathered from the statements as to his writings. In the division περὶ πίστεων probably the theory of knowledge was treated, and in the preceding one the theory of motion.

[1] *Cic.* Acad. ii. 46, 143: aliud judicium Protagoræ est, qui putet id cuique rerum esse, quod cuique videatur: aliud Cyrenaicorum, qui præter permotiones intimas nihil putant esse judicii. Ibid. 7, 20: de tactu, et eo quidem, quem philosophi interiorem vocant, aut doloris aut voluptatis, in quo Cyrenaici solo putant veri esse judicium. *Plut.* adv. Col. 24, 2, p. 1120: [οἱ Κυρηναϊκοὶ] τὰ πάθη καὶ τὰς φαντασίας ἐν αὑτοῖς τιθέντες οὐκ ᾤοντο τὴν ἀπὸ τούτων πίστιν εἶναι διαρκῆ πρὸς τὰς ὑπὲρ τῶν πραγμάτων καταβεβαιώσεις ἀλλ' ὥσπερ ἐν πολιορκίᾳ τῶν ἐκτὸς ἀποστάντες εἰς τὰ πάθη κατέκλει-

CHAP. XIV.

other people. There may be common names, but there are no common feelings, and when two persons

σαν αὐτούς. τὸ φαίνεται τιθέμενοι, τὸ δ' ἐστὶ μὴ προσαποφαινόμενοι περὶ τῶν ἐκτός . . . γλυκαίνεσθαι γὰρ λέγουσι καὶ πικραίνεσθαι καὶ φωτίζεσθαι καὶ σκοτοῦσθαι τῶν παθῶν τούτων ἑκάστου τὴν ἐνέργειαν οἰκείαν ἐν αὐτῷ καὶ ἀπερίσπαστον ἔχοντος· εἰ δὲ γλυκὺ τὸ μέλι καὶ πικρὸς ὁ θαλλὸς κ.τ.λ. ὑπὸ πολλῶν ἀντιμαρτυρεῖσθαι καὶ θηρίων καὶ πραγμάτων καὶ ἀνθρώπων, τῶν μὲν δυσχεραινόντων [add τὸ μὲν] τῶν δὲ προσιεμένων τὴν θαλλίαν, καὶ ἀποκαομένων ὑπὸ τῆς χαλάζης, καὶ καταψυχομένων ὑπὸ οἴνου, καὶ πρὸς ἥλιον ἀμβλυωττόντων καὶ νύκτωρ βλεπόντων. ὅθεν ἐμμένουσα τοῖς πάθεσιν ἡ δόξα διατηρεῖ τὸ ἀναμάρτητον· ἐκβαίνουσα δὲ καὶ πολυπραγμονοῦσα τῷ κρίνειν καὶ ἀποφαίνεσθαι περὶ τῶν ἐκτός, αὐτήν τε πολλάκις ταράσσει καὶ μάχεται πρὸς ἑτέρους ἀπὸ τῶν αὐτῶν ἐναντία πάθη καὶ διαφόρους φαντασίας λαμβάνοντας. *Sext.* Math. vii. 191, who gives the fullest account, but probably to a great extent in his own language: φασὶν οὖν οἱ Κυρηναϊκοὶ κριτήρια εἶναι τὰ πάθη καὶ μόνα καταλαμβάνεσθαι καὶ ἄψευστα τύγχανειν, τῶν δὲ πεποιηκότων τὰ πάθη μηδὲν εἶναι καταληπτὸν μηδὲ ἀδιάψευστον· ὅτι μὲν γὰρ λευκαινόμεθα, φασί, καὶ γλυκαζόμεθα, δυνατὸν λέγειν ἀδιαψεύστως . . . ὅτι δὲ τὸ ἐμποιητικὸν τοῦ πάθους λευκόν ἐστι ἢ γλυκύ ἐστιν, οὐχ οἷόν τ' ἀποφαίνεσθαι. εἰκὸς γάρ ἐστι καὶ ὑπὸ μὴ λευκοῦ τινα λευκαντικῶς διατεθῆναι καὶ ὑπὸ μὴ γλυκέος γλυκανθῆναι, just as a diseased eye or a mad brain always sees things different from what they are. οὕτω καὶ ἡμᾶς εὐλογώτατόν ἐστι πλέον τῶν οἰκείων παθῶν μηδὲν λαμβάνειν δύνασθαι. If, therefore, we understand by φαινόμενα individual impressions (πάθη), it must be said πάντα τὰ φαινόμενα ἀληθῆ καὶ καταληπτά. If, on the contrary, every name means the thing by which the impression is produced, all φαινόμενα are false and cannot be known. Strictly speaking, μόνον τὸ πάθος ἡμῖν ἐστι φαινόμενον· τὸ δ' ἐκτὸς καὶ τοῦ πάθους ποιητικὸν τάχα μέν ἐστιν ὂν οὐ φαινόμενον δὲ ἡμῖν. καὶ ταύτῃ περὶ μὲν τὰ πάθη τά γε οἰκεῖα πάντες ἐσμὲν ἀπλανεῖς, περὶ δὲ τὸ ἐκτὸς ὑποκείμενον πάντες πλανώμεθα· κἀκεῖνα μέν ἐστι καταληπτά, τοῦτο δὲ ἀκατάληπτον, τῆς ψυχῆς πάνυ ἀσθενοῦς καθεστώσης πρὸς διάγνωσιν αὐτοῦ παρὰ τοὺς τόπους, παρὰ τὰ διαστήματα, παρὰ τὰς κινήσεις, παρὰ τὰς μεταβολάς, παρὰ ἄλλας παμπληθεῖς αἰτίας. See Pyrrh. i. 215; *Diog.* ii. 92: τά τε πάθη καταληπτά. ἔλεγον οὖν αὐτά, οὐκ ἀφ' ὧν γίνεται. Ibid. 93: τὰς αἰσθήσεις μὴ πάντοτε ἀληθεύειν. Ibid. 95 of the School of Hegesias, which does not in this respect differ from others: ἀνῄρουν δὲ καὶ τὰς αἰσθήσεις οὐκ ἀκριβούσας τὴν ἐπίγνωσιν. Aristotle in *Eus.* Præp. Ev. xiv. 19, 1: ἑξῆς δ' ἂν εἶεν οἱ λέγοντες μόνα τὰ πάθη καταληπτά. τοῦτο δ' εἶπον ἔνιοι τῶν ἐκ τῆς Κυρήνης (which in the face of the definite statements of Cicero, Plutarch and Sextus, does not prove that this doctrine did *not* belong to the whole School, nor can this be intended. Conf. c.

say that they have felt the same thing, neither of them can be certain that he has experienced the same sensation as the other, since he is only conscious of his own state and not of that of the other.[1]

Thus, like Protagoras,[2] the Cyrenaics regard all notions as relative and individual; their view differing from his in this respect only that they refer notions more directly to internal feelings, leaving out of sight[3] Heraclitus' doctrine of perpetual flow

18, 31) . . . καιόμενοι γὰρ ἔλεγον καὶ τεμνόμενοι γνωρίζειν, ὅτι πάσχοιέν τι· πότερον δὲ τὸ καῖον εἴη πῦρ ἢ τ τέμνον σίδηρος οὐκ ἔχειν εἰπεῖν. *Sextus*, Math. vi. 53, says: μόνα φασὶν ὑπάρχειν τὰ πάθη, ἄλλο δὲ οὐθέν. ὅθεν καὶ τὴν φωνήν, μὴ οὖσαν πάθος ἀλλὰ πάθους ποιητικήν, μὴ γίνεσθαι τῶν ὑπαρκτῶν. But this is inaccurate. The Cyrenaics, we gather from the above, cannot have denied the existence of things, but only our knowledge of their existence. This whole theory probably belongs to the elder Aristippus, as will be probable from a passage in Plato soon to be mentioned. Against *Tenneman's* notion (Gesch. d. Phil. ii. 106) that it first came from Theodorus, see *Wendt*, Phil. Cyr. 45.

[1] *Sext.* Math. vii. 195; ἔνθεν οὐδὲ κριτήριόν φασι εἶναι κοινὸν ἀνθρώπων, ὀνόματα δὲ κοινὰ τίθεσθαι τοῖς κρίμασι. λευκὸν μὲν γάρ τι καὶ γλυκὺ καλοῦσι κοινῶς πάντες, κοινὸν δέ τι λευκὸν ἢ γλυκὺ οὐκ ἔχουσιν· ἕκαστος γὰρ τοῦ ἰδίου πάθους ἀντιλαμβάνεται. τὸ δὲ εἰ τοῦτο τὸ πάθος ἀπὸ λευκοῦ ἐγγίνεται αὐτῷ καὶ τῷ πέλας, οὔτ' αὐτὸς δύναται λέγειν, μὴ ἀναδεχόμενος τὸ τοῦ πέλας πάθος, οὔτε ὁ πέλας, μὴ ἀναδεχόμενος τὸ ἐκείνου . . . τάχα γὰρ ἐγὼ μὲν οὕτω συγκέκριμαι ὡς λευκαίνεσθαι ὑπὸ τοῦ ἔξωθεν προσπίπτοντος, ἕτερος δὲ οὕτω κατεσκευασμένην ἔχει τὴν αἴσθησιν, ὥστε ἑτέρως διατεθῆναι, in support of which the example of a jaundiced or diseased eyesight is adduced. It follows then: κοινὰ μὲν ἡμᾶς ὀνόματα τιθέναι τοῖς πράγμασι, πάθη δέ γε ἔχειν ἴδια.

[2] *Zeller's* Phil. d. Griech. i. 869.

[3] The last point has been too much lost sight of by *Schleiermacher* (Plato's Werke, ii. 1, 183), who considers the description of the Protagorean teaching in the Theætetus to be chiefly meant for Aristippus, whose view does not absolutely coincide with that of Protagoras. See *Wendt*. Phil. Cyr. 37. On the other hand, the difference between them is exaggerated by the Academician in *Cic.* (see p. 349, 1), who ascribes to Protagoras a view entirely different from that of the Cyrenaics, and by *Eus.* Pr. Ev. xiv. 19, 5, who after discussing the Cyrenaics introduces Protagoras

CHAP. XIV.

as not wanted for their purposes and transcending the limits of human knowledge.[1] If knowledge, however, be confined to knowledge of feelings, it follows on the one hand that it would be absurd to seek for a knowledge of things, such knowledge being once for all impossible; and thus the sceptical attitude assumed by the Cyrenaics in respect to knowledge was the ground of their conviction of the worthlessness of all physical inquiries.[2] For this very reason feeling only can supply the rule by which the aim of actions is determined and their value tested. For things being only known to us

with these words: *ἕπεται τούτοις οὖν συνεξετάσαι καὶ τοὺς τὴν ἐναντίαν βαδίζοντας, καὶ πάντα χρῆναι πιστεύειν ταῖς τοῦ σώματος αἰσθήσεσιν ὁρισαμένους*, for Protagoras only asserted the truth of all perceptions in the sense that they were all true for him who perceived them, that things were to each one what they appeared to him to be. In this sense the Cyrenaics, as Sextus has rightly shown, declared all to be true, but both they and Protagoras said nothing about objective truth. Hermann's objection here in Ges. Ab. 235, on the ground that Protagoras was far more subjective than Aristippus, since Aristippus presupposed an agreement amongst men in describing their impressions, is still more at variance with the statements of Cicero and Eusebius, to which Hermann appeals, for they do not make Protagoras more subjective than Aristippus, but Aristippus more subjective than Protagoras. In the next place it is not correct. Of course Protagoras did not deny that certain names were used by all, he even treated himself of the *ὀρθότης ὀνομάτων* (*Zeller's* Phil. d. Griech. i. 933, 1), but what is the use of agreeing in names when the things differ? The Cyrenaics are only more accurate than Protagoras in asserting that perceptions which are called by the same name are not the same in different persons. But there is no disagreement in the teaching of the two.

[1] Had they acted consistently they must have regarded as such every attempt at a natural explanation of our perceptions. We must, therefore, not be misled by *Plut.* N. P. Suav. Vivi Sec. Epic. 4, 5, p. 1069, so as to attribute to them the view of Democritus about pictures and emanating forms.

[2] As *Diog.* ii. 92 remarks. (See p. 347, 1).

by our own feelings, the production of certain feelings is all that can be attained by action; hence the best thing for us will be what is most gratifying to the feelings.[1] Here from the Cyrenaic theory of knowledge follow those ethical principles, which in other ways also it was their main object to establish.

(3) Pleasure and pain.

All feeling, as Aristippus asserts following Protagoras, consisting in an emotion in him who experiences it, if the motion be gentle, there arises a feeling of pleasure; if it be rough and violent,[2] of pain; if again we are in a state of repose, or the

[1] *Sext.* Math. vii. 199: ἀνάλογα δὲ εἶναι δοκεῖ τοῖς περὶ κριτηρίων λεγομένοις κατὰ τούτους τοὺς ἄνδρας καὶ τὰ περὶ τελῶν λεγόμενα· διήκει γὰρ τὰ πάθη καὶ ἐπὶ τὰ τέλη. Ibid. 200.

[2] *Euseb.* Pr. Ev. xiv. 18, 32, says of the younger Aristippus on the authority of Aristocles: τρεῖς γὰρ ἔφη καταστάσεις εἶναι περὶ τὴν ἡμετέραν σύγκρασιν· μίαν μὲν καθ' ἣν ἀλγοῦμεν, ἐοικυῖαν τῷ κατὰ θάλασσαν χειμῶνι· ἑτέραν δὲ καθ' ἣν ἡδόμεθα, τῷ λείῳ κύματι ἐφομοιουμένην· εἶναι γὰρ λείαν κίνησιν τὴν ἡδονὴν οὐρίῳ παραβαλλομένην ἀνέμῳ· τὴν δὲ τρίτην μέσην εἶναι κατάστασιν, καθ' ἣν οὔτε ἀλγοῦμεν οὔτε ἡδόμεθα, γαληνῇ παραπλήσιον οὖσαν. *Diog.* ii. 86, says almost the same thing of the older Cyrenaic school: δύο πάθη ὑφίσταντο, πόνον καὶ ἡδονήν, τὴν μὲν λείαν κίνησιν τὴν ἡδονήν, τὸν δὲ πόνον τραχεῖαν κίνησιν. Ibid. 89, 90: μέσας τε καταστάσεις ὠνόμαζον ἀηδονίαν καὶ ἀπονίαν. *Sext.* Pyrrh. i. 215: [ἡ Κυρηναϊκὴ ἀγωγὴ] τὴν ἡδονὴν καὶ τὴν λείαν τῆς σαρκὸς κίνησιν τέλος εἶναι λέγει. Math. vii. 199: τῶν γὰρ πάθων τὰ μέν ἐστιν ἡδέα, τὰ δὲ ἀλγεινά, τὰ δὲ μεταξύ. That these statements come, on the whole, from the elder Aristippus, appears to be established by several passages in the Philebus. After Socrates (p. 31, B.) has there shown that pain consists in a violation, and pleasure in a restoration, of the natural connection between the parts of a living being, he appends (p. 42, D.) the question: What would happen if neither of these changes were to take place? The representative of the theory of pleasure having answered in a way afterwards repeated by Plato, Rep. ix. 583, C., that in this case there would be neither pleasure nor pain, he continues: κάλλιστ' εἶπες· ἀλλὰ γάρ, οἶμαι, τόδε λέγεις, ὡς ἀεί τι τούτων ἀναγκαῖον ἡμῖν συμβαίνειν, ὡς οἱ σοφοί φασιν· ἀεὶ γὰρ ἅπαντα ἄνω τε καὶ κάτω ῥεῖ. Accordingly the answer is modified to mean that great changes produce pleasure and pain, but small ones neither. To the same view he comes back (on p. 53, C.),

CHAP XIV.

motion is so weak as to be imperceptible, there is no feeling either of pleasure or pain. Of these three states, only that of pleasure is absolutely desirable. Hereto nature bears witness; all following pleasure as the highest end, and avoiding nothing so carefully as pain,[1] unless indeed their judgment be perverted by unfounded fancies.[2] To put freedom from pain in the place of pleasure would not be correct, for where there is no emotion, enjoyment is

with the words: ἆρα περὶ ἡδονῆς οὐκ ἀκηκοάμεν, ὡς ἀεὶ γένεσίς ἐστιν, οὐσία δὲ οὐκ ἔστι τὸ παράπαν ἡδονῆς; κομψοὶ γὰρ δή τινες αὖ τοῦτον τὸν λόγον ἐπιχειροῦσι μηνύειν ἡμῖν, οἷς δεῖ χάριν ἔχειν. These latter words clearly prove that the assertion, all pleasure consists in motion, had been made by some one else, when Plato wrote the Philebus; and since with the exception of Aristippus no one is known to whom it can be referred (Protagoras did not draw the ethical conclusions of his principles); since moreover this assertion is universally attributed to the School of Aristippus; since too the epithet κομψὸς suits him best; it is most probable that both this passage and the passage connected with it on the two kinds of motion and rest, are his. The same observation applies to the remark, that small changes make no impression. Likewise, *Diog.* ii. 85, says of Aristippus: τέλος δ' ἀπόφαινε τὴν λείαν κίνησιν εἰς αἴσθησιν ἀναδιδομένην, according to which not every slight motion is felt or produces pleasure. Perhaps it is in reference to this that *Arist.* Eth. N. vii. 13, 1153, a, 12, says: διὸ καὶ οὐ καλῶς ἔχει τὸ αἰσθητὴν γένεσιν φάναι εἶναι τὴν ἡδονήν. Nor can we allow that there is a discrepancy (as *Susemihl*, Genet. Entw. d. Plat. Phil. ii. 35, note, 120 asserts) between the language of Plato, p. 42, D., and the statements which attribute to Aristippus the assumption of an intermediate state between pleasure and pain. Hence we cannot countenance the conjecture that Aristippus acquired from Plato the more accurate limitation of his teaching. Why did not Aristippus say: We are at all times in a state of gentle or violent motion, but pleasure or pain only arises, when we become conscious of this motion? Yet this is exactly what he did say according to Diogenes, and what Plato makes his representative say, though certainly not without some conversational help.

[1] *Diog.* 88; 87; *Plato*, Phil. 11, B. See above, p. 348, 1.

[2] *Diog.* ii. 89: δύνασθαι δέ φασι καὶ τὴν ἡδονήν τινας μὴ αἱρεῖσθαι κατὰ διαστροφήν.

as little possible as pain, the condition being one of insensibility, as in sleep.[1] Thus the good comes to be identical with what is agreeable—with pleasure; the evil, with what is disagreeable, or unpleasant; what affords neither pleasure nor pain can be neither good nor evil.[2]

(4) *The highest good.*

From this view it follows, as a matter of course, that individual feelings of pleasure must, as such, be the ends of all actions. Simple repose of mind, that freedom from pain in which Epicurus at a later time placed the highest good, cannot, for the reason just given, be the good.[3] To the Cyrenaics it also appeared unsatisfactory that the happiness of the whole of life should be considered and the aim of mankind accordingly represented as being to procure for

[1] *Diog.* 89: ἡ δὲ τοῦ ἀλγοῦντος ὑπεξαίρεσις (ὡς εἴρηται παρ' Ἐπικούρῳ) δοκεῖ αὐτοῖς μὴ εἶναι ἡδονή, οὐδέ ἡ ἀηδονία ἀλγηδών. ἐν κινήσει γὰρ εἶναι ἀμφοτέρα, μὴ οὔσης τῆς ἀπονίας ἢ τῆς ἀηδονίας κινήσεως. ἐπεὶ ἡ ἀπονία οἷον καθεύδοντός ἐστι κατάστασις. Such explicit statements probably belong to a later time, and are due principally to the School of Anniceris in contrast to Epicurus, according to *Clemens*, Strom. ii. 417 B.

[2] *Sext.* Matt. vii. 199: τὰ μὲν ἀλγεινὰ κακά φασιν εἶναι, ὧν τέλος ἀλγηδών, τὰ δὲ ἡδέα ἀγαθά, ὧν τέλος ἐστὶν ἀδιάψευστον ἡδονή, τὰ δὲ μεταξὺ οὔτε ἀγαθὰ οὔτε κακά, ὧν τέλος τὸ οὔτε ἀγαθὸν οὔτε κακόν, ὅπερ πάθος ἐστὶ μεταξὺ ἡδονῆς καὶ ἀλγηδόνος. See p. 353, 2.

[3] See p. 301, 1. *Diog.* ii. 87: ἡδονὴν μέντοι τὴν τοῦ σώματος ἣν καὶ τέλος εἶναι, καθά φησι καὶ Παναίτιος ἐν τῷ περὶ τῶν αἱρέσεων, οὐ τὴν καταστηματικὴν ἡδονὴν τὴν ἐπ' ἀναιρέσει ἀλγηδόνων καὶ οἷον ἀνοχλησίαν, ἣν δ' Ἐπίκουρος ἀποδέχεται καὶ τέλος εἶναί φησι. Perhaps the words in *Cic.* Fin. ii. 6, 18 (after his having said similar things, i. 1, 39), are taken from a kindred passage: aut enim eam voluptatem tueretur, quam Aristippus, i.e. qua sensus dulciter ac jucunde movetur . . . nec Aristippus, qui voluptatem summum bonum dicit, in voluptate ponit non dolere. 13, 39: Aristippi Cyrenaicorumque omnium; quos non est veritum in ea voluptate quæ maxime dulcedine sensum moveret, summum bonum ponere, contemnentes istam vacuitatem doloris.

CHAP. XIV.

themselves the highest sum total of enjoyments that can be had in this life. Such a principle requires the past and the future as well as the present to be considered in the pursuit, neither of which are in our power, and which certainly afford no enjoyment. A future feeling of pleasure is an emotion which has not yet begun; a past one is one which has already ceased.[1] The one only rule of life is to cultivate the art of enjoying the present moment. The present only is ours. Forbear then to distress yourself for what is already past or for what may never be yours.[2]

[1] *Diog.* 87: δοκεῖ δ' αὐτοῖς καὶ τέλος εὐδαιμονίας διαφέρειν. τέλος μὲν γὰρ εἶναι τὴν κατὰ μέρος ἡδονήν, εὐδαιμονίαν δὲ τὸ ἐκ τῶν μερικῶν ἡδονῶν σύστημα, αἷς συναριθμοῦνται καὶ αἱ παρῳχηκυῖαι καὶ αἱ μέλλουσαι. εἶναί τε τὴν μερικὴν ἡδονὴν δι' αὑτὴν αἱρετήν· τὴν δ' εὐδαιμονίαν οὐ δι' αὑτήν, ἀλλὰ διὰ τὰς κατὰ μέρος ἡδονάς. 89: ἀλλὰ μὴν οὐδὲ κατὰ μνήμην τῶν ἀγαθῶν ἢ προσδοκίαν ἡδονήν φασιν ἀποτελεῖσθαι, ὅπερ ἤρεσκεν Ἐπικούρῳ. ἐκλύεσθαι γὰρ τῷ χρόνῳ τὸ τῆς ψυχῆς κίνημα. Ibid. 91: ἀρκεῖ δὲ κἂν κατὰ μίαν [ἡδονὴν] τις προσπίπτουσαν ἡδέως ἐπανάγῃ. *Athen.* xii. 544, a: ['Αρίστιππος] ἀποδεξάμενος τὴν ἡδυπάθειαν ταύτην τέλος εἶναι ἔφη καὶ ἐν αὐτῇ τὴν εὐδαιμονίαν βεβλῆσθαι καὶ μονόχρονον αὐτὴν εἶναι· παραπλησίως τοῖς ἀσώτοις οὔτε τὴν μνήμην τῶν γεγονυιῶν ἀπολαύσεων πρὸς αὐτὸν ἡγούμενος οὔτε τὴν ἐλπίδα τῶν ἐσομένων, ἀλλ' ἑνὶ μόνῳ τὸ ἀγαθὸν κρίνων τῷ παρόντι, τὸ δὲ ἀπολελαυκέναι καὶ ἀπολαύσειν οὐδὲν νομίζων πρὸς αὐτόν, τὸ μὲν ὡς οὐκ ἔτ' ὄν, τὸ δὲ οὔπω καὶ ἄδηλον. *Ælian.* V.H. xiv. 6: πάνυ σφόδρα ἐρρωμένως ἐῴκει λέγειν ὁ 'Αρίστιππος, παρεγγυῶν, μήτε τοῖς παρελθοῦσιν ἐπικάμνειν, μήτε τῶν ἀπιόντων προκάμνειν· εὐθυμίας γὰρ δεῖγμα τὸ τοιοῦτο, καὶ ἵλεω διάνοιας ἀπόδειξις· προσέταττε δὲ ἐφ' ἡμέρᾳ τὴν γνώμην ἔχειν καὶ αὖ πάλιν τῆς ἡμέρας ἐπ' ἐκείνῳ τῷ μέρει καθ' ὃ ἕκαστος ἢ πράττει τι ἢ ἐννοεῖ· μόνον γὰρ ἔφασκεν ἡμέτερον εἶναι τὸ παρόν, μήτε δὲ τὸ φθάνον μήτε τὸ προσδοκώμενον· τὸ μὲν γὰρ ἀπολωλέναι, τὸ δὲ ἄδηλον εἶναι εἴπερ ἔσται. There can be no doubt that Aristippus had already propounded these views, his whole life presupposing them, and his other views immediately leading to them, p. 353, 2. The precise formularising of them may very possibly belong to the period of Epicurus.

[2] *Diog.* 66: ἀπέλαυε μὲν γὰρ ['Αρίστιππος] ἡδονῆς τῶν παρόντων, οὐκ ἐθήρα δὲ πόνῳ τὴν ἀπόλαυσιν τῶν οὐ παρόντων· ὅθεν καὶ

The character of the things whence the feeling of pleasure arises is in itself unimportant. Every pleasure as such is a good, nor is there in this respect any difference between one enjoyment and another. They may spring from various, even from opposite sources, but considered by themselves, they are all alike, one is as good as the other, a pleasurable emotion, and as such always a natural object of desire.[1] The Cyrenaics therefore never allow that there are pleasures not only declared by law and custom to be bad, but bad by their very nature. In their view pleasure may be occasioned by a disreputable action, but in itself it is nevertheless good and desirable.[2]

(5) Modified form of this extreme view.

At the same time this principle received several limitations by means of which its severity was toned down, and its application restricted. In the first place, the Cyrenaics could not deny that notwith-

Διογένης βασιλικὸν κύνα ἔλεγεν αὐτόν.

[1] *Diog.* 87: μὴ διαφέρειν τε ἡδονὴν ἡδονῆς, μηδὲ ἥδιόν τι εἶναι. *Plato*, Phileb. 12, D., where the champion of pleasure answers the objection of Socrates that good pleasures must be distinguished from bad ones thus: εἰσὶ μὲν γὰρ ἀπ' ἐναντίων . . . αὗται πραγμάτων, οὐ μὴν αὐταί γε ἀλλήλαις ἐναντίαι· πῶς γὰρ ἡδονὴ γε ἡδονῇ μὴ οὐχ ὁμοιότατον ἂν εἴη, τοῦτο αὐτὸ ἑαυτῷ, πάντων χρημάτων; Ibid. 13, A.: λέγεις γὰρ ἀγαθὰ πάντα εἶναι τὰ ἡδέα, how is this possible in the case of the worst pleasures? to which Protarchus replies: πῶς λέγεις, ὦ Σώκρατες; οἴει γάρ τινα συγχωρήσεσθαι, θέμενον ἡδονὴν εἶναι τἀγαθόν, εἶτα ἀνέξεσθαί σου λέγοντος τὰς μὲν εἶναί τινας ἀγαθὰς ἡδονάς, τὰς δέ τινας ἑτέρας αὐτῶν κακάς. Just as little will Protarchus (36, C.) allow that there is imaginary pleasure and pain. See p. 348, 1.

[2] *Diog.* 88: εἶναι δὲ τὴν ἡδονὴν ἀγαθὸν κἂν ἀπὸ τῶν ἀσχημοτάτων γένηται, καθά φησιν Ἱππόβοτος ἐν τῷ περὶ αἱρέσεων. εἰ γὰρ καὶ ἡ πρᾶξις ἄτοπος εἴη, ἀλλ' οὖν ἡ ἡδονὴ δι' αὑτὴν αἱρετὴ καὶ ἀγαθόν. To the same effect is the passage already quoted from the Philebus, Conf. p. 359, 1.

standing their essential likeness there were yet differences of degree in feelings of pleasure: for allowing that every pleasure as such is good, it does not follow that the same amount of good belongs to all: as a matter of fact one affords more enjoyment than another, and therefore deserves to be preferred to it.[1] Neither did it escape their notice, that many enjoyments are only purchased at the cost of greater pain; hence they argue unbroken happiness is so hard to gain.[2] They therefore require the consequences of an action to be taken into account; thus endeavouring to secure by an indirect method the contrast between good and evil which they would not at first allow to attach to actions themselves. An action should be avoided when more pain follows therefrom than pleasure; hence a man of sense will abstain from things which are condemned by the laws

[1] *Diog.* 87 says that the Cyrenaics denied a difference in degrees of pleasure, but this is undoubtedly a mistake. *Diog.* ii. 90, says that they taught that bodily feelings of pleasure and pain were stronger than mental ones. See p. 359, 3. *Plato* too, Phil. 45, A.: 65 E., in the spirit of this School, talks of *μέγισται τῶν ἡδονῶν*, nor is there the slightest reason for equalising all enjoyments in their system. They could not allow that there was an absolute difference of value between them, some being good and others bad; but they had no occasion to deny a relative difference between the more or less good, and they might even allow of different kinds of pleasure, those of the body, for instance, and those of the mind. *Ritter's* remarks on *Diog.* ii. 103, do not appear satisfactory. Not more satisfactory are those of *Wendt* (Phil. Cyr. 34, Gött. Aug. 1835, 789). According to Diogenes the Cyrenaics only denied that any object taken by itself and independently of our feelings was more pleasant than another.

[2] *Diog.* 90: *διὸ* [?] *καὶ καθ' αὑτήν αἱρετῆς οὔσης τῆς ἡδονῆς τὰ ποιητικὰ ἐνίων ἡδονῶν ὀχληρὰ πολλάκις ἐναντιοῦσθαι· ὡς δυσκολώτατον αὐτοῖς φαίνεσθαι τὸν ἀθροισμὸν τῶν ἡδονῶν εὐδαιμονίαν ποιούντων.* See p. 356, 1.

of the state and public opinion.[1] Lastly, they also directed their attention to the difference between bodily and mental pleasures.[2] Holding bodily pains and pleasures to be more pungent than those of the mind;[3] perhaps even attempting to show that all pleasure and its opposite are in the last resource occasioned by bodily feelings;[4] they nevertheless contended that

[1] *Diog.* 93: μηδέν τι εἶναι φύσει δίκαιον ἢ καλὸν ἢ αἰσχρὸν, the value of every action depending on the pleasure which follows it, ἀλλὰ νόμῳ καὶ ἔθει, ὁ μέντοι σπουδαῖος οὐδὲν ἄτοπον πράξει διὰ τὰς ἐπικειμένας ζημίας καὶ δόξας. *Wendt* (Phil. Cyr. 25) calls this statement in question without reason. It is quite consistent in Aristippus, and is met with in Epicurus; *Zeller*, Stoics, &c.; but he is right (Ibid. 36, 42) in rejecting Schleiermacher's hypothesis (Pl. W. ii. 1, 183; ii. 2, 18), that in the Gorgias Aristippus is being refuted under the name of Callicles, and in the Cratylus 384, Diogenes under that of Hermogenes.

[2] Which, strictly speaking, they could only have done by saying that one portion of our impressions *appears* to us to come from the body, another not; for they had long since given up all real knowledge of things. But their consistency hardly went so far as this.

[3] *Diog.* ii. 90: πολὺ μέντοι τῶν ψυχικῶν τὰς σωματικὰς ἀμείνους εἶναι καὶ τὰς ὀχλήσεις χείρους τὰς σωματικάς· ὅθεν καὶ ταύταις κολάζεσθαι μᾶλλον τοὺς ἁμαρτάνοντας. (The same, Ibid. x. 137.) χαλεπώτερον γὰρ τὸ πονεῖν, οἰκειότερον δὲ τὸ ἥδεσθαι ὑπελάμβανον· ὅθεν καὶ πλείονα οἰκονομίαν περὶ θάτερον ἐποιοῦντο.

[4] This is indicated by the expression οἰκειότερον in the above passage also. See p. 360, 2. To say that not all pleasure and pain is connected with bodily states, may be harmonised with this statement by taking their meaning to be, that not every feeling has its *immediate* object in the body, without, however, denying more remote connection between such feelings and the body. Joy for one's country's prosperity might in their minds be connected with the thought that our own happiness depends on that of our country. It can only be considered an opponent's exaggeration for Panætius and Cicero to assert that the Cyrenaics made bodily pleasure the end of life. (See p. 355, 3.) *Cic.* Acad. iv. 45, 139: Aristippus, quasi animum nullum habeamus, corpus solum tuetur. The highest good Aristippus declared consists not in bodily pleasure, but in pleasure generally. If he regarded bodily pleasure as the strongest, and in this sense as the best, it by no means follows that he excluded mental pleasures from

CHAP. XIV.

there must be a something besides sensuous feelings, or it would be impossible to explain how unequal impressions are produced by perceptions altogether alike:—the sight, for instance, of the sufferings of others, if they are real, gives a painful impression; if only seen on the stage, a pleasurable one.[1] They even allowed that there are pleasures and pains of the mind which have no immediate reference to any states of the body. The prosperity, for instance, of our country fills us with as much pleasure as does our own.[2] Although therefore pleasure is in general made to coincide with the good, and pain with evil, the Cyrenaics are far from expecting happiness to result from the mere satisfaction of animal instincts. For a true enjoyment of life, you not only need to weigh the value and the consequences of every enjoyment, but you need also to acquire the proper frame of mind. The most essential help to a pleasant life is prudence,[3] not only because it supplies that presence of mind which is never at a loss for means,[4] but, mainly, because it teaches how to make a right

the idea of good. Indeed, his remarks respecting the value of prudence make this probable. See *Wendt*, 22.

[1] *Diog.* 90: λέγουσι δὲ μηδὲ κατὰ ψιλὴν τὴν ὅρασιν ἢ τὴν ἀκοὴν γίνεσθαι ἡδονάς, τῶν γοῦν μιμουμένων θρήνους ἡδέως ἀκούομεν, τῶν δὲ κατ' ἀλήθειαν ἀηδῶς. The same is found in *Plut.* Qu. Conv. v. 1, 2, 7, p. 674. Here belongs *Cic.* Tusc. ii. 13, 28.

[2] *Diog.* 89: οὐ πάσας μέντοι τὰς ψυχικὰς ἡδονὰς καὶ ἀλγηδόνας ἐπὶ σωματικαῖς ἡδοναῖς καὶ ἀλγηδόσι γίνεσθαι· καὶ γὰρ ἐπὶ ψιλῇ τῇ τῆς πατρίδος εὐημερίᾳ ὥσπερ τῇ ἰδίᾳ χαρὰν ἐγγίνεσθαι.

[3] See p. 348, 2.

[4] See the anecdotes and proverbs in *Diog.* 68; 73; 79; 82, and what *Galen.* Exhort. c. 5, vol. i. 8, K., and Vitruv. vi. Præf. i., say of his shipwreck. Conf. Exc. e Floril. Joan. Damasc. ii. 13, 138.

use of the good things of life;[1] overcoming the prejudices and fancies which stand in the way of success, such as envy, passionate love, superstition;[2] preserving from regret for the past, from desire for the future, from dependence on present enjoyment; and guaranteeing that freedom of soul of which we stand in need would we at every moment rest contented with our present lot.[3]

Hence the cultivation of the mind is warmly advocated by these philosophers,[4] philosophy being specially pointed to as the way to a truly human life.[5] They even assert that therein lies the essential condition of happiness; for although mankind are too far dependent on external circumstances for the wise man to be invariably happy, and the foolish man invariably miserable,[6] yet as a rule so it is. No

[1] *Demetr.* (Elocut. 296) mentions as an εἶδος τοῦ λόγου Ἀριστιππεῖον· ὅτι οἱ ἄνθρωποι χρήματα μὲν ἀπολείπουσι τοῖς παισὶν ἐπιστήμην δὲ οὐ συναπολείπουσι τὴν χρησομένην αὐτοῖς. The thought is Socratic. See p. 142, 1.

[2] *Diog.* 91: τὸν σοφὸν μήτε φθονήσειν μήτε ἐρασθήσεσθαι (on this point compare the language used by Aristippus respecting his relations to Lais) ἢ δεισιδαιμονήσειν, whereas he is not preserved from fear and sorrow as being natural consequences.

[3] See p. 356, 2.

[4] Many expressions to this effect are on record, particularly those of Aristippus, *Diog.* ii. 69, 70, 72, 80. *Plut.* Frag. 9, 1, and comment. in Hes.

[5] See the saying of Aristippus in *Diog.* ii. 72; *Plut.* Ed. Pu. 74. He is also mentioned by Diogenes ii. 68 (Conf. Exc. e Floril. Joan. Damasc. ii. 13, 146) as the author of the saying, which *Cic.* Rep. i. 2; *Plut.* adv. Col. 30, 2, p. 1124, attribute to Xenocrates, that the conduct of the philosopher would remain the same, supposing all laws to be abolished.

[6] *Diog.* 91: ἀρέσκει δ' αὐτοῖς μήτε τὸν σοφὸν πάντα ἡδέως ζῆν, μήτε πάντα φαῦλον ἐπιπόνως, ἀλλὰ κατὰ τὸ πλεῖστον. In the same way the Cyrenaics would not deny that the ἄφρονες were capable of certain virtues. Probably this was only expressly stated by later members of the School in agreement with the Cynics and Stoics.

CHAP. XIV.

departure is here made from the fundamental principle of the School, the pursuit of pleasure; but certainly something very different has come of it from what might at first have been expected.

C. *Practical life of the Cyrenaics.*

With this accords all that is further known as to the views and conduct of Aristippus. His leading thought is comprised in the adage, that life offers most to him who, without ever denying himself a pleasure, at every moment continues master of himself and his surroundings. The Cynic freedom from wants is not his concern. Prudent enjoyment he says is a greater art [1] than abstinence. He lived not only comfortably, but even luxuriously.[2] A good table he enjoyed,[3] wore costly clothing,[4] scented himself with perfumes,[5] and caroused with mistresses.[6]

[1] *Stob.* Floril. 17, 18: κρατεῖ ἡδονῆς οὐχ ὁ ἀπεχόμενος, ἀλλ' ὁ χρώμενος μὲν μὴ παρεκφερόμενος δέ. *Diog.* 75: τὸ κρατεῖν καὶ μὴ ἡττᾶσθαι ἡδονῶν κράτιστον, οὐ τὸ μὴ χρῆσθαι.

[2] *Xen.* Mem. ii. 1, 1, already calls him ἀκολαστοτέρως ἔχοντα πρὸς τὰ τοιαῦτα [προς ἐπιθυμίαν βρωτοῦ καὶ ποτοῦ καὶ λαγνείας], etc. He says himself then, 1, 9, that his object is ᾗ ῥᾷστά τε καὶ ἥδιστα βιοτεύειν· and Socrates asks whether he depended for his homelessness on the circumstance that no one would like to have him even as a slave? τίς γὰρ ἂν ἐθέλοι ἄνθρωπον ἐν οἰκίᾳ ἔχειν πονεῖν μὲν μηδὲν ἐθέλοντα, τῇ δὲ πολυτελεστάτῃ διαίτῃ χαίροντα; this picture was afterwards more deeply coloured by later writers, and certainly not without exaggeration. See *Athen.* xii. 544, 6, e, according to Alexis; Ibid. viii. 343, according to Soter; Timon in *Diog.* ii. 66; Ibid. ii. 69, iv. 40; *Lucian.* V. Auct. 12; *Clemens*, Pædag. ii. 176, D.; *Eus.* Pr. Ev. xiv. 18, 31; *Epiph.* Exp. Fid. 1089 A.; *Steele*, p. 41: 71.

[3] See the anecdotes in *Diog.* ii. 66, 68, 69, 75, 76.

[4] *Max. Tyr.* Diss. vii. 9; *Lucian*, l. c.; Ibid. Cic. Acc. 23; *Tatian* adv. Græc. c. 2; *Tert.* Apol. 46.

[5] That he made use of fragrant perfumes, and defended this practice, is told by *Seneca*, Benef. vii. 25, 1; *Clem.* Pæd. ii. 176 D., 179 B., *Diog.* 76, all apparently from the same source, the others mentioned by *Stein*, 43, 1, probably doing likewise.

[6] His relations to Lais are well known. Hermesianax in

Nor were the means neglected by which this mode of life was rendered possible. For he argued that the more of these you possess the better for you: riches are not like shoes, which when too large cannot be worn.[1] He accordingly not only demanded payment for his instruction;[2] but did not hesitate to enrich himself by means, and for this purpose to submit to things, which any other philosopher would have considered below his dignity.[3] The fear of

Athen. xiii. 599, b, 588 c; xii. 544, b, d.; *Cic.* ad Fam. ix. 26; *Plut.* Erot. 4, 5, p. 750; *Diog.* 74, 85; *Clemens*, Strom. ii. 411, C.; *Theod.* Cur. Gr. Aff. xii. 50, p. 173; *Lact.* Inst. iii. 15. A few other stories of the same kind may be found, *Diog.* 67; 69; 81; iv. 40.

[1] *Stob.* Floril. 94, 32.

[2] See p. 340, 5.

[3] Here belong many of the anecdotes which relate to Aristippus' stay at the court of Dionysius. According to *Diog.* 77, Aristippus is said to have announced to Dionysius, on his arrival, that he came to impart what he had, and to receive what he had not; or, according to a more probable version, Ibid. 78, when he wanted instruction he used to go to Socrates for it; now that he wanted money, he had come to Dionysius. To the same person, too, according to *Diog.* 69, his remark was addressed that the reason why philosophers appeared before the doors of the rich, and not the contrary, was because philosophers knew what they wanted, whilst the rich did not. The same story is found in *Stob.* Floril. 3, 46, and in a somewhat different connection, *Diog.* 70 and 81. Yet *Schleiermacher* has no reason to refer to this remark, on the strength of *Arist.* Rhet. ii. 16, 1391, a, 8, the passage in Plato's Republic, vi. 489, but he is quite right in setting down the Scholiast who wished to attribute the remark of Socrates to Aristippus. Of the liberal offer made by Dionysius to Plato, he observes in *Plut.* Dio. 19: *ἀσφαλῶς μεγαλόψυχον εἶναι Διονύσιον· αὐτοῖς μὲν γὰρ μικρὰ διδόναι πλειόνων δεομένοις, Πλάτωνι δὲ πολλὰ μηδὲν λαμβάνοντι.* Dionysius at first refusing to give him any money because the wise man, on his own showing, was never in difficulties, he replied, Give me the money this once, and I will explain to you how it is; but no sooner had he got it, than he exclaimed, Ah! was I not right? *Diog.* 82, *Diog.* 67, 73, and *Athen.* xii. 544, tell further, on the authority of Hegesander, that once having been placed at the bottom of the table by Dionysius because of some free expression, he contented himself

CHAP. XIV.

death too, from which his teaching professed to deliver,[1] was not so fully overcome by him that he could face danger with the composure of a Socrates.[2]

It would, nevertheless, be doing Aristippus a great injustice to consider him an ordinary, or at most a somewhat more intellectual pleasure-seeker. Enjoy he will, but, at the same time, he will be above enjoyment. He possesses not only the skill of adapting himself to circumstances and making use of persons and things,[3] not only the wit which is

with remarking, To-day, this is the place of honour which he assigns. Another time he is said to have taken it quite quietly when Dionysius spat in his face, observing: A fisherman must put up with more moisture, to catch even a smaller fish. Once, when begging a favour for a friend, he fell at the feet of Dionysius, *Diog.* 79, and when reproached for so doing, Wherefore, he asked, has Dionysius ears on his legs. It is a common story that Dionysius once asked him and Plato to appear dressed in purple: Plato refused to do so, but Aristippus acceded with a smile. *Sext.* Pyrrh. iii. 204, i. 155; *Diog.* 78; *Suid.* Ἀρίστ.; *Stob.* Floril. 5, 46; *Greg. Naz.* Carm. ii. 10, 324: the latter unskilfully places the incident at the court of Archelaus. *Stein*, 67. The observation in *Diog.* 81, is likewise referred to Plato, that *he* allowed himself to be abused by Dionysius for the same reasons that others abused him: a preacher of morals after all is only pursuing his own interests. He is represented as a flatterer and parasite of Dionysius, by *Lucian* V. Aut. 12; Parasit. 33, Bis Accus. 23; Men. 13.

[1] See *Diog.* 76: at the same time the Cyrenaics consider fear to be something natural and unavoidable. See p. 361, 2.

[2] On the occasion of a storm at sea he was charged with displaying more fear than others, notwithstanding his philosophy, to which he adroitly replied: οὐ γὰρ περὶ ὁμοίας ψυχῆς ἀγωνιῶμεν ἀμφότεροι, *Diog.* 71; *Gell.* xix. 1, 10; *Ælian*, V. H. ix. 20.

[3] *Diog.* 66: ἦν δὲ ἱκανὸς ἁρμόσασθαι καὶ τόπῳ καὶ χρόνῳ καὶ προσώπῳ, καὶ πᾶσαν περίστασιν ἁρμοδίως ὑποκρίνασθαι· διὸ καὶ παρὰ Διονυσίῳ τῶν ἄλλων εὐδοκίμει μᾶλλον, ἀεὶ τὸ προσπεσὸν εὖ διατιθέμενος. A few instances of this skill have been already seen (p. 363, 3). Here, too, belongs what is told by *Galen.* and *Vitruv.* (see p. 341), that after having suffered shipwreck, and lost everything, he immediately contrived in Syracuse or Rhodes

never at a loss for repartee,[1] but he possesses also calmness of mind and freedom of spirit, which can forego pleasure without a pang, bear loss with composure, be content with what it hath, and feel happy in any position. His maxim is to enjoy the present, ignoring care either for the future or the past, and

to procure an ample supply of necessaries. Further, it is stated in *Plutarch*, Dio. 19, that he was the first to notice the growing estrangement between Dionysius and Plato. In *Diog.* 68, he answers the question, What good he has got from philosophy, by saying: τὸ δύνασθαι πᾶσι θαῤῥούντως ὁμιλεῖν—and *Diog.* 79, relates that when brought as a captive before Artaphernes, some one asked him how he liked his situation, to which he replied, that now he was perfectly at rest. Well known is the answer which he is reported to have given to Diogenes (which, however, is told of others), *Diog.* vi. 58, ii. 102: εἴπερ ᾔδεις ἀνθρώποις ὁμιλεῖν, οὐκ ἂν λάχανα ἔπλυνες. *Diog.* 68; *Hor.* Ep. i. 17, 13; *Valer. Max.* iv. 3, Ext. 4.

[1] See p. 363, 1; 364, 2. In a similar way he could defend his luxuriousness. When blamed for giving fifty drachmæ for a partridge, Aristippus asked if he would have given a farthing for it. The reply being in the affirmative; I, said Aristippus, do not care more for fifty drachmæ than you do for a farthing. *Diog.* 66, 75; or with a different turn, *Athen.* viii. 343, c, where the story is told of him and Plato *àpropos* of a dish of fish: ὁρᾷς οὖν . . . ὅτι οὐκ ἐγὼ ὀψοφάγος, ἀλλὰ σὺ φιλάργυρος. Another time he argued that if good living were wrong, it would not be employed to honour the festivals of the gods. Ibid. 68. Another time, when some one took him to task for his good living, he asked him to dinner. The invitation being accepted; he at once drew the conclusion that he must be too stingy to live well himself. Ibid. 76. When Dionysius offered him the choice between three mistresses, he chose them all, with the gallant observation, that it had been a bad thing for Paris to prefer one of three goddesses, but bade them all farewell at his door. Ibid. 67. When attacked for his relations to Lais, he answered with the well-known ἔχω καὶ οὐκ ἔχομαι. The same relation is said to have given rise to other light jokes; it was all the same to him whether the house in which he lived had been occupied by others before; he did not care whether a fish liked him, if he liked the fish. The Cynicism is betrayed by the anecdotes in *Diog.* 81, p. 342, 4, although they are not otherwise at variance with Grecian morals.

CHAP. XIV.

under all circumstances to keep cheerful.[1] Come what may, there is a bright side to things,[2] and he knows how to wear the beggar's rags and the robe of state with equal grace.[3] Pleasure he loves, but he can also dispense therewith.[4] He will continue master of his desires.[5] His temper shall not be ruffled by any risings of passion.[6] Some importance is attached to riches, but hardly any independent value,[7] and therefore the want of them is never felt. He is lavish of them because he does not cling to them.[8] If necessary, he can do without them,[9] and

[1] See pp. 356 and 361.

[2] *Hor.* Ep. i. 17, 23: omnis Aristippum decuit color et status et res, tentantem majora fere, præsentibus æquum. *Plut.* de Vit. Hom. B., 150: Ἀρίστιππος καὶ πενίᾳ καὶ πόνοις συνηνέχθη ἐῤῥωμένως καὶ ἡδονῇ ἀφειδῶς ἐχρήσατο. *Diog.* 66, p. 163, 3; 355, 2.

[3] According to *Diog.* 67, Plato is said to have remarked to him: σοὶ μόνῳ δέδοται καὶ χλανίδα φέρειν καὶ ῥάκος. The same remark, and not the story of the purple dress, is referred to by *Plut.* Virt. Alex. 8, p. 330: Ἀρίστιππον θαυμάζομαι τὸν Σωκρατικὸν ὅτι καὶ τρίβωνι λιτῷ καὶ Μιλησίᾳ χλάμυδι χρώμενος δι' ἀμφοτέρων ἐτήρει τὸ εὔσχημον, and *Hor.* Ep. i. 17, 27, on which passage the Scholiast tells how Aristippus carried off the surcoat of Diogenes from the bath, leaving his purple cloak instead, which Diogenes refused to wear at any price.

[4] *Diog.* 67, p. 364, 4.

[5] ἔχω οὐκ ἔχομαι. *Diog.* 69, tells a saying of the same kind which Aristippus uttered on paying a visit to his mistress, to the effect that there was no need to be ashamed of going there, but there was of not being able to go away.

[6] See p. 361, 2 & 3. *Plut.* N. P. Suav. V. sec. Epic. 4, 5, p. 1089: οἱ Κυρηναϊκοὶ . . . οὐδὲ ὁμιλεῖν ἀφροδισίοις οἴονται δεῖν μετὰ φωτός, ἀλλὰ σκότος προθεμένους, ὅπως μὴ τὰ εἴδωλα τῆς πράξεως ἀναλαμβάνουσα διὰ τῆς ὄψεως ἐναργῶς ἐν αὐτῇ ἡ διάνοια πολλάκις ἀνακαίῃ τὴν ὄρεξιν. The same way of thinking is expressed in his definition of pleasure as a gentle motion of the mind. The storms of passion would change this gentle motion into a violent one, and turn pleasure into pain.

[7] See p. 348, 1.

[8] See p. 304, 3, and the story that he bade his servant who was carrying a heavy burden of gold cast away what was too much for him. *Hor.* Serm. ii. 3, 99; *Diog.* 77.

[9] Finding himself on board a

is readily consoled for their loss.[1] To him no possession appears more valuable than contentment,[2] no disease worse than avarice.[3] He lives an easy life, but he is not on that account afraid of exertion, and approves of bodily exercise.[4] His life is that of the flatterer, but he often expresses himself with unexpected candour.[5] Freedom he esteems above all things,[6] and hence will neither rule nor be ruled, nor belong to any community, being unwilling to forfeit freedom at any price.[7]

pirate vessel, he threw his money into the sea with the words: ἄμεινον ταῦτα δι' Ἀρίστιππον ἢ διὰ ταῦτα Ἀρίστιππον ἀπολέσθαι. *Diog.* 77; *Cic.* Invent. ii. 58, 176; *Auson.* Idyl. iii. 13; *Stob.* Floril, 57, 13, taking care to read with Menage and Stein, p. 39, τὸ ἀργύριον for ἀγρὸς.

[1] In *Plut.* Tranq. An. 8, p. 469, Aristippus having lost an estate, one of his friends expressed sympathy with him, upon which Aristippus replied: Have I not now three estates, whilst you have only one? Ought I not rather to sympathise with you?

[2] *Hor.* see p. 366, 2; *Diog.* ii. 72: τὰ ἄριστα ὑπετίθετο τῇ θυγατρὶ Ἀρήτῃ, συνασκῶν αὐτὴν ὑπεροπτικὴν τοῦ πλείονος εἶναι. Hence the same story in Ep. Socrat. 29, the compiler of this late and miserable forgery not having used the earlier genuine letters to Aret. mentioned by Suid Ἀρίστ.

[3] See further details in *Plut.* Cupid. Div. 3, p. 524.

[4] See p. 366, 2, *Diog.* 91: τὴν σωματικὴν ἄσκησιν συμβάλλεσθαι πρὸς ἀρετῆς ἀνάληψιν.

[5] Several free expressions of his towards Dionysius are told by *Diog.* 73, 77; *Stob.* Floril. 49, 22; conf. *Greg. Naz.* Carm. ii. 10, 419, vol. ii. 430 Codd.; not to mention the anecdotes in *Diog.* 75, repeated Ibid. vi. 32; *Galen.* Exhort. ad Art. c. 8, i. 18, k.

[6] On the principle mentioned by *Hor.* Ep. i. 1, 18: nunc in Aristippi furtim præcepta relabor, et mihi res, non me rebus subjungere conor. According to the context, however, the principle should not be confined to Aristippus' relations to outward possessions. Here, too, the saying belongs *Plut.* in Hes. 9, vol. xiv. 296, Hu.: συμβούλου δεῖσθαι χεῖρον εἶναι τοῦ προσαιτεῖν. Conf. p. 364, 3.

[7] *Xen.* Mem. ii. 1, 8. In reply to Socrates, who asked whether he considered himself among the number of those who rule, or those who are ruled, Aristippus states: ἔγωγ' οὐδ' ὅλως γε τάττω ἐμαυτὸν εἰς τὴν τῶν ἄρχειν βουλομένων τάξιν. For, as is explained here and p. 17, there is no man who is more troubled than a statesman: ἐμαυτὸν τοί-

CHAP. XIV.

Still less did he allow himself to be restrained by religious considerations or traditions. We have at least every reason for asserting this both of Aristippus personally, and of his School.[1] Theodorus was probably the first to gain notoriety for his wanton attacks on the popular faith;[2] still a connection between the Cyrenaic philosophy and the insipid rationalism of Euemerus[3] is far from certain. Nor ought it to be forgotten, that Aristippus strove to make life easy not only for himself, but also for

νυν τάττω εἰς τοὺς βουλομένους ᾗ ῥᾷστά τε καὶ ἥδιστα βιοτεύειν. When Socrates met this by observing that those who rule are better off than those who are ruled, he rejoined: ἀλλ' ἐγώ τοι οὐδὲ εἰς τὴν δουλείαν αὖ ἐμαυτὸν τάττω· ἀλλ' εἶναι τίς μοι δοκεῖ μέση τούτων ὁδός, ἣν πειρῶμαι βαδίζειν, οὔτε δι' ἀρχῆς οὔτε διὰ δουλείας, ἀλλὰ δι' ἐλευθερίας, ἥπερ μάλιστα πρὸς εὐδαιμονίαν ἄγει. And after further objections: ἀλλ' ἐγώ τοι, ἵνα μὴ πάσχω ταῦτα, οὐδ' εἰς πολιτείαν ἐμαυτὸν κατακλείω, ἀλλὰ ξένος πανταχοῦ εἰμι. Quite in keeping with this homeless life is the language used by Aristippus, according to Teles in *Stob.* Floril. 40, 8, vol. ii. 69, Mein., that to him it was of no moment to die in his country; from every country the way to Hades was the same. His address to Dionysius in *Stob.* Floril. 49, 22, is also quite in harmony with Xenophon's description: Had you learnt aught from me, you would shake off despotic rule as a disease. Being obliged, however, to live under some form of government, a good one is naturally preferable to a bad one; and accordingly the saying attributed to him in *Stob.* Floril. 49, 18, touching the difference between a despotic and a monarchical form of government has about it nothing improbable. Nevertheless, at a later period Aristippus may have relaxed his views on civil life to a certain extent. At any rate he formed a connection with a family with which he would previously have nothing to do. Certainly *Diog.* 81, proves nothing. See p. 342, 4.

[1] It was a natural consequence of their scepticism, that they followed Protagoras in his attitude towards religion; and by means of their practical turn that freedom from religious prejudices was decidedly promoted, which they especially required in the wise man. *Diog.* 91, see p. 361, 2. *Clemens*, Strom. vii. 722, D., says more generally that they rejected prayer.

[2] Particulars of this below.

[3] See p. 344, 5.

others. Possessed of pleasing and attractive manners,[1] an enemy of vanity and boasting,[2] he could comfort friends with sympathy,[3] and bear injuries with calmness.[4] He could avoid strife,[5] mitigate anger,[6] and conciliate an offended friend.[7] The most extraordinary spectacle to his thinking is said to have been a virtuous man steadily pursuing his course in the midst of the vicious; [8] and that such was really his opinion is shown by his reverence for Socrates. It may therefore be true,[9] that he congratulated himself on having become, thanks to Socrates, a man capable of being praised in all good conscience. In a word, with all his love of enjoy-

[1] ἥδιστος is the name which *Greg. Naz.* 307, gives him, and Ibid. 323, he commends him for τὸ εὐχάριστον τοῦ τρόπου καὶ στρωμύλον.

[2] See *Arist.* Rhet. ii. 23; *Diog.* 71, 73. See also p. 364, 3.

[3] *Aelian.* V. H. vii. 3, mentions a letter of sympathy addressed to some friends, who had met with a severe misfortune. He quotes from the introduction the words: ἀλλ' ἔγωγε ἥκω πρὸς ὑμᾶς οὐχ ὡς συλλυπούμενος ὑμῖν, ἀλλ' ἵνα παύσω ὑμᾶς λυπουμένους. In theory, Aristippus could only estimate the value of friendship by its utility, as Epicurus did at a later time. *Diog.* 91: τὸν φίλον τῆς χρείας ἕνεκα, καὶ γὰρ μέρος σώματος, μέχρις ἂν παρῇ, ἀσπάζεσθαι. Something similar is also found in Socrates, see pp. 152, 3; 223, 3; and he employs the same argument *Xen.* Mem. i. 2, 54.

[4] *Plut.* Prof. in Virt. 9, p. 80.

[5] *Diog.* 70; *Stob.* Floril. 19, 6.

[6] *Stob.* Floril. 20, 63.

[7] See the adventure with Æschines in *Plut.* Coh. Ira. 14, p. 462, *Diog.* 82, which *Stob.* Flor. 84, 19, probably by mistake, refers to the brother of Aristippus.

[8] *Stob.* Floril. 37, 25: Ἀρίστιππος ἐρωτηθεὶς τί ἀξιοθαύμαστόν ἐστιν ἐν τῷ βίῳ; ἄνθρωπος ἐπιεικής, εἶπε, καὶ μέτριος, ὅτι [ὃς or ὅστις?] ἐν πολλοῖς ὑπάρχων μοχθηροῖς οὐ διέστραπται.

[9] Which is told by *Diog.* 71. Few of the anecdotes about Aristippus rest on good authority. Agreeing, however, as they all do, in portraying a certain character, they have been used as the material for an historical sketch. They may be spurious in parts, but on the whole they give a faithful representation of the man.

CHAP. XIV.

ment, Aristippus appears to have been a man of high feelings and a cultivated mind, a man knowing how to preserve calmness and freedom of mind amidst the perpetual change of human affairs, how to govern his passions and inclinations, and how to make the best of all the events of life. A strength of will which can beard destiny, the seriousness of a high mind bent upon great purposes, a strictness of principles may not be his; but he is a proficient in the rare art of contentment and moderation, while the pleasing kindness and the cheery brightness of his manners attract far more than the superficial and self-indulgent tone of his moral views repel.[1] Nor are these traits purely personal; they lie in the very nature of his system and its requirement that human life should be regulated by prudence. Theory and practice overlap quite as much with Aristippus as with Diogenes, and in either case one may be explained by the other.

D. *Position of their system to that of Socrates.*

From Socrates indeed both are far enough removed. His was a theory of knowledge of conceptions; theirs a most downright subservience to the senses. His was an insatiable thirsting for know-

[1] Cicero, who is not generally his friend, says (Off. i. 41, 148), that if Socrates or Aristippus placed themselves in antagonism with tradition, they ought not to be imitated therein: magnis illi et divinis bonis hanc licentiam assequebantur; and he also quotes (N. D. iii. 31, 77) a saying of the Stoic Aristo: nocere audientibus philosophos iis, qui bene dicta male interpretarentur: posse enim asotos ex Aristippi, acerbos e Zenonis schola exire. The same is attributed to Zeno by Ath. xiii. 566, d, on the authority of Antigonus Carystius: those who misunderstood him might become vulgar and depraved, *καθάπερ οἱ τῆς Ἀριστίππου παρενεχθέντες αἱρεσέως ἄσωτοι καὶ θρασεῖς.*

ledge, an untiring critical exercise; theirs a total renunciation of knowledge, an indifference to all theoretical inquiries. His was a scrupulous conscientiousness, an unwavering submission to moral requirements, an unceasing working of man upon himself and others; theirs was a comfortable theory of life, never going beyond enjoyment, and treating even the means thereto with indifference. On his side were self-denial, abstemiousness, moral strictness, patriotism, piety.; on theirs were luxurious indulgence, frivolous versatility, a citizenship of the world needing no country, and a rationalism needing no Gods. Still it cannot be said that Aristippus was only a sportive pupil of Socrates, or that his teaching had only been touched surface-deep by that of his master. Not only was he classed among followers of Socrates by the unanimous voice of antiquity, which, no doubt, has more immediate reference to his outward relations with him; not only did he always call himself a pupil of Socrates and speak of his teacher with unchanging devotion[1]—a proof stronger than the former, and showing that he was able to appreciate the greatness of his friend—but his philosophy leaves no doubt that the spirit of the master had in him been mightily at work. The intellectual convictions and the intellectual aims of Socrates he did not share;[2] Socrates, on the one

[1] See above, p. 338, 5.

[2] *Hermann's* remarks (On Ritter's Dar. d Socr. Sys. 26; Gesch. d. Plat. Phil. 263), intended to bring the intellectual teaching of Aristippus into closer connection with that of Socrates, do not appear satisfactory, even when supported by the additional arguments in

CHAP. XIV.

hand, straining every nerve to attain to knowledge; Aristippus, on the other, denying that knowledge

his Ges. Abh. 233, nor are they regarded as satisfactory by *Ritter*, Gesch. d. Phil. ii. 106. Hermann thinks that Aristippus was only lacking in the religious and moral tone of Socrates, but that he steadily adhered to his logical principles. Socrates declared all judgments to be relative, and only conceptions to be universally valid; in the same way, the Cyrenaics only denied the universal validity of judgments, but not that of conceptions; for they allowed that all men receive from the same things the same impressions, as to the names of which they were agreed. These names, however, were identical with the conceptions of Socrates, conceptions having been by them as by the Cynics and Megarians reduced to empty names and deprived of all real substance. There is indeed a noticeable advance in entirely separating conceptions from appearances, and in more precisely defining the highest good as the first judgment universally valid. But in the first place it never occurred to Socrates to deny the universal validity of judgments; and it is as certain that he allowed universally valid judgments as that he allowed universally valid conceptions—such, for instance, as 'All virtue is knowledge,' 'every one pursues the good;' and if he called some judgments relative—such as, 'This is good,'—it is no less certain that he declared the corresponding conceptions—for instance, that of the good—to be relative. In the next place it is equally untrue to say that the Cyrenaics only denied the universal validity of judgments but not that of conceptions; for they declared most emphatically that all our notions only express our personal feelings. They did not even allow that all feel the same impressions in the same way: unless in this passage we are to understand by impressions, feelings themselves, in which case this language would be as unquestionable as it would be unmeaning; but they maintained that we cannot know whether others have the same feelings as ourselves. And that they practically admitted the common meaning of names the use of which they could not deny, is of little account; for they left it an open question, whether common impressions and notions corresponded to these names. It will be seen at once that the progress which Hermann finds in Aristippus is imaginary. A clear distinction between conceptions and appearances can least of all be attributed to the Cyrenaics, seeing that they know of nothing but appearances; and after what has been said, it will appear to be equally a mistake to say that 'Pleasure is the highest good' is the first judgment universally valid.

was possible; Socrates taking up a new position and a new method of gaining knowledge; Aristippus allowing of no knowledge which does not serve a practical end.[1] Still he was in a great measure indebted to his teacher for that critical skill for which we must give him credit,[2] and for that unprejudiced sobriety which stamps his whole bearing.

The same remark applies to his moral teaching and conduct. How far in this respect he was below Socrates is obvious. Yet in truth he was nearer to him than will be at first sight believed. For Socrates, as we have seen, made utility the ground of moral duties: and might not Aristippus believe that he was in accord with Socrates as to the final end in view, if in some respects he held a different opinion from his instructor as to the means to a pleasant life? Besides, there was about Aristippus much which is truly Socratic—that composure with which he rises above circumstances, that independence with which he is master of himself and his surroundings, that uninterrupted cheerfulness which engenders a kindliness of feeling, that quiet repose which grows out of confidence in strength of mind. Knowledge is with him the most important element. By culture and prudence he would

[1] We cannot accordingly agree with *Brandis*, Gr. Röm. Phil. ii. a, 96, who says: Aristippus appears to have held firm to the view that the impulses to action must be found within the sphere of knowledge; and, in investigating what can be known, to have arrived at a conclusion opposite to that of Socrates.

[2] See *Xen.* Mem. ii. 1; iii. 8, and the stories told by *Diog.* ii. 13; compare *Athen.* xi. 508, c, on the form of dialogue observed in his writings.

CHAP. XIV.

make men as independent of outward circumstances as their nature permits. Nay, so far does he go in this direction that he not unfrequently trenches on the ground of the Cynics.[1] As a matter of fact his School was also logically connected with theirs. Both Schools propose to philosophy the same problem, how to acquire practical culture,[2] rather than theoretical knowledge. Both, therefore, neglect logical and physical inquiries, justifying their procedure by theories, based it is true on different principles, but leading in the end to the same sceptical results. Both in their ethics compass the same aim—the emancipation of man by means of prudence, and the raising him above external surroundings and occurrences. One thing only makes them opponents—their pursuing this common end by means the most opposite. The Cynic School follows the path of self-denial, the Cyrenaic that of self-indulgence; the Cynic dispenses with the outer world, the Cyrenaic employs it for its own purposes.[3] The object of both Schools being, however, one and the same, their principles come back again to the same point. The Cynics derive the highest pleasure from their self-denial; Aristippus dispenses with property and

[1] This relationship appears in the tradition which attributes the same maxims at one time to Aristippus, at another to Diogenes.

[2] The standing expression is παιδεία, and what they say in favour of it is much to the same effect. See what has been said, pp. 295 and 361, 4, and 5.

[3] To make this difference clearer, *Wendt* (Phil. Cyr. 29) quotes the contradictory statements of Antisthenes and Aristippus in *Diog.* ii. 68, vi. 6. Antisthenes says that to philosophy he owes τὸ δύνασθαι ἑαυτῷ ὁμιλεῖν, Aristippus, τὸ δύνασθαι πᾶσι θαῤῥούντως ὁμιλεῖν.

enjoyment, in order the more thoroughly to appreciate them.[1]

Their attitude towards political life and religious traditions is a kindred one, and for a kindred reason. Conscious of mental superiority, needing no country, feeling himself unfettered by the beliefs of his fellow-men, the individual withdraws himself from the outer world; so little troubling himself about others that he never attempts any moulding influence on the sphere either of politics or of religion. Thus, notwithstanding their marked disparity, there is a family likeness between these Schools betraying a common descent from the Socratic philosophy alloyed with Sophistry.

It must unhesitatingly be granted that Aristippus departed far more from the original ground of the Socratic teaching than Antisthenes. The utilitarian view of life, which with Socrates was only an auxiliary notion invoked to justify the practice of morality before the tribunal of reason, was here raised to be a leading principle, and the knowledge of Socrates impressed into its service. Philosophy became with Aristippus, as with the Sophists, a means for furthering the private objects of individuals. Instead of scientific knowledge, personal culture was pursued, that personal culture being considered to consist in knowledge of the world and in the art of enjoyment. The few remarks of Aristippus on the origin and truth of impressions, borrowed for the most part from Protagoras, and ultimately leading to

[1] *Hegel*, Gesch. d. Phil. ii. 127. See above, pp. 309 and 365.

CHAP. XIV.

a wholly un-Socratic overthrow of all knowledge, were only intended as helps to moral doctrines. If not wholly lost, the deeper meaning of the Socratic philosophy was here at least subordinated to a bare outwork which Socrates regarded as almost an obstruction to his leading thought. If Aristippus was not a false follower, he was certainly a very imperfect follower of Socrates,[1] or rather the one among all the imperfect followers of Socrates who least succeeded in reaching the kernel of his master's teaching.

Points of resemblance.

Side by side with this foreign element, the genuine Socratic teaching cannot be ignored. Two elements are in fact present in the Cyrenaic School, the combination of which constitutes its peculiarity. One of these is the doctrine of pleasure as such, the other, the limitation of that doctrine by the Socratic demand for intellectual circumspection—the principle that prudence is the only means for arriving at true pleasure. Taken alone, the former element would lead to the conclusion that sensual enjoyment is the only object in life; the latter, to the strict Socratic doctrine of morals. By uniting both elements Aristippus arrived at the belief—which is stamped on all his language, and on which his personal character is a standing comment—that the surest way to happiness lies in the art of enjoying the pleasures of the moment with perfect liberty of soul. Whether this is indeed possible, whether the two leading thoughts in his system can

[1] As *Schleiermacher* maintains, Gesch. d. Phil. 87.

CHAP. XIV.

be harmonised at all, is a question which it seems never occurred to Aristippus. We can only answer it in the negative. That emancipation of soul, that philosophic independence at which Aristippus aimed, can only be secured by soaring above the impressions of the senses and the particular circumstances of life until happiness becomes independent of all surroundings and feelings. Conversely, when the enjoyment of the moment is the highest object, happiness can only be felt when circumstances give rise to agreeable feelings; all unpleasant impressions will be disturbers of happiness, since it is impossible to abandon the feelings freely to the enjoyment of what is present, without at the same time being disagreeably affected by what is unpleasant. Abstraction, whereby alone this might be done, is distinctly forbidden; Aristippus requiring the past and the future to be ignored, and the present only to be considered. Apart therefore from other faults, this theory involves a contradiction in fundamental principles, the injurious effects of which on the whole system were inevitable. In point of fact they soon made their existence felt in the teaching of Theodorus, Hegesias, and Anniceris; and hence the interest which the history of the latter Cyrenaics possesses.

E. *The later Cyrenaics.* (1) *Theodorus.*

About the same time that Epicurus was working up the philosophy of pleasure into a new form, Theodorus, Hegesias, and Anniceris were advocating, within the Cyrenaic School, views partly agreeing with those of Epicurus, partly in advance of the

CHAP. XIV.

doctrine of pleasure. Theodorus, on the whole, adhered to the principles of Aristippus, not hesitating without compunction to push them to their most extreme consequences.[1] The value of an action depending upon its results to the doer, he concluded that any and every action might under circumstances be allowed. If certain things pass for immoral, the reason why this is so is to restrain the masses within bounds; the wise man tied by no such prejudices need not, if occasion require, be afraid of adultery, theft, and sacrilege. If things exist for use, beautiful women and boys are not made only for ornament.[2] Friendship, it seemed to him, may be dispensed with; for the wise man is self-sufficing and needs no friends, and the fool can make no sensible use of them.[3] Devotion to country he considered ridiculous; for the wise man is a citizen of the world, and will not sacrifice himself and his

[1] θρασύτατος is the term used of him by *Diog.* ii. 116; and this epithet is fully justified by a passage like that, vi. 97.

[2] *Diog.* ii. 99. That Theodorus said this and similar things, cannot be doubted after the definite and explicit testimony of Diogenes. It is true that, in *Plut.* Tranq. Anim. 5, p. 567, Theodorus complains that his pupils misunderstood him—a statement which, if it be true, probably refers to the practical application of his principles. He may have led a more moral life than Bio (*Diog.* iv. 53; *Clemens*, Pædag. 15, A.), and yet have expressed the logical consequences of the Cyrenaic teaching. But it is undoubtedly an exaggeration to charge him, as *Epiphanius* (Expos. Fid. 1089, A.) does, with inciting to theft, perjury, and robbery.

[3] *Diog.* 98, and *Epiphanius*, l. c. in still stronger terms: ἀγαθὸν μόνον ἔλεγε τὸν εὐδαιμονοῦντα, φεύγειν (l. φαῦλον) δὲ τὸν δυστυχοῦντα, κἂν ᾖ σοφός· καὶ αἱρετὸν εἶναι τὸν ἄφρονα πλούσιον ὄντα καὶ ἀπειθῆ (ἀπαθῆ?) This statement, likewise, seems to be rather in the nature of a hasty conclusion, for Theodorus makes happiness depend on intelligence, and not on things without.

wisdom to benefit fools.[1] The views of his School respecting the Gods and religion were also expressed without reserve;[2] Bio[3] and Euemerus[4] herein fol-

[1] *Diog.* 98, *Epiph.* l. c.

[2] The atheism of Theodorus, which, besides an indictment at Athens, gained for him the standing epithet ἄθεος (he was called θεὸς according to *Diog.* ii. 86, 100, in allusion to a joke of Stilpo's, but probably κατ' ἀντίφασιν for ἄθεος), will be frequently mentioned. In *Diog.* 97 he says: ἦν . . . παντάπασιν ἀναιρῶν τὰς περὶ θεῶν δόξας· καὶ αὐτοῦ περιετύχομεν βιβλίῳ ἐπιγεγραμμένῳ περὶ θεῶν οὐκ εὐκαταφρονήτῳ· ἐξ οὗ φασὶν Ἐπίκουρον λάβοντα τὰ πλεῖστα εἰπεῖν. The last remark can only apply to the criticism of belief in the Gods generally, for Epicurus' peculiar views about them were certainly not shared by Theodorus. *Sext.* Pyrrh. iii. 218; Math. ix. 51, 55, mentions him among those who deny the existence of the Gods, with the addition: διὰ τοῦ περὶ θεῶν συντάγματος τὰ παρὰ τοῖς Ἕλλησι θεολογούμενα ποικίλως ἀνασκευάσας. *Cic.* (N. D. i. 1, 2) says: nullos [Deos] esse omnino Diagoras Melius et Theodorus Cyrenaicus putaverunt. Ibid. 23, 63: Nonne aperte Deorum naturam sustulerunt? Ibid. 42, 117: Omnino Deos esse negabant, a statement which *Minuc. Fel.* Oct. 8, 2, and *Lact.* Ira Dei, 9, probably repeat after him. Likewise *Plut.* Comm. Not. 31, 4, p. 1075, says: Even Theodorus and those who shared his views did not declare God to be corruptible, ἀλλ' οὐκ ἐπίστευσαν ὡς ἔστι τι ἄφθαρτον. *Epiph.* (Expos. Fid. 1089, A.) also asserts that he denied the existence of a God. In the face of these agreeing testimonies, the assertion of *Clemens* (Pædag. 15, A.), that Theodorus and others had wrongly been called atheists, and that they only denied the popular Gods, their lives being otherwise good, can be of little value. Theodorus no doubt denied the Gods of the people in the first place, but it was not his intention to distinguish between them and the true God. The anecdotes in *Diog.* ii. 101, 116, give the impression of insincerity.

[3] *Diog.* iv. 54: πολλὰ δὲ καὶ ἀθεώτερον προσεφέρετο τοῖς ὁμιλοῦσι τοῦτο Θεοδώρειον ἀπολαύσας· but in his last illness he was overcome with remorse, and had recourse to enchantments. The argument quoted by *Sen.* Benef. vii. 7, 1, to prove that every one and that no one commits sacrilege is more a rhetorical and intellectual work of skill.

[4] The view of Euemerus respecting the Gods is briefly as follows: There are two kinds of Gods—heavenly and incorruptible beings, who are honoured by men as Gods, such as the sun, the stars, the winds; and dead men, who were raised to the rank of Gods for their benefits to mankind. Diodorus in *Eus.* Pr. Ev. ii. 2, 52. To

CHAP. XIV.

lowing his example. For all that, the theory of Aristippus did not altogether satisfy him. He was fain to admit that pleasure and pain do not merely depend on ourselves and our inner state, but also in a great measure on external circumstances; and he therefore sought such a definition of the highest good as should secure happiness to the wise man, and make that happiness dependent on prudence.[1] This result seemed attainable by making happiness consist, not in individual pleasures, but in a cheerful state of mind—and conversely evil, not in individual feelings of pain, but in an unhappy tone of mind; for feelings being the effects of impressions from without, states of mind are in our own power.[2] Accordingly, Theodorus asserted that in themselves pleasure and pain are neither good nor bad; goodness consists in cheerfulness, evil in sadness; the

the latter class of beings Euemerus referred the whole of Mythology, and supposed it to be a history of princes and princesses, Uranus, Cronus, Zeus, Rhea, &c. For further particulars respecting this rationalising history of the Gods, consult *Steinhart*, Allg. Encyclo. Art. Euhemerus. V. *Sieroka*, De Euhemero.

[1] These reasons are not given in so many words, but they follow from Theodorus' position about the highest good, and also from the stress which, according to *Diog.* 98, he laid on the αὐτάρκεια of the wise man, and the difference between wisdom and folly.

[2] Probably what *Cic.* (Tusc. iii. 13, 28; 14, 31) quotes as Cyrenaic doctrine belongs to Theodorus: that not every evil engenders sorrow, but only unforeseen evils, that many precautions can be taken to prevent sorrow by familiarising ourselves with the thought of future evils. What control of outward impressions he considered possible by prudence, appears also from the explanatory remarks in *Stob.* Floril. 119, 16; the wise man has never sufficient reason to put an end to his own life, and it is inconsistent to call vice the only evil, and then to put an end to life to avoid the sufferings of life.

former proceeds from prudence, the latter from folly; pursue therefore prudence and justice, eschew ignorance and wrong-doing.[1] Occasionally he displayed a fearlessness and an indifference to life[2] which would have done honour to a Cynic. The theory of pleasure was not therewith surrendered, but the older setting of that theory was abandoned. In place of individual pleasures, a state of mind was substituted unconditioned by the mere feelings of enjoyment and pain. Instead of being a cheerful resignation to the impressions of the moment, the highest good was made to consist in rising superior to circumstances.

(2) *Hegesias.*

Hegesias went a step further. He, too, adheres to the general position of Aristippus. With him good is identical with pleasure, evil with pain: all that we do, we do only for ourselves; if services are rendered to others, it is only because advantages

[1] *Diog.* 98: *τέλος δ' ὑπελάμβανε χαρὰν καὶ λυπήν· τὴν μὲν ἐπὶ φρονήσει, τὴν δ' ἐπὶ ἀφροσύνῃ· ἀγαθὰ δὲ φρόνησιν καὶ δικαιοσύνην, κακὰ δὲ τὰς ἐναντίας ἕξεις, μέσα δὲ ἡδονὴν καὶ πόνον.* That justice should be reckoned among good things may be brought into agreement with what is quoted p. 267, 3. It is to be recommended, because it protects us from the unpleasant consequences of forbidden actions, and from the disquiet which the prospect of these consequences produces, although such actions are not in themselves inadmissible.

[2] When at the court of Lysimachus, he so enraged the latter by his frankness (*Diog.* 102; *Plut.* Exil. 16; *Philo*, Qu. Omn. Pr. Tib. p. 606, 884, C.) that Lysimachus threatened to crucify him, upon which Theodorus uttered the celebrated saying, that it was indifferent to him whether he went to corruption in the earth or in the air. *Cic.* Tusc. i. 43, 102; *Valer. Max.* vi. 2, 3; *Plut.* An. Vitios. 3, p. 499; *Stob.* Floril. 2, 23, attribute another saying to him on the same occasion, giving Anaxarchus the credit of the above passage in *Stob.* Floril. 2, 23.

CHAP. XIV.

are expected in return [1] But on looking round to discover wherein true pleasure is to be found, Hegesias met with no very consoling answer. For life, he says, is full of trouble; the numerous afflictions of the body affect the soul also and disturb its peace; fortune in numberless ways crosses our wishes; man cannot reckon upon having a net outcome of satisfactory experiences, in a word, upon happiness.[2] Even the practical wisdom, upon which Aristippus relied, affords to his mind no security; for feelings, according to the old Cyrenaic maxim, not showing us things as they are in themselves, who can be sure, if he is always obliged to act according to probabilities, that his calculations will come true?[3] If happiness cannot be had, it is surely foolish to try for it; enough if we can but fortify ourselves against the sufferings of life; freedom from pain, not pleasure, is our goal.[4] How may this goal be reached

[1] *Diog*. ii. 93 : *οἱ δὲ Ἡγησιακοὶ λεγόμενοι σκοποὺς μὲν εἶχον τοὺς αὐτοὺς ἡδονὴν καὶ πόνον, μήτε δὲ χάριν τι εἶναι μήτε φιλίαν μήτε εὐεργεσίαν, διὰ τὸ μὴ δι' αὐτὰ ταῦτα αἱρεῖσθαι ἡμᾶς αὐτὰ, ἀλλὰ διὰ τὰς χρείας αὐτάς* [probably *αὐτῶν*], *ὧν ἀπόντων μηδ' ἐκεῖνα ὑπάρχειν*. Ibid. 95 : *τόν τε σοφὸν ἑαυτοῦ ἕνεκα πάντα πράξειν· οὐδένα γὰρ ἡγεῖσθαι τῶν ἄλλων ἐπίσης ἄξιον αὐτῷ· κἂν γὰρ τὰ μέγιστα δοκῇ παρ' αὐτοῦ καρποῦσθαι, μὴ εἶναι ἀντάξια ὧν αὐτὸς παράσχῃ*. *Epiph*. Exp. Fid. 1089, B., says the same, but less accurately.

[2] *Diog*. 94 : *τὴν εὐδαιμονίαν ὅλως ἀδύνατον εἶναι· τὸ μὲν γὰρ σῶμα πολλῶν ἀναπεπλῆσθαι παθημάτων, τὴν δὲ ψυχὴν συμπαθεῖν τῷ σώματι καὶ ταράττεσθαι, τὴν δὲ τύχην πολλὰ τῶν κατ' ἐλπίδα κωλύειν· ὥστε διὰ ταῦτα ἀνύπαρκτον τὴν εὐδαιμονίαν εἶναι*. See p. 344, 1.

[3] *Diog*. 95 : *ἀνῄρουν δὲ καὶ τὰς αἰσθήσεις οὐκ ἀκριβούσας τὴν ἐπίγνωσιν, τῶν τ' εὐλόγως φαινομένων πάντα πράττειν*. We insert this sentence in connection with the doctrine of Hegesias, where it most probably belongs, without, however, guaranteeing for it this position.

[4] *Diog*. 95 : *τόν τε σοφὸν οὐχ οὕτω πλεονάσειν ἐν τῇ τῶν ἀγαθῶν αἱρέσει, ὡς ἐν τῇ τῶν κακῶν φυγῇ, τέλος τιθέμενον τὸ μὴ ἐπιπόνως ζῇν*

in a world where so much trouble and pain falls to our lot? Clearly not at all so long as peace of mind depends upon outward things and circumstances; contentment is only then sure, when we are indifferent to everything which produces pleasure or pain.[1] Pleasure and pain depend ultimately, as Hegesias observes, not upon things, but upon our attitude towards things; in itself nothing is pleasant or unpleasant; it makes a varied impression, according to our tone and condition.[2] Neither riches nor poverty affect the happiness of life; the rich not being happier than the poor. Neither freedom nor slavery, high rank or low degree, honour or dishonour, are conditions of the amount of pleasure we receive. Life itself only appears a good thing to a fool; to the wise man it is a thing indifferent.[3] No Stoic or Cynic could more sternly denounce the value of external things than the pupil of Aristippus here does. With these principles is connected the noble and thoroughly Socratic saying that faults do not call for anger, nor human beings for hatred, but only for instruction, since no one intentionally does what is wrong;[4] desiring what is pleasant, everyone desires what is good; and as the wise man does not

μηδὲ λυπηρῶς· ὃ δὴ περιγένεσθαι τοῖς ἀδιαφορήσασι, περὶ τὰ ποιητικὰ τῆς ἡδονῆς.

[1] See preceding note.

[2] *Diog.* 94: φύσει τ' οὐδὲν ἡδὺ ἢ ἀηδὲς ὑπελάμβανον. διὰ δὲ σπάνιν ἢ ξενισμὸν ἢ κόρον τοὺς μὲν ἥδεσθαι τοὺς δ' ἀηδῶς ἔχειν.

[3] Ibid. 95: καὶ τῷ μὲν ἄφρονι τὸ ζῆν λυσιτελὲς εἶναι, τῷ δὲ φρονίμῳ ἀδιάφορον· which probably only bears the sense given in the text. Similarly *Epiphanius*, l. c.; conf. p. 344, 1.

[4] Ibid.: ἔλεγον τὰ ἁμαρτήματα συγγνώμης τυγχάνειν· οὐ γὰρ ἑκόντα ἁμαρτάνειν, ἀλλά τινι πάθει κατηναγκασμένον· καὶ μὴ μισήσειν, μᾶλλον δὲ μεταδιδάξειν.

CHAP. XIV.

allow his peace of mind to depend on things external, neither does he allow it to be ruffled by the faults of others.

The theory of Hegesias illustrates more decidedly than that of Theodorus how unsatisfactory is the principle of the doctrine of pleasure. It even expressly admits that human life has about it more of sorrow than joy, and hence insists upon a perfect indifference to things outward. But what right has Hegesias to identify pleasure with the good, and pain with evil? After all, the good is that which is the condition of our well-being; if this be indifference rather than pleasure, indifference and not pleasure is the good; the doctrine of pleasure has come round to its opposite—the Cynic independence of everything external. As a general principle the Cyrenaic School could not avow this without surrendering its own position; still within that School it is distinctly admitted that pleasure is not in all cases the highest motive. Anniceris maintained that the aim of every action is the pleasure resulting therefrom; and, like the older Cyrenaics, he would not hear of a general aim of life, nor substitute freedom from pain in the place of pleasure.[1] He

(3) *Anniceris.*

[1] *Clemens*, Strom. ii. 417, B.: *οἱ δὲ Ἀννικέρειοι καλούμενοι . . . τοῦ μὲν ὅλου βίου τέλος οὐδὲν ὡρισμένον ἔταξαν, ἑκάστης δὲ πράξεως ἴδιον ὑπάρχειν τέλος, τὴν ἐκ τῆς πράξεως περιγινομένην ἡδονήν, οὗτοι οἱ Κυρηναϊκοὶ τὸν ὅρον τῆς ἡδονῆς Ἐπικούρου, τουτέστι τὴν τοῦ ἀλγοῦντος ὑπεξαίρεσιν, ἀθετοῦσι νεκροῦ κατάστασιν ἀποκαλοῦντες*. See p. 355, 1. This would justify the inaccurate statement in *Diog.* ii. 96: *οἱ δ' Ἀννικέρειοι τὰ μὲν ἄλλα κατὰ ταὐτα τούτοις*—(*i.e.* the School of Hegesias)—and also the assertion (*Suid.* Ἀννίκ.) that Anniceris, although living, according to Suidas, in the time of Alexander, was an Epicurean.

observed that by pleasure only our own pleasure can be understood; for of the feelings of others, according to the old teaching of his School, we can know nothing.[1] Yet pleasure results not only from enjoyments of the senses, but from intercourse with other men and from honourable pursuits.[2] Hence, Anniceris allowed to friendship, gratitude, family affection, and patriotism an absolute value, quite apart from the benefit resulting from these relations. He even went so far as to say that the wise man would make sacrifices to secure them, believing his happiness would not suffer from so doing, even if there remained to him but little actual enjoyment.[3] He thus came round to the ordinary view of life, still further approximating thereto by attaching less value to discernment, the second element in the Cyrenaic doctrine of morals, than Aristippus had done. He denied, in fact, that discernment alone is sufficient to make us safe and to raise us above the prejudices

Cicero and Diogenes likewise affirm that his School declared pleasure to be the good.

[1] *Diog.* 96: τήν τε τοῦ φίλου εὐδαιμονίαν δι' αὑτὴν μὴ εἶναι ἀρετήν, μηδὲ γὰρ αἰσθητὴν τῷ πέλας ὑπάρχειν. See p. 351, 1.

[2] *Clemens*, l. c. continues: χαίρειν γὰρ ἡμᾶς μὴ μόνον ἐπὶ ἡδοναῖς, ἀλλὰ καὶ ἐπὶ ὁμιλίαις καὶ ἐπὶ φιλοτιμίαις. Comp. *Cic.* Off. iii. 33, 116. See p. 348, 2. The expression in Clement, τὴν ἐκ τῆς πράξεως περιγινομένην ἡδονήν, probably refers not only to the pleasure resulting from an action, but to the pleasure immediately bound up therewith.

[3] *Diog.* 96: ἀπέλιπον δὲ καὶ φιλίαν ἐν βίῳ καὶ χάριν καὶ πρὸς γονέας τιμὴν καὶ ὑπὲρ πατρίδος τι πράξειν. ὅθεν, διὰ ταῦτα κἂν ὀχλήσεις ἀναδέξηται ὁ σοφός, οὐδὲν ἧττον εὐδαιμονήσει, κἂν ὀλίγα ἡδέα περιγένηται αὐτῷ. Ibid. 97: τόν τε φίλον μὴ διὰ τὰς χρείας μόνον ἀποδέχεσθαι, ὧν ὑπολειπουσῶν μὴ ἐπιστρέφεσθαι· ἀλλὰ καὶ παρὰ τὴν γεγονυῖαν εὔνοιαν· ἧς ἕνεκα καὶ πόνους ὑπομένειν, καί τοι τιθέμενον ἡδονὴν τέλος, καὶ ἀχθόμενον ἐπὶ τῷ στέρεσθαι αὐτῆς ὅμως ἑκουσίως ὑπομένειν διὰ τὴν πρὸς τὸν φίλον στοργήν.

CHAP. XIV.

of the masses; there must be practice as well, to overcome the effect of perverse use.[1]

Thus the Cyrenaic doctrine is seen gradually to vanish away. Aristippus declared that pleasure was the only good, understanding by pleasure actual enjoyment and not mere freedom from pain; making, moreover, the pleasure of the moment, and not the net outcome of experiences, to be the aim of action. One after another these limitations were abandoned. Theodorus gave up the last one, Hegesias the second, and even the first was assailed by Anniceris. It thus appears how impossible it is to combine the Socratic demand for insight and superiority to the external world with the leading thought of the theory of pleasure. The Socratic element disintegrates that theory and turns it into its opposite. But as the process takes place without the mind being conscious of it, no new principle is evolved thereby, and the very men in whom this result is made to appear, persistently adhere to the doctrine of Aristippus in the most inconsistent manner.

[1] Ibid. 96: μὴ εἶναί τε αὐτάρκη τὸν λόγον πρὸς τὸ θαῤῥῆσαι καὶ τῆς τῶν πολλῶν δόξης ὑπεράνω γενέσθαι· δεῖν δ' ἀνεθίζεσθαι διὰ τὴν ἐκ πολλοῦ συντραφεῖσαν ἡμῖν φαύλην διάθεσιν.

CHAPTER XV.

RETROSPECT.

CHAP. XV.

A. Inconsistencies of the imperfect Socratic Schools.

INCONSISTENCIES appear to have been common to all the Socratic Schools. It was, without doubt, an inconsistency on the part of the Megarians to confine knowledge to conceptions, and at the same time to do away with all possibility of growth and with anything like multiplicity or definiteness in conceptions; to declare that being is the good, and, at the same time, by denying variety and motion to being, to deprive it of that creative power which alone can justify such a position; to begin with the Socratic wisdom, and to end in unmeaning hair-splitting. It was an inconsistency on the part of Antisthenes to endeavour to build human life on a foundation of knowledge, whilst at the same time he dissipated all knowledge by his statements respecting the meaning and relation of conceptions. It was no small inconsistency both in himself and his followers to aim at a perfect independence of the outer world, and yet to attribute an exaggerated value to the externals of the Cynic mode of life; to declare war against pleasure and selfishness, and at the same time to pronounce the wise man free from the most sacred moral duties; to renounce all enjoyments,

CHAP. XV.

and yet to revel in the enjoyment of a moral self-exaltation. In these inconsistencies and in this involuntary self-contradiction the unsatisfactory nature of the principles from which all these Schools started is manifested. It is seen how far they were removed from the perfect proportion, from the ready mental susceptibility, from the living versatility of Socrates, attaching themselves as they all did to particular sides of his genius without grasping it as a whole.

B. *These Schools are more followers of Socrates than of the Sophists.*

The same fact will doubtless also explain that tendency to Sophistry which is so striking in these philosophers. The captious reasoning of the Megarians, the indifference of the Cynics to all speculative knowledge, and their contempt for the whole theory of conceptions, Aristippus' theory of perceptions and doctrine of pleasure, savour more of the Sophists than of Socrates. Yet all these Schools professed to follow Socrates, each one of them placing some element of the Socratic philosophy at the head of its system. It seems therefore hardly correct for modern writers to see nothing but Sophistical views in their teaching, supplemented and modified by what is Socratic, and, instead of deducing their variety from the many-sidedness of Socrates, to attribute it to the diversities of the Sophists leading up from various detached points towards the Socratic philosophy.[1] With decided admirers of Socrates,

[1] K. F. *Hermann*, Ges. Abh. 228, who, amongst other things, states that the agreement in matter between these Schools and the Socratic teaching ought to be regarded as a corrective, modifying more or less strongly their fundamental views de-

such as Antisthenes and Euclid, this is out of the question. The one desire of such men being faithfully to reproduce the life and teaching of Socrates, they must have been well aware that to him they were first indebted for an intellectual centre, and that from him they had first received the living germ of a true philosophy;—indeed, the influence of Socrates as the starting-point of their systems is unmistakable. In their case, instead of speaking of the ennobling influence of Socrates on Sophistical principles, we ought rather to speak of the influence of Sophistry on their appreciation of the teaching of Socrates. Socrates, as it were, gave the substance of the teaching, Sophistry only supplied a narrower limitation of the platform; for this reason a School like that of the Stoics was able in the end to join itself on to that teaching.

The case of Aristippus is slightly different. Yet even in respect of him it has been already established, not only that he professed to be a follower of Socrates, but that he really was one, albeit he least of all those followers penetrated into the heart of the Socratic teaching, and allowed the greatest play to Sophistical influences. Possibly the possession of inferior mental

rived from the Sophists; they are the pioneers of advancing Sophistry, endeavouring to act as an equipoise to Socratic teaching, &c. Yet this remark agrees ill with those steps in advance of Socrates which Hermann thinks to discern in many Sophistical assertions of Antisthenes and Aristippus (see pp. 297, 1; 371, 2), and with the proof of the difference in principle between the Eristic of the Sophists and that of Megara. (Ges. Abh. 250, f.) Far more correct and more in keeping with our view was that expressed by Hermann at an earlier time. (Plat. 257.)

CHAP. XV.

capacities or else a previous training in Sophistry may account for the failure of the founders of the imperfect Schools to enter into the spirit of their master so deeply and so thoroughly as Plato did; but it is also possible that in a great measure Socrates was himself the cause of diversity in the Schools which attached themselves to him. So rich a field was presented in his personality that it stimulated investigation in all directions; and yet so immature and so unsystematic was the shape of his philosophy that it afforded the widest scope for treatment.[1]

C. *Importance of these Schools.*

This disintegration of the Socratic Schools is accordingly not without importance for the further progress of philosophy. Bringing out the separate elements which were united in Socrates, and connecting them with the corresponding elements in the pre-Socratic philosophy, it exposed them to a thorough scrutiny; problems were set for all subsequent thinkers to discuss; the logical and ethical consequences of the Socratic maxims were brought to light. At the same time the outcome was made apparent of isolating separate elements in the teaching of Socrates, and combining them with other theories, without first recasting these theories in the

[1] *Cic.* de Orat. iii. 16, 61, observes with some justice, but somewhat superficially: Cum essent plures orti fere a Socrate, quod ex illius variis et diversis et in omnem partem diffusis disputationibus alius aliud apprehenderat, proseminatæ sunt quasi familiæ dissentientes inter se, &c. For instance, Plato and Antisthenes, qui patientiam et duritiam in Socratico sermone maxime adamarat, and also Aristippus, quem illæ magis voluptariæ disputationes delectarant.

Socratic mould. Thus the very imperfection of the smaller Socratic schools was indirectly instrumental in forcing on the demand for an all-round treatment which should connect the different aspects of the Socratic philosophy more closely with each other and with earlier systems, assigning to each one an importance relatively to the rest. In both ways these Schools influenced Plato and Aristotle, Euclid supplying to Plato the outline for his theory of ideas, Antisthenes and Aristippus the groundwork for his theory of the highest good.

Of greater importance is the fact that these followers of Socrates prepared the way for the course taken by philosophy after the time of Aristotle. For although the post-Aristotelian systems do not coincide with the imperfect Socratic Schools, and would have been impossible without Plato and Aristotle; still it must not be forgotten that they owe much to these Schools. The predominance of practical above speculative interests displayed by the post-Aristotelian philosophy; the moral contentment with which the wise man withdrawing from things external falls back again into the consciousness of his freedom and virtue; the citizenship of the world which can dispense with country and political activity—all these peculiarities of later times are foreshadowed in the lesser Socratic Schools. The Stoa adopted the moral principles of the Cynics almost in their entirety, only toning them down and expanding them in application. The same School takes its logic from the Megarians no less than from Aristotle. From the Megarians comes the scepticism of Pyrrho and the Academy branching off in a somewhat different direction. The teaching of Aristippus reappears in Epicurus, only somewhat changed in details. In short, tendencies, which at an earlier period only secured a qualified recognition, became dominant when strengthened, recast, and supplemented by other elements.

True it is that this result was not possible until the intellectual vigour of Greece was on the wane, and her political condition had become so far hopeless as to favour the idea that indifference to things external can alone lead to peace of mind. Whilst the intellectual sense was still quick, and the Greek spirit still keen, the issues of the Socratic philosophy were allowed to run to waste. That philosophy from its own true bent could not fail to issue in a science of conceptions such as Plato and Aristotle built up. It was only by isolating the several inwardly connected elements of the Socratic teaching, by confounding the garb in which Socrates clothed his teaching with that teaching itself, by mistaking defects in his manner for defects in his matter, that it was ever possible for philosophy to be limited to such abstract metaphysics and so empty a criticism as the Megarian, to so unintellectual and negative a morality as the Cynic, or for a doctrine like that of Aristippus to pass current for truly Socratic. Whilst therefore these Schools are not without importance for the progress of Greek philosophy, their intellectual results cannot be valued very highly. A truer understanding and a more comprehensive treatment of the Socratic philosophy, was the work of Plato.

INDEX.